D1156784

CARDINAL
WYSZYŃSKI

HARCOURT BRACE JOVANOVICH, PUBLISHERS
SAN DIEGO   NEW YORK   LONDON

Andrzej Micewski

CARDINAL WYSZYŃSKI

A Biography

Translated from the Polish by
William R. Brand and Katarzyna Mroczkowska-Brand

Requests for permission to make copies of any
part of the work should be mailed to:
Permissions, Harcourt Brace Jovanovich, Publishers,
Orlando, FL 32887

The publisher wishes to thank
Reverend Walter J. Ziemba
for his dedicated editorial assistance in this publication.

LIBRARY OF CONGRESS CATALOGING IN PUBLICATION DATA

Micewski, Andrzej, 1926
Cardinal Wyszyński. Translation of: Kardynał Wyszyński, prymas i mąż stanu.
Includes index.
1. Wyszyński Stefan, 1901–   . 2. Cardinals—
Poland—Biography. 3. Statesmen—Poland—Biography.
I. Title.
BX4705.W86M5213   1984   282'.092'4 [B]   84-4683
ISBN 0-15-115785-5

Designed by Mark Likgalter

Printed in the United States of America

First edition

A B C D E

Photo Courtesy Lochon/Gamma–Liaison

CONTENTS

Introduction:
Human Greatness

Stefan Wyszyński was not yet forty-five years old when, in 1946, he became Bishop of Lublin and the youngest member of the Polish Episcopate. Three years later, having become Archbishop of Gniezno and Warsaw, he received the highest distinction in his country's Church and became the Primate of Poland. Hardly anyone then knew that a heavy cross would befall him: the Primate would be imprisoned by his own government.

Was imprisoning him really necessary? Although it went against common sense, the interests of the nation and even the interests of the communist government, such an act lay within the logic of the totalitarian Stalinist system. Initially then, Primate Wyszyński ruled the Polish Church for only five years, during which time he was elevated to the rank of cardinal. Less than a year and a half after becoming Archbishop of Gniezno and Warsaw, he contracted the first agreement in history between the Catholic Church and a communist government. Three years later, the same government arrested the man who had dared to make that experiment. At the moment of his arrest, the Primate did not know whether prison alone awaited him, or a martyr's death. He entrusted himself to Christ and His Mother; the government had to free him three years later.

Under the influence of external events and public pressures, the Stalinist system in Poland broke down. The ruling Communist Party had to set right its greatest violations of law, especially those that had most provoked public opinion. Hardly had Cardinal Wyszyński left prison when he had to calm an agitated nation in order to prevent a disaster like the one that had gripped Budapest in 1956. Far from showing gratitude, those in power soon commenced a new struggle—less drastic in appearances but no less vexing—against the Church. Once again the Primate became the main target. The iron curtain had been raised slightly and humanity was hoping for peaceful coexistence; within this context, the authorities began to portray the Primate as a hardened conservative who might be capable of martyrdom but could not live up to the demands of détente or the Vatican Council reforms, which called for openness and subtle diplomacy rather than uncompromising resistance. It soon became apparent, however, that those who were supposedly attacking the Primate's conservatism actually were in favor of forced laicization and materialistic indoctrination of society, as well as a further limitation of church prerogatives. The Primate turned out to be "not only" a martyr; he won victory for the Church in all its conflicts with the government between 1957 and 1970.

The bloody events on the Polish coast in December 1970 led to a new political crisis. Again Cardinal Wyszyński calmed public opinion to prevent more bloodshed; his authority was once more unquestionable. After a few years, however, another wave of discontent crested, and a prolonged internal crisis began. Now even the state authorities, needing support, stressed the Primate's merits, his patriotism, and his understanding of the requirements of the Polish *racja stanu.** Since

Racja stanu, raison d'état (reason, interest, or good of the state). Because Polish history involves so many attacks by its enemies, so many persecutions, partitions, and threats to existence, the term *racja stanu* has taken on a broader meaning in Poland to include

open conflict with the Church was no longer possible, the confrontation assumed a different, ever subtler character. Nevertheless, the Primate enjoyed no respite. The country remained on the edge of a precipice, and church affairs waited in vain for their resolution. Everyone, however, now spoke of Cardinal Wyszyński as a great man.

What is greatness? It is relatively easy to define human greatness within the conditions of a totalitarian system, which, especially during the Stalinist period, provided the context for our consideration of Cardinal Wyszyński's greatness. Historical greatness is a result of steadfastness of principle combined with flexibility of action. Steadfastness of principle, which is bound up with great, deep faith, is first of all a grace, a gift from God. Flexibility of action results from foresight, imagination, and qualities of mind. In Stalinist Poland, only Wyszyński knew how to combine these two characteristics and virtues. Let us compare him, for example, with Cardinal Mindszenty —a man of great character and principles, but entirely devoid of flexibility.* Mindszenty thus had to lose, and despite his personal heroism he achieved for the Hungarian Church not even a fraction of what Wyszyński achieved for the Polish Church. Readiness for martyrdom does not in itself constitute greatness. Both cardinals had that readiness. Wyszyński, though, knew how to be more than a martyr. Without altering his principles, he could anticipate developments. When it became obvious that coexistence was the only alternative to nuclear annihilation, he was able to address the issue this time as a statesman, not as a martyr. Had he not possessed unshakable faith and principles, he could have played no role; he would have become the chaff of history, like so many who, having no

---

its right to exist, to be independent, to defend itself, to be sovereign, and not to be threatened from without or within by anyone.

*József Cardinal Mindszenty (1892–1975) was bishop of Veszprém in 1944 when he was imprisoned by the Fascists. He was archbishop of Esztergom and Primate of Hungary (1945) when he was arrested by the Communists and sentenced to life imprisonment. He was freed from custody by the Hungarian insurrectionists in 1956 and given asylum in the American Embassy in Budapest, where he remained a virtual prisoner for fifteen years. President Nixon persuaded him to leave, and he died in exile in Vienna in 1975.

ideas of their own, enter into agreements with the communists that are doomed to defeat. On the other hand, if he had been incapable of anticipating and reacting flexibly to the changing situation, the Polish Church would have lost its leader (and probably the whole leadership of the Episcopate) in 1950, when Wyszyński signed that unprecedented, "risky" agreement with a communist government. The Primate lasted out the ups and downs of church-state relations and "chose" imprisonment only when no other dignified solution was left. Fortunately, the decline of classical Stalinism began soon after Stalin's death, and the Polish Church survived because of its primate's actions. The Church managed to preserve its hierarchy, its structure, and its numerous institutions.

Wyszyński is the only primate who won every confrontation with a succession of governments. Because of him, the Church is strong and popular in a communist country. In some other countries ruled by the same system, government employees still sit in bishops' offices, and certain clergymen are vassals.

Naturally, there is more to Poland's exceptional status than Cardinal Wyszyński's actions. It has also to do with our belonging to Western culture and our past historical greatness, which the nation has remembered through partitions, annexations, Nazi occupations, and postwar dependence. But Cardinal Wyszyński's special role was to personify Polish historical greatness for more than thirty years, referring constantly to our national and Catholic traditions and setting those traditions against every attempt to undermine the Christian and national Polish identity. Wyszyński never allowed a shadow of doubt that culturally we belong to the West, to Europe—but he always left the communists a way out. Whenever the threat of bloodshed arose, he calmed the people and began talks with the successive leaders of the Communist Party.

One might ask why the greatest Pole of our generation was a clergyman and not a politician. Yet Wyszyński did not want to be a political man and always stayed clear of the practice of politics.

Unwillingly, however, he became not only a prince of the church but also a Polish statesman whom even his communist opponents had to accept. He defended church rights, human rights, and the national right to independence, inevitably entering into conflict with a system that threatened all these rights and values. Finally, faithful to our cultural links with the West and to the concept of Europe, he was the first to stretch out his hand in reconciliation to the Germans; in response, the dogmatists unleashed an insane political campaign against him.

Thus, this clergyman who did not practice politics became our only postwar statesman against his own will and in fact performed the function of national leader.

Writing a book about him is a necessity, an obligatory witness to truth. Wider international opinion has not been well informed about the dramatic history of Polish Catholicism after the war. Polish society, especially the younger generations, needs to know about this period more than any other period of our history. It is, of course, much too early for a full biography of Cardinal Wyszyński. The Polish Episcopate cannot make public most of the relevant documents, which are still politically sensitive, if not explosive. Historians may be able to examine them in twenty-five or fifty years. But we lay Catholics witnessed these events, stood alongside the Cardinal, argued with him, and usually realized that he was right. Our own sources and documents may be incomplete or random, but as participants in history we can attempt a synthesis, an introductory sketch of his biography. For the time to realize this project has come: the Primate of Poland has died.

The election on October 16, 1978, of Karol Cardinal Wojtyła as the first non-Italian pope in 455 years, and the Pope's subsequent visit to Poland, brought Cardinal Wyszyński's life new meaning. John Paul II said so himself in his inaugural message to the Poles:

Honorable and beloved Primate! Allow me to say simply what I am thinking. In the Chair of Peter there would not be a Polish pope who today, full of the fear of God but also full of confidence, begins a new pontificate, if it had not been for your faith, which never retreated during imprisonment and suffering, your heroic hope, your unceasing trust in the Mother of the Church, if there had not been Jasna Góra and that whole period in the history of the Church in our homeland that is linked to your ministrations as bishop and primate.

It is hard to add anything to those words. The historian can only try to corroborate their literal accuracy with facts.

Cardinal Wyszyński, already advanced in years and having undergone several major operations, experienced great emotion at the time of John Paul II's election and enthronement. No one knows what role he played in the conclave; it was certainly not small. It was he who shaped the Church that gave the world a new pope. There turned out to be a second spiritual greatness in Poland, consciously remaining in the Primate's shadow. The son is never the same as the father. Pope Wojtyła is certainly a different man from Primate Wyszyński. Yet he is much more the son of the Primate than anyone can imagine. To the Poles who had come to Rome he said, "Listen to the Primate. I always listened to him, and things worked out well for both of us." The stirring scene during the inauguration at the Vatican, when the son-Pope rose from his throne to kiss the hand of the father-Primate, thrilled Poland and the entire Christian world. These two men belonged to different generations—nineteen years separated their births—and they must have held many different ideas. Yet the same simplicity, kindliness, and Christian humility brought them simultaneously to their knees during the meeting with the Polish faithful. The emotions they were experiencing at that moment spread to millions.

Within months, John Paul II made his visit to the same Poland whose government had earlier refused to admit Paul VI. So much had changed during thirteen years that the intolerable became the possible. The leaders of the Polish Communist Party must have learned something from old mistakes, from the precarious situation in their country, from the great social influence and strength of the Church. This strength is indissolubly linked with the name of Stefan Cardinal Wyszyński.

One might ask whether, in regard to a priest, bishop, and prince of the Church, it would not be more correct to speak of holiness than of human greatness. Certainly. But we are talking about a man who, even though he always set for himself religio-social, rather than political, goals, fulfilled the mission of defending not only church rights, but also human rights and the moral rights of a nation. Saying, "The Mother of God—that too is my politics," he became not only a prince of the Church, but also a statesman who expressed national traditions, the national identity, human needs, though his greatness has its deepest springs in the supernatural order—in religious inspiration.

The following work stresses the temporal, sociopolitical role of the Primate of Poland. However, even the most skeptical and critical mind will see a supernatural radiance and an intersection of the human and the divine in the way he fulfilled that role. It was that spiritual attitude before which totalitarianism, and even Stalinism, proved helpless and was forced to surrender, first morally and finally politically.

A. Micewski

CARDINAL
WYSZYŃSKI

1

Childhood
to Priesthood
and Mitre (1901-1948)

The first emotion of a child, the first memory of home—how fruitful it would be in spiritual development and religious formation. Stefan Cardinal Wyszyński told us of it in a speech given in his native parish:

> My father enjoyed going to Jasna Góra, and my mother to Ostra Brama.* Then they would meet back in the village on the banks of the Bug, where I was born, and

*Jasna Góra and Ostra Brama are Marian shrines in Częstochowa and Wilno (at present in the Lithuanian S.S.R.)—the traditionally pre-eminent pilgrimage places and centers of Polish Catholic devotion. Jasna Góra ("Bright Mountain") is often referred to by the name of the Silesian industrial city, Częstochowa, within which stands the Pauline monastery housing the famous "Black Madonna" icon, which legend claims to be a portrait of the Virgin painted on a tabletop by Saint Luke. Jasna Góra is linked to Polish patriotic traditions because the monastery held out against a Swedish siege in 1655 when almost all of Poland had been inundated by the invasion from the north; after the defense by a small garrison of monks and soldiers, the Poles turned the tide and drove out the invaders. The "Black Madonna" is painted with dark skin, forming the contrast to the "White Lady" of Wilno, whose icon hangs in Ostra Brama, "The Pointed Gate," in a street of the old town.

exchange impressions from their pilgrimages. I, a little sprout, eavesdropped to learn what they had brought back. They brought a lot, because they both had outstanding, deep reverence and love for the Most Holy Mother; if there was any difference between them on that subject, it was in the unending dialogue about which Mother of God is more efficacious, the one who shines in the Pointed Gate at Ostra Brama or the one who brightly guards Częstochowa. . . .

And at home two pictures hung above my bed: the Blessed Virgin of Częstochowa and the Blessed Virgin of Ostra Brama. Even though I was not very good at praying then—my knees always hurt, especially during the evening rosary that was a custom in our home—on waking up I would nevertheless always gaze for a long time at that Black Madonna and that White one. What intrigued me was that one was black, and the other white. Those are my earliest memories.

Devotion to Mary was thus the first and strongest feeling that Stefan Wyszyński acquired in his family home. There is nothing accidental about this. Let us remind ourselves what epoch that was, and what Poland. For over a hundred years the country had been divided among three occupiers. It was subjected to continual Russification and Germanization. The Catholic religion, the universal faith of Poles, welded them together, and devotion to the Virgins of Częstochowa and Wilno united the people of the different regions. It was a matter of religious and national survival.

Stefan Wyszyński's grandfather Piotr came from Podlasie—the region centering on Białystok, in the Russian partition—where Catholicism was persecuted more harshly than anywhere else. After the January Uprising of 1863, the tsarist authorities dissolved the diocesan structure of Podlasie. Several bishops who protested were banished, and many priests who had taken part in the uprising were exiled. One hundred twenty-nine monasteries were closed, and thirty-eight were denied the right to accept novices. Monks of different orders were thrown together. By 1870 not a single bishop from the area under Russian control was left in his own diocese.

Almost simultaneously, persecutions of the Church were developing in Prussian Poland as part of the *Kulturkampf** that began in 1871. For propaganda purposes, the Prussians fabricated a threat to their rule from "Polish-Catholic-Austrian machinations" that became a pretext for persecuting the Church and everything Polish. The Polish language was banned from all schools and offices. Many who taught religion in their own language were punished. Clerical positions were open only to citizens of the Reich. In 1874, Cardinal Mieczyslaw Ledóchowski was imprisoned as a result of a conflict over seminary administration, and after his release he was forbidden to return to his archdiocese, where a German had been installed in his place.

In Podlasie, Russification was energetically enforced, along with efforts to tear priests and lay people away from the Church. Piotr Wyszyński had to leave Podlasie: he had been active in defending the Uniate Catholics.† He bought some farmland on the Liwiec, near Łochów, in Kamieńczyk parish. Stefan's father, Stanisław Wyszyński, was raised in Kamieńczyk, on the border of Podlasie and Mazovia (the central region that includes Warsaw). The story of grandfather Piotr, who did not have the right to visit his native Podlasie, was remembered in the family. Piotr's son, the future Primate's father, studied music and then worked as an organist in Gałkowek

---

*The conflict between the German civil government of Bismarck (1st chancellor of German Empire—1871–1890) and Polish religious authorities, especially over the control of education, church appointments, and use of the Polish language, in order to destroy Polish culture.

†Members of the Orthodox Church (which broke from the Roman Church in the eleventh century), who at the Synod of Brest (Lithuania) in 1596 acknowledged the primacy of jurisdiction of the Roman Pope over the whole Church, preserving the liturgical form of the eastern rites and their own church hierarchy. The union was supported by several orthodox bishops. The Uniates together with their hierarchy became the subjects of severe persecution, especially during the time of the Polish partitions (1772–1918). In the Russian partition they ceased to exist by a decree of the Czar. In spite of these difficulties they survive to this day in Poland, where the Primate is their protector.

(near Łódź), in Prostynia (on the Bug), and finally in Zuzela, where Stefan came into the world. Zuzela lies in the Nurska region, where the Bug divides Podlasie and Mazovia.

Stanisław Wyszyński was thus linked to Mazovia, where his parents had tilled the land. In 1899, in the parish of Prostynia, he married Julianna Karp, of Kamieńczyk. From this marriage Stefan was born in Zuzela on August 3, 1901. A daughter, Anastazja, had been born first, and there would be two more girls, Stanisława and Janina, and another son, Wacław, who died when he was eleven.

Life in the small Mazovian village was peaceful, though not free from the psychological consequences of the last uprising. The country's defeat had become intertwined with religious persecution, a connection that projected itself onto everyone's mind, and especially the minds of the young.

The modest home of Stanisław and Julianna Wyszyński shaped the personality of their son Stefan. It may well be that the Cardinal's first memories, his parents' impressions from their pilgrimages, spring from the period of his very early childhood—when feelings of horror at the country's predicament must also have first reached the child's soul. At the same time, the family atmosphere softened such fears. His sisters surrounded young Stefan with loving tenderness, a feminine kindness and delicacy that he never forgot. "I know the female of the species," he would say later. "I had so many sisters, didn't I?" He was most deeply molded, however, by the absolute authority of his parents, by trust and respect for his father and tenderness for his mother. In a subjugated and persecuted country the family fills the principal role in education, replacing almost everything else. And this religious family tied its members, above all, to the Church. It also taught love of the homeland, of its crops and fruits. Cardinal Wyszyński later reminisced about being ordered to pick up a crust of bread he had dropped and kiss it. At Częstochowa in 1975 he recalled, as he had in many sermons, that his parents had instilled in him a reverence for human labor, bread, and grain—*zboże* in Polish, a word similar to *z Boże,* which means "from God."

At home he learned respect for people. Often he had to kiss the work-hardened and sometimes dirty hands of Mrs. Jesionek, who helped his mother with chores. On Christmas Eve, he had to get up from the family table and, carrying dinner, trot beside his father to a place near the cemetery where, regardless of the weather, they spoon fed a lonely and seriously ill old man.

From 1910 on, Stanisław Wyszyński worked in the hamlet of Andrzejewo, which lay in the same county of Ostrów Mazowiecki. Stefan attended third grade in the Russian-language elementary school there. A tension existed in the atmosphere between the students and their teachers at the Russian state schools. The severe preceptor ordered Stefan to kneel in the corner after some mischief, during a time when Stefan's mother was gravely ill. The punishment consisted of kneeling and going without midday dinner. While Stefan was kneeling, his younger sister, Stasia, came into the classroom, and the worried boy thought she was bringing news of his mother's death. But it turned out that his father was calling him to dinner. The hard-nosed teacher leaped toward the door and held Stefan back, saying, "I am telling you that you will stay here without dinner."

Then the nine-year-old Stefan showed his character; "I've had enough of your teaching, sir!" he announced.

"What did you say?"

"I've had enough of your teaching," young Wyszyński repeated.

"So don't come to school any more."

"I won't."

Nor did he. Stefan's father, understanding his son and the situation, hired a tutor rather than send his son back to the Andrzejewo classroom. When he was promoted to the fourth grade, Stefan continued his schooling at the Wojciech Górski school in Warsaw.

But it was in Andrzejewo that Stefan first encountered real tragedy. On October 31 he lost his mother, who died at thirty-three after giving birth to a last daughter, Zofia, who also died a month later. For a boy of nine, the loss of his mother was a great blow. Telling circumstances preceded it. The dying mother called her son close to her and said, "Stefan, get dressed." He began to pull on his coat, thinking his mother was sending him to the druggist's for medicine. "Get dressed," she said again, "but not like that. Dress yourself differently." Differently! The boy was taken aback and did not know what to do. His father said that he would explain later, but Stefan began to sense his mother's intention. She must mean that he should dress or change his clothes for God, by becoming a priest. In a family with close ties to everyday liturgical routines, it was easy to understand "Get dressed"; Stefan understood, although he told nobody. The Primate would say later that he had a calling from his first moment of conscious reflection on the matter. Once, before his mother died, he dreamed of being married; when he woke up he was crying because he thought he would not be able to become a priest. He told no one of the dream.

His mother's death shook Stefan, but did not shake his faith. He had prayed fervently for her recovery. His family, however, had bred in him the conviction that God's will must be accepted. Many times in later life he would have to demonstrate that acceptance. Surrendering to the will of God shaped his spiritual life; he emerged from his first great misfortune unscathed. Years later he said, "I never had doubts within my faith." That confidence stemmed from his being placed firmly within a family and national environment, tinged though the latter was by restlessness and the desire for independence, in which religion and the Church were the crown of the natural human order. A man whose destiny was to reconcile himself voluntarily to the thought of martyrdom would need to have unshakable faith.

In 1911, needing a wife to care for his five children, Stefan's father remarried. Eugenia Godlewska, his bride, was a friend of his first wife. Circumstances made the union understandable, but he longed for his own mother; the grown-up Stefan

Wyszyński was to say, "I went to Jasna Góra to say my First Mass so that I could have a Mother, a Mother who is forever and does not die." In Mary he saw throughout his life a Mother of his own, who would not abandon him. From his love for her he would draw the courage he needed when he had to risk everything, including his own life. Devotion to her became one of the leading motives in his religious life, recompensing him for his personal misfortunes and the affecting tragedies of the nation, giving him strength combined with feminine kindness and tenderness. One can hardly overvalue the import of these early events in his life—as the whole later career of the bishop, primate, and cardinal confirms.

Stefan Wyszyński attended Russian-language elementary school, but—as parents had been doing throughout the period of the partitions—his father took care to teach him the Polish language and literature.

From 1912 to 1915, Stefan attended the well-known Wojciech Górski *gimnazjum* in Warsaw. Here he came to know not just city life, but also the reality of the nation's bondage, which was more visible in Warsaw than in the provinces. Once again, the influence of specifically Polish circumstances on a young psyche becomes apparent. Games between Polish and Russian students developed into fights; they battled, for instance, to capture the gravel mound in the Saxon Gardens* "for Poland." Historians studying the generation preceding Stefan Wyszyński's have concluded that Poles born in the eastern lands had strong anti-Russian feelings, while those born under Prussian sway in Silesia or Poznań detested Germans. In Stefan Wyszyński one sees neither extreme, for the greatest influence on him was his religion, which determined everything else. In a close second place came his passionate affirmation of Polishness; yet, it must be emphasized, this affirmation never assumed a nationalistic character. The spirit of Christian love into which he had entered, and the deep respect for every person

---

*A park in Warsaw near the Tomb of the Unknown Soldier.

his family had cultivated in him, protected young Stefan from conflicts with his schoolmates, or from antipathy toward anyone.

Andrzejewo was burned down at the beginning of the war: the front passed through in August 1915. Stefan, who was on vacation, was cut off from Warsaw and the possibility of returning to his *gimnazjum*. Thanks to the efforts of Father Leonard Załuski, all those from Andrzejewo who had been studying in Warsaw were taken to Łomża and enrolled in the *gimnazjum* there, Stefan among them. In Łomża, he had his first painful experience with Germans. Stefan belonged to a troop of Boy Scouts who met in the woods. The German authorities sentenced boys caught at such meetings to a flogging of ten to twenty-five lashes. Stefan did not escape this punishment, and it lodged deep in his memory.

But he managed to avoid anti-German, anti-Russian, and anti-Semitic feelings—strong in Warsaw, where Jewish exiles, speaking only Russian or Yiddish, were streaming in from the East. It was his priestly calling that played the greatest role in shaping his attitudes. Felt from the time of his earliest memories and unmarred by any vacillations even during his childhood, the desire to prepare for the priesthood was so strong in Stefan that in 1917 he decided to transfer from the Łomża *gimnazjum* to the Pius X Lyceum, a minor seminary adjoined to the Major Seminary in Włocławek. Priests from Andrzejewo who had attended that seminary influenced his choice. Stefan's father initially opposed the decision, but Stefan managed to obtain permission to transfer to the Minor Seminary, where he stayed for three years before moving on to the Major Seminary. (His father, incidentally, changed jobs for the last time in 1918, settling in Wrociszew, on the Pilica River, where he was to stay until he died in 1970—at the age of ninety-four.)

Stefan's move to the major seminary happened in 1920, a time when all of his generation was caught up in the dramatic events occurring in Poland, and across Europe, in the wake of the First World War. While Stefan was growing up, his country recovered its independence, in 1918, after 123 years of partitions and subjugation; then came the Polish-Soviet War and the unusually dramatic Polish victory of 1920. During the decisive months the Polish bishops (Edmund Dalbor, Aleksander Kakowski, Józef Bilczewski, Józef Teodorowicz, Adam Sapieha, Marian Leon Fulman, Henryk Przeździecki) helped the cause. They called for social unity in a pastoral letter dated July 6: "In these difficult times, let us not allow pettiness into our hearts; on the contrary, let us give to the country what it deserves in accordance with God's will. . . . Restrain for its sake all partisan envy, all resentment. . . . Not with words, but with deeds, assert your love." And on August 9, a few days before the Battle of Warsaw, a proclamation by Cardinal Kakowski was read in all the churches of the capital, calling on the faithful to join the ranks of the defenders. "Forward, to your battle stations, under the banner of God and country!"

Stefan, at the Włocławek seminary, was eager to fight in defense of the homeland, but his priestly vocation was stronger than all other impulses, so he stayed where he was.

The juxtaposition of the words "God" and "country," which Cardinal Wyszyński would later make his motto, was harshly criticized, both within the country and abroad, and particularly among people ignorant of the historical context. But, then, at the time of the battle for Warsaw—which ultimately determined that revolution would not swallow up all Europe, and which was called the "miracle of the Vistula"*— the phrase "God and country" was no platitude. It expressed faith in the need to defend religion and the nation, European culture, the Church, and human freedom. How could that faith and the drama of those events fail to make an impression on

---

*A popular label used to identify the event which occurred in 1920 when the Communist Bolshevik army of Russia attacked Poland and proceeded to the very gates of Warsaw. At that point the Polish Army repulsed the attack, defeated the Russians, and pursued them well beyond the eastern borders of Poland. The apparently impossible victory came on the Feast of the Assumption of the Virgin Mary, August 15th, and the turning of the tide of battle was ascribed to her "miraculous" intervention.

Stefan's young, sensitive psyche? Would they not reinforce in his soul the ideas and values he had brought from his home and from the earliest years of his life?

* * *

His studies at the major seminary in preparation for the priesthood called for great determination: Stefan was struggling against weak health, but despite all obstacles he completed his philosophical and theological studies in 1924.

The other seminarians were ordained on June 24, 1924, but Stefan was obliged to defer the sacrament because he had to be hospitalized for a lung condition. On his birthday, August 3, he was ordained in the chapel of the Blessed Virgin in Włoc-ławek Cathedral, by Auxiliary* Bishop Wojciech Owczarek. During the ceremony he was so weak that when the moment came to lie down with arms outstretched as on a cross, he felt too weak to stand.

The dramatic beginning of his priesthood once again tied him to the Virgin Mary. Immediately after his ordination, he left for Częstochowa so that he could offer his First Solemn Mass, on August 5, before the miraculous icon of the Madonna of Jasna Góra, Queen of Poland. During this Mass he once again felt so weak that he barely managed to stay on his feet. At the time he prayed fervently to Mary, asking only to be a priest for at least a year. His sister Stanisława, who was witness to that First Mass, could not stop crying at the sight of her brother's physical weakness.

After his ordination, Father Wyszyński had to take a cure, so that he did not begin his priestly work until October. Evidently enjoying a splendid reputation among his clerical superiors, he was entrusted with three positions at once: as a vicar in the Włocławek Cathedral, a prefect of evening courses for adults, and editor-in-chief—at the age of twenty-three—of the

---

*Or "suffragan."

diocesan newspaper, *Słowo Kujawskie* (The Kujawy Word).

After a year of work in the diocese, the young priest was directed by Bishop Stanisław Zdzitowiecki of Włocławek to study further, at the Catholic University of Lublin (commonly known by its Polish initials, KUL). From 1925 to 1929 he was enrolled in the department of canon law and, simultaneously, studying Catholic social science and economics under Father Antoni Szymański in the department of law and socioeconomic science. Upon defending a thesis entitled *The Rights of the Family, the Church, and the State in Relation to Schools* in June 1929, he received his doctorate in canon law.

During his studies at KUL, Father Wyszyński was active in the Catholic academic youth association, "Rebirth," a center for innovation in Polish Catholicism. Such innovative currents found expression in the strictly religious realm—great stress was put upon new liturgical forms, like the recited Mass—as well as in social matters. Rebirth opposed the nationalistic manifestations endemic to the Catholic world and espoused personalist philosophy. The organization produced an elite that played a great role in shaping Polish Catholicism after the Second World War. Father Wyszyński owed much of his ideology to it. In turn, his powerful personality and thorough knowledge sketched out directions for Rebirth to follow. He always stressed national values in combination with individual ones—an outgrowth of Catholic personalism.

Father Wyszyński always remained an intransigent foe of totalitarianism. At the same time, he understood the importance of Polish religious, national, and cultural identity as few others did. These qualities made up the spiritual personality that enabled him to become a defender of religion and everything Polish, or human rights and man's individual worth in the face of a totalitarian system.

Father Władysław Korniłowicz* was one of those who had a great influence on the future primate. A profound relationship

---

*The personal spiritual director of the Primate. He had been chaplain of the students at the Catholic University of Lublin at the time that Cardinal Wyszyński was a priest-student there.

sprang up between the two priests, spiritual father and son, because of which Wyszyński became—apart from his work in Rebirth and the student Fraternal Aid organization—associate director of the priests' residence and the representative of the student priests for four years. Finally, showing great social sense and an activist's disposition, the young priest took an active part in developing and strengthening the young Catholic University, pleading its cause in the magazine *Ateneum Kapłańskie* (The Priests' Atheneum). In his articles he not only urged that the idea of a Catholic university be accepted by the clergy, but also pleaded for its full legal accreditation.

Father Korniłowicz also influenced Wyszyński's pastoral style. The future primate understood the relation of Catholic clergy to the faithful as a relation of father to sons and daughters. In later life, those closest to him never addressed him as Your Eminence, but simply as "Father." Those who loved him cherished this intimacy. When he became Bishop of Lublin, Wyszyński wrote in *Tygodnik Powszechny:*

> Father Korniłowicz's fatherhood had a distinctly supernatural character. He gave birth to people for God, and once he had won them over he was never indifferent to even the most minute problems of his spiritual children. He was father to the Franciscan Sisters of the Cross [who ran an institution for blind children at Laski, near Warsaw], to a small group of Brothers of the Third Order [of Saint Francis], to a Thomistic circle, to the blind children, to students, to many converts, to Jews he baptized, to the Lublin academic priests, to all among whom he worked and who saw God through the Father's service.

This obituary of Father Korniłowicz—the "hunter of souls" who, spending most of his time in the confessional, reconciled with God many of the leading personalities of his day, invigorated participatory liturgy, stimulated Thomistic thoughts, preached, and led retreats indefatigably—testifies to Korniłowicz's influence on the younger priest's pastorship.

In the meantime, however, the son had to leave his spiritual father. From Lublin he carried away the experience of a religiosity as fervent as his own that was open-minded and tinged with a special warmth for people regardless of their origins, race, social background, or intellectual accomplishments. Characteristically, the Bishop of Lublin did not shy away from mentioning hostility toward the "liberal" Father Korniłowicz when he wrote his preceptor's obituary in 1946. "This quiet animosity, however, existed only among lukewarm Catholics who sensed a threat to their own comfort and a spur to efforts they would rather avoid." The lay opposition to Father Korniłowicz came from nationalists who resented his special devotion to converts. These were the lukewarm Catholics, more interested in developing a predominate national Catholicism than in the deepening of faith. But Catholic universalism has room both for warmly, even intensely, affirming the nation and for accepting converts and brothers of whatever background.

After defending his dissertation, Wyszyński received a traveling scholarship that allowed him to study the state of the Christian social sciences in Austria, Italy, France, Belgium, Holland, and Germany. This journey, in 1929–30, widened the young priest's intellectual horizons and led to his first publications in the field of social Catholicism: *The Work of Cardinal Ferrari: Ideals and Socio-Apostolic Action* (1930), and *The Main Types of Catholic Action Abroad* (1931). Above all, the foreign journey reinforced his passion for the social sciences. The world was entering a great economic crisis. Could there have been a more inspiring moment for dedicating oneself to the Christian teachings about society?

* * *

On his return to Poland, Father Wyszyński began outlining lectures on social science for the seminary and published the results of his travels in *Ateneum Kapłańskie* and *Prąd* (Current).

He concentrated on pedagogical matters and the work of Catholic Action.

In the fall of 1930, after working temporarily as vicar at Przedcz Kujawski, Wyszyński returned to his post as vicar in Włocławek Cathedral. A multitude of duties now fell upon him. In 1931 he became secretary of the Pius X Lyceum and lectured on social economy in the seminary. He also directed the diocesan missions office in 1931–32. From 1932 until the outbreak of the war, he was editor-in-chief of *Ateneum Kapłańskie*. At the same time, until 1938, he filled the post of promoter of justice and defender of the matrimonial bond in the diocesan curia, and from 1938 on he was a judge in the Bishop's Tribunal.

All these functions were part of an educated and enthusiastic priest's normal career path. But Wyszyński, interested above all in Christian social science, did not stop there. He was not satisfied to lecture on sociology, Catholic social science, Catholic Action,* and canon law, and to found a sociological workshop in the seminary in 1937. To engage himself directly with the workers, he headed the Christian Workers' University. From 1932 on, he was active in the Christian trade unions and organized the Catholic Union of Young Workers.

Father Wyszyński was capable of combining his activities among the workers with a role in the Marian Society of Landowners of the Kujawy-Dobrzyń region, although the landowners were dissatisfied to a certain extent at having a labor activist minister to them. But before the war it was characteristic for Father Wyszyński to engage himself as much with workers and the unemployed as with proprietors and gentry.

He was engrossed in social theory as well as in social practice. Under the direction of the respected Rector Antoni Szymański, he began preparing his *habilitacja*† at KUL on

---

*A highly organized and very active Catholic social movement in Poland under the direction of the Church that worked to inculcate a Catholic social ethics in society, especially among youth, workers, and intelligentsia.
†The highest academic achievement in Poland, which requires, after the usual doctoral dissertation, a considerable body of published research and a colloquium with the university faculty.

work that he wrote up as *The Moral Environment of Factory Work.* Concurrently, he was developing a program of talks for Rebirth and keeping in touch with Father Korniłowicz.

What were Wyszyński's social views in the thirties? He was definitely regarded as a progressive priest, although by no means as an extremist. For communism he never had the slightest sympathy, not even of the sort to which many distinguished minds reconciled themselves after the war. This lack of illusions resulted not just from his exemplary knowledge of the Church's social teachings, but still more from his knowledge of the workers, of their true needs and interests. In an article in *Schönere Zukunft* titled "The Wandering Unemployed at the Doors of the Rectory" in which he reviewed the Reverend F. Kerer's work Wyszyński deliberated over the extent to which the priest should "deproletarianize the body" and "deproletarianize the soul." In another article, "The Pastor and the Unemployed," he suggested retreats for the unemployed, extending spiritual care to them by—among other means— involving them in parish work, maintaining personal contact with them, visiting them at home, providing spiritual support, and leading common charitable activities in the parish. He demanded material and moral help for the unemployed, the satisfaction of their cultural needs, and above all the assurance of care for their children.

Wyszyński's views oscillated between two principal tendencies. On the one hand he warned against the influence of communist ideology on the workers, and on the other hand he firmly supported policy and structural changes to answer workers' needs. In 1931 he wrote that the current economic crisis

> is not a temporary interruption of the economic boom, but in large part a necessary consequence of the world capitalist economy. . . . All pomp and modern luxury is open only to the privileged, who enjoy it in the presence of the proletariat with the frivolity and thick skin typical of plutocrats and the boorish *nouveaux riches*. Endlessly

created artificial needs have a negative effect on the capacity for charity. . . . Lacking other methods, one can easily end up on the side of lawlessness! . . . They talk about the decline of morality among the working class in order to prepare an adequate number of prison cells. . . . They talk about the increase in communism, and yet they do not want to believe that the reason for this growth is not so much Bolshevik propaganda as the lack of work, of bread, and of a roof over one's head.

Two years later, Father Wyszyński warned that "close contact with working people teaches us that the influence of Russia, fighting against God, is stronger here than we appreciate."

But in 1934, Father Wyszyński demanded in *Ateneum Kapłańskie,* concrete changes to benefit the working class: "The enormous salaries of high officials . . . so absorb institutional budgets that there is nothing left over to pay junior officials and workers. . . . Such a state of things does not accord with Catholic ideas of just distribution. . . . Violating the balance of incomes in society is bound to lead to a shaking of the whole social order; these are the causes of an inclination toward Bolshevism."

He proposed the following solutions: "Acknowledging the need for differences of salaries, substantiated by the inequality of services to society, we must firmly establish the permitted extent of these differences. . . . Help can come only from a financially independent state, unbeholden to bankers and financiers, by raising the moral level and moral requirements of the people who direct economic life."

These postulates signify a departure from liberal economics and a declaration for active state social policies, for limited intervention in economic life to aid the most impoverished levels of society. But Wyszyński was far from assigning all responsibility for economic life to the state. Writing about the causes of the continuing economic malaise under the pseudonym of "Doctor Zuzelski" in *Kurier Warszawski,* he underscored the unanimous agreement of scholars, writers, and politicians who

> acknowledge that the lack of ethical norms is the basic source of the crisis. What is more, many warn of the indispensable connection of economic ethics and religious life. We must energetically set about renovating whatever shows itself to be obsolete in our economic structure, conforming it to new conditions of life, while seeking in the unavoidable struggles of reconstruction that which unites, rather than that which divides.

Critics often accuse Christian social science of wanting to substitute moralizing for social change. Wyszyński, however, forthrightly acknowledged in his writings the inevitability of change. He also knew that the Christian reformer often faces charges of promoting communism hurled by the conservatives, only to turn around and find the communists distorting his views because they want to hold on to their revolutionary monopoly on social transformation. He resolved the two tendencies in 1937, speaking to the Catholic Action pastoral course in Płock:

> It is necessary to realize *what is, and what is not communism.* The name of communism is often applied to all reforms intended to improve the lot of workers and peasants, to all calls for social justice, better distribution of income, agricultural reform, and so on. . . . The Church fights socialism because that doctrine warps the view of the nature of society, of its sense of purpose, and of the purpose and character of social man, which it presents out of accord with Christian truth. . . .
>
> The class struggle proclaimed by communism keeps the "future state" in constant turmoil, while the revolutionary method makes it impossible for even today's oppressed classes to develop in social well-being. It links to such

development the destruction of several social levels on the road of revolutionary transformation which *destroys the basic principles of the past* once and for all.

Communism *proclaims an idea of false liberation*. . . . The inequality created by communism lies on a different plane [from that of capitalism], perhaps a more acute one, because it is enforced by a complete monopoly of food supply. Communism sees the person only as a wheel in a collective mechanism, entitled to the basic means of life only in proportion to his productive utility.

While he firmly opposed revolutionary change, Wyszyński pointed in this same speech to the need for restructuring Polish agriculture. In some regions of the country, unemployment and poverty were worse in the villages than in the cities, although this was not immediately apparent. Wyszyński cited the causes of the emerging peasants' political movement: "The imperfect division of land, leaving 34 percent of the farms undersized; the civic and social degradation of farm people— despite constitutional guarantees of equality; the economic gap between organized urban industries and the dispersed productivity of the villages, etc." To satisfy the demands of a peasant youth movement for education, Wyszyński proposed the creation of Catholic peasant universities. He also supported the striving of the village people for their due respect from society, and their demands for land ownership, because "the peasant loves land, and that love guards him from communism. The Polish village will not be at peace as long as it has today's examples of social greed before its eyes." This was a decisive call for agricultural reform, all the more important because it was made within the forum of Catholic Action, a movement closely connected to the church hierarchy.

These sketchy examples of Wyszyński's social views testify to his social radicalism and his conviction that a third road exists between liberal capitalism and revolutionary Marxism. His early conviction later blossomed into the idea that Poland, lying between East and West, has a definite, well-understood mission: to create—based on the social strength of a Catholicism that had stood firm through the long battle with atheism —a political system that opposed not only the inherent mistakes of collectivism but also the structural weaknesses and egotistical tendencies of capitalism. The social teaching of the Church provides a basis for such solutions. Such a system has not yet been realized, for which the major Christian countries of the West certainly bear a great responsibility. Faith in Poland's mission to realize such a system, despite the country's membership in the Eastern bloc, seems noble—although one might doubt the prospects for quick success. Looking, however, at the dangers to humanity and the hopes presented in Pope John Paul II's first encyclical, *Redemptor hominis,* we recognize the distinct universal echoes of Stefan Wyszyński's efforts within the Polish Church.

Between 1931 and 1939, the future primate brought out 106 publications, of which the overwhelming majority dealt with the economic crisis, unemployment, and social justice. Pius XI's encyclical *Quadragesimo anno* (1931), with its references to the epochal *Rerum novarum* of Leo XIII (1891), spurred new interest in social problems throughout the Christian world. Father Wyszyński tried to give this interest a special and original expression in Poland, which, during those years, found itself mired in a particularly difficult social situation.* In 1937, Wyszyński was made a member of the Primate's Social Council. The council managed, before the war, to issue a declaration on agricultural matters and worker enfranchisement. Today the West is still seeking a realization of the latter concept in "comanagement" and "co-ownership." In agricultural policy, the council demanded compensated redistribution of large estates, following the principles that Wyszyński had been expressing.

Wyszyński's most significant efforts, however, took place

---

*Because of more than one hundred years of partitions, there were in the 1920s in Poland widespread poverty, belated industrial development, and a generally backward situation, e.g. the absence of safety rules for workers. For these reasons Cardinal Wyszyński championed the cause of the workers and laboring classes.

among the workers of Włocławek. At the time, Włocławek was a highly industrialized city, with celluloid and paper mills, ceramics plants, and food-processing factories. The Christian trade unions there counted five thousand members before the war and controlled a fifth of the seats on the village council— a degree of power they had not obtained anywhere else in the country. The socialist unions were also strong in Włocławek and worked closely with the Christian unions; communist, nationalist, and Jewish unions were relatively weaker than elsewhere in Poland. Within this variegated workers' movement, Wyszyński strove to create a new atmosphere of cooperation among unions and independence from political parties. The Christian group cooperated with other unions in negotiating contracts, organizing strikes, monitoring labor cases in the courts, trying to gain accident insurance, and so on. A sort of "social peace" resulted from this affiliation of diverse organizations. At the height of the economic crisis, over the winter of 1933–34, Wyszyński managed to bring about a meeting of employers and workers that succeeded because the workers, under his guidance, refrained from advancing economic demands that the employers could not have met in the circumstances. Instead, the workers demanded and obtained measures of respect for their personal dignity, measures much needed in a period of usually contemptuous attitudes by employers.

Father Wyszyński's efforts succeeded because he lived the principles of Catholic social thought instead of merely preaching them. He even devoted his personal financial resources to his work with the proletariat. When the Marian Society of Landowners raised funds for his medical expenses—he never enjoyed good health—he put the money instead toward the erection of a Christian Unions Building. (The edifice still stands, though, paradoxically, today it houses the offices of the communist-directed unions.)

Later, Father Wyszyński was always to remember with great sentiment this phase of his activities, to which the war put an irrevocable end. "The work undertaken from my own predilections and the impulses of my heart in the Christian trade unions, where I left my soul, my heart, and a good deal of my health, gave me great joy," he said. "How well I remember today the fellowship of workers who, with the song 'We Want God' [the anthem of the Catholic Action movement] on their lips, obediently followed the voice of the Holy Church, believing that in the spirit of its social teachings true justice fortified by love would conquer the world."

*   *   *

Toward the end of August 1939, Father Wyszyński returned from Zakopane to Włocławek, where the outbreak of war found him. Bishop Karol Radoński placed the senior class of the seminary under Wyszyński's protection and ordered them to travel to Lublin, to be ordained as quickly as possible. They got only as far as Łuck, however, for the Red Army was entering eastern Poland. Mixed with the flood of refugees on the roads, they straggled back to Włocławek in small groups. Father Wyszyński returned from Łuck in a horse-drawn cart, holding the reins himself, and picking up priests along the way. People in Włocławek still had some illusions about the Germans. Bishop Michał Kozal and a few professors tried to reopen the Major Seminary; since Wyszyński knew German, he handled the negotiations with the occupiers. By October 15, however, priests were being arrested, and the earlier illusions vanished. Because of his prewar publications on Nazism, Father Wyszyński himself was in danger. Rector Józef Korszyński of the seminary told the young professor to leave Włocławek, but Wyszyński, feeling a sense of duty, refused to leave until Bishop Kozal personally gave the order. In 1956, as Auxiliary Bishop of Włocławek, Korszyński recalled with pride how he had helped preserve the Church's future leader: "I knew for sure that this was a man needed for the future, that God was going to ask great things of him."

Wyszyński had already left Włocławek when he realized that he had forgotten an important book. He turned back, but at the train station someone warned him that the Gestapo had searched his apartment and was looking for him—thus, the warnings of his superiors proved correct. He was to spend the rest of the war moving from place to place, hiding from the Gestapo and living with the uncertainty of a man whose life is in constant danger.

After staying for a few days with his friend Father Michał Szwabiński in Grabkowo, he paid a visit to his family; when he returned he found that Father Michał Szwabiński had been arrested by the Gestapo. The road to Włocławek was closed, and there was no option besides the risky one of returning to his father, stepmother, and sisters in Wrociszew by Warka. In the village he did not show himself except to go to church. He dreamed of returning to Włocławek until news came that the entire seminary staff—clerics, professors, and Bishop Kozal, forty-four people in all—had been arrested.

Wyszyński had no choice but to carry on his work in his parents' home. Although he had no library, he managed to compose four series of *Social Sermons* between November 1939 and July 1940. Eventually, however, the Gestapo started looking for him around Wrociszew; this, plus Wyszyński's sense of unfulfilled obligation, made him decide to move on.

In July 1940, while he was staying temporarily with his sister Janina Jurkiewicz, a teacher, a nun arrived, sent by Father Korniłowicz to ask Father Wyszyński to take over the spiritual care of a group of sisters and blind children who had been transferred to an estate in Kozłówka. Father Wyszyński set out immediately. Since Polish conspiratorial activity was beginning in the vicinity, he also became chaplain to the partisans and to fugitives from the Germans. After the owner of the estate, Count Andrzej Zamoyski, was arrested, Wyszyński continued to care for his housemates, giving lectures for the intelligentsia and reading papers on Catholic social theory and philosophy. As had been his habit before the war, he brought gentry and workers together in retreats, giving spiritual support to everyone and sharing his will to endure and survive.

In October 1941, a recurrence of his lung disease forced him

to travel to the mountain town of Zakopane. There the Gestapo caught up with him, arrested him, and took him to the
Glaspalast, their punishment center for Poles. After several
hours, during which he was already preparing for death, the
Germans unaccountably released him. He ascribed his deliver-
ance to the prayers of the Ursuline Sisters, with whom he had
been staying.

From November 1941 until June 1942, Father Wyszyński
lived in Żułów, where he watched over a group of sisters and
blind people, conspired in the clandestine teaching of young
people, and carried relief to nearby victims of typhus. One day
he stumbled upon the forest hut of a woman the villagers called
"the last resort" who was condemned by the locals for her
loose behavior. The astonished Father Wyszyński discovered
the emaciated woman lying on a disordered straw bed in the
extremities of labor. He wanted to send for help, but it was too
late. The woman desperately grabbed hold of his cassock and
begged him not to leave. Holding him by the hand, she summoned her last strength and brought a child into the world.
The priest, who had never before witnessed such an event,
acted as midwife and nurse, and experienced the Mystery of
the Visitation in a way he had never anticipated.

In June 1942, he went to Laski, to fill the shoes of another
close associate of Father Korniłowicz, Father Jan Zieja, who
had fled when the Gestapo picked up his trail. The Laski
Institute for the Blind, of which Wyszyński became chaplain,
had attracted Catholic students, former members of the Rebirth group who had been associated with care of the sightless,
gentry, and Warsaw intellectuals. Father Wyszyński became
the spiritual guide for this whole wartime aggregation, and he
would not have been himself if he had not begun presenting
lectures on Catholic social thought and organizing conferences
on the Church as the Mystical Body of Christ.

In addition, it was not long before Wyszyński had entered
the whirlpool of Warsaw social and political work. He became
active at the house of the Resurrectionist Sisters on Chłodna
Street, where students of the secret Warsaw University and the

University of the Western Lands (also operating in the capital) gathered. Here he became a magnet for thinking people of all ages who were eager for social reform in a future Poland, and for the reinvigoration of Catholic thought. On Kredytowa Street he held classes for a Pauline circle, which was studying Saint Paul's epistles. He organized a year-round schedule of retreats in convent chapels, especially those of the Gray Ursulines on Wiślana Street, and of the Kuźniczanki Ladies* on Mirowski Place. Workers, the young, gentry, teachers, and scholars came together at these retreats to listen, confess, discuss, and convert. Later, many of them followed the muddy road to Laski. A legend was slowly growing around Father Wyszyński.

Wyszyński chose for himself the underground pseudonym Sister Cecilia, and before long people were asking, "Is Sister Cecilia saying Mass today? When is she hearing confessions?" Even as life got worse under the Germans and the dangers increased, Father Wyszyński kept at his work, with confidence in the Virgin Mary as his guarantee of security. He was discreet about his special devotion to Mary, although one of the students remembered that he often sang the relatively unfamiliar hymn "Beautiful Splendid Star, Mary of Częstochowa."

He was still in Laski when the Warsaw Uprising began on August 1, 1944. Everyone realized the gravity of the drama being played out in the capital, and the possibility of a tragic ending. A group of young women staying at Laski for a few days experienced a conflict of conscience that they could not solve: should they join the uprising or not? They approached Father Wyszyński for his spiritual and paternal advice; he told them he would give them an answer the next day. After a night in the grip of this awful responsibility, he told them, "Were I in your place, I would go—people are dying there. But don't

---

*A term used to designate the graduates of the school founded by Jadwiga Zamojska (d. 1923), "The School of Housekeeping," first in Kórnik, near Poznań, and later, because of Prussian persecution in that area, in Kuźnice, a small town near Zakopane in southern Poland. More than 3,000 young women completed this program of Christian family formation.

shoot. You are to carry life. The greatest need there is for prayer." Today some might question this advice, but a man who understands his own life as an offering to God cannot advise others to renounce danger. As it turned out, the whole group survived and made it back to Laski. Then the sort of tension in which Father Wyszyński had been living became plain. As he welcomed them, tears fell onto his cassock. He could manage but four words: "My children have returned."

The uprising transformed the Institute for the Blind into a hospital, a home for fugitives, and a contact point for underground groups. Under the pseudonym Radwan 2, Wyszyński served as chaplain for the Żoliborz military district. Under constant bombardment, he also served as chaplain to the wounded and fugitives in Laski. It was an extraordinary pastoral experience to be in contact with suffering people day and night, offering them the spiritual help that they, oppressed in the uprising, needed more than at any other time in their lives.

Help meant all sorts of things in those weeks. Once, in the forest, Father Wyszyński came across a wounded, half-conscious courier girl who had lost so much blood that she could not move. The frail and sickly priest picked up the well-grown girl and carried her on his back to the institute, more than two kilometers away. The drama of suffering and death produced many instances of such dedication. The first time he took part in an operation, Father Wyszyński almost fainted from the sight and smell of blood, but later he assisted the surgeons whenever he could. One boy agreed to have a shattered leg amputated only if the chaplain were present. Wyszyński held his hand until he fell asleep, then went to attend others who were in danger of death, and returned by the time the amputee woke up. A soldier of sixteen kept singing religious songs until the moment of death; later Wyszyński recalled, "I buried him in the cemetery near Izabelin, in a little sand mound without a coffin—we had run out of coffins. At least he had beautiful flowers for his grave. He is still there, near Warsaw." A nineteen-year-old named Jurek was in despair after the resection of his intestines. He was an only son, pampered, and bore his situation very badly; it was Wyszyński who had to tell him that death lay ahead. When Jurek complained, "I've had enough lying around; I want to go to the front," the priest answered, "Jurek, before long you'll be going to the front where Our Lady is." Amazingly, these words calmed Jurek. As Father Wyszyński had predicted, Jurek died on September 7, the eve of Our Lady's Feast Day (Nativity of Mary, September 8).

In an uprising during which 240,000 people perished, every priest came across similarly dramatic incidents. Their situation was often more difficult than that of the soldiers. Besides attending to Polish soldiers, the chaplains had also to minister to enemy German, Hungarian, and Ukrainian soldiers who were dying. Such help was never refused. In the meantime, the city and the uprising were dying. Father Wyszyński stood motionless for hours at night, blessing the burning capital. When he thought no one was watching, he would lie prone in the form of a cross on the floor of the chapel, praying for both the dying and the ones fated to survive. He prayed for those spiritual children of his for whose participation in the battle he took moral responsibility. The wind carried ashes all the way to Laski from the capital. Once, toward the end of the uprising, Father Wyszyński found a shred of paper on which the fire had left only three words: "Thou shalt love." Was it not his motto? The priest showed it to the nuns and said, "The burning capital could not have sent us anything more dear."

* * *

A short account can only hint at the true effect the five long years of war had on Stefan Wyszyński. During that period, a Catholic priest confronted new psychic shocks, unexpected problems, and ultimate, existential situations almost every day. Small incidents are perhaps the most revealing. A nun who had worked with him at Laski, Sister Vianney (Jadwiga Szachno) recalled in 1978 her own days with the future primate:

From the fall of 1944 until the end of the occupation, there were two German priests using the chapel of the institute. One of them, a clerk, had a fixed hour for saying Mass; the other, an orderly, said Mass at various hours, whenever he could find the time. I often saw him carting straw and barrels of water during the course of the day. He was a good, fervent priest. I was a witness in the sacristy once when, already dressed for Mass, he stood gazing at the crucifix and crying. Since I was in charge of the Mass intentions, I sometimes had a chance to see Father Wyszyński's attitude toward these German priests in the sacristy. On the one hand, I observed the great dignity of a Pole, and on the other I sensed a certain sacerdotal camaraderie that linked him to these priests. There was the supernatural brotherly respect for priesthood, and at the same time a certain delicate distancing. For example, Father Wyszyński liked to joke at times, but I noticed that in the presence of the German priests he was solemn and never joked.

All sorts of people, groups, and church organizations sought out Father Wyszyński during his enforced stay at Laski to ask for his religious services. Some he had to refuse, with pain in his heart. His popularity was greater than the amount of time he had, and an excess of duties weighed down on him. There were times, however, when he seized on new ideas and requests that were presented to him. On November 1, 1942, for instance, he gave a lecture, "The Competence of the Church in the Socioeconomic Sphere," to a group directed by Maria Okońska.

Maria Okońska gathered around herself girls who wanted to devote themselves entirely to religious social work, renouncing married life but still remaining lay people. First the members of the group had to develop a wider knowledge of sociology and a more profound religious faith. Then they were to embark upon professional careers and spread among their colleagues the higher Catholic culture they had acquired. Father

Wyszyński's lecture made such an impression on its female audience that the group decided to ask him to become its spiritual adviser. And because the idea of a "lay apostolate" in conformity with Christian social teachings interested Father Wyszyński a great deal, on August 10, 1943, he agreed to take over the spiritual direction of the group. A long association was thus born.

Because of its initial size, the group became known as the Eight. During the war its members made far-reaching plans for the cultural training of young Polish women in accordance with Catholic doctrine. A Girls' City was even projected, in which young women would be prepared for the wider world. Postwar conditions forced the group to limit its earlier plans, but even in a communist state Maria Okońska's Eight did not give up their ideas. They soon undertook educational work among young people in a Catholic spirit and organized many youth groups and camps.

*   *   *

The end of the war presented Stefan Wyszyński with a choice. He could stay in Laski, which had become an important Catholic center, a place of conversions and the home of a radiant spirit of Christian openness, to which he felt strongly attached by the war experience. He also received various offers from Warsaw. However, he decided to return to Włocławek, his mother diocese and the place of his impressive prewar academic and pastoral beginnings.

Thus he set out in an overcrowded railroad car with one of the sisters from Laski. Clearing a path through the passengers, he asked people to move out of the way. One man, without looking to see who was trying to pass through, growled, "Move where? You're stupid." The answer came calmly, in Wyszyński's characteristic sad tone of voice: "Oh, if you only knew how stupid!" The passengers immediately found a place for the priest and the sister.

The seminary building in Włocławek had been destroyed, the library burned, and the professors had not yet returned from the concentration camps. Father Wyszyński organized the temporary establishment of the seminary in the parish of Lubraniec, thirty kilometers away, and on March 19, 1945, he became rector. Everyone was hungry, and the seminarians depended on the local parishioners for food. On one occasion the parishioners brought seventy loaves of bread. Then a little girl appeared, carrying one more loaf. When she was told that it was not needed, she began to cry and said that they did not want to take bread from her because she was poor. Father Wyszyński could do nothing but take her loaf.

Thirty students enrolled in the seminary, covering two years' worth of material in one. Besides being rector, professor, and spiritual father to the seminarians, Stefan Wyszyński also worked as vicar in Lubraniec and as pastor of the parishes of Kłobia and Zgłowiączka. Each Sunday included many kilometers of travel on foot. As parts of the seminary were gradually re-established in Włocławek, there was even more traveling to do. He commuted to town in a horse cart until the autumn of 1945, when all the departments of the seminary returned to the prewar building. Still, no matter how much Father Wyszyński loved work, he had to turn down an offer of appointment to yet another parish, Świerczyn: he had taken over the old church printing shop, set up a diocesan weekly, *Ład Boży* (God's Order), for which he wrote a column, "Order in Thought," and revived the diocesan curial publishing house and its *Ateneum Kapłańskie*. He retrieved part of the library and the diocesan archives. On August 15, 1945, he was named canon capitular* of the Włocławek Cathedral. As at Laski during the war, he became a magnet for nuns, youth, intelligentsia, and workers.

These new duties influenced Stefan Wyszyński's attitudes. Before the war he had been fascinated by academic work; now,

---

*A member of the clergy attached to a cathedral or other large church, with specific duties such as the choral recitation of the Divine Office

by necessity and by the choice of those around him, he became first of all a pastor and "Father." That word came to define his ideal of priestly service; in his book *Our Father* he considered the word "father":

> Jesus began his prayer with a word that opens the most unskilled, shy, and tightly drawn lips. Who among the sons of Eve does not know that word? It shatters all ice, victoriously overcomes the vastest spaces, stretches out its arms and reaches for the heart. Father! It is a triumphant, possessing, captivating word. It is a codex of rights for everyone who opens his lips. It never contains a threat, sometimes perhaps a reproach or a reminder, always a plea and a right.

The psychological switch from academe to pastoral activity was not easy, but the principle of *res sacra homo* (man is sacred) won out. People always managed to tear Stefan Wyszyński away from his books. He threw his soul into ministering to priests and workers, but he did not believe he understood the psychology of women. However, Father Korniłowicz would tell him, "Stefek, there is no Church of men or Church of women. There is only one—the Church of Christ." Father Wyszyński followed Korniłowicz's wisdom, and he turned out to have a great, unconscious influence on women's religiosity. He became religious director to many womens' circles and a specialist in womens' souls. They were drawn to him by his delicacy in matters of conscience and the inner strength that radiated from his whole personality. People easily entrusted him with their spiritual secrets; women students who would confess to no one else lined up outside his confessional; lapsed Catholics would summon him to their deathbeds. Father Wyszyński reconciled hundreds or even thousands to God, but this "success" wore him down. He was so chronically exhausted that more than once he had to ask his penitents to wake him up if he should doze in the confessional.

On March 25, 1946, Cardinal Hlond, the Primate, summoned

FatherWyszyński and Bishop Radoński of Wrocław to Poznań. Father Wyszyński feared that he was going to have his ears boxed for an article, "The Problem of the Vatican," that he had written for a Warsaw weekly. Bishop Radoński supposed the same. However, Cardinal Hlond greeted them with the words, "I have a matter that pertains only to Father Wyszyński." The Cardinal then informed the young priest that Pope Pius XII had nominated him Bishop of Lublin on March 4.

Stefan Wyszyński's recent work, of which Cardinal Hlond was obviously proud, justified the nomination, but Wyszyński himself could not imagine leaving Włocławek, where he had just been setting so many religious activities in motion. He said that he could not leave the seminary, most of whose professors had not yet returned from the camps. Cardinal Hlond had an irrefutable answer: "One does not say no to the Pope." Hlond could sense the nominee's internal conflict. "Tomorrow morning I leave to take possession of the Archdiocese of Warsaw by the will of the Holy Father. The archbishop of Gniezno ceases to be Archbishop of Poznań and becomes the Archbishop of Warsaw. This is an absolute secret, but I am taking over in Warsaw. So it should be easier for you to decide, Father Professor. We will be together in one metropolitan area.* My decision is not easy, either. But one does not refuse anything the Holy Father asks."

Father Wyszyński wanted time to think, and Cardinal Hlond said that he could wait until early the next morning, when he had to set out for Warsaw. The night was a difficult one. In its course Father Wyszyński remembered being amused when Father Korniłowicz first put on the purple robes of a monsignor. "Don't think I make light of this," the older priest said then. "On the contrary—I cherish it. Is not each step

---

*Refers to a geographical province which includes an archdiocese, usually centered in a large city, and one or more dioceses. E.g. Detroit is an archdiocese, Michigan is a metropolitan area that includes Detroit and all other dioceses in Michigan (Saginaw, Kalamazoo, Lansing, Grand Rapids, Gaylord, and Marquette). The Archbishop is called the Metropolitan. (In Poland Poznań is an archdiocese and a metropolitan see with no other dioceses attached to it to make a metropolitan area. It is an exception.)

upward in the hierarchy a greater fullness of the priesthood and a greater unity with Christ?"

Such reasoning seemed abstract when juxtaposed with the beloved Włocławek Cathedral, the seminary, the *Ateneum Kapłańskie*, the workers, and the "children." All this would have to be left behind. Later, Wyszyński said that if he had been able to choose in strictly human terms, he would have stayed in Włocławek as a professor, editor, and social activist. These were the passions of his life. But the conviction that Christ and the Holy Father cannot be refused proved stronger in the end. The secret longings of Stefan Wyszyński's soul and the actions life would demand of him were mutually exclusive. Yet his choice in 1946 for the fullness of the priesthood seems inevitable when set against the whole course of his destiny.

He set May 12 as the date of his consecration, and of course he chose Jasna Góra, where he had said his First Mass, as its site. Stefan Wyszyński included the Madonna of Jasna Góra— Virgo Auxiliatrix—in his coat of arms. Later, he would say that the device was not a decoration, not a symbol, but a program of his work in the Church.

Between the time of his nomination and his consecration, Stefan Wyszyński returned to Włocławek to put the affairs of the seminary and of *Ateneum Kapłańskie* in order. He led retreats that drew great numbers of participants; every action had the character of a farewell. As the nominee bishop's consecration drew near, a new worry came over him. The former professors of the seminary had still not returned from the camps, and finally Stefan Wyszyński "made a deal" with the Virgin Mary: if the professors did not return by May 3, the day he planned to leave for his final preconsecration retreat in Częstochowa, he would stay in Włocławek. Unexpectedly, five professors, including Rector Franciszek Korszyński, returned from Dachau on May 2. Mary had given a sign. Perhaps it was when he was gazing for the last time at the spires of Włocławek Cathedral from his room there that the motto *Soli Deo* (from 1 Tim. 1:17 and Jude 25), which he also placed on his bishop's arms, was born.

Although Stefan Wyszyński had been engrossed in pastoral matters since the end of the war, his earlier calling as author and scholar still manifested itself. At the end of the war he had published a book titled *The Spirit of Human Work,* based on lectures delivered during the occupation and later published in seven other languages, as well as many Polish editions. In it he wrote:

> Work is man's duty. . . . Man's mind and will should gain something from work. Orders given must be evaluated by reason. . . . So-called blind obedience in work, exempting man from thought, will be harmful in all but exceptional circumstances. . . . Only when work involves all our powers does it acquire a human character.
>
> Owning some sort of property is closely tied to God's way of arranging the world; the conditions of human life are connected with possession. No wonder, then, that the Church defends the *right* of private ownership, although on the other hand it discourages the "proprietary" *spirit* as an abuse of the right.
>
> The main basis of a well-arranged society is private ownership and public use of things.
>
> Daily work should be such as simply to secure the greatest material and economic efficiency and to justify man's right to decent pay . . . and it should leave enough energy for performing the other tasks of everyday life.
>
> Economic forces alone cannot determine the length of the workday, for they are not the highest human value.

Father Wyszyński also took special pains to reassure the country about the attitudes of Pius XII and the Apostolic See toward Poland, both during and after the war. Writing under the pseudonym of Dr. Stefan Zuzelski in an article entitled "The Apostolic See and the Postwar World," he stressed Rome's conviction that the new political system be based on religious freedom, respect for social justice, international security, and the avoidance of total war. An indispensable union of law and morality would have to support the new system. These comments were addressed in large part to those who were currently coming to power in Poland: a revolution had followed the war's conclusion.

In an article titled "Pius XII and Poland," published after Wyszyński's nomination as bishop of Lublin, he quoted a statement Pius had made on June 2, 1943:

> Our thoughts and our feelings go out to those smaller nations that, because of their geographical and geopolitical situations vis-à-vis today's contempt for moral principles and international law, are endangered and tormented by the affairs of the Great Powers, are suffering defeat on their own lands, have become the theatres of destructive battles, and have been condemned to unspeakable terror against their civilian populations and to the massacre of the flower of their youth and intelligentsia.

During the occupation the Pope never ceased to recognize Poland's sovereignty, as many of the Vatican's actions testify. Rome recognized the government-in-exile and maintained relations with it. No personal or territorial changes were made in the Polish Church, and the Vatican press still wrote about Poland "as of a country standing in the ranks of free states fighting for a better future for themselves. News about Poland was frequent and not at all subservient to Axis intentions. Nor had the Vatican radio stopped its Polish-language broadcasts. "If sometimes news about Poland was scarce and tragic moments were passed over in silence, this was done only on the request of Polish circles who had discovered that the Germans took revenge on our prisoners for programs about their exploits in Poland."*

---

*The quote is most likely from Cardinal Wyszyński. In 1945 he wrote an article on the subject of Polish-Vatican relations in the *Ateneum Kapłańskie*, which later was separately printed as a pamphlet.

* * *

Before his consecration as Bishop of Lublin, Father Wyszyński carried out an eight-day retreat in Częstochowa that did not
entirely dispel his anxieties or his nostalgia for the life he was
leaving. But he remembered that the episcopacy is the fullness
of priesthood and that the bishop's ring is a symbol of nuptials
within the church, of its bearer's being wedded to a diocese.
When he receives the ring, the bishop is told, "Take this ring,
the sign of faith, so that, adorned with intrepid faith, you may
watch over the Holy Church, God's Bride without blemish."
The consecration fell on May 12, 1946, the Feast of Our Lady
of Grace; so many important events in Stefan Wyszyński's life
occurred on Marian feasts. Sometimes this concurrence resulted from choice, but more often not, and the coincidences
strengthened his sense of living under the Virgin's special care.
Later as Primate, instead of precious stones and saints' relics
Wyszyński's ring carried a likeness of the Madonna of Częstochowa. Eventually, he would expand his personal motto
from *Soli Deo* to *Per Mariam Soli Deo*. His consecration picture
bore the inscription "Mother of God's Grace!"

After being consecrated at the hands of August Cardinal
Hlond, Bishop Wyszyński made his formal ingress to Lublin
on May 26, 1946. The populace turned out in crowds to give
its new pastor an enthusiastic reception—after all, a legend
was already growing around his person. Young—not yet forty-
five—he was well known as a Catholic sociologist, a social
worker, and a pastor of great individuality. It was very significant that a specialist in Catholic social sciences was elevated
to bishop at the moment the communist system was being
imposed.

As well as multitudes of citizens, the administrative, military, school, judicial, and municipal authorities took part in the
ingress. The Catholic University was represented—and so was
the state university. This was characteristic of the authorities'
attitude at a time when the government, locked in battle with
the implacable political opposition, wanted to neutralize the

Church at any price. Of course, the sight of the new communist authorities courting church dignitaries only enhanced the standing of the Church in public opinion.

Trying to make up for time lost during the war, the new bishop quickly set to work confirming, inspecting parishes, and supervising KUL. He preached and led retreats in the working-class districts; on Sundays he would drop in on city churches and deliver lectures to the intelligentsia. Remaining faithful to his prewar views, he carried out an active pastorship among all classes.

One amusing but completely true anecdote illustrates the new bishop's popularity. In winter, he had to avoid going into the streets any more than necessary: so many people greeted him that in continually lifting his hat to reply he ended up almost going bareheaded, leading to the colds to which his weak constitution was prone.

In those first years after the war, both Church and people still bore grievous, fresh wounds from the war. When the prewar ordinary, Bishop Fulman, returned from the concentration camp, he was invited to address a youth meeting at one of the schools. Exhausted and wasted by a long illness, he arrived at this assembly devoted to healing the sufferings of the Polish clergy, but he could not speak. He looked in silence at the young people, saying not a word, before blessing them and leaving. Never able to return to normal life and work, he died before long.

Among Wyszyński's greatest tasks were those connected with his responsibilities as great chancellor of KUL. He was linked very closely to the university by his scholarly interests, and perhaps even more by his cooperation with two university people who seemed to have the greatest spiritual influence on him. These were the prominent social scientist Father Antoni Szymański and his friend and "father" from the student priests' residence, Father Władysław Korniłowicz. Bishop Wyszyński had to oversee scholarly matters as well as the practical needs of the university. In 1947–48 he lectured in the department of law and socioeconomic studies, in addition to his work in the

Institute of Higher Religious Culture, preaching, and leading retreats at this, the only Catholic university between the Elbe and Vladivostok. He was also the main initiator of the new department of Christian philosophy. The *Catholic Encyclopedia* was conceived during his term of office.

Drawing on his Włocławek experiences, the Bishop of Lublin did not limit himself to ordinary diocesan and university matters. He devoted much time to charitable activities, lectures to workers, and cooperation with religious orders. By attending meetings of religious superiors, he worked toward their participation in the affairs of the diocese and the hierarchy. He re-established and ratified the bylaws of the Caritas society, called the first postwar Theological Congress of Professors of Theology in Diocesan and Religious Seminaries and issued important pastoral letters titled "On the Christian Liberation of Man" and "On the Catholic Will to Live." In May 1946, on the day of his consecration, he issued a letter to the clergy, and then another to clergy and faithful on the day of his ingress; in July he created a department of educational affairs; and in August he issued a pastoral letter on the day of the dedication of the Polish nation to the Immaculate Heart of Mary, explaining how this dedication springs from history. He also addressed the diocese on the care of cemeteries, graves, and execution sites, called for cooperation with the Majdanek* Preservation Society, asked the clergy to regulate the employment status of church organists in an equitable way, and organized a convention to deal with pastoral formation.

He personally prepared almost half of each issue of the *Lublin Diocese News,* including even the layout and choice of type. His old affection for editing kept recurring.

In 1947 he summoned an extended meeting of the cathedral chapter that planned the next year's work and established a pastoral department in the Bishop's Curia.†

---

*A German concentration camp near Lublin during the Second World War.
†A collective name for all administrative offices of a diocese. The Tribunal is the matrimonial court that handles marriage cases. It is usually located in the Curia building.

The Bishop of Lublin also organized catechism courses, created three new deaneries and several new parishes, issued one pastoral letter to school-age Catholics and another concerning the daily recitation of the Rosary, and convened the Tenth Rosary Congress on July 2, 1947. In 1948 he published regulations for parochial day celebrations, for church singing, for organizing the religious vocations week; he led quarterly retreats for nuns and, on September 7–8, convened the First Marian Congress in Chełm. Not wishing to tire the reader with a detailed list of his pastoral activities, I will only add that he had several hundred speaking engagements a year and generally exceeded the limits of his weak constitution. Often he would attend and address ten different ceremonies and meetings in a single day.

A passion for incessant activity characterized Stefan Wyszyński's entire ministry. His ardor, initiative, and pastoral verve had no equal. His indefatigable will to serve continued into his later years as Primate, but then—in outward appearance—it was bent principally toward the struggle for church freedom, toward a sort of politics—even though he declared himself to be an apolitical hierarch. In the Lublin period, political matters had not yet imposed themselves so visibly, and those around him could better see the extent of his pastoralism. No matter how frenzied his schedule, he always concentrated on and paid attention to everyone he cooperated with, as Bishop Zdzisław Goliński, the first postwar Auxiliary of Lublin, remembers.

Bishop Wyszyński was exemplary in his attitude to the auxiliary. When he assigned work he forced you to think independently, to look for means, and to develop your initiative. He gave you freedom, rather than thwarting your individuality. Imperceptibly directing and correcting, he gave more and more difficult assignments; grading their difficulty, he educated the auxiliary to become an ordinary.

When he was elevated to bishop, Father Wyszyński did not stop directing the Eight. Many outstanding church dignitaries considered the group an extraordinary one and recommended that its spiritual direction remain in the hands of the Lublin bishop. The new bishop's longtime spiritual guide, Father Korniłowicz, seems to have intervened in the matter just before he died, so that on September 8, 1946, the day of the dedication of Poland to the Immaculate Heart of Mary, Cardinal Hlond asked Bishop Wyszyński not to abandon the Eight.

Nevertheless, other quarters criticized Bishop Wyszyński's relationship to the group and even subjected him to unpleasantnesses on its account; after all, the Eight were a complete *novum* in the Church, and priests needed time to accept this form of the lay apostolate. Bishop Wyszyński imposed formidable demands on the group. Apart from their professional university studies, its members had to finish degrees in theology and sociology. Maria Okońska was arrested in March 1948 for her work with young people, but after three and a half months she was released; Bishop Wyszyński had intervened by sending a letter to Stanisław Radkiewicz, the minister of Security. The Eight continued to occupy themselves with educational work—mostly among female university students—as well as the organization of youth camps and their own studies right up until 1953, when their spiritual director, by then Primate of Poland for five years, was himself arrested.

Now we must ask, how did the youngest member of the Episcopate, with less than three years of experience as a bishop, become the Primate of Poland? Even those convinced of the Holy Spirit's presence in the Church's actions will find Stefan Wyszyński's three-year progress from Włocławek through the bishopric of Lublin to the archbishoprics of Gniezno and Warsaw remarkable. Of course, in 1946, and more so in 1948, Stefan Wyszyński was well known in Poland: his legend had begun before the war, encompassed his actions during the occupation, and extended into his postwar management of Włocławek and Lublin. It was no secret that he was one of Poland's outstanding clergymen. Still, it is a long road from such a reputation to the office of primate. Only those who knew Bishop Wyszyński personally realized his true nature.

It was difficult to define the qualities of the man who would have to lead the Polish Church through one of the most difficult periods in its history. Being a scholar, a social activist, a writer and editor, a pastor, and a pedagogue would not have been enough: many priests combined these talents. For the task that would fall on the shoulders of Stefan Wyszyński, a special charisma and grace were needed. And these characteristics must have radiated from him, because people were suggesting Bishop Wyszyński's candidacy for Cardinal Hlond's post to Hlond himself, before his death.

Monsignor Bolesław Filipiak, protonotary apostolic, judicial assessor, auditor, vice-dean of the Roman Rota, and later curial cardinal, spoke on Vatican Radio on November 13, 1963, on the fifteenth anniversary of Stefan Wyszyński's nomination as primate. He recalled a conversation with August Cardinal Hlond, who had mentioned a visit from the Bishop of Lublin. The Primate said that Bishop Wyszyński had made a great impression on him: "Young, intelligent, brave. I am glad that such an important see is being taken over by Father Wyszyński."

Without stopping to think, Monsignor Filipiak said, "Eminence, I know now who is to be the future primate."

The reaction was lightning-quick and very understandable in human terms: "Father, I am still alive."

"It is not easy to be a prophet. Your Eminence knows how much I love him. This would be after the longest life of Your Eminence."

Later, Monsignor Filipiak heard the Cardinal muse, "Father Wyszyński—not a bad proposition. Excellent."

Three years passed quickly. Primate Hlond was dying and, as his archives in Warsaw indicate, he dictated a letter to Pope Pius XII through his secretary, Father Antoni Baraniak, in which he asked that the Bishop of Lublin be named his successor.

So it was the dying primate who made the suggestion to the Holy Father. Unaware of this, the Polish Episcopate also forwarded Stefan Wyszyński's name to Rome. The choice proved a good one: the new primate would lead the Church through incredibly varied situations. He served when there was a "need for a martyr," during the "guerrilla war" of attrition in the sixties, and in the phase of subtle diplomacy in the seventies.

Father Wyszyński's personal traits allowed many Catholics to see in him a "man of the future." When Cardinal Hlond died, people who could not have known of his will mentioned Bishop Wyszyński as a candidate. Already, people saw that in addition to his scholarship, activism, and fervent pastorship he possessed the spiritual strength crucial to the defense of principles. His moderation, levelheaded judgment, lack of illusions, openness, and ability to grasp a complex situation were all visible. This predestined him for activity among imponderabilia, where flexibility was needed. Polish Catholicism was not ready for its confrontation with communism—a confrontation no one had anticipated or desired. Inevitably, the event produced varied, and even extreme, reactions. Bishop Wyszyński's reactions were foreseeable to a degree, calculable. On the one hand, as an involved spokesman of Catholic social science, he was immune to communism, so to speak. He knew the ideology and harbored no illusions about it. On the other hand, he was a man who had moved with equal ease and closeness among varied social and cultural groups, among gentry and workers. Dedication to Polish tradition and the historical values of our religiosity, and his goal of melding national and Catholic values, were important elements of his spiritual profile. At the same time, Bishop Wyszyński criticized the mistakes of the past, liberal philosophy, the capitalist system, and all the evils that stemmed from practical materialism, egotism, and the pursuit of the easy life.

In 1948, many Polish priests certainly had a similar spiritual and intellectual formation, but none of them could express it with Stefan Wyszyński's originality, give it his personal and unique assessment. Originality accompanied by balanced opinions is the commonest sign of greatness, just as platitudes and the repetition of hackneyed thoughts symptomize mediocrity. Those who knew Bishop Wyszyński in those early days confirm the uniqueness of his words and reactions.

Thus, I think that the Holy Spirit did not really face many difficulties in the nomination of a new Primate of Poland in 1948. A merely human eye could spot the right candidate, even if there were many spiritual mysteries along the road from a small Mazurian village to the highest dignity of the Polish Church.

Cardinal Hlond died like a Biblical patriarch, in calm dignity and unshakable faith. Unlike the many people who have too little courage to think about their own death until it is too late, he took the time to indicate his successor. With his eyes rather than with a gesture, he summoned Father Baraniak and told him, "Write to the Pope. Say I have always been loyal to him. And the other matter—my successor—Bishop Wyszyński."

From Monsignor Filipiak's Vatican-radio address, and from other accounts, we know that the dying Cardinal Hlond's spiritual testament read, "Keep working under the protection of Our Blessed Mother. Victory, when it comes, will be the victory of the Most Blessed Virgin. *Nil desperandum!* [Never despair!]"

The convergence of his own life's Marian program with his predecessor's spiritual testament must have greatly strengthened Bishop Wyszyński's convictions about the road he and the Polish Church ought to follow. No one can be surprised that later he considered himself simply the executor of his great predecessor's last will.

At the end of August 1948, Bishop Wyszyński had undergone surgery for appendicitis, then journeyed to Zakopane for a period of convalescence. While he was there, upsetting news about Cardinal Hlond's illness reached him. But then came word of an improvement. Yet, when Bishop Wyszyński returned to Lublin on October 23, his valet, Janek, greeted him with a long face.

"Cardinal Hlond?" the bishop asked.

"Yes," came the answer. "He died yesterday in Warsaw, at 10:30 A.M."

The news was a shock. After standing in the hall for a long

time, the bishop went to his chapel, put on a black chasuble, and began saying a Mass for the soul of the late primate.

That day Bishop Wyszyński wrote, "So often I took joy in the thought that our Church was blessed with a helmsman who could lead it through its torments with a firm hand. A man felt strangely calm in the presence of Primate Hlond."

The funeral of Cardinal Hlond was one of the greatest occasions the capital ever saw. All Catholics were spontaneously paying tribute to their primate while at the same time looking to the future with heavy hearts. Who, everyone wondered, could be such a worthy helmsman now, in the existing conditions? Everyone could see that the postwar transition period, during which the small minority represented by the communist authorities were feeling slowly for the reins of power, was coming to an end. The communists had already managed to eliminate the great Peasants' Party of Stanisław Mikołajczyk, former premier of the London government-in-exile. The three-year plan of economic reconstruction was ending, and the first five-year plan, intended to communize the country, collectivize agriculture, and establish the pre-eminence of state-owned heavy industry over consumer goods, was being introduced. Changes were also taking place within the Communist Party. Politicians imported from the Soviet Union, ready to realize the program of Stalinist totalitarianism, were coming to full power. It took no unusual prescience to see that the sharp blade of party policy would now swing toward the only strong, independent social force left in the country: the Catholic Church. The existing models of communist church-state politics were well known; no one yet realized what sort of force the Polish Church was, and what sort of individual its new leader would turn out to be. When the eagerly awaited nomination by the Holy See quickly came, many people in enlightened Catholic circles could not help wondering whether elevation to the highest church dignity would not also be a condemnation to martyrdom.

2

Unwilling
Politician (1948-1951)

In a consistory in Rome on November 12, 1948, the Feast
Day of the Five Martyred Polish Brothers, Pius XII named the
Most Reverend Dr. Stefan Wyszyński to be Archbishop of
Gniezno and Warsaw, Primate of Poland. The nominating
bull was signed on November 16, the feast day of the Blessed
Virgin of Ostra Brama, to whom the Primate's mother had
such great devotion.

The nomination, awaited by many, took the nominee by
surprise. Once again, he defended himself from a new honor
—this time the highest one in the Polish Church. He traveled
to Cracow several times, asking Cardinal Sapieha, the senior
and most authoritative member of the Polish hierarchy, to
convince the Pope that the new post would be too much for
him to bear. He went so far as to ask that the Pope reverse
himself. Was it possible? Bishop Wyszyński himself realized
that for the first time in his life he was saying no to God and
the Holy Father. Inwardly terrified, he withdrew into himself

and became depressed before deciding to give in. Then Bishop Michał Klepacz delivered a letter from Rome in which the Pope decisively repeated his position. The matter was settled —Gniezno and Warsaw were no longer "orphan" dioceses, and Poland had a new primate.

Police chicanery awaited the new primate along the road to Gniezno: his car was repeatedly stopped, and his identity checked, although everyone knew well who the traveler was.

Archbishop Wyszyński's ingress to Gniezno occurred on Candlemas, the Feast of the Purification of the Blessed Virgin Mary, February 2, 1949. Fittingly, almost everyone in the Cathedral of the Assumption carried a lighted taper, and thousands of candles burned at the sepulcher of Saint Wojciech. Gniezno welcomed its new archbishop enthusiastically, with the beautiful candles and fervently sung hymns. Over the following years he paid Gniezno back with efforts to restore the original Gothic interior of the cathedral, which had been covered by the remodeling of later centuries. The new primate also set himself the task of "re-Gothicizing" the national spirit before the thousand-year anniversary of Polish Christianity. Remaining faithful to this program, he brought about an extraordinary rebirth within the Church. From the very beginning, we can distinguish two leading ideas that the Primate wanted to bestow on the Church—the Marian idea and the victory of the endangered national faith. Through love of Mary and her strength, he wanted to light a beacon of faith in a nation lost in the postwar tragedies and spiritual discords. Facing a new historic trial, society had to oppose Poland's subjugation and its surrender to Marxist indoctrination. Faith and hope, supported by great spiritual traditions, became the *sine qua non* of survival. Thus Wyszyński decided, as he said himself, to light "a torch" for the nation—one of faith, hope, and love.

The nation's devotion to Mary came first. At the time of his ingress to Gniezno, the Primate had already decided to place the day-to-day affairs in the hands of the Blessed Virgin of

Jasna Góra, whose image he wanted to continue carrying on his seal.

Archbishop Wyszyński made his ingress to Warsaw on February 6. To the people of the capital he said:

> From today begins my road through Warsaw. I know her well, I am linked closely with her. She was closest to me, perhaps, when she dripped with the blood of the uprising, when I looked from Izabelin on the sacrificial smoke above the great altar of the holocaust. Today I must fall in love with Warsaw and render unto her my strength and life. Oh, how much more easily today than ever! May God who is Love bestow upon this pastoral love His fatherly image.

On February 9, the Primate went to Jasna Góra for a retreat, prior to taking up his pastoral obligations. In Częstochowa he decided to include in his primatial coat of arms the Madonna of Jasna Góra, but without her crown. Poland, he remarked, was too poor at the time for her Queen to wear a crown.

When he returned from Jasna Góra, the Primate began to fulfill his duties, which included not only leading the two archdioceses, Gniezno and Warsaw, but also directing the whole work of the Polish Church. To his roles as primate and head of the Episcopate, the Holy See had added authority over church administration in the Western Lands.* Additionally,

---

*The Western Lands are the territories, formerly under German sovereignty, placed in Polish hands at the end of hostilities in 1945 and formally recognized as Polish by the West German state in 1971. The Western Lands include former portions of Germany proper that lie west of the Odra-Nysa (Oder-Neisse) line, as well as the part of East Prussia that was not absorbed into the Soviet Union in 1945. As Micewski's narrative indicates, the Western Lands posed a sensitive problem for the Polish Church and for the Vatican: for more than a quarter of a century, until the conclusion of the Polish–West German treaties, these lands were "only" under "temporary" Polish administration, even though the population and the reconstruction efforts within them were Polish. Therefore, the Vatican had to regard the German Episcopate as still having a claim on the dioceses there and could not appoint a permanent Polish hierarchy. The state authorities in Warsaw, who preferred the term "Recovered Lands," contended with reason that the territories were historically Polish and ought to be under Polish spiritual as well as secular control. Thus, the communists were able to keep the Polish Church between a rock and a hard place, between the claims of nationality and the Vatican's necessity for adjusting ecclesiastical boundaries in con-

Warsaw, including most of its churches and its cathedral, still lay in ruins. More than fifty churches, which had taken centuries to erect, needed rebuilding—now the work of a single generation. Archbishop Wyszyński took personal charge of the Primate's Council for Rebuilding the Churches of Warsaw.

The dioceses of Gniezno and Warsaw, actually separate entities, had been placed under the administration of a single archbishop for the first time under Wyszyński's predecessor, Cardinal Hlond. The mentalities of both clergy and faithful in the two cities differed: the results of Prussian control still showed in the hard-working, solid population of Gniezno, accustomed to organized activity; around Warsaw, the people were rather warm, impetuous, patriotic, and not always systematic in their work. These characteristics demanded different pastoral approaches.

In the pastoral letter issued on the occasion of his ingress, Primate Wyszyński described himself and his mission: "I am not a politician, not a diplomat, I am neither an activist nor a reformer. I am, however, your spiritual father, the pastor and bishop of your souls. I am the apostle of Jesus Christ. My mission is priestly, pastoral, apostolic, grown from the eternal thoughts of God, from the redeeming will of the Father who joyously shares his happiness with man. . . ."

Despite his wishes, the archbishop had quickly to show that he could be both politician and diplomat. He began his work with exclusively religious motives, filled with the spirit of the fullness of the priesthood and a Christian apostolic mission, and he tried above all to be close to his priests. He paid particular attention, in a Church that had to make up for the loss of over three thousand priests in the war, to the seminaries. He personally led retreats in the seminaries and was there for all important feasts and holidays, and, commuting constantly between Warsaw and Gniezno, he attended all meetings of the deans in the deaneries of both dioceses.

---

formity to international treaties. Nevertheless, the desired schism never came about, and since 1971 the Western Lands have been universally recognized as canonically Polish territory.

He also found a way to unite himself with the faithful of Warsaw and Gniezno. These were years when every word spoken from the pulpit could be risky and have far-reaching political consequences. Nevertheless, the Primate could preach clearly to ordinary people while avoiding unnecessary troubles with the state authorities. Each of his public appearances drew great attention. He never hesitated to speak the truth, yet he tried at the same time to express moderation and reason. No one else in Poland commanded such unlimited trust. Having entered upon his duties in great humility, he earned within his first years the reputation of greatness, an extraordinary, rare achievement within the highly individualistic society of Poland. It was his very humility that enabled him to fill the ancient role of the Polish primate as *interrex*.

The use of the ancient term became common during the Stalinist era, more because of the faith people had in Wyszyński than because of his popularity. When a Polish king died in early times, the primate served as *interrex* until a successor was elected. Primate Wyszyński never allowed himself any pretensions to such a title, or to the title "leader of the nation," which some applied to him. But because the postwar government struck most of society as an imposed government, the Primate, regardless of his will, became with each year more of a political figure and an embodiment of society's most secret, profound longings. Wanting to be only the pastor of the nation, he became in fact the symbol of its spiritual desires and thirst for independence.

Primate Wyszyński had his own conception, far removed from political aspirations, of his office and mission. He plainly wanted to preserve the close bonds between the Church and the people. As we have mentioned, his pastoral concepts were bound up with the idea of fatherhood. The mystery of fatherhood was, for him, born of the Heavenly Father. Yet Wyszyński reckoned that the religious mission could not be entirely divorced from the historical. He regarded his task as the charge given him by God. Fulfilling his supernatural fatherhood in these specific historical circumstances, in a nation that felt itself to be deprived of independent leadership, he became more and more the representative of the nation. This was not done unconsciously: when life placed before the Primate the burden of a great political responsibility—a consequence of his feeling of spiritual fatherhood vis-à-vis the nation—he could not refuse the burden, and he did not want to. But the pastoral burden he assumed almost exceeded human strength. He was in two, even three places at once, inspecting, confirming, dropping in on parish churches and monasteries, meeting with young people. By not sparing himself even the greatest efforts, he quickly found himself close to "the little ones," the faithful, and great masses of people. This personal, everyday contact quickly bore fruit. Soon the parishes and outposts of the Church were creating occasions just so the Primate could be invited to them, and his pastoral-fatherhood concept was being realized.

The political results of this pastoral work were inevitable in the circumstances, as the Primate was aware. A program of spiritual fatherhood, addressing the faithful as "my children" and underlining the connection, both historical and contemporary, between the fate of the Church and the fate of the nation, was bound to meet with criticism. And criticism, completely antagonistic, came from many sides. The communists feared that such a course would progressively usurp their authority in the nation. Democratic circles in the West were uneasy about the vitiation of pluralism in Poland if the Primate's importance to the people was unrivaled. Finally, some Catholic circles within the country, following French influences, feared anachronism and particularly the renewal of nationalistic tendencies within the Church. Like other contemporary European societies, Poland is indeed pluralistic and ought to have an open character in which freedom and human rights are central values. However, Wyszyński's "fatherly" pastoral conception evolved in a situation that was unquestionably threatening basic human and national rights. It was by addressing this issue that the Polish Church gained such great strength. Paradoxically, the idea underlying Wyszyński's pastoral work was questioned, while its results were praised. Countries that differ greatly cannot always be judged by the same standard. After the Second World War, Polish society was relatively less advanced than its Western counterparts, and at the same time, in Stalinism, it faced far greater dangers of subjugation to Marxist dogma. Stalinism took aim not only at individuals, but at all social structures, at whatever was spiritually, culturally, or nationally Polish. From the society's viewpoint, the alternative, a system of parliamentary democracy, also entailed the protection of the Polish national and spiritual identity. Polish identity came under the providential care of the Church when almost all other social structures had disintegrated or been reduced to a bare minimum.

However, the Church never sought temporal riches, power, or influence. It never threatened nonbelievers or those of different convictions in the postwar period. Polish national feelings, distorted by nationalist politics before the war, were now channeled into religious rather than political directions, into the inculcation of a Christian spirit that mitigated the earlier traits of aggressiveness and nationalistic hatred. As a result of the links—upsetting to many political circles—between the feelings of Polishness and Catholicism, one hears more about dignity, freedom, and human rights in Poland than in any other country of the Eastern bloc. In West Germany, democratic political parties served to confine radicalism and extremism to the margins of society; in Poland, I think, the Church played the same role. Nowhere in Europe did national feelings and politics give way to an ideology of complete universalism, as official accusations of imperialism flew back and forth, perhaps with good reason. Those who worry about the stress placed on national matters by the Polish Church ought to consider the fact that in this country more than anywhere else, society accepted the loss of territory over which it had historically exercised great influence, the displacement of millions of people, and the impossibility of acting in accord with earlier visions of historical greatness in the East.

These remarks are not intended to question today's ideological and cultural pluralism or to justify an increase in national-

ism; they serve here merely to present the historical context of
Stefan Wyszyński's pastoral concepts. Of course, it is probably
too early for any final words; the matter demands a long historical perspective.

Finally, the nationalistic Church of Poland produced a pope.
That this pope felt at home in the Vatican from the first day
and quickly made a name for himself in the worldwide church
is more than a historic paradox. While stressing its attachment
to the nation, the Church in Poland never for a moment lost
its universalism and relied exclusively on faithfulness to the
spirit of the Gospel, which is the same for all peoples and
nations.

* * *

Primate Wyszyński wanted to continue Cardinal Hlond's
policies and practices. He made no changes in the primatial
residence, in the personnel of the secretariat, or even among
the Sisters of Saint Elizabeth who supervised the household.
Nor did he alter the composition of the metropolitan curia.

The Primate set the construction of the Warsaw and
Gniezno cathedrals as his first task. Rebuilding in Warsaw took
until January 1953. The return of the Gniezno Cathedral to its
Gothic form, undertaken in 1951, lasted beyond the Primate's
return from prison, up to 1966, the Millennium of Polish Christianity. Wyszyński also planned to rebuild the primatial residence on Miodowa Street in Warsaw, but it was not until
January 3, 1953, that he moved there from his temporary residence in the papal nunciature on Szucha Avenue.

From the first, the new primate did all he could to ensure
frequent meetings (four times a year, eventually every two
months) of the Episcopate and to foster close harmony and
unity among his bishops. The success of the Church in a new,
threatening situation depended in large measure upon this
unity.

In the Podgórze district of Toruń, at the first parish church he visited on the way to his ingress to Gniezno, Primate Wyszyński received from the parishioners a painting representing Christ the King, his hands bound, with a soldier holding him by the shoulders. The Primate hung it in his office in Gniezno, where it was to become a symbol of his fate, although never of his plans. Yet those around the Primate—his father, bishops, many clergy and faithful—thought from the beginning that imprisonment awaited him, given the increasing distortions of Stalinist power. One bishop presented Wyszyński with a copy of Father Klimkiewicz's book about Cardinal Ledóchowski,* in the conviction that reading it might prove useful.

When he himself was in prison, Primate Wyszyński asked himself whether he had succumbed to the atmosphere of fear. He decided that subjectively he had been ready for anything; objectively, however, he had determined to work so that the worst, when it came, would come as late as possible. It was the government that accused the Primate of wanting to be a martyr. He himself was far from such thoughts, even though as a priest and bishop he could not rule them out. He felt, however, that the Polish Church had already shed too much blood in the German concentration camps to expend the blood of its remaining priests so thoughtlessly. Martyrdom seemed like an honor, a grace, to Wyszyński, but the Primate believed at the same time that God led the Church not only down the extraordinary road of martyrdom, but also down the ordinary road of apostolic work. Primate Wyszyński later presented this latter road as his program when he met Pius XII and Monsignor Tardini in the Vatican.† When he set out for Warsaw, the new primate was planning to begin his work by visiting the president of the republic. The police actions in Gniezno and the

---

*Witold Klimkiewicz, *Kardynał Ledóchowski na Tle Swej Epoki: 1822–1902* (Cardinal Ledóchowski and His Times: 1822–1902). Mieczysław Ledóchowski, a count, Archbishop of Poznań and Gniezno from 1866 to 1886, was imprisoned by the Prussians (1874–76) for his opposition to the May laws during the *Kulturkampf*. He was named a cardinal in 1875 and served as the prefect of propaganda at the Vatican from 1892 to 1902.

†Monsignor Dominici Tardini was undersecretary of State under Pius XII in 1953.

hostile attitude of the official press changed his mind; he decided to wait and see.

Wyszyński took over the leadership of the Church in the same year as the Congress of Party Unification, which merged the Polish Socialist Party into the communist movement and created the PZPR (Polska Zjednoczona Partia Robotnicza, Polish United Workers' Party). In a speech to the unification congress on December 17, 1948, Aleksander Zawadzki, a leader of the PZPR, said:

> . . . among the masses one hears demands for the separation of Church and state, for the laicization of education. . . . For members of the party, those demands are justified by the attitude of a part of the clergy who, behaving as antagonists or outright enemies of the democratic-popular state, are trying to take advantage of their clerical positions for antistate political actions. In discussions in almost all pre-congress party conferences, remarks were made on the damaging activities of the reactionary segment of the clergy, its politicization, the fact that individual priests and religious are linked to the underground, the depravation of youth by some representatives of the secular clergy and religious. . . . We will be opposing that and only that activity which is damaging in the eyes of every progressive man.

Zawadzki's speech represented a clear harbinger of an assault on the Church, of a policy of dividing the clergy into reactionaries and patriots, of suggesting links with the political underground. The remark about the depravation of youth provided a basis for subsequent provocations and false charges.

The turn of the years 1948 and 1949 marked a threshold in the political stage, not only in Poland, but all across the Eastern bloc, as the tragic events in Hungary show.

Cardinal Mindszenty stood for a policy of adamant opposition, and was much less flexible in his tactics than Cardinal

Wyszyński. Mindszenty, born Jozef Pehm in the village of Csehimindszent in 1892, adopted the name of his native village as his surname. Ordained in 1915, he became a bishop in 1926 and was named Archbishop of Esztergom, Primate of Hungary, upon the death of Justinian Cardinal Seredi in 1945. Shortly afterward, the communists took power.

The Hungarian primate would not make any compromises or come to any agreement with the communists. He was arrested on December 26, 1948, marking the beginning of the Stalinist persecution of the Church in his country. After a show trial, he was sentenced to life imprisonment. Hungarian church-state politics were far more brutal than in Poland. On the night of June 9, 1950, approximately one thousand nuns and male religious were arrested, along with many more secular priests. Church property was confiscated. The Priests of Peace, a movement of patriotic priests, was created, and a "progressive" journal called *Kereszt* (The Cross) was launched, to combat Stalinist injustices. But an understanding with the state was forced upon the Church on July 30, 1950.

The Polish situation was less drastic, not only because of the strength of Catholicism, but also because the new primate combined definite opposition with progressive flexibility. The authorities, however, intended to follow the example of Hungary. How uncomfortable the Polish Episcopate's situation was is evident in this communiqué from Władysław Wolski, minister of Public Administration, to Bishop Zygmunt Choromański, secretary of the Episcopate, dated March 14, 1949:

> For some months there has been a noticeable intensification of unfriendly activities by certain factions of the clergy in relation to the people's government and state. A part of the higher church hierarchy has been trying through pastoral letters and confidential instructions to bring about a state of mental agitation and unrest over spurious threats to religion, *for which there is no real basis.*
> ... There often occur incidents in which priests patronize

or engage in outright cooperation with various criminal, antistate groups which are agents of Anglo-American imperialism. . . .

In the face of such spurious charges, the Church nevertheless went about its tasks of inculcating religious precepts in the young, trying to support Christian values in the family, and upholding the national tradition of faith.

The political accusations served as a pretext for a campaign that would attempt to crush the Church. It was inevitable that opposition from the masses to establishment of totalitarian rule should include some priests who had decided to undertake secret or political activity. The accusation that bishops were giving political instructions to their priests was, however, trumped up by people without consciences who, on command, launched violent press attacks upon the Church. The day after Minister Wolski's communiqué, the newspaper *Życie Warszawy* (Warsaw Life) wrote: "The silence of the church hierarchy on the matter of participation by priests in underground actions, the lack of any condemnation of such incidents, must leave the impression that the underground—the open agent of foreign imperialism—is tolerated and even supported by the church hierarchy."

Under Stalinism, the accusation that the hierarchy tolerated "agents of foreign imperialism" could lead to the mass arrest of bishops, and such attacks multiplied in the press. In May, *Życie Warszawy* accused the Church through an "opinion poll" of creating intolerance by means of "clerical propaganda against people of other convictions," and went on to mention "medieval fanaticism" and "religious war." It was like a cat chasing its tail, and I could cite many more absurd accusations, which often ended in trials and prison sentences for priests engaged in the struggle over ideology. Such struggles were unavoidable, since the government leaders insisted upon a materialistic, totalitarian state ideology, which had nothing to do with an ordinary citizen's view of life. In the midst of this, the Episcopate strove to channel the unavoidable struggles within limits that would not disrupt the normal life of the nation. The Primate had thought of attempting to normalize affairs even more, until the Vatican's decision of July 1949 to excommunicate people who cooperated with the communists made the situation more acute. A violent campaign in the Polish press naturally ensued.

From his first weeks at the head of the Church, Wyszyński began to familiarize the bishops with this "hazardous" program: he wanted to work toward creating a permanent body to maintain an understanding between the Episcopate and the government. This plan was realized in the form of the so-called Mixed Commission, on which the Primate placed great hopes.

Full information about the early work of the Mixed Commission is not yet publicly known. We do know that it began its work five months after the Primate took office, meeting four times in the next three months, to deal with the developments in government tactics. Bishops Choromański, Klepacz, and Zakrzewski represented the Episcopate. Meanwhile, the Primate endeavored to prepare for the commission's meetings, conferring over the most important matters with the bishops who took part. After each meeting the bishops not only discussed with the Primate what had happened, but also wrote out the minutes. When the Polish Church is able to open its archives, the future historian will strike an extraordinary lode of source material.

From its inception, the Mixed Commission began taking on the character of a preparatory group for an agreement between the Church and the state. Thus the Primate, within a few months of taking office, was already thinking of some sort of *modus vivendi* with the government. The Mixed Commission continued to meet even when the government confronted the Church with the *fait accompli* of limitations on church property ownership. When it served his side's purposes, Franciszek Mazur, head of the government delegation to the commission —also a member of the legislature and the party official responsible for church-state affairs—would not call a meeting for months. It would be difficult even to reach him. Still Primate Wyszyński did not give up on the talks with the authorities.

The Primate was the firmest proponent of concluding an agreement between the Church and a communist government. At times, even such a consistent supporter of the agreement as Bishop Michał Klepacz of Łódź broke down in the face of obstacles created by the government. But the Primate, realizing that the project had its opponents, emphasized his personal responsibility for the conclusion of this first accord.

The well-known emigrant writer Józef Mackiewicz put anticommunist emotion ahead of religious considerations when he wrote that, while the Polish hierarchy had not reached the same complete subjugation as the Moscow patriarchate and other episcopates in some subjugated communist countries, "the rule is: compromises and concessions are exactly the *price* that the Church pays for 'rescuing Catholicism.' "

Fully aware of such criticism, the Primate never concealed his reasons for favoring the agreement. For one thing, the Church and the Polish nation had sacrificed so much blood during the war that allowing any more to be spilled would directly threaten the survival of Poland and her religion. After vegetating in subjugation for 150 years, the Polish Church had enjoyed barely twenty years of freedom, during which time it had just begun to make up for its weaknesses and prepare itself for work when the Nazi occupation dealt it such a horrible blow. The seminaries and theological faculties had been staffed, a Catholic press set up, and new parishes erected, but before the war most of the clergy was still following obsolete or borrowed models in their work. A Polish pastoral theology had not yet been worked out. The war had interrupted the work of the seminaries; many parishes were left without pastors and thousands of priests never returned from the concentration camps. The Primate had to consider the objective situation: under the "new reality," a conflict between Catholicism and communist materialism would occur; the Church needed to buy time and prepare itself to survive the confrontation.

Because its support in society was so fragile, the government also had an interest in concluding an agreement, though it had made the task more difficult by abrogating, for doctrinal reasons, the prewar concordat between Poland and the Vatican. While working toward an agreement, the state authorities also wanted to reap as many propaganda benefits as possible. For this reason they stepped up the pressure on the Episcopate just after Wyszyński had come into office. Nor did the authorities stop their efforts to limit the freedom of the Church and its institutions. Such government actions did little to allay the fears and strong doubts within the Episcopate itself.

Minister Wolski's previously cited communiqué also contained the first threats to particular bishops, questioning the attitudes of Bishops Czesław Kaczmarek (of Kielce) and Stanisław Adamski (of Katowice) toward Poland during the occupation, and accused some priests of cooperating with antistate groups. And although the communiqué concluded with a propitiatory offer to regulate church-state relations, at the same time it made clear that any agreement would be expressed in the state constitution then being prepared and that "within the area of the church hierarchy's prerogatives, it will be based on experience and reflect the attitudes of the clergy and hierarchy toward the people's state." By tying the situation of the Church to "support" of the "people's" state, the government was threatening and tempting at the same time.

This variety of "dialogue" did not make Primate Wyszyński's final decision any easier. Nor did an international situation that, like the domestic one, was becoming particularly acute. The cold war and the lowering of the iron curtain cut the Polish bishops off from Rome and forced them to make important decisions on their own. Within the country, Stalinist totalitarianism was being articulated in concrete and highly dangerous steps: the forced collectivization of agriculture, the introduction of state capitalism, the elimination of private property and services, the spreading terror of the security forces. Scholarship, culture, and the media were submitted to purely political control and the most rigid version of Marxist orthodoxy. Everything was brought into line with the economic and political dictates of the Eastern bloc, without regard to Polish sovereignty or national interests.

Despite all this, and as stated earlier, Polish Stalinism was less rigorous than that of any other country in the bloc. The explanation lay in the strength of the Church, in the extraordinary national adherence to tradition, in peasant resistance to collectivization, and in the general resistance, partly active and partly passive, to giving up on Polish independence. The government imagined that an agreement with the Church would mean the Church's capitulation to and acceptance of "People's Poland." When this illusion encountered resistance, the authorities resorted to drastic forms of pressure. One of the sharpest and longest-lasting tactics was the creation, in September 1949, of a group of "patriotic priests" in a Priests' Committee within ZBoWiD.* The "patriotic priests," recruited from the margins of the clergy where there was the least resistance to pressure, were set the task of swaying the bishops in a direction favorable to the authorities.

The government applied other means of "persuasion" to the bishops. The meeting of the Episcopal Steering Committee in Cracow on October 26, 1949, revealed the bishops' unanimous opinion that the government's declaration of a state monopoly of the media was unacceptable. The Primate wanted some form of coexistence, but he did not intend to capitulate or make any declarations benefiting the authorities, even after the "patriotic priests" had been set up as a diversion within the

---

*ZBoWiD is an acronym of Związek Bojowników o Wolność i Demokrację, the Association of Fighters for Freedom and Democracy, the official organization of Second World War partisan and army veterans. During the Stalinist period, the group rigidly excluded and even helped persecute all ex-partisans and soldiers except those who had served on the procommunist or Soviet side. Later, with the ending of such persecution and the gradual rehabilitation of former partisans who had paid allegiance to the London government-in-exile, ZBoWiD became a stronghold of "nationalist" communists and was to form the power base of such politicians as General Mieczysław Moczar, whose attempts at seizing power led to more than one bitter political struggle, as in 1968. In its early days, through its committees of "patriotic priests" (i.e., clerics who supported, for one reason or another, the communist state), ZBoWiD attempted to lend a veneer of nationalistic "respectability" to the People's Republic while, as a not unintentional side effect, creating divided allegiances among certain church elements.

Church. Nevertheless, the steering committee decided to continue talking to the government, and the bishops who took part in the Mixed Commission drafted a new proposal for a declaration under the Primate's personal supervision.

At the same time, the bishops decided not to command religious orders to report to the authorities for the purpose of "settling their legal status" in accordance with the Regulation of the Minister of Public Administration of August 6, 1949 (§5 and §6). Such a command, the committee decided, would run counter to canon law and the principles of the Church. A struggle against religious order has always been part of the repertoire when a regime represses the Church; the communists were following the tsarist and Prussian example. On the other hand, the Episcopate also refrained from ordering the religious *not* to report to the authorities, both to avoid negative consequences for the monasteries and to indicate respect for their autonomy. The Episcopate decided to limit itself to an advisory role and remained within the spirit of the law.

The Church went on trying to defend its prerogatives and institutions from government control, and the government went on applying pressure by way of rigorous laws, and by trying to force the bishops to make political declarations or face a dismantling of the church organizations. These organizations were finally eliminated, though some of them continued to operate informally for some time.

The Catholic Church received a great shock in January 1950, when the authorities took away the Caritas church union in a brutal and illegal way. The government then set up a state-controlled Caritas of its own to act in political support of the authorities. This action deprived the Church of most of its charitable institutions. The Caritas affair would still be causing irritations and anxieties between Church and state twenty years later.

At a meeting of the Episcopal Steering Committee in Cracow on January 28–29, 1950, Bishop Klepacz reported on a meeting he had had with Minister Wolski. The minister accused the Church of stalling because events were running against it; the bishop countered that the government was stalling and people were astonished at the government's attacks on the Church at a time when the hierarchy was acting in good faith and had not even revealed the full extent of government actions. When the issue of whether or not the bishops would have to use the term "People's Poland" arose, the minister said that the bishops must understand the present realities. "What exactly is the Episcopate counting on?" he asked. "On America? On the Vatican? Or perhaps on a war? If the agreement is signed, there won't be any attacks against the Church."

Hoping to win recognition from the bishops, the government promised them things it had no intention of carrying out. But the bishops realized that the alternative to a *modus vivendi* or "declaration" would be further blows against the Church. Bolesław Piasecki, leader of the "progressive Catholics" and intermediary in the negotiations, was convinced that the arrest of the Primate was already being considered at the time. It was because of this that Bishop Klepacz went to Minister Wolski twice in January 1950, carrying new drafts of a declaration written in cooperation with the Primate and Bishop Choromański. On January 23 the authorities arrested three Jesuits, one of them the provincial, and carried out their takeover of Caritas. Klepacz protested that such actions made an understanding impossible, to which Wolski replied, "If the declaration had been signed, all that need not have happened, *but in the present situation more things are possible*" (emphasis added). This was an obvious threat.

The Episcopal Steering Committee questioned Piasecki's role as a go-between; Bishop Klepacz clarified that Piasecki was mediating between Wolski and himself, rather than between Church and state. The bishops hoped "that in the future this type of person would not be involved," referring to both Piasecki and his organization, Today and Tomorrow (later Pax).*

---

*This officially sanctioned "Catholic" group, allowed to publish books, print newspapers, and run shops selling religious items, played a political role similar to that of ZBoWiD's "patriotic priests" in the postwar period. Rather than military connections, however, Pax stressed its support for the Soviet-led international peace movement of

Subsequent dramatic events would confound the wishes of the bishops. For the present, they decided that the group and its publications "have gone far enough and ought to be dealt with," either by the Archbishop of Warsaw or by the Episcopate as a whole. For the time being, Piasecki continued in his role, although the bishops trusted him no more than they trusted the government.

After its January meeting, the Episcopate issued a communiqué to the faithful and a memorandum to the government on the seizure of Caritas. The government addressed its reply to Cardinal Sapieha, the supervisor of Caritas. The authorities naturally maintained their position. Taking Piasecki's intermediary role into account, the Primate limited himself for the moment to warning Today and Tomorrow about its role in the Caritas affair.

In January the bishops felt that they were near enough to concluding the *modus vivendi* to set Bishop Choromański to work with Franciszek Mazur on a final draft. Instead of an agreement, however, further attacks against the Church ensued. On February 28, 1950, the Polish Press Agency blamed the lack of an accord on the Episcopate. Their main accusation was the failure to agree to the use of the phrase "People's Poland," along with canonical action against the "patriotic priests" and "taking advantage of religious sentiment" to the detriment of People's Poland. At the beginning of March, Bishop Kazimierz Kowalski of Pelplin was arrested. This alarming act demonstrated the extent to which rulers were counting on a "declaration," and also the means they would resort to if a *modus vivendi* was not achieved.

After carrying out these attacks, the government seemed

---

the forties and fifties. The group was allowed to elect a handful of delegates to the *Sejm* (the highest political body), and its power increased as it devoted its less public energies to a growing chain of light industries, more or less privately owned, that produced everything from fountain pens to fishing line, in addition to devotional trinkets. Piasecki is one of the more interesting political figures in recent Polish history. A leader of the ultra-rightist Polish Falange before the war, he underwent Soviet captivity and emerged as a shrewd supporter of the new order. He fought a running battle with the Church, tried to establish a slice of political power for himself, endured the kidnapping and murder of his son, and died a very wealthy but widely disliked man in 1980.

inclined to talk, counting on a diminution of the bishops' resistance. Their calculation, as usual, was a delusion: the Primate
still wanted an accord, not a capitulation. The negotiations
dragged on. The Mixed Commission met on March 11 and 28;
Choromański and Mazur discussed the draft agreement on
March 30 and April 1. On April 3 the Episcopate met in Cracow
and decided to sign a joint declaration with the government,
reserving the right to certain amendments of the text. According to Bishop Choromański's minutes, "With the exception of
one vote against, everyone agreed to sign on the condition that
the joint declaration insured an improvement of the atmosphere between church and state."

The bishops hoped that such a change in the atmosphere
would be made possible through the settlement of the Caritas
matter, through the exemption of seminarians, religious, and
priests from military service, and through certain concessions
by the government in the confiscation of church lands. They
did not hope to recover Caritas, but counted on its liquidation
and, at least, an end to the abuse of its name. All this turned
out to be unrealistic. Still, the decision was made in principle.
When the Primate presented the pros and cons of the signing,
Archbishop Walenty Dymek stated that the pros outweighed
the cons. The Primate had staked all his authority on that side
of the scale.

The Episcopate also asked all bishops to send lists of imprisoned priests and religious to the secretariat, expecting that after
the signing of the agreement with the government they would
be freed. The next day, April 4, the Mixed Commission held
a meeting in Warsaw. Everything pointed to the signing, but
the pact's fate remained unclear even on April 14, the day of
its acceptance, when the commission debated over the final
formulation of this, the first understanding in history between
a Catholic episcopate and a communist government.

In view of the authorities' prior hostile steps against the
Church, public opinion was skeptical. The clergy remained
particularly distrustful. But the Primate held to his position
that the Church never says no when it can move toward peace

and harmony. He reminded everyone that the harshest persecutions of the Church in France, Bismarck's Germany, Mexico, and Spain all ended in armistices. At the last instant, the word "understanding" instead of "declaration" was chosen to define the agreement with the government. It was not a concordat that had been agreed upon, then, but a *modus vivendi,* a limited understanding to protect the Church against further, rapid, drastic destruction.

Wyszyński naturally realized that, while he was acting from principle, the other side was trying to compromise the Church in the eyes of conservative circles, to buy time, and to strengthen its own position. But as the Primate had explained in Cracow on April 3, when he threw all his authority behind the understanding and took personal responsibility for it, he was acting from conviction. His whole spiritual nature and the Catholic social teachings he had studied demanded that peace and harmony be sought. Paradoxically, the very Catholic social teachings that the communists regarded as so offensive thus led to the first church agreement with a communist regime. For Wyszyński, it had been a matter of principle.

The Episcopate realized that, if the agreement had not been signed, the coexistence of Church and state, which was unavoidable, would have been unregulated, precarious, and volatile. With the understanding signed—no matter how often the regime violated its provisions—there always existed a certain brake on antichurch activities. If the government wanted to "catch up" with the other Eastern-bloc countries, it would have to reckon with the fact that, in the eyes of the public, it was the authorities that were breaking an agreement. The government thus had to act cautiously and could not start an open conflict with the Church for some time. The understanding slowed destructive actions against church institutions for the first five years of Wyszyński's leadership.

The Primate also took into consideration the Russian experience. Even the arbitrary postrevolutionary government had gradually to move away from its harsh persecution of the Orthodox Church and toward a "tacit agreement." The Primate correctly saw that, although the political systems in the communist countries would not change, the governments in those countries would from time to time have to seek compromises with their people.

Given Polish conditions, the Primate realized, the struggle against religion might turn out differently from the way it had in Russia or in Hungary. He was convinced that social reform was inevitable. Even though he was far from agreeing with the goals the communists had set for themselves, he thought that Poland needed socioeconomic reconstruction, and he did not automatically condemn everything that was being done in the country. The official position favoring atheism stood as a barrier between the government camp and progressive Catholic circles that, while disapproving of revolutionary methods, did not always oppose all the postulates of socialism. "If it were not for this narrow-minded atheism," the Primate wrote,

> which so often takes on the dimensions of a war against religion, this Polish society with its cultural and historical inclinations toward democracy would be the most hospitable field for the work of a sensible government. Of course, such a government would have to be wise, free of demagoguery, predominantly oriented toward social issues, and free of the sort of outside pressures that deprive it of popularity among the society that has to make sacrifices on its account.

Meanwhile, however, the government was weak and even lacked legitimacy in Polish opinion; it was for this reason that it relied on political repression and might. Thus the tormented nation opposed even some of its correct aspirations. The government compounded matters by glorifying Soviet reality and trying to force a Eurasian system onto an individualistic, Western-Latin culture. The introduction of a totalitarian, ideological state denied social pluralism, liquidating political parties, labor unions, and all the richness of social life. This system naturally had to take aim at the Church as well. Tearing society apart, it could only use force. The Primate anticipated the use of force and an ever-wider battle against religion. Therefore he tried, through the understanding with the state, to make things easier for individual parishes and for the whole Church.

All these arguments came up in the March 1950 meetings of the Episcopate, before the understanding was concluded. To Wyszyński, it was important that "Cardinal Sapieha, when he went to Rome, knew well of the Episcopate's position and shared it." But Primate Wyszyński made the final decision himself. The agreement was signed in the evening hours of April 14, 1950. With no concordat, facing a government that did not recognize the prewar constitution, never mind canon law, the bishops from that moment on had nothing but the understanding to fall back on in their fight for the rights of the Church.

* * *

In the short term, the understanding was a propaganda victory for the government. In the long term, it gave the Church a protective shield. The government did everything it could to find at least indirect support for its political program in the document. The Church had obligated itself to "tell the clergy that their pastoral work, in accordance with church teachings, should foster respect for the laws and prerogatives of the state among the faithful." This might seem like too much of a concession, but a comparison of the wording in the Polish agreement with the one forced on the Hungarian Church makes it clear that the bishops had not gone too far. Article 1 of the Hungarian accord reads, "In accordance with its civic duties, the Episcopate recognizes and agrees to support the *state political system of the Hungarian People's Republic* and its constitution" (emphasis added). Agreeing to respect the laws is completely different from approving of the communist system. Cardinal Mindszenty's uncompromising tactics had led to his own removal and to his Church's loss of independence.

Mindszenty obtained nothing in return for the far-reaching Hungarian declaration; the Polish Church held on to a certain independence and dealt with the government as an equal.

The Polish understanding conformed in many points to the national interest. The bishops called for "intensive work to rebuild the country" and stated that "the laws of economics, history, culture, and religion, along with historical justice, demand that the Recovered Lands [Western Lands] belong to Poland forever." They also declared, "Proceeding from the assumption that the Recovered Lands form an inseparable part of the republic, The Episcopate will request of the Apostolic See that the church administration, enjoying the right of residential bishops, be changed to one of permanent bishops ordinary." The government would later attack the Church in connection with this provision, but the Episcopate obtained all it could from the Vatican. The understanding also condemned German revanchism within the western dioceses. Finally came an unusually precise and effective declaration: "The principle that the Pope is the competent and highest church authority applies to matters of faith, morality, and church jurisdiction; in other areas the Episcopate will guide itself by the Polish *racja stanu.*" There was much opposition in public opinion to the part of the understanding promising to explain to the clergy "that they should not oppose the enlargement of the cooperative movement in the villages," but the same point addressed the principle of free choice. When the communists violated this principle in the attempt at collectivization, the Episcopate turned out to have made an important reservation. The pronouncement against "misusing religious sentiments for anti-state ends" in no way contradicts Catholic principles. The declaration favoring efforts toward peace and against the armed underground was certainly a government success, but in the actual situation the armed underground was damaging not only to the government, but also to the very life of the much-bloodied nation. In short, the Episcopate agreed to nothing that cannot be justified even today, more than thirty years later.

At the same time, the Church gained certain concrete concessions from the government. Religious education in the schools was assured. Students would not be hindered from religious practice outside of school. The continuation of Catholic schools was guaranteed; indeed, they were to benefit from state law. The existence of the Catholic University of Lublin and the work of Catholic associations were assured. The Church would be allowed to develop its charitable, benevolent, and catechetical activities. The government agreed to the freedom of the Catholic press and publishing houses, and to noninterference in public worship, processions, and pilgrimages. The matter of pastoral care in the army, prisons, and hospitals was to be settled, and freedom of action to be guaranteed to religious orders. A joint protocol appended to the understanding covered the conditions under which the Episcopate could permit priests to work if they chose in Caritas, and also regulated the matters of church claims of mortmain, the creation of a church fund, the delay of military obligations for seminarians, and the exemptions of priests and religious from military service.

The ostensible balance of the understanding certainly favored the Church, even if it was known that the government would not always follow the document loyally. To the charge, "You can't do business with the devil," the Primate replied, "With the devil you can't, but with people you can."

The bishops at Warsaw did not think that the understanding would end the struggle against the Church, but, rather, that it would provide a breathing space. In the Vatican, Monsignor Tardini was at first "overcome by pain" on learning that the understanding had been signed, but Pius XII was later to give it his full approval. For the government the agreement was only one move in a game designed to atheize the people and eliminate religion. Immediately further declarations appeared for the bishops to sign, but only those that did not contradict the Catholic religion were accepted. They issued a communiqué on international peace, they signed the so-called Stockholm Petition* after concerted, long-term pressure, and they issued a declaration on the occasion of the Second World Congress of the Defenders of Peace.

By the second half of 1950, the atmosphere was growing cloudy. The continual demands for peace declarations were becoming tiring to the bishops. Even though the idea of peace has its deepest roots in the Gospel, the peace extravaganzas of the Stalinist period were the main façade behind which the communists concealed domestic violence and the true foreign politics of their camp. However, the Primate stood firmly by the signed understanding and tried to exhibit the maximum good will.

The end of the year brought an increase in church-state tensions. The Episcopate met and continued discussions within the framework of the Mixed Commission on November 16 and 28 and December 4. In January, unhappy with the results of its tactics and its efforts to disorganize the Church, the government resorted to pressure. On January 20 Bishop Czesław Kaczmarek was arrested and his trial announced. The matter would have far-reaching consequences, but worse was to come. On January 28, the government announced that the apostolic administrators in the Western Lands had been barred from their church functions. The chapters were forced to elect vicars capitular—a canonically invalid action.† Father Teodor Bensch was removed from Olsztyn, Father Bolesław Kominek

---

*A campaign launched in Stockholm, Sweden, in 1950, by the World Peace Congress of the Partisans for Peace to gain signatures to ban the atomic bomb. The effort was dominated by the U.S.S.R. and imposed on all the Soviet Bloc countries.

†In the new Western territories, sees (dioceses) did have ordinaries (head bishops) because the Holy See was waiting for a peace treaty between Poland and Germany before appointing official ordinaries. In the meantime it named apostolic administrators. The Polish government did not recognize these because it wanted ordinaries named by the Holy See in order to give the territories greater stability. As a result, it nullified the appointed apostolic administrators and, contrary to canon law, which specifies that chapters elect vicars-capitular *only after the death* of an ordinary, forced the chapters to elect vicars-capitular to fill the vacancies created by the removal of the apostolic administrators.

from Opole, Father Karol Milik from Wrocław, Father Edmund Nowicki from Gorzów, and Father Andrzej Wronka from Gdańsk. The act did not end the temporary ecclesiastical administration, as the government claimed, but confirmed its temporary character. Even those ignorant of canon law can plainly see that an apostolic administrator is worth more within the Church than a vicar capitular, especially if the latter has been invalidly elected.

A brief recapitulation of events in the Polish church administration of the Western Lands since 1945 is in order here. On August 15, 1945, upon the conclusion of the Potsdam Conference, which awarded the "formerly German territories" beyond the Oder and Neisse rivers to Poland, Cardinal Hlond —endowed by Pius XII with extraordinary powers—established five Polish prelates as apostolic administrators of the territories in question. This was done as a pastoral necessity. The proclamations and letters of Pius XII confirm that he approved of, and even praised, Cardinal Hlond's actions in the Western Lands.

Primate Wyszyński, following in Cardinal Hlond's footsteps, acted to strengthen Polish church administration in the Western Lands as soon as the communists stopped creating artificial obstacles and when international circumstances allowed. In the meantime, the government placed the destruction of the Church above Polish interests and chose this matter of church administration as one of its main propaganda tools in the battle against the Church, particularly in its effort to isolate the Polish Church from the Apostolic See. Government propaganda suggested that the Episcopate, prompted by the Vatican, wanted to keep the Polish church administration of these territories temporary. When the government went beyond propaganda and attempted to force an end to the apostolic administration in January 1951, the Episcopate lodged a protest against this violent act, but decided not to make the protest public in order not to inflame the situation (*ad maiora mala vitanda*, to prevent a greater scandal of the innocent). To avoid a schism in the Church, the Primate granted jurisdiction to the vicars capitular. In the situation, the bishops decided that a visit to Rome by the Primate was urgent.

He set out on April 3, taking with him a handful of Polish soil and a picture of Our Lady of Jasna Góra. It was his first visit *ad apostolicam sedem*, even though he had been a bishop for five years and primate for more than two. Wyszyński acquainted Pius XII with the complexity of Polish church problems and especially the Western Lands question. The Pope approved and blessed all the conduct and methods of the head of the Polish Church. During their meeting, the Holy Father spoke the historic words *Polonia fara da se,* Poland will take care of itself. In the matter of the Western Lands, the Pope did all he could, given the absence of a treaty between Poland and West Germany. He agreed to the nomination of titular bishops to administer the dioceses of the Oder-Neisse territories. This was a considerable step toward reinforcing the position of the Polish Church in these lands. The government, however, rejected the idea. (In 1956, after the political upheaval, the communists agreed that they had made a grave mistake and accepted the solution that President Bolesław Bierut and the Stalinists had rejected.)

In 1951, the Primate met with President Bierut at Belvedere Palace, both in February and May, before and after his visit to Rome. Extraordinarily loyal to all his interlocutors, the Primate never revealed anything about these meetings, the second of which went on for three hours.

Wyszyński not only made every effort to show the matter of the Western Lands in the proper light during his journey to Rome, but also systematically and constantly made visitations to the parishes there, devoting as much time to them as to the parishes of his own two archdioceses. Thus, by personal contact and supervision, he underlined the importance of the new territories to the Polish Church. Following one of his inspection trips, an interview with the Primate was published in *Tygodnik Powszechny* (Universal Weekly) on December 16, 1951. He reminded the interviewer of the efforts put into these territories by the clergy and said that the Polishness of the

Western Lands was obvious and appreciated by the Holy See. This interview later became a pretext for furious attacks by the government and its collaborators. The first sign of the new onslaught was an article by Bolesław Piasecki in *Słowo Powszechne* (Universal Word), the organ of Pax, on January 1, 1952. Piasecki accused the Vatican of having "a negative attitude toward the needs of contemporary Poland" and of giving in to "the influence of German revanchists and the NATO alliance." This pronouncement by the head of Pax heralded a new and difficult stage in the history of the Church and the life of Stefan Wyszyński.

3

Unavoidable
Imprisonment (1952-1956)

The Primate of Poland must have looked upon the beginning of 1952 with concern. On New Year's Day he expressed thoughts that testify to his great determination: "Whatever God demands—I shall fulfill. It is all the same to me whether I have to sow words and examples, or my own blood. As long as Poland remains Christ's Kingdom." What strikes one here is the reference to blood. It shows not only that he was ready to suffer martyrdom, but also that he had discerned, whether by intuition or logic, that he was facing a situation in which martyrdom could not be ruled out.

He went to Cracow on January 2 to speak at a conference on the situation of clergy facing the transformation of the political system. From Monsignor Tardini in Rome had come a question about a *terno* (legal) nomination for the Cracow archbishopric, but the Primate was in no hurry. Archbishop Eugeniusz Baziak, formerly the metropolitan of Lwów, was reigning energetically in Cracow. But the state authorities wanted to see a "rival" to the Primate in the Cracow see. Stefan Wyszyński already knew well the current variations on the eternal tactic *divide et impera* (divide and conquer).

On returning to Warsaw, the Primate kept appointments concerning business matters and participated almost every day in pastoral duties. The new rector of KUL, Father Józef Iwanicki, discussed institutional business. Father Roman Szemraj, one of the leading "patriotic priests," and other army chaplains applied for an extension of their jurisdiction, Szemraj himself pledging "by the honor of my officer's uniform" that he was not writing for the ZBoWiD Priests' Committee's publication, *Citizen Priest.* The Primate explained that "priestly honor" would be more convincing: the uniform could come off; priesthood was forever.

The Primate's regular evening conversation on January 6 (Epiphany) with Bishop Choromański, secretary of the Episcopate, reviewed what the Church's situation really was. They discussed the attitude to be taken toward the projected new constitution as well as the consequences of a demonstration in Wrocław that priests were forced to attend and witness an attack on the Episcopate by representatives of the authorities. Finally, they had to evaluate the echoes in the press of the Primate's "Discussion" (of the Western Lands) that had appeared in *Tygodnik Powszechny* on December 16, 1951. "Remarks of the Episcopate on the Draft of the New Constitution," transmitted to the authorities by Konstanty Łubieński of Pax, had met with a negative reaction, and the Primate's remarks in *Tygodnik Powszechny* had also been received critically by the government.

All these matters, as well as the occurrence of a series of assaults on church property, were the subject of a steering-committee meeting on January 14. Bishop Choromański recounted his discussion with Minister Antoni Bida, the chief of Polish internal security, in which he had protested against press attacks on Bishop Kowalski, against the violent treatment of priests at the time of the Wrocław demonstration, and against the Politburo's association of the clergy with the underground. Minister Bida had been upset by the Pope's New Year message. The steering committee ascertained that the government was acting mainly against bishops—by imprisoning Bishop Kaczmarek, for instance—while showing restraint toward the clergy. Bishop Klepacz believed that as heads of the party, Edward Ochab, Roman Zambrowski, and Franciszek Jóźwiak favored a hard line against the Church, while Bolesław Bierut, Jakub Berman, and Hilary Minc were more moderate; he also thought that the most liberal communists were those at the very top. Nevertheless, the government was trying to set bishops and clergy at odds; the moves in Kielce were probably a trial run of this policy. The cathedral there had been searched without witnesses; a trial of Bishop Kaczmarek was being prepared; priests were still being arrested. The steering committee decided to send a letter concerning the affair to President Bierut and to scold Pax's publishers for bringing out Father Żywczyński's *The Church and the French Revolution* since the false analogies made in the book could not be answered in the face of state censorship.

Bishop Klepacz's five-hour meeting with delegate Mazur (returning to work after a long illness) reinforced the impression of growing tension. Mazur, who liked long expositions, spoke for three and a half hours; his accusations against the Episcopate included engaging in "conspiratorial activity," "ambushing" the government, and regarding the present authorities as "temporary." He blustered somewhat comically that the main enemies of the Polish Church were the United Nations and the Vatican (!). "There are Masonic forces at work in the United Nations," he said, "who express astonishment to Polish communists that the Polish Church 'is not bleeding.' Good conditions and relations in Poland make them sad, and the bishops' defensive statements cheer them up. Episcopal statements and protests play into their hands." The Vatican, according to Mazur, wished the martyrdom of the Polish Church for its own political ends. The government thought either that it was talking to the very naïve, or that the Church would buy its anti-Masonic arguments. Mazur revealed himself further by saying of the *Tygodnik* interview with the Primate, "If he hadn't talked about the Pope, we would approach these matters differently."

Thus, everything presaged trouble, and facts answered forebodings in short order. January 21 brought news that priests and religious sisters were being ejected from the Coast* under varied pretexts. On January 24, the hospital of the Sisters of Saint Elizabeth in Warsaw was nationalized. On the same day, four Bernardine Fathers, two of them new administrators, were jailed.

The Primate did not change his course at all. He drafted a letter to the government about the abusing and threatening of clergy at the Wrocław meeting. He sent the letter on January 23, but at the same time he held up Bishop Klepacz's projected letter to the clergy on the subject of the constitution. Bringing up the matter publicly would be extremely ticklish for the government, besides dangerous to the Church. On January 29 the Primate showed similar realism. Bishop Herbert Bednorz reported to him the proposal of Bishop Adamski of Katowice to organize "universal prayers that Poland remain Catholic." Wyszyński advised him to wait at least until the meeting of the Episcopate.

These cautious tactics joined principled action with matters crucial to the Church. The Primate spent all of February 1 working on a memorandum to the government in connection with the constitution. Its main idea concerned the fact that the projected constitution guaranteed the Catholic community no basis for organizing and meeting. The Church was not even acknowledged as a public institution, yet how could it allow itself to be considered as only a common association? Significantly, this matter recurred in the Primate's demands more than a quarter of a century later: it had still not been settled. On Candlemas, February 2, he went to Gniezno, where he was informed for the first time that an attempt had been made on his life at the time of his ingress to Warsaw on February 5, 1949

---

*The Coast here means the Baltic Coast. The Polish term, Wybrzeże, is often used to designate the two agglomerations of Szczecin and the Tri-Cities (Gdańsk-Gdynia-Sopot), which have frequently played a leading role in social protest, notably in 1970 and 1980.

—a steel cable had been stretched across his route at the height of a car's windshield, but fortunately he had taken another road.

Stalinist tactics against the Church relied not only on trying to drive a wedge between the clergy and the Episcopate, but also on attempting to divide the bishops themselves. This last goal had minimal chances of success, but we shall see how artfully it was attempted. Bishop Choromański met with delegate Mazur, who again grew angry and blustered. Interestingly, Mazur was amicable when he spoke to Bishop Klepacz, but with Choromański he moved to the familiar "you," rude under the circumstances—"you'll see," "we'll show you," "we're not afraid." He was trying to frighten the Episcopate by permitting himself an attitude of overfamiliarity. Then he settled down to making further threats.

Soon afterward the Primate spoke with Father Eugeniusz Dąbrowski, principal speaker at the Wrocław meeting. The priest explained that he had entered into political affairs so that he would be able to publish his academic works. Dąbrowski had in fact managed to have hundreds of thousands of New Testaments in his translation published through Pax, and also his own Biblical commentaries. The government had been willing to pay a high price for the temporary services of an eminent scripture scholar. Their gamut of ways to divide the Church was inexhaustible.

The steering committee met on February 10, the full Episcopate the next day. The general situation and the evident hardening of the government line as reflected in the meetings with Mazur were discussed. Bishop Franciszek Korszyński had come from Włocławek with news of the arrest of Father Jan Grajnert, chancellor of the curia there, and the interrogation of other priests. Eight priests from the diocese were already in prison. Mazur's threats were coming to life. The Episcopate decided to submit the memorandum on the constitution to the government and to send a copy to the clergy, a mild response to the situation. Earlier, a public declaration or communiqué had been considered, but the Primate wanted to act as patiently and moderately as possible. The Episcopate also decided to send letters to the imprisoned priests and to help them financially out of curia funds. Priests were not to be allowed to submit articles to Pax's *Słowo Powszechne* without the agreement of the Warsaw curia, books could be published by Pax only after the *nihil obstat** of the Warsaw curia was sought, and other bishops would not grant permission for material to be published in Warsaw. The Primate was firmly gathering the means of controlling church activity into his own hands in this explosive situation. The Episcopate charged Bishop Zdzisław Goliński with composing a memorandum to the commission working on the penal code to protest the loose provisions relating to the protection of children—the penalty for abortion was less than that for destroying trees.

The next day the memorandum on the constitution, signed by the Primate and the bishops, was delivered to the president's office.

On the morning of February 12 the Primate received Bolesław Piasecki. Bishop Klepacz was present as a witness, because the Primate had learned how a tête-à-tête could later be misrepresented in Pax forums and create misunderstandings. Piasecki acknowledged that the attack on the Primate in *Słowo Powszechne* had been a mistake. He claimed its publication had been forced upon him. Government functionaries had allegedly been considering at the time whether to let the Primate back into the country, and according to Piasecki the attack in *Słowo Powszechne* "eased" the decision about Wyszyński's returning. The argument was hardly convincing, but Piasecki's information on plans to banish the Primate was truly sensational. It was interesting that the head of Pax had not shared it with anyone within his own group. At this time, *Pravda* was interfering in Polish affairs by attacking the Primate; the Soviet articles proved to the Primate that Moscow, not the Polish

---

*Literally, "nothing stands in the way," a term used on the verso of the title page of a book to indicate that a person delegated by an ordinary (head bishop) verifies that the material is free from doctrinal or moral error and approves it for publication.

party, was organizing the struggle against the Church. The PZPR was acting as factotum.

Piasecki put his group's doctrinal mistakes down to inexperience, asserted with something less than candor that young members of Pax were learning Catholic social teachings, and agreed to withdraw from sale two pro-Pax books that would have a deleterious effect in a totalitarian society, where the free play of criticism was forbidden. Disagreeing with the Primate only over Pax's right to criticize the Vatican Secretariat of State, Piasecki conducted himself amicably, asked to keep in contact, and said that he did not want to "intrude" himself upon the Church. It was decided that he would stay in touch with Bishop Klepacz and see the Primate only under exceptional circumstances.

Each day of the difficult new year (1952), meanwhile, was marked by more arrests of priests and religious, interference in church affairs, divisiveness on the part of the "patriotic priests," and the removal of religion from the schools. Meeting with Bishop Klepacz, Mazur would not agree to Father Bensch's accession in Gorzów. A congress of the ZBoWiD Priests' Committee attacked the Episcopate's "Wrocław Memorandum" in a meeting to which Minister Bida's presence added weight. That was on February 20–21; on the 25th, Jerzy Turowicz and Jerzy Zawieyski informed the Primate that the censor would not allow *Tygodnik Powszechny* to publish the Episcopate's memorandum on the constitution. These innumerable blows all caused additional stress on Stefan Wyszyński, who could see that the actions intended to crush the Church were only beginning. Already he recognized the danger to himself. He remained peaceful and did not give up the "dialogue" with the government, however, realizing that the communists, wary of society's reaction, could not move too quickly to ultimate measures. Above all, the Primate's strength flowed from his faith and hope in the Virgin Mary's grace and intercession. The Marxists would be amazed that in resisting them he counted on supernatural forces.

In March the government's minions mounted new attacks on the Pope, linking him to American capital, financiers, and bankers. In the press they undertook indirect arguments with the Episcopate's memorandum on the constitution. At the same time, they intensified pressure by taxation, presenting priests with demands for payment. On March 8 *Słowo Powszechne* announced a declaration in favor of the new constitution by the Commission of Intellectuals, which was more and more evidently rivaling the discredited ZBoWiD Priests' Committee in its politics. Over the next weeks, the Primate received numerous reports of the nationalization of Catholic kindergartens that refused to submit to the government's Caritas association. The government also began a program of inspecting minor seminaries, then started stepping it up.

In this atmosphere of incessant limitation of church prerogatives, the Mixed Commission met on March 20, 1952, with Choromański, Zakrzewski, and Klepacz representing the Episcopate, and Mazur and Bida the government. During the seven-hour session, Minister Bida accused the bishops of sabotaging the understanding, and he polemicized over the memorandum on the projected constitution. Mazur claimed that the Primate was "undermining" the vicars capitular in the Western Lands and stated, "The government does not recognize the special rights of any ordinary or plenipotentiary in the Western Lands, not even if he were the very Archbishop of Gniezno. We are treating them as legitimate vicars capitular." The government, having forced the election of the vicars, pretended not to understand that if the Primate did not recognize these vicars they would represent nothing less than a schism in the Polish Church. The government was thus acting more and more ruthlessly. Mazur asserted that the publication of Episcopate letters in regard to political matters (i.e., the constitution) was forbidden, and he spoke directly of personal responsibility. However, the bishops judged the situation of the Church in the Western Lands to be more dangerous than such threats. Unfortunately, those interesting historical documents are still unavailable today.

During a retreat for young academics at Saint Anne's Church in Warsaw on March 23, the Primate, certainly having the progovernment "intellectuals" in mind, advanced what he himself termed "a rather extreme position." He said, specifically, that "Poland still has no Catholic intelligentsia of its own, because that sphere always came under the influence of intellectual and moral relativism. This shows particularly during crises, when the intelligentsia disappears from the field of battle for Catholic ideals." These stern words come from a man tortured by blows against the Church, who now has had a log rolled under his feet in the name of abstract ideals by so-called progressive Catholics. Fortunately the *Tygodnik Powszechny* group and Catholic intellectuals in prison redeemed the honor of the laity. It goes without saying that intellectuals found themselves in a particularly difficult situation, depending as they did on one employer—the communist state.

The Episcopate Steering Committee met more often under this increasing pressure. On March 26 it heard Monsignor Tardini's letter reiterating the Vatican's earlier position that new dioceses could not be created in the Western Lands in the absence of international treaties. Since the government would not recognize the Primate's authority in the Western Lands, he informed the steering Committee that he would use the *facultates specialissimae** he had obtained from Rome on April 18 of the previous year to name the vicars his special delegates, with the rights of resident ordinaries. Above all, this action preserved canonical order.

The authorities' intention to frighten the bishops, signaled by Minister Bida's threats over letters to the clergy, continued. On March 27 Bishop Choromański reported that Bida had asked him whether the Episcopate would calm the nuns whose kindergartens had been seized. What could he have expected but the negative answer he received?

The next day Father Antoni Marchewka of Częstochowa,

---

*"Most special faculties" refers to certain special powers reserved to the Holy See but in this case granted to Cardinal Wyszyński.

editor of the magazine *Sunday,* reported that Bida had ordered him to condemn the Nazis for the Katyń massacre.* The same day, Turowicz and Stanisław Stommat told the Primate that Bida had commanded their publications, *Tygodnik Powszechny* and *Znak,‡* to denounce the use of bacteriological weapons in Korea.

On March 31, in a letter he sent to President Bierut, Archbishop Wyszyński protested the plundering of monasteries under the pretext of nationalizing those that had not submitted to the government's Caritas.

On April 8 the Primate held discussions, arranged by Bishop Choromański, with Franciszek Mazur. Meeting in Wilanów Palace, the two talked for five and a half hours, mostly about the Western Lands and about coordinating their actions should a church post fall vacant there. It must have been humiliating for the Primate to attend such a meeting while church institutions were being attacked, monastic houses seized, kindergartens liquidated, and so on. The next day he said:

> A year ago I visited the Holy Father; what an impression this anniversary makes upon me. I cannot overcome my desire to be there again. I need Rome like the air, like drops of water on thirsty lips. All day I suffer from this insuperable longing. I pray for the Holy Father all day. His prepossessing figure appears before my eyes. I see the Pope. I see his good, penetrating eyes. And yet—I cannot go to Rome. In such moments I understand that I am the slave of that "cannot."

---

*Katyn is a forest area near Smoleńsk (Russia) where in April 1943 the Germans announced that they had discovered mass graves of 4,143 bodies of Polish military officers, all shot in the back of the head. Eyewitnesses stated that in April and May of 1940 they had seen a series of transports with prisoners heading for that area, after which they had heard shots. Numerous international investigations concluded that the Germans could not have murdered the Poles since they did not occupy the area until 1941.

†Stomma: Professor of Law at the Catholic University of Lubin and University of Warsaw; chairman of the Znak group in the Polish Parliament; and adviser to Cardinal Wyszyński in legal matters referring to church-state relations.

‡"The Sign," a publication issued by the independent Catholic group Znak.

At last, the strong and peaceful primate allowed himself to admit that he was tired. It was no accident that this occurred after his discussions with Mazur: he had no chance of traveling, for the tension was increasing from day to day and his freedom to return could not be assured.

It was characteristic of Stefan Wyszyński's realism that, despite the tense situation, he sent his wishes to Bolesław Bierut on April 18, 1952, the president's sixtieth birthday. He wanted to create the appearance of respect for the head of state, regardless of Bierut's personal convictions or his function as leader of a Marxist party.

On April 19 the Primate and Mazur met again at Wilanów, to conclude the business of their previous session. The main subject was the nomination by the Holy See of successors to vacant bishoprics. Mazur explained that the government wanted only one candidate named for Wrocław and one for Cracow. He did not want to hear about the normal practice of presenting a *terno* (legal nomination) to the Pope. This constituted an assault on canonical principles and an attempt to dictate personnel matters to the Church. The Primate had to protest. It was an exceptionally unpleasant meeting, from which the Primate came away with the impression that attacks were being prepared against monasteries, seminaries, curias, and chapters. For instance, the government wanted to politicize the seminaries by introducing courses on contemporary Poland, though the opposition of the Episcopate would frustrate such plans.

The steering committee met on April 24 to discuss the situation and to approve the added powers given to the leaders of the dioceses in the Western Lands. The bishops decided to stick up for the right to nominate new bishops through a *terno*, and they stressed the importance of unity and contact with the Holy See. They agreed to courses on contemporary Poland in the seminaries as long as the courses did not in any way represent communist indoctrination. Finally, the Episcopate was disposed to renew its appeal to society on how best to work for the good of the country. Such actions combined principles and flexibility.

At the beginning of May 1952, Primate Wyszyński made a grand pastoral tour of the Western Lands, preaching, inspecting, and in particular confirming. He met thousands of the new residents who were streaming in from all over the country. On May 3 he stated his principal impression:

> Above all other considerations shines the fact that the Church is here again. And it is the most important, the most necessary unifying force. Everything else is weak here. The administration is in tatters, the economy has been cut off at the roots by doctrine and *kolhozes*, the people feel temporary. But the priests are carrying on within the church organization; the prayers have not stopped. The Church is not in politics here—the Church is praying and bringing people together. In this way it is also doing a service to the state that has come here.

Hardly had the Primate returned to Warsaw on the evening of May 5 when he encountered bad news and unpleasantness. Bishop Choromański informed him that Minister Bida had protested the transfer of "patriotic priests" to other posts. The authorities demanded the registration of all duplicating machines belonging to the Church. On April 26 the Pax organ *Słowo Powszechne* had printed a declaration of the University of Warsaw's theology department "on internal peace." The document apparently was based on word of mouth rather than a meeting of the department; it constituted an argument against the "Discussion" between the Primate and Jerzy Turowicz which had been published in *Tygodnik Powszechny* on April 27, 1952. The Primate's statements were also dealt a sharp attack by *Trybuna Ludu* (The People's Tribune) on May 7. Unable to break the Primate by talking to him, the party was turning to media pressure and attempts at intimidation. The state radio also carried the *Trybuna Ludu* article.

All year the Primate carried out visitations in both his archdioceses, confirming children, meeting crowds. Everywhere he was greeted with great affection, even though the authorities had returned to the tactics of two years earlier by forbidding the erection of welcoming gates, banners, and public demonstrations for the Primate. Wyszyński counseled priests who had been harassed by the authorities to keep their religious celebrations within the church buildings, but as it turned out, the enthusiasm at the sight of the Primate was so great that his reception always became public.

On May 21 Primate Wyszyński signed a document ratifying the vacancy in the Wrocław chapter and a decree on the composition of a new chapter. He then took part in the celebrations that installed the new chapter. Father Kazimierz Lagosz was chosen as the new vicar capitular—the Primate had accepted this one change in personnel as the price for a new chapter; the government would have ejected a different chapter by force. The new one, it is true, would provoke dissatisfaction among the most unbending conservatives, and the lack of German priests would not make the Germans happy. But the Primate felt he had done the right thing. The faithful gained legal pastors, and the Church a canonically correct solution. The government and official press passed over these events in silence; it was not convenient for them that the Church was accomplishing things in the Western Lands.

The steering committee met in Warsaw on June 3, and the next day the full Episcopate discussed the Wrocław celebrations and various pastoral documents. The Episcopate approved the text of a communiqué to the faithful on a series of profanations of churches and the Blessed Sacrament, which had had occurred too frequently and too intensively to seem accidental. Archbishop Walenty Dymek of Poznań expressed the general conviction of the bishops when he said, "The communist government is systematically, deliberately, and persistently undercutting the status of the Church and its possibilities of working." The Primate responded with the words *gaudia vitae* (joy of life).

The Polish proverb "If you strike the table, the scissors will rattle" has to do with the idea that guilt always reveals itself; the proverb seemed to be fulfilled when Minister Bida "asked" Bishop Choromański to call off the Episcopate's communiqué on the profanations. At the same time, it was announced in the press that the perpetrators of the worst profanation, in Wita- szyce, had been apprehended. Bida also wanted the Corpus Christi procession limited to one day, but the bishops turned him down. Later an attempt would be made to limit even the number of altars and Masses along the route of the procession in Warsaw. Finally, Bida demanded that the chancellor of the Olsztyn curia, Father Kobyłecki, be dismissed for sheltering chaplains from the diocese of Łuck.

Machinations by progovernment agents among the clergy appeared in the form of a visit to the Primate on June 13 by Father Jan Piskorz* from Wrocław. In Father Lagosz's name he proposed that politically engaged priests, including Fathers Jan Czuj and Eugeniusz Dąbrowski, be named honorary can- ons for their services to the Western Lands. The Primate did not formally refuse him, explaining instead that he could not answer at that time. Instead of granting church honors, the Primate approved Bishop Choromański's April 20 letter to Pax on the matter of errors still being propagated in *Today and Tomorrow* and *Słowo Powszechne*, even after the meeting with Piasecki. So again caution was combined with decisiveness.

During June the Primate carried out inspections, marked by celebrations, meetings, confirmations, speeches, and preach- ing, to the dioceses of Warmia-Mazuria and Opole, where he was still the canonically valid ordinary. The results were satis- factory: religion was strengthening Polishness. Attacks on reli- gion made the residents long for a return to German rule. Monsignor Wojciech Zink of Olsztyn, whom Bida sneered at as "the little German," was able to work with great dignity in a difficult situation.

On July 1, while he was taking part in a retreat at Jasna Góra

---

*A professor of Catechetics in the Kielce Seminary with pro-government leanings. Later the government arranged for him to be elected the vicar-capitular in Katowice. He was from Wrocław.

with priests from Warsaw, Archbishop Wyszyński first heard the news, later repeated in the capital, that the government was liquidating minor seminaries, particularly those for religious. Together with Father Bronisław Dąbrowski, the Primate drafted a letter of protest to President Bierut. It was sent on July 8, but they had to wonder whether he would even read it. After all, the "Red aristocracy" had already achieved a numbness to the affairs of ordinary people that rivaled the indifference of the prewar "blue and scarlet aristocracy."*

The seizure of the seminaries was accompanied by numerous arrests. Simultaneously news came that the government, which had never confirmed the professors at KUL, was now demanding that many of them, including Fathers Pastuszko and Nowicki and Professor Strzeszewski, be removed. The Primate sent Father Zink, the vicar capitular of Olsztyn, to the president's office in order to explain to the authorities what a defeat for the Polishness of the Western Lands the liquidation of seminaries was. Before the move against the seminaries, the authorities had liquidated the Institutes for Advanced Religious Studies.† The state censor began to cross out the *nihil obstat* from all religious books on the pretext that only the state could censor texts. On July 10 the Primate again protested the liquidation of the minor seminaries, this time in a private letter to Bida that also sharply criticized all of the latter's policies toward the Church. Unfortunately, these were policies not only of the Bureau of Religious Affairs, but also of the party and the state. Poland was moving quickly to make up for ground lost through the authorities' weakness and the Church's strength.

The government wanted to go still further. On July 11 the Primate received an anonymous suggestion—clearly a provo-

---

*"Red aristocracy" refers to the top communists in power in Poland; "blue and scarlet aristocracy" refers to the higher and lower aristocracy of old Poland: "blue" to the "magnates" and "scarlet" to the "nobility."

†These were affiliated with the Catholic University of Lublin. They provided courses in theology for the laity, had the power to grant degrees, and included courses by correspondence. They were liquidated (before the seminaries) to prevent the formation of a theologically educated Catholic intelligentsia.

cation—that he call a meeting of the Episcopal Steering Committee and issue a declaration on the seminary affair. Wyszyński remained calm.

The various religious orders sent letters similar to his memorandum to Bierut. On Sunday, July 13, the Primate consecrated a church built without official permission in Izabelin, near Warsaw. In the evening he went to Laski to chat with people there about Father Korniłowicz's pastoral methods. Attacked from all sides, he maintained extraordinary calm. At the same time he acted realistically, secretly preparing twenty documents concerning the brutal actions against the seminaries, which he supplied to prominent political figures to show them what was going on in the country.

In July 1952, the new constitution was approved. The national holiday was celebrated on the 22nd, and a youth festival in Warsaw was arranged. The organized joy contrasted to the raging lawlessness. Along with the seminaries, several monastic novitiates were dissolved, the houses and all their furnishings confiscated. On July 30 the steering committee discussed the inevitable liquidation of the Catholic press, harassed by the censor and by the deliberate inefficiency of Ruch, the nationalized distributors. A government decree abolishing foundations endangered many church institutions. The censor began to cross out the phrase "With permission of the ecclesiastical authorities" so that religious literature could not be distinguished from the politicized, "progressive," and pseudo-religious.

None of the Church's interventions in the matters of the minor seminaries or the plundering of the monasteries did any good. Bida answered that the government was defending law and order; President Bierut did not answer at all. A letter sent by the Episcopate to the Council of State was unsuccessful. Some of the institutions at Laski were now threatened.

At Częstochowa on August 15, the Primate preached the rights of man, the nation, and the Church in words that anticipated statements being made today.

Let us remind others of the human rights: the right of life and a livelihood, the right to God, the right to truth, the right to love. Let us remind others of family rights: the right to freedom, to the choice of life, to a vocation; the right to domestic peace, the right to property, the right to raise children and to a choice of schools. Let us remind others of the rights of the nation: the right to a free country, to fidelity to country, to a place in our country, to history, language, and culture. Finally, the synthesis and protective force of these rights: the Church, upon which is grounded the European culture that depends on the protection of these rights derived from Christ. The Church has the right to proclaim the Gospel from the pulpit, in the press, in books. The Church has the right to educational freedom and to Catholic schools! If our Polish relatives in America have more than a thousand Catholic schools, then we in our free homeland should not be worse off—but we have barely a few!

The defense of these rights leads to domestic peace. Whoever defends these rights renders a service to order and social success.

What could be a better, more principled, more peaceful answer to the assaults of the last year? Ten days later, talking to Bishop Choromański, Minister Bida called it "a gamble." Since informing society of the Church's losses was forbidden, this was indeed a real, specific gamble on the Primate's part. However, it was also an obligation.

* * *

Risking so much in defense of the Church and its institutions, lodging protests against authorities who considered protest a crime and criticism of the government an antistate activity, the Primate of Poland tried appealing as a citizen to prove to the authorities that he did not want to exacerbate the situation. After the approval of the constitution, elections to the Sejm* were to be held. The Primate knew perfectly well that the elections were a fiction and that a second list of candidates to oppose that of the coalition National Front would not even be put up. Bolesław Piasecki warned Bishop Klepacz, and Minister Bida warned Bishop Choromański, that the government was troubled by the Episcopate's attitude toward the National Front. The Primate thus firmly opposed the candidacy of priests, let alone of bishops. And the Marxists had too little courage even to run any candidates from among the "patriotic priests." However, the steering committee faced the problem, in its meeting of September 18–19, of formulating an attitude toward the elections, which, although a fiction, provided an opportunity for the government to accuse the bishops of opposing elections and intending a boycott. The Episcopate did not want to boycott them if only because, within the framework of the constitutional obligation, they might become more authentic.

Accordingly, the Primate gave instructions to Catholic editors on September 22. Despite the threat to the existence of these publications, beset by difficulties with Ruch, he counseled them to keep publishing even if they were losing money. He proposed that the Catholic press treat subjects pertinent to the national good, such as the rebuilding of Warsaw, the Polish rights to the Western Lands and their economic reconstruction, social and economic questions, and any positive information that could be found in the lay press.

The state authorities, however, did not want to see gestures of good will from the Episcopate. In October there were new unfriendly steps: the provincial government councils refused to recognize the new parishes created by the Primate and other

---

*The Polish legislature, presided over by a marshal and including delegates from the "leading" National Front, a "transmission belt" coalition of communist and fellow-traveler parties (the communist PZPR, the Democratic Party [SD], and the Peasants' Party [ZSL]), Pax, and, according to the political weather, the independent Catholic group Znak (The Sign) as well as "nonparty" individuals.

bishops. Nevertheless, the Church presented the authorities with a *fait accompli* instead of retreating. On this matter, the Primate warned, the authorities were copying the old tsarist prohibition *Swoda Zakonów.** The Warsaw authorities turned their attention to church building, closing and sealing off newly constructed annexes to chapels and churches, but the Primate's energetic protests achieved the revocation of several such orders.

Throughout 1952, attempts were made to organize sports and artistic events in competition with religious festivities, especially those at which the Primate appeared. The secular shows lost the competition, however, as huge crowds—particularly of the young—turned out for the Primate's visitations.

The Primate's impressions of one visitation he made in a working-class parish in Żyrardów, near Warsaw, are characteristic:

> The day passes at a Żyrardów church among crowds of people who, it seems, keep the building constantly full. . . . Today Żyrardów looks much changed; the "veneer of government" has made the town its domain. All the Red houses around the church, occupied in days of yore by German and Czech socialists, and later, between the wars, by trade-union dignitaries, are filled today by the communist gentry. But working people, the ones in overalls, only go along with the politicking so that they can hold their jobs. In the factories they are Red; in the churches they are enthusiastic and faithful. We can see this double Żyrardów all too well. We can sense plenty of spies in the crowd—they mill around in their typical shuffle, with dragging feet and swiveling necks, always ready to spot something to the right or the left. . . . The entrance to the church is full of children, even though they were ordered to "debate the National Front" after athletic exploits at the

---

*The tsarist *Monastic Codex*, a set of state rules governing the laws of the religious.

stadium. There is no lack of them here. Altar boys and girls in white, with their own banners and canopies, lead the way for us.

That was on October 5.

It later turned out that Minister Bida, amusingly enough, had been in Żyrardów that same day, as if doomed to follow the Primate around. The numbers of workers who took part in the religious ceremonies in Żyrardów must have made the party nervous. Cars with loudspeakers drove around the church during High Mass, and the Primate had to ask that the doors be closed. But the Church always won social confrontations with the Marxists.

Also in October of this difficult year, the Primate finally allowed himself an eighteen-day vacation, which he spent in Krynica with Bishop Baraniak and Father Zaręba. It was not entirely a time of rest, however. The Primate received the editors of the persecuted and endangered *Tygodnik Powszechny:* Turowicz, Stomma, Zawieyski, Gołubiew,* and Woźniakowski.† In a daylong discussion, he encouraged them to keep publishing in spite of their difficulties:

> The Church will not become extinct as long as one bishop is left. . . . From my first moment in command of Gniezno and Warsaw I worked for the "understanding," even though the government was hostile to me from the beginning—no, more than that: they did not even refrain from insults and laying ambushes. But that could not influence my attitude toward the government. As I see it, the "understanding" is needed by both sides. Whatever the future brings, it is worth remembering that a large

---

*Antoni Gołubiew: Catholic writer, member of Znak group in Parliament, and famous as the author of monumental historical novels, e.g. *Bolesław Chrobry* (second Polish king) in six volumes.

†Jacek Woźniakowski: professor of the History of Art at the Catholic University of Lublin, author of many books on aesthetics, member of the editorial staff of *Znak*, and director of Znak publications.

number of their so-called social achievements have the character of permanent achievements. Among them, I count the public ownership of heavy industry and the larger estates. The Polish Church is not going to fight for the restoration of the landed estates, not even of its own farms. If God demands martyrdom of us yet again, we will not hold back our blood. But it seems to me that today's ideal must be the "ability of the Church and Poland to live," rather than the ability to die—because we showed in Dachau and in the Warsaw Uprising that we have learned how to die for the Church and for Poland. Today we have to show something else. Martyrdom is always a grace and an honor. But when I weigh the present great needs and demands of Catholic Poland, I want martyrdom only as a last resort. I said the same thing in Rome to Monsignor Tardini and to the Holy Father. Our tactics here should be the same. I want my priests at the altar, in the pulpit, and in the confessional—not in prison.

Before a year had passed, the Primate who spoke thus would be in prison. Yet how very different was his program from Cardinal Mindszenty's, and how much more effective it turned out to be!

On October 25, the day before the fictitious "elections" to the Sejm, the Primate returned to Warsaw. One bishop commiserated with him over the necessity of voting, which took the Primate aback: he went to the polling place in accordance with the Episcopate's declaration. When he was given the ballot, he asked where the booth was, went in, and cast his vote, following his conscience.

Daily realities stripped the Church of all illusions. On October 28, a representative of the Bureau of Religious Affairs informed the provincial of the Pallotine Fathers that the people's state, concerned about training priests to a high standard, would no longer consent to the granting of high-school diplomas within the seminaries, thus taking another step toward eliminating as many seminaries as possible. At the same time, numbers of drunken men dressed in cassocks, behaving crudely and offensively, ordering taxis to drive them to houses of prostitution, attracted notice in Warsaw. Old methods of discrediting the cassock in the public eye were being reprised.

During a visit to the Archdiocese of Gniezno at the beginning of November, the Primate consulted architects, auxiliaries, and other experts and then set about rescuing one of the country's finest architectural sites, re-Gothicizing Gniezno Cathedral—a difficult, costly task, projected over many years, but of the greatest importance to Polish culture. Bad news tore the Primate away from these sublime plans, however. Authorities in Szczecin sent word that they did not wish him to visit that area. Bishop Lucjan Bernacki of Gniezno came under threat of arrest. A telephone call from Bishop Choromański presaged another disaster, confirmed in his November 6 letter: Minister Bida had demanded "the stepping-down from church office of the leadership of the Katowice curia," in response to Bishop Adamski's initiative in having parents in that Silesian city circulate petitions urging the Council of State to restore religious instruction in the schools. Legally, nothing could be said against this action, though politically it was a challenge to the Stalinists, who regarded it as antistate activity. The Primate, recognizing the gravity of the situation, sought enlightenment in prayer. He ordered a reply to Minister Bida, stating that the Episcopate could not dismiss bishops—that right belonged to the Holy Father alone, with whom the Episcopate had no contact. At the same time he sent a dispatch to President Bierut, asking for an audience. On November 7 the Primate returned to Warsaw, where Bishop Bednorz, it turned out, had been arrested even before Bishop Choromański's discussions with Bida. The security authorities informed Bishop Juliusz Bieniek, who was visiting Warsaw, that he could not return to Katowice. Bishop Adamski was also ordered to leave the diocese. Thus the authorities created a *fait accompli* of their own, although they wanted the Episcopate to take the responsibility for it—which was, of course, out of the question. Bishop Adamski's move had been brave, even hazardous, for the communists have always feared an appeal from the bishops to the nation like fire. Yet there had been no other way. Religion had already been thrown out of a third of the schools, and the expulsions were continuing; protests did no good.

The next day, November 8, the Primate learned of a discussion between Bishop Wacław Majewski, Auxiliary of Warsaw, and the leader of the Warsaw Provincial Council, Jerzy Albrecht. The latter demanded the dismissal of Father Sprusiński, parish priest at Mother of God in Leszno, while on the other hand defending one of the "patriotic priests" and protesting the "wild" building and renovating of church buildings. Albrecht, later a Party liberal, naturally refused to see Father Sprusiński. More bad news came the same day from the president's office: the meeting with the Primate would take place after the Mixed Commission had established its theme. Having ejected the Silesian bishops, the government had foreseen such a meeting.

The Episcopal Steering Committee and the Mixed Commission both met on November 11—the latter for five hours. The steering committee decided that the Katowice chapter should elect a vicar capitular, but the government refused its consent and ordered the bishops to condemn their Silesian colleagues. Taking the position that Bishop Adamski had been defending religion by legal means, the Episcopate absolutely refused to do so.

On November 14, the government increased the pressure on the Catholic press. The intention was clearly its liquidation, to be brought about by financial hardships, harassment by the censor, and sabotaged distribution. At a meeting with the Primate, the editors reported that the censors had cut even the articles on the Western Lands from *Tygodnik Powszechny*, which was being held to a circulation of 42,000. *God's Order* was restricted to 14,000 copies, the *Sunday Guest* in Katowice had been suspended by the authorities, and *Sunday* in Częstochowa had been trimmed from 100,000 to 10,300 copies. In Gorzów, the censors were clipping more than 60 percent of each week's text in the *Catholic Weekly*. By these methods the authorities hoped to drive the publications into bankruptcy, but the Primate reminded the editors that out of apostolic considerations they should keep operating, even at a loss. Every day brought new evidence of the government's offensive. On November 15, Monsignor Zink from Olsztyn reported that the authorities had demanded the right to approve all appointments of parish pastors. This was a clear precedent for later actions.

In Katowice, the failure to establish diocesan leadership was becoming critical. Doing everything to prevent a schism there, the Episcopate submitted three new candidates for vicar capitular, and the government rejected all three. So the Primate drew up a list of six more priests, which the authorities ignored. On November 18 the Episcopate approved a declaration defending bishops' right to protect religious liberty; Mazur replied with his own, unacceptable proposal, a declaration condemning the Silesian bishops.

The Primate sent a letter to President Bierut on the Katowice affair, and on November 24, after two days of prayer at Jasna Góra, he informed the president of the Council of Ministers that, in accordance with his special rights, he was naming Monsignor Stanisław Bross to lead the Katowice diocese. This candidate, too, was rejected; the next day, news came from Katowice that the security authorities had dropped hints about the candidacy of Father Filip Bednorz, a "patriotic priest" from ZBoWiD.

On November 26, the Primate traveled to Gniezno for a pastoral visit. Sticking to normal duties despite the earthquakes around him showed his steel nerves and uncommon faith in Divine Providence. While there, the Primate conferred again with experts in church art and with the cathedral staff, and finally inaugurated the work of re-Gothicizing Gniezno Cathedral, so that "the Primate's basilica can appear in her Gothic robes for the thousandth anniversary of Polish Christianity [1966]." Before leaving Gniezno, Primate Wyszyński sent inquiries to the Ministry of Public Security about the reasons for Bishop Bednorz's arrest and his place of confinement. On the same day, *Trybuna Ludu* ran an article titled "The Ambassador and the Bishops" that clearly suggested that the bishops were engaging in espionage activities. This was the party organ's response to protests against such insinuations, lodged by the Episcopate in its November 18 letter to President Bierut. On the morning of the 27th, the radio reported the election of Father Filip Bednorz as vicar capitular of Katowice. The election of this "patriotic priest" had been a pretense, held under direct pressure from the state security authorities. Nevertheless, Father Bednorz had been sworn in at the curia, late on the night of the 25th.

On November 29, the Primate set out for Szczecin. When he arrived, at six in the evening, a group of priests led by Monsignor Zygmunt Szelążek was waiting with congratulations: according to the radio, he had been elevated to the rank of cardinal. The Primate received the news coolly, remarking that the radio had transmitted a good number of falsehoods, and went off to the basilica for a meeting with young students. He began Sunday, November 30, by saying a seven o'clock Mass for the students, followed by a Mass for the professors and, finally, a High Mass in the basilica. Later Father Goździewicz, who worked in the secretariat, presented him with a telegram from Monsignor Montini;* the Holy Father, it confirmed, would elevate Stefan Wyszyński to the College of Cardinals during a secret consistory on January 12, 1953. The radio had been telling the truth this time.

On this important day, the newly created cardinal reflected:

Omnia—soli Deo. It strikes me that this news could not have come at a more fitting season than now, in Szczecin, during a time of hectic work against the background of the Katowice affair. Before the High Mass I inform the faithful of my nomination. I give the sermon after thanking them for their congratulations. My own thanks I give

---

*Monsignor Montini: Giovanni Battista (1897–1978). At that time he was secretary of state of the Vatican; he was elected pope in 1963 and became Pope Paul VI.

to the Heavenly Father, to Christ, to the Church, to my Catholic homeland, and to my parents. I underline the joyful fact that it is precisely from Szczecin that I have sent a telegram of thanks to the Holy Father, from this Szczecin about which—together with Wrocław, Opole, Gorzów, and Olsztyn—I have spoken often to the Holy Father. He knows how I understand the matter of the Western Lands. If, therefore, he bestows the scarlet on me today, I take it as an approval of these ideas.

Characteristically, Stefan Wyszyński thought at this moment of God, the Church, and Poland, rather than of his triumph over the authorities. His elevation was very inconvenient for them, and caught them off guard, but they did not intend to yield.

Together with the joyous telegram came news that Mazur had lodged a declaration on behalf of the government stating that with the election of Father Filip Bednorz, the Katowice affair was to be considered over. On November 30, the Primate informed Bednorz by telegram from Szczecin that his forced election was invalid. Besides recognition of Bednorz's election, meanwhile, the authorities were now demanding the election of a vicar capitular in Cracow, where the staff of the curia had been arrested—the Katowice solution was to become a model. The Primate agreed to send a delegation to Katowice to study the election and its circumstances. For the temporary incumbent in Cracow he thought of Bishop Klepacz—the Primate insisted that Cracow be ruled by a bishop, not by a vicar capitular. Klepacz began holding discussions with General Ochab on Katowice and Cracow, with Piasecki also present to serve as intermediary. A solution gradually took shape through an exchange of messages between December 6 and 9. The Primate was inclined to sanction the invalid election in Katowice, especially since inquiries showed that the chapter was as blameworthy as Father Bednorz. On the other hand, the government gave up its hopes to install a "patriotic priest" in Cracow rather than a bishop designated by the Episcopate.

On December 12, the Primate explained his position in a long discourse to the Council of Bishops:

We may have the right to sacrifice ourselves, but we may not sacrifice the dioceses, the Church, and the faithful. Where bishops and priests disappear, so does the Church. It is up to us to defend a clergy that has been exhausted by the war and the concentration camps and today shows itself more ready to come to an agreement [with the government] than ever. The behavior of the Katowice chapter is an example of this lessened resistance. What will happen if bishops go to prison? At the moment, the Polish nation is leaning on the maternal shoulder of the Church. We must act, therefore, in such a way that the nation does not lose its grip on this shoulder.

This argument testifies to the new cardinal's restraint, showing him as a statesman as well as a religious and national leader. The Episcopate, won over, placed most of the responsibility for the decision on the Primate's shoulders. The conference of the Episcopate was by no means a capitulation. On the contrary, the Episcopate took a firm stand against any repetition of the Katowice incident. Ordinaries were to meet immediately with their chapters, deans, and as many priests as possible. Diocesan archives were to be examined, and priests warned against holding foreign currency or having contacts with the underground, so as not to give the authorities a pretext for further assaults.

On the day the conference ended, December 12, the Primate informed Bishop Jan Kanty Lorek of Sandomierz that his auxiliary bishop, Franciszek Jop, would take over in Cracow as vicar capitular. In Warsaw on December 16, the Primate handed Father Filip Bednorz a decree validating his election and declaring him exempt from *inhabilitates* (the illicit act), thus at the same time authorizing him to continue his duties at the head of the Katowice diocese. On the same day, Father Iwanicki, the rector of KUL, came to Warsaw with news that the university had been assessed a tax of over 300,000 złoty for the years 1945–46. On December 18, the Primate sent a letter to the Council of State—Premier Bierut was also president at this time—requesting a meeting about this. After four days Kazimierz Mijal* (later head of a pro-Chinese faction in the party and eventually a defector to Albania) telephoned on Bierut's behalf to authorize a meeting with Mazur, vice-Marshal of the Sejm.

In the talks, at Wilanów Palace on December 23, the Primate led off with a ninety-minute exposition of church-state problems. Mazur spoke next, though the Primate broke in, by mutual consent, to argue specific points. After first touching upon general matters, the Primate went on to the details of the Cracow and Katowice incidents, showing that it was the Marxists, not the Episcopate, who were destroying "internal peace." Calmly but decisively, he pointed out that such disturbances threatened the government's interests. In Cracow, the investigation of curial priests was still under way. The Primate went on to say that if bishops did not enjoy the freedom to carry out their church jurisdictions, the understanding signed in 1950 would be considered broken. In Czechoslovakia and Hungary, he reminded Mazur, dioceses had been deprived of their bishops. Events in Cracow and Katowice set precedents, as did the aggressiveness of ZBoWiD's "patriotic priests," who were already arguing over which dioceses would fall to them. The Primate also asked that Bishop Kaczmarek, imprisoned for two years, be pardoned and released.

Mazur replied, "There will be a trial."

Speaking of bishops, the Primate noted that Archbishop Baziak, who had been unseated in Cracow, was one of the most moderate men in the Episcopate and a great supporter of the 1950 understanding. If there had been any disorder in the Cracow curia, it had come about solely because Baziak, knowing his post as vicar capitular was temporary, had tried to avoid

---

*A Polish Stalinist who held the position of Minister of Public Administration in the Polish government.

touching any of Cardinal Sapieha's old papers and belongings. Mazur promised to pass this information along to the government. Bishop Adamski, the vice-marshal said, was comfortable in his new situation. Theoretically, little was known of the Katowice auxiliaries. On the subject of religion in the schools, Mazur said that the government had nothing against "positive" religious instruction. The Primate reminded him that every limitation of church activities in the Western Lands was an assault on Polishness there. In answer, Mazur demanded that the Vatican establish new dioceses in the west; he also touched upon the matter of the remnants of eastern dioceses whose sees were now in the Soviet Union. To the Primate's reproaches about the Bureau of Religious Affairs and the lack of Catholic books, Mazur replied with murky promises. He skirted the issue of creating new parishes and building new churches, putting the blame for a lack of building on the Bureau of Architecture. In short, every answer was no.

On the subject of the Primate's going to Rome to receive his cardinal's hat in a consistory, the answer was also negative—allegedly because the Vatican had sided with Washington, instead of remaining neutral in international affairs as the communists had expected. Besides, Mazur said, the cardinal's hat would serve to strengthen Wyszyński's hand in his struggle with the government. The Primate categorically denied this charge. He said he would not take responsibility for the repercussions in the world press of his absence from Rome, which would be damaging to Poland. When Mazur charged that the Primate was doing nothing about the Western Lands, the latter replied, "I have traveled to almost every town there, speaking hundreds of times. No member of the party has done that." Despite all of the Primate's efforts, however, nothing more was achieved than a decision to meet again after the feast of Epiphany in the new year.

The next day, Christmas Eve, Bolesław Piasecki appeared; from their conversation the Primate concluded that the government was preparing a new, crucial showdown on the theme "to be or not to be with Rome." The state leadership had illusions that the Primate could name bishops and create dioceses on his own, without regard to the Pope's authority. They wanted to take advantage of Wyszyński's good will by demanding the impossible. But the Primate never defied the Vatican, and, on the other hand, the Vatican could not remain neutral in the face of raging Stalinist terror.

One bright spot for Stefan Wyszyński among the darkening clouds during this Christmas season was his consciousness of pastoral achievements: during the year, the Primate had spoken 618 times around the country. With great faithfulness, he was realizing his motto: *Soli Deo.*

* * *

Cardinal Wyszyński began 1953, probably the most difficult year of his life, with pastoral duties in Gniezno. On January 3 he returned to Warsaw and the restored home for the archbishop at 17 Miodowa Street. Everything had been moved there from the papal-nunciature building that had served as a residence during the reconstruction of Miodowa.

In preparation for the next meeting between the Primate and Vice-Marshal Mazur, Bolesław Piasecki came to report on his own talks with high party officials. Piasecki had some ideas about what the Primate should do "so that the government will talk with the bishops and not with the vicars capitular"; of course, what the government wanted was more concessions as a price for not removing bishops. The second question was how to deal with Rome in such a way as to create new dioceses and bishops in the Western Lands without causing a schism. Piasecki was hardly disinterested, but the Primate thought that he could at least listen to him at this stage. Piasecki's great game had contributed in some degree to the conclusion of the understanding of 1950, but it ended in the catastrophe of the Primate's arrest.

On the evening of January 12, the Primate—with Bishop

Klepacz in attendance this time—had one more conversation with the head of Pax. Wednesday the 14th brought a six-hour meeting with Mazur in Wilanów Palace. Believing that he should present the whole truth and presume the good will of the other side, the Primate began with what he described as a "professorial" lecture of three hours, during which Mazur listened with grudging patience, swallowing pills, giving the impression of an ailing, suffering man. The Primate pointed out that his absence from the consistory undermined the agreement and blackened the name of Poland in the eyes of the world, while making it difficult to realize the *racja stanu* in the Western Lands and impossible to settle complex church problems. The Primate also asked a question to which he expected no answer: was the government unwilling, or unable, to look after the national interest?

He also spoke frankly of the relation between Catholicism and Marxism, which latter he described as indigenous to an Anglican-Protestant background and applied on the terrain of the Orthodox Church, and therefore inimical to Catholicism. A Polish road to Marxism would require a revised, less hostile attitude toward the Church. The baggage of the nineteenth century, when Freemasonry and individualist philosophy had warred with the Church, constituted an obstacle. The Primate concluded that there was no necessary connection between atheism and Marxism or between atheism and the new political system. Furthermore, he said, it should be understood, despite old prejudices, that Catholicism was not the enemy of progress and that its social teachings lay closer to the dreams of socialism than to the aims of capitalism. Recounting the social achievements of the Church, he asserted that Marxism delays social change and the realization of welfare for the masses. The fight against the Church was driving the best people away from the idea of social change while creating divisiveness and soullessness in social life.

Finally, the Primate asked, what would it be? Caesaropapism, venality, and the subjugated conscience of the Russian

Orthodox Church, or the independence and socially useful moral instruction of Roman Catholicism? State religion, he said, is the worst form of civic slavery.

Attacks on the Pope and calumnies on the theme of a Washington-Vatican connection, the Primate said, served the interests of Poland's enemies and communism's enemies as well. Wise politics avoids the multiplication of opponents. The Primate reminded Mazur that he, and not the party, was trying to establish Vatican representation in Warsaw. Bishop Dąbrowski, assigned to discuss that matter among others in Rome, had been denied a passport.

The Primate further demanded the demobilization of the antichurch administrative machinery. Press attacks on the Church as antistate or even anti-Polish ought to cease. "Your writers know too little about Polish history," he said, pointing out that in its songs and books the Church had never Latinized, Germanized, or Russified, but had, on the contrary, done much to promote the Polish language. Yet the authorities would not allow the printing of Polish religious books in formerly German territories.

The Primate stressed that, despite the party's accusations, he was not playing for time. Believing that the Church would survive in any epoch, he said, he was following two courses at once: introducing the supernatural powers of the Church into everyday life, and following common sense in managing church affairs. He said that he wanted a dialogue on fundamentals, but not a conjunctural dialogue with the communist state.

Finally, he mentioned the lines in front of the shops, the work camps, and the employment of women in the mines, "which Europe has not known for seventy years." The Primate said that he would try to change the recalcitrant attitudes of the clergy if he had guarantees against further attacks or attempts to divide the Church internally. He expected, he told Mazur, "fundamental explanations."

Naturally, Mazur could not provide them. The old communist knew that the Primate's heroically frank arguments had to be cast aside, no matter if they were convincing. Carrying even a portion of them into a party forum would catapult Mazur out of office. Indeed, the facts clearly showed that the government intended these talks as a sounding on how best to handle the Church.

Nevertheless, the discussions produced a certain softening of the attacks. The next day, Mazur phoned the Primate with the news that Archbishop Baziak and the aged Bishop Rospond* would be excluded from the coming trial of the Cracow curia—if they left the city.

While these dramatic church-state matters were unfolding, it must be stressed, the Primate was still spending the great majority of his time in pastoral work, visitations, consultations with priests and religious, and visits to social institutions like the one for blind children at Laski. On the human level, his statesmanlike maneuvers may have decided the Church's fate, but in the order of grace, constant prayer and religious fervor characterized Polish Catholicism in this crucial period.

The Episcopal Steering Committee met on January 22, with only Bishops Choromański, Zakrzewski, Klepacz, and Kałwa attending, besides the Primate: Archbishop Jałbrzykowski was ill, Archbishop Dymek was recovering from an illness, and Archbishop Baziak was excluded because of the situation in Cracow. Wanting to avoid an open conflict, the Primate proposed a series of constructive acts to be discussed by the full Episcopate and decided to compose an article on church unity in the present Polish and international situation for *Tygodnik Powszechny*.

The show trial of the Cracow curia, a painful spectacle, included accusations—even by certain priests—against the curia and against the late Cardinal Sapieha. In fact, those involved in politics had not been members of the curia, and the Episcopate had issued a declaration against misusing the Church for antistate purposes in December 1952. Still, the government, apparently contemplating more such trials, made the

---

*Rospond was the auxiliary bishop of Cracow. After the death of Cardinal Adam Sapieha, he was elected vicar capitular of the Archdiocese of Cracow and governed it during the Stalinist era.

Cracow performance into a platform for attacking the Vatican.

In the aftermath of the trial, the Primate and Vice-Marshal Mazur met for several hours in Wilanów on Friday, January 30. Their discussions lacked the "theoretical" nature of the previous meeting. The Primate concentrated on the abuses perpetrated in the Cracow show trial: the arbitrary broadening of charges, the use of witnesses with only tenuous connections to the curia, the suggestions, implicating the Vatican, of hostility to People's Poland. Everything had been adduced without the support of facts or any proof of lawbreaking. Not even the dead—men like Monsignor Mazanek and Cardinal Sapieha, perhaps the greatest moral authority in Poland after the war—had been spared. The Primate could see no interest on the government's part in better church-state relations. Mazur repeated the newspaper accounts with little conviction and made no special effort to defend the trial. At the same time, he revealed the authorities' intentions, saying that they would demand the right to approve appointments to church positions. This illuminated the true purpose of the show trial. Indeed, it was through such trials that the Stalinist system made policy.

Aware of the grave situation, the Primate made every effort to convince Mazur of the Episcopate's good will. He emphasized their readiness to instruct the clergy to suspend all opposition to political activities and mentioned the instructions that had been given to the Catholic press about making allowance for the *racja stanu.* In exchange, he said, he expected the government to refrain from direct interference in church personnel affairs and to use its veto only in exceptional cases, on personal grounds. Furthermore, he wanted the harassment of the Catholic press through censorship and sabotaged distribution to cease. He concluded by raising the issues of church construction, the return of religious instruction to the schools, and the repeal of current policies that forced young people to spend holy days at entertainment and sports events, thus denying them freedom of religious practice. He also complained of the unresponsiveness of the Bureau of Religious Affairs and the lack of prayer books and catechetical materials.

Mazur clarified the extent of the government's plans to interfere in personnel matters by insisting that Bishop Jop in Cracow have two progovernment vicars: Father Stanisław Huet from the Intellectuals' Commission and Father Bonifacy Woźny from the ZBoWiD* Priests' Committee. The Primate pointed out that there had previously been only one candidate, Father Czuj, mentioned for vicar, and that Father Woźny, as an ex-religious, was a questionable choice. He promised to discuss the matter with Bishop Jop. Despite the tensions, the two men agreed to meet again.

The same day, the Primate learned that Minister Bida had insisted on the appointments of the two vicars general a few days earlier. Bishop Choromański met with Mazur the next day and learned that the government would not withdraw its nominations. The Primate was farsighted enough to see that a concession was both necessary and acceptable, since the priests of Cracow could be counted on to gather around Bishop Jop, not the two imposed vicars general.

The Primate was on a pastoral journey to Gniezno and elsewhere when, on February 6, he learned that the press was attacking him for alleged cooperation with Cardinal Frings of the HKT.† In Włocławek, ZBoWiD priests had intruded themselves into the curia. The editors of *Tygodnik Powszechny* sent word that the government was ordering them to denounce the Cracow curia, of which they were the press organ. The official press was condemning the curia as a whole, not the individuals found guilty in the show trial. A general assault on the hierarchy was obviously under way.

---

*Związek Bojowników o Wolność i Demokrację: Union of Fighters for Freedom and Democracy, a government organization for groups of veterans.
†The acronym, from the names of three of its early activists, of an anti-Polish association established in 1894 during the *Kulturkampf*. This was one of the first German organizations intent upon expelling an "alien" people—in this case the Poles of the Poznań region—from the Reich. HKT functioned as a lobbying group and fathered discriminatory legislation that forbade Poles to inherit or buy land, to conduct business, and to use their language within the Reich. After the Second World War, communist propagandists used HKT as a smear against anyone suspected of opposing the postwar arrangement by which the Polish People's Republic included sometime German territory.

On Saturday, February 7, Bolesław Piasecki appeared, to explain to the Primate that the government had suspended the intrusive action against the Włocławek curia the preceding Wednesday. The Primate replied that those who had participated were excommunicated for plotting against the church authorities, as were those who had taken part in the last extended meeting of the ZBoWiD Priests' Committee.

On February 9, first the steering committee and then the full Episcopate met throughout the day. The Primate explained the government's position on filling church vacancies, about which he had sent a memorandum to the state authorities. His own proposal was to arrange appointments confidentially between the local ordinary and the local head of the provincial council, with higher authorities to be brought in only in the case of disagreements. The Primate appealed to the bishops not to let priests discuss potentially dangerous matters in the curias. The Episcopate worked on instructions to the clergy and the school prefects in the spirit of the 1950 understanding. The intention was to keep priests from giving the authorities any pretexts for further attacks. The bishops, it was decided, would summon any ZBoWiD priests who had fallen under church penalties and inform them of the fact. Members of that organization, it now emerged, had made intrusions and demanded personnel changes in Opole and Płock as well as in Włocławek.

The government had no intention of relenting. On that same day, February 9, it issued a decree claiming the right to approve church appointments. This was one of the most painful blows dealt by Stalinism. Jerzy Albrecht, head of the Warsaw Provincial Council, immediately started summoning bishops to discuss personnel matters, apply ideological pressure, and decry the "wild" building of churches. Piasecki called on the Primate five days after the issuing of the decree and spent an hour and a half discussing it. Undaunted by the pressure, the Primate decided that Bishop Choromański would lodge a protest with Minister Bida the next day.

The militia tried the tactic of humiliating the Primate personally. When he came to pick up his identity card on February 16, two young policemen who knew well who he was dragged him rudely through their standard run of questions, addressing him with insulting familiarity: "What's your surname? Given name? The names of your mother and father?" And so on, until: "Sign here." The Primate answered coolly, using the polite form and addressing them as "sir."

This small incident, another form of pressure, probably had some connection with the fact that the Primate had an appointment with Mazur at Wilanów the next day. The Episcopate's position, as the Primate presented it to Mazur, the decree of February 9 did not accord with canon law, the state constitution, or the church-state understanding. It had been issued on the very day that the Episcopate was agreeing on instructions to calm the clergy. Mazur, of course, tried to play down the decree's importance.

The diversionary activities of the ZBoWiD priests formed the second main point on the agenda. The Primate pointed out that the Episcopate had forbidden the splitting of the Church, but had not outlawed political work in general. When Mazur made it clear that the government would "defend" any of its priests who fell under Church penalties, the Primate asked, "Will you defend them against their own consciences?" The Episcopate considered the following acts as machinations *contra legitimas auctoritates ecclesiasticas,* which fell *ipso facto* under the Holy See's authority to excommunicate: (1) the decrees of the expanded Priests' Committee from January 30, 1953, against the curias and the seminaries; (2) the article in *Citizen Priest* on January 15, 1953, demanding that the leadership of the Polish Church be transferred into different hands; and (3) the intrusions into curias and demands for personnel changes by provincial delegations of ZBoWiD priests.

Mazur again tried to trivialize the matter, although he seemed calm and ill-convinced, insisting only that he would defend the progovernment priests.

While stressing the treacherousness of the government's decree, the Primate returned to his principle of seeking a compromise. He handed Mazur a three-part memorandum that covered the Episcopate's efforts to establish good church-state relations, the Church's expectations of the government, and the attitude of the Episcopate toward the "patriotic priests." Instead of discussing these issues, however, Mazur claimed that the Americans were trying to protect the Polish Church and that the Primate ought to distance himself from such efforts. Wyszyński denied that the Americans were doing anything special to defend the Polish Church; besides, since the government had answered the good-will gesture of the Episcopate's instructions to the clergy with the February 9 decree, it seemed like a poor time for further political declarations.

The communists clearly wanted to subjugate the Church and make it their mouthpiece, or to split it. In Warsaw, it was no secret that the arrest of the Primate was being considered. Something was holding the government back, though, and for the moment its efforts were bent on making the Primate denounce the United States. On February 19, Piasecki and Father Eugeniusz Dąbrowski came to apply pressure on that theme. That same day, the Primate talked to Father Wacław Radosz about the writing he had done for the Pax paper *Słowo Powszechne*, and to Father Antoni Lemparty, who admitted that the ZBoWiD Priests' Committee included some "degenerate" people who were "ready for anything." During their meetings, the ZBoWiD priests had raised outright demands for a change of primates.

Stefan Wyszyński tried to go on with normal life, but an urgent letter from Bolesław Piasecki forced him to break off his retreat at Laski and to meet there with the head of Pax on February 25. Mazur, it seemed, had begun making threats in connection with the hostility between the ZBoWiD priests and the bishops. The Primate told Piasecki that priests who related to the state authorities their conversations with their bishops deserved little compassion (or protection from excommunication), but that, out of his regard for the souls of the priests, he would agree to meet the leaders of the ZBoWiD priests.

He managed two more days of retreat at Laski before meeting, on February 28, with the ZBoWiD priests—Fathers Szemraj, Lemparty, Kulawik, Owczarek, Kroczek, and Pancer. Reverend Colonel Roman Szemraj protested that the organization was simply a patriotic association; the Primate replied that while organizations cannot be excommunicated, any priest who plots against the church authorities must be. Piasecki showed up on the same day, to sound out the Primate on his next meeting with Mazur, but the head of Pax did not mention an article he was preparing for the March 2 edition of *Słowo Powszechne*, which was intended to put more pressure on Wyszyński.

On March 3, the Primate and Mazur met yet again in Wilanów. From the Church's point of view, efforts at compromise had been answered with the recent seizure of a convent in Cracow, the terrorization of priests and nuns by the security police, and efforts by the ZBoWiD priests to buy off the clergy with promises of promotions. The government, on the other hand, worried about recent Western statements on liberating the Church from communism, asked again for an anti-American declaration, which the Primate refused to make.

The talks reached a deadlock over the "patriotic priests." Mazur defended them energetically; to the Primate they constituted a tactic for splitting the Church. Neither side would bend, and a crisis was clearly coming. Wyszyński refused to compromise in matters of conscience and excommunication, though it meant ending an important chapter in the history of the Polish Church. When Mazur coldly said, "Good-bye," the Primate replied, "My respects, sir."

That evening, having gone to Gniezno, he learned that Stalin was ill. Returning to Warsaw on March 5, he learned that the dictator had died. But Stalin's death would not change the fate of the Polish Church or its leader. Mazur's attitude had shown that the authorities were ready, under the pretext of the *racja stanu*, to violate priests' consciences and force them into excommunication. Stalin's death brought only one immediate effect: the authorities pressed to have the church bells rung at the time of his funeral. The Primate, ever hopeful of reaching a *modus vivendi*, decided not to put up a fight.

The government, however, had no interest in reconciliation. The February 9 decree signaled a widespread assault. Every day brought reports from bishops that the authorities were demanding the removal of a certain number of priests from their posts. In Warsaw, Jerzy Albrecht was making such demands to Bishop Majewski. The Primate calmly recommended that official letters defending the accused priests be sent to the authorities. The authorities were trying to provoke him into some rash action; he determinedly followed the terms of the church-state understanding. The Catholic press continued to dwindle; when *Tygodnik Powszechny* failed to print an obituary of Stalin, it was closed down. Hoping that this decision would not be final, the Primate began preparing a new "Discussion" with Jerzy Turowicz, which was intended—as far as possible—to meet the government's demands for a political declaration.

The Episcopal Steering Committee met on March 13 and decided to send a protest to the Council of State over the interference in personnel matters. The bishops were to collect declarations from all the priests whose removal had been requested, and to send them to the president of the Council of State along with copies of appeals that had already been sent to the local authorities. It was also decided to leave posts vacant rather than fill them with "canonically unworthy" candidates. Finally, the steering committee approved the "Discussion" with Jerzy Turowicz, which the Primate intended as an answer not only to Mazur's demands, but also to Piasecki's article "The Two Paths of Catholicism."

In Włocławek, the authorities were pushing for the resignation of the ordinary. The Primate went there to oppose it: he himself had no plans to resign and thought no other bishop should do so. The line beyond which there could be no more concessions was approaching.

On Tuesday, March 31, Piasecki came to justify his article, which had in effect backed the design of turning the Church into an adjunct of party propaganda. The Primate was no more interested in Piasecki's rationalizations than in his attempts to talk politics and to gossip about Mazur. Pax was now doing what Wyszyński had warned the "patriotic priests" not to do. The party was obviously mustering its forces for an attack on all Catholics who did not fall into line. On April 2, Maundy Thursday, Antoni Gołubiew and Father Andrzej Bardecki of *Tygodnik Powszechny* reported that the new "Discussion" had been confiscated by the censor: Mazur wanted the right to approve the text. This was his answer to an honorable, unslavish declaration. The editors were waiting for the Primate to take the next step, but he was not ready to do so: he preferred not to have it printed at all.

On Easter Tuesday, April 7, Piasecki came to renew the demands for an anti-American declaration. The Primate refused. He could do nothing more.

The government's intention of liquidating the Catholic press became obvious during a meeting of Catholic editors at the Primate's residence on April 10. The censor had already seized three or four issues of each publication. Debts were growing. The censor had even cut an article about peace from *The Pulpit* on the grounds that it was intended to disarm Poland and leave the country prey to America. The decision was made to have a steering-committee meeting on the Catholic press, but its fate was already sealed. The meeting took place on April 14, at a time when people were noticing the first signs in the Russian—but not the Polish—press about the citizen's right to law and order and defense against abuses of the security apparatus. The Russian doctors were being rehabilitated.* But there were no signs in Poland of liberalization toward the Church. The steering committee discussed the declaration made by the ZBoWiD Priests' Committee in response to the excommunication of some of its members. The bishops unanimously agreed that the authors of the declaration had made

---

*Refers to the restoration of rights to Russian physicians who had previously been arrested. The majority of these were Jews.

themselves liable to new church penalties. Next came the "swearing-in" of priests, a method by which the government could control clerical appointments. Because the swearing-in involved a very general text, the steering committee decided to allow priests to take the oath, although a protest was sent to the government about the unilateral and somewhat conspiratorial way in which the regulation had been introduced.

Finally, the steering committee decided to cover the deficit of *Tygodnik Powszechny,* whose hard times had been brought on by the necessity of laying off its employees. Antoni Gołubiew had made such a plea several days earlier, and in view of the paper's merits it was complied with. That evening, Jerzy Turowicz and Stanisław Stomma reported that their talks with the government had been fruitless: the most important Catholic paper in the country had ceased to exist.

The general situation remained deadlocked. Stymied by the ineffectiveness of its pressure, the government was thinking out new steps. For the moment, certain priests were being pressured not to take the oaths, an obvious threat to their positions.

The Primate did not allow the impasse to derail him from his pastoral duties. He set out on a grand tour of the Coast, Gniezno, and Poznań, preaching, celebrating Mass, and meeting great crowds of the faithful everywhere. Official harassment followed his steps, making it difficult for young people and even priests to take part in the celebrations. One priest had his identity papers checked by a militia officer who was a personal acquaintance. "But you know me," the priest said. "Yes, but I have my instructions," came the reply. "And I am being watched."

Nevertheless, the faithful of all ages were enthusiastic in their welcome. The harder things became for the Church, the more the nation stood behind it. Yet some pessimists had predicted the opposite, fearing that the Episcopate was not taking a hard enough line. During this trip, the Primate reflected on the history of the Church and the nation. At first the state had supported the Church; later, as now, the Church supported the nation when there was no state or when the state was dependent on foreign forces.

The Primate had just returned to Warsaw when he learned what new "threats" were in store. Two letters were waiting from Father Lagosz, the vicar capitular of Wrocław. One dealt with the statutes of the Wrocław chapter and the enlarging of its membership. The second was a memorandum about creating a "bishop for Wrocław," combined with a proposal for including the administration of Opole and Gorzów within the Archdiocese of Wrocław. This would be an obvious step backward, from both a pastoral and a Polish point of view. The Primate explained as much to Father Piskorz, who had come on Lagosz's behalf. One amusing aspect of the April 30 talk with Father Piskorz was Lagosz's personal dilemma over how to dress for the celebrations of Saint Stanisław in Cracow: entitled only to the robes of a protonotary apostolic, Lagosz wanted to come in a bishop's vestments, for which a consecration would be necessary. These remained worries for the "bishop for Wrocław," who was obviously acting on the instructions of the government.

* * *

It is no exaggeration to state that the Plenary Session of the Episcopate, held in Cracow on May 8–9, was historic. It began on the seven hundredth anniversary of the canonization of Saint Stanisław. After Bishop Chorománski and Primate Wyszyński spoke on the predicament of the Church, the Episcopate decided to send the government an extensive memorandum dealing with the most important violations of the three-year-old understanding.

This memorandum, addressed to Bolesław Bierut, president of the Council of Ministers, is perhaps the most impressive postwar statement by the Polish bishops. Written and signed by Primate Wyszyński, it became one of the main reasons for his arrest. As if he foresaw this, the Primate wrote:

If it happens that external actions make it impossible for us to appoint our own competent people to church positions, we have decided to leave those positions vacant rather than to place the church administration in undeserving hands. Anyone who considers taking over any church positions otherwise ought to know that he will fall under the sentence of excommunication. Similarly, if we are given the choice between personal sacrifice or turning the church administration into a tool of the secular authorities—we shall not waver. We shall follow the apostolic voice of our calling and priestly conscience, with inner peace and the consciousness that we have not given the least reason for our persecution, that suffering shall become a part of our share in the affairs of Christ and Christ's church. We cannot place what belongs to God on the altar of Caesar. *Non possumus!* [We cannot!]

Conscious of the dire consequences hanging over them, the Primate and the bishops committed that dramatic *non possumus* to history in the conviction that they could no longer remain silent and bear without protest the continuing struggle against, and limitations upon, the Church. The bishops wrote that they stood by the 1950 understanding and were still ready for reconciliation, but that the Church

has been deprived over several years of things that are needed for its normal life and development, that are simply indispensable, that the Polish Church has always possessed and that are still possessed elsewhere. It is enough to mention the seizure of landholdings, houses, the charitable organization Caritas, foundations, brotherhoods, associations, hospitals, schools, day-care centers, nurseries, printing presses, publishing houses, and the press.

They protested the expulsion of bishops, priests, religious, and nuns, the destruction of the Polish church administration—so important to the sense of Polishness and the national interest

—in the Western Lands, the division of the Church by the "patriotic priests" and lay people from Pax. The letter enumerated the major illegal acts and deceits that the Church had experienced; it detailed all the miseries that must be encountered in a system of militant atheism and Stalinist totalitarianism that was a parody of ideas like Marxism, socialism, and progress. At the same time, the Episcopate cited all the important evidences of its own good will, its readiness for talks, its patience in face of injuries, and even its human respect for its adversaries. The bishops declared themselves ready for further, evenhanded adherence to the 1950 understanding, if only the government would join in the effort. But the government was no longer interested in an understanding, and the words *non possumus* were most timely.

The Episcopate next discussed the swearing-in oath that the government expected of bishops. It was regarded as basically applying to men taking over new positions, but the bishops decided not to refuse to take it in the current crisis, on the condition that they were assembled collegially with the Primate at their head.

During the meeting, the Primate returned to the church administration in the Western Lands. He had already told Father Lagosz that he would defend the administrative separateness of Opole and Gorzów, which in fact were normal dioceses and would eventually receive canonical recognition. In the context of what was going on in the Western Lands, he emphasized to the bishops that two years earlier the Holy Father had named bishops for the dioceses there: Father Kominek for Wrocław, Father Jop for Opole, Father Bensch for Gorzów, Father Nowicki for Gdańsk, and Father Wilczyński for Olsztyn. These names, until now held in strict confidence, made a great impression on the bishops. The authorities had refused to admit nominated bishops to their offices or even to their dioceses, although the Primate had informed the government of the nominations as soon as he returned from Rome two years earlier. To consolidate dioceses now, the Primate emphasized, would ruin the pastoral efforts and the Polishness of the Western Lands. Now, for the first time, he openly stated that he would rather go to prison than betray the needs of the Church and the national interest in the Western Lands. Unfortunately, the government was so intent upon having its "bishop for Wrocław" that it took no account of the national interest.

The Primate also informed the bishops of the debilitation of the Catholic press—even *Tygodnik Powszechny* seemed beyond help. In closing, he exhorted them to persevere in their offices, no matter if it was at the price of freedom. The situation of bishops preserving their freedom by abandoning their dioceses could not be repeated, he said.

The specter of imprisonment was facing the hierarchy, although not all its members realized it yet. The traditional procession from Wawel to Skałka* on the seven hundredth anniversary of Saint Stanisław's canonization occurred without problems, before great masses of people. The authorities had concocted the usual "military training" for youth, entertainment for schoolchildren, meetings of factory councils and work groups, free excursions to the mountains, and so on, but the streets of Cracow were so crowded that the procession could only advance slowly and with great difficulty. The people chose to stand by the Church. In their own way, the Saint Stanisław celebrations were a social plebiscite.

Immediately after the Cracow observances, the Primate left for Zakopane to make a canonical visitation, and afterward he fulfilled his pastoral obligations in the parishes outside Warsaw. At this time came news that Canon Zygmunt Kaczyński, a minister in the wartime government-in-exile in London, had died in prison. The fact that he had been feeling well and died "suddenly" made the embarrassment to the authorities all the greater.

On May 21, the Primate sent the *non possumus* memorandum to Bolesław Bierut. The next day, he sent the president another letter, about the brutality and illegal actions of the Bureau of

---

*Skałka is the Church of the Rock in Cracow, the site of Saint Stanisław's martyrdom.

Religious Affairs in monastic houses. The Primate also answered Father Lagosz's statement on the chapter statutes and the "bishop for Wrocław"—in the negative, of course.

The government's next move was to announce in *The Monitor* instructions related to the February 9 decree. These instructions were in fact an answer to the Episcopate's objections; ominously, they introduced new bureaucratic hurdles in the assumption of ecclesiastical offices: applications, questionnaires, and résumés to be filled out by priests. Nominations were to become more dependent upon the government.

As an observer of Cardinal Wyszyński's life at this period, I continue to be struck by his ability to make difficult decisions on church-state relations while also attending to normal pastoral duties and personal contacts. All bishops and archbishops have such duties, but the daily stresses on the Primate—even today one cannot write of all that happened—were such that his ease in carrying out the normal pastoral tasks is amazing. Only rarely in the course of his countless visitations did his anxieties creep into his sermons, like the ones he gave in Bydgoszcz and Solec Kujawski on May 24. "It is almost madness," he said, "to demand that a whole nation renounce Christianity only because a small group of people believe the reconstruction of a society is impossible without a materialist ideology."

During meetings with the deans and curia in Gniezno, he learned of more duplicity on the part of the Bureau of Religious Affairs. Not only were the officials demanding, as they had the year before, that the Corpus Christi procession be confined to the very day; now they had added the illegal stipulation that preachers at the celebration submit their sermons for censorship. After ordaining priests and discussing the re-Gothicization of Gniezno Cathedral, he left for Olsztyn, where, on May 31, he ordained more priests. The next day, Monsignor Zink made a report on the state of the diocese, a testimony to persecution in Warmia. The chancellor of the curia had been expelled, the minor seminary confiscated along with all its contents (including the personal belongings of the students), the church lands seized, the parish priest of the cathedral and another chancellor driven away. Nevertheless, Warmia kept fighting for church freedom, and the diocese was healthy; the Primate told the deans and cathedral priests that he hoped political wisdom would ultimately triumph over bureaucracy. He stressed, too, that the Church could point to successes as well as losses. After the loss of religion in the schools, extracurricular instruction had been organized, proving more attractive to the children and their parents and involving them in a more direct way. Having lost its press, the Church achieved closer contact with the people through the direct, spoken word. Having lost its estates, the Church succeeded in social charity. And abroad there was talk of a new "Miracle of the Vistula." When they heard about this speech, people might have asked where the man found such optimism, spiritual peace, and faith. Indeed, it was difficult to understand merely within the natural order.

When the Primate returned to Warsaw on June 2, he learned that the government was regarding his latest memorandum as an exploitation of its own difficult situation. International and domestic considerations were making a sharp retort impossible. It is more than a rhetorical question to ask whether anything but a difficult situation could exist under Stalinism and its irrational economic methods. The Episcopate, on the other hand, had acted according to the current tragic predicament of the Church, not according to the permanently bad situation of the state. It emerged that the government did not want to talk to the bishops any more; this was fine with the Primate, who, after the February 9 decree and his last discussion with Mazur, was also in no mood for talks. He did not want tensions to worsen, but he had to stand firm. In his sermon during the June 4 Corpus Christi procession, he told the huge crowds in Warsaw that Christ had locked himself in the Upper Room with the disciples during the Last Supper and there established the priesthood that was transferred to the apostles. Jesus had recognized no intermediaries. A priesthood free of bureaucracy was the litmus test for freedom of conscience. This was moderate and dignified, but also a clear answer to the attempt at interfering in church personnel affairs.

After Corpus Christi, the Primate made a visitation in Kalisz, and then returned to Warsaw by way of Łódź, where the steering committee met on June 9. News came from government circles that the authorities were unhappy with the Corpus Christi sermon, as well as with the last memorandum. An antichurch campaign was stirring in the periodicals, especially the Marxist *Philosophical Thought*. The steering committee decided to send the government a new letter in connection with its May instructions for executing the February decree. Bishops were also warned to be prudent in all ecclesiastical nominations. Should the authorities turn down a nominee, the bishops should demand the reasons, according to provisions in the decree. The caution was well founded: a few days later, Bishop Majewski reported that Jerzy Albrecht, head of the Warsaw Provincial Council, had demanded the expulsion of several parish priests. It was decided to regard these demands as a grossly loose interpretation of the decree.

At the same time, the Primate paid attention to a second drastic occurrence—the banning of religion from the schools. The government, in meetings with the clergy, suggested that each parish set aside catechetical materials, build or assign places for teaching, and have instructors and teaching materials on hand.

The incessant pressure destroyed people as well as institutions. On June 17, for example, the Primate learned about a certain unnamed priest who, after being hounded by the security police, had disappeared for several days and afterward gone into hiding, afraid to meet other priests. Eventually he went mad and was committed to a mental institution, where he persisted in his fear of priests and always dressed himself for an "appointment at headquarters."

The same day, Bishop Ignacy Świrski informed the Primate that Albrecht had declared the Episcopate memorandum "treasonous," because it had called the February decree unconstitutional. Bishop Jop reported on official maneuvers to publish a "new" *Tygodnik Powszechny* under a progovernment editorship. The Catholic editors decided, however, that they could not print material that was not in accord with the Episcopate's guidelines.

On June 26, the Primate left for Opole, where he was to take part in celebrations at Saint Anne's Mountain and ordain new priests. The authorities had also approached the Opole curia, insisting that disseminating the latest Episcopate memorandum had been "unconstitutional."

At the same time, however, the authorities had produced a joint memorandum of the Intellectual Priests* and the ZBo-WiD Priests' Committee ("patriotic priests"), dated June 18, which was critical of Episcopal policies. On July 2, the Primate led a steering-committee meeting that decided to send Father Czuj a canonical warning† in connection with the June 18 declaration.

The Primate spent the beginning of July in Warsaw and then led a retreat for eighty priests from Gniezno at Częstochowa on July 7–10. In every free moment he counseled priests and lay people. The work seemed insubstantial, but it helped many to overcome the psychological pressures created by the authorities.

The government's church policy in the year of Stalin's death fluctuated according to the political weather, both domestic and international. The richness of meanders and vacillations in 1953 has remained secret until this day. Sometimes the line toward the Church softened, in fact or at least in appearance; on July 17, for example, Father Bronisław Dąbrowski informed the Primate that Minister Bida, in a conversation, had criticized his own provincial Religious Affairs employees and actually announced that he was rebuking them and issuing instructions more favorable to the Church—a *novum*, indeed. The next day, Father Bross informed the Primate of difficulties that the Archdiocese of Gniezno was having in nominating priests: the religious territory straddled two civic provinces, Bydgoszcz

---

*A sub-group of the Intellectuals' Commission.
†A special provision in canon law used to warn priests who become involved in political matters, thereby becoming disloyal to the Ordinary.

and Poznań. One provincial office would agree to the appointment of a vicar in town X, while the other would refuse to let the same priest be transferred out of town Y. This is what the "approval" of clerical nominations had led to in practice. However, Minister Bida had clearly passed from the "hawks" to the "doves" and informed Bishop Choromański that Mazur was interested in a new meeting of the Mixed Commission. This was puzzling, since the government in the past had regarded asking first as a loss of face. Besides, the recent policy had been one of *faits accomplis* rather than of negotiations. The meeting was set for July 24; beforehand, the Primate sent a letter to the Council of State asking that Bishop Kaczmarek be freed, and a private letter to Bierut asking that the Church of Saint Martin's in Warsaw be restored.

After visitations in Łomża, Białystok, and Drohiczyn, the Primate was back in the capital in time for the meeting, at which Bida, Mazur, and Mijal represented the government and Bishops Choromański, Klepacz, and Zakrzewski the Episcopate. The government attacked the Episcopal memorandum and the Primate's Corpus Christi sermon as acts directed by reactionary circles in the West; the bishops replied that the reasons for these acts could be found in the decree and the continuing harassment carried out by the state authorities. At least the government agreed to provide reasons when a nomination to a clerical post was questioned. The meeting of the Mixed Commission had obviously been called in order to frighten the Episcopate and assure the party against troubles in its own backyard. Mazur, who had asked for the session in the first place, remarked that it had been convened at the request of the Episcopate. Hopes for a further softening of the official line were diminishing. They were dashed by an attack on the Primate in the July 25 *Życie Warszawy* (Warsaw Life) that accused the Primate of having attempted to foment a demonstration on Corpus Christi in Warsaw.

That summer, the Primate allowed himself ten days for a much-needed vacation. On August 16, after dedicating a new church in Chotomów, he met Bolesław Piasecki at the latter's request. The head of Pax suggested four scenarios for the future of Poland: (1) the continuation of Marxist socialism; (2) the return of prewar capitalism; (3) a significant evolution of socialism, or (4) an improved version of capitalism. Piasecki declared that Pax was counting on the third possibility and asked the Primate for his own prediction. Cardinal Wyszyński's reply indicated that there were more than political scenarios: "When a politician sees four outcomes, he is not so badly off. But a Catholic bishop sees one more."

"Which one?" Piasecki asked.

"Prison," the Primate replied. "The experience of the Church teaches that, in all predictions, to x you can always add y." The Primate made Piasecki aware that his remarks at the June 18 meeting had been false, creating artificial charges against the hierarchy, accusing it, among other things, of desiring a return to capitalism. The Primate categorically disassociated himself from such ideas and declared himself a proponent of social change. On the other hand, he criticized Piasecki for always talking of some ambiguous "socialism" instead of the existing Marxist system, including the struggle against religion that was going on behind the socioeconomic scene. Finally, he reproached Pax for intruding upon grounds restricted to church jurisdiction. The Episcopate rebuked the organization for (1) its pronouncements against the Holy Father in the New Year's edition of *Słowo Powszechne*, (2) its false interpretation of the February decree at a rally of the Intellectuals' Committee in Lublin, and (3) the joint declaration by its priests' groups on June 18. No more such interference would be brooked, he warned his interlocutor.

Piasecki also brought the Primate news from Mazur, who judged the Episcopate memorandum and the recent Mixed Commission meeting so negatively that he saw only two alternatives: Either the Episcopate should back off from its position in the memorandum, or an unrestrained conflict would erupt. The threat was unmistakable. The Primate made it clear to Piasecki that any modification of the memorandum would mean agreeing to government interference and was therefore impossible. Piasecki also announced that the Intellectuals' Committee and the ZBoWiD Priests' Committee would be merged into a single organization called the Lay and Clerical Activists' Committee of the National Front. Piasecki gave assurances that he would enforce a proper attitude toward the Episcopate in this new body, and also that the reorganization would reduce the police's influence on the clergy. Organizing the clergy was superfluous in any case, the Primate averred, since politics was for lay people. Considering that Piasecki had admitted some mistakes and brought useful information, the Primate decided to receive him every two weeks. The decisive showdown was coming, and Piasecki was a well-informed spectator, if not a disinterested one.

At the beginning of the school year, on September 1, official pedagogical conferences announced a struggle for a "scientific view of the world" and "socialist morality"; from all over the country reports came in to the Primate of prefects being denied certification in the schools. So, while the government may have been angry at the Episcopate's memorandum, it would not change the policies that made the memorandum necessary. In Wrocław, seminarians were being torn away from studies and assigned manual labor, including the clearing of rubble. During a pastoral visit to the Archdiocese of Gniezno, the Primate was circumspect but unable to disregard the Church's predicament. In Łabiszyn he compared the Church to an oak, hundreds of years old, growing in the village, which had stood firm against all evil and survived all injuries. He answered the enthusiastic farewell cries of the parishioners by joking, "I thought that here at least people would not be shouting at me." They smiled, understanding.

Back in Warsaw, the Primate awoke on September 9 to learn that the authorities, with Minister Bida's personal participation, had confiscated the Catholic House in Łomża.* In Cracow, the Black Ursulines were being threatened with the loss

*Before World War II Catholic Action in Poland built a Catholic Home in each diocese and used it for meetings and celebrations, both religious and national, e.g. the Feast of Christ the King.

of their boarding-school buildings. Worst of all was the news that the trial of Bishop Czesław Kaczmarek, ordinary of Kielce, was proceeding.

On September 12 the prewar head of the conservative camp, Prince Janusz Radziwiłł, came to share his supporters' views with the Primate. These people did not always recognize the gravity of the situation. The prince was worried about the growth of pro-German sentiment in Wrocław, and about Father Lagosz's effect on church affairs in Lower Silesia. None of this was news to the Primate; he seized the opportunity to share some critical remarks on the Catholic intelligentsia, which made great demands on the clergy but was never there itself. Radziwiłł defended the intellectuals, citing their need for bread; he had a point in a country where the state was unfortunately the only employer. The Primate remarked that while the intellectuals were privately "offended" by communism, many of them also became its suppliers by writing antichurch brochures to order. The Primate knew that such people said, "Only the Church . . . " and yet they themselves did not go to Mass. They looked to the Church for political thrills, but not for the grace that was its mainspring. Although the two men differed on many issues, the Primate appreciated Prince Janusz for his patriotism, style of life, and above all for his regular presence at the communion rail. He was, finally, a sincere man.

In the capital, meanwhile, the show trial of Bishop Kaczmarek had been announced.

On Saturday, September 12, Monsignor Cymanowski of Gdańsk appeared with news that students from his diocese who had been studying at the Wrocław seminary wanted to leave because of Father Lagosz's actions. The government was also harrying a Greek Catholic priest because his denomination was not recognized by the state. Thus, the Polish communists were becoming the handmaidens of Russian Orthodoxy in persecuting any Eastern Uniate churches that did not pay fealty to the Patriarch of Moscow. Such are the ironies of fate. Monsignor Cymanowski had another interesting bit of news: a government representative had told him, "The Primate ought to put up a fight over Bishop Karol Maria Splett." A German from Gdańsk, Splett was the other imprisoned bishop besides Kaczmarek. The suggestion had surely been a provocation, intended to show the Primate as a supporter of German interests. The "German card" still had some psychological impact in 1953, but the government would keep trying to play it when it had become ridiculous. The authorities were making additional trouble by spreading rumors that the scraps of the Pińsk diocese remaining within Polish borders would be joined to the diocese of Siedlce, and those of Wilno to Łomża. One had to admire the complexity of their stratagems.

On September 14, *Trybuna Ludu* published wide-ranging accusations against Bishop Kaczmarek. The trial had been in preparation for two and a half years; it was beginning now not by coincidence but for clear political reasons. To the authorities it meant nothing that the trial was colliding with distinct possibilities of social change. Press attacks began upon the Vatican, the Episcopate, and particularly against the Primate. When he set out for an Episcopal retreat that would last from September 14 to 17, Wyszyński encountered signs of the "new course" along the road to Częstochowa as the militia repeatedly stopped his car and asked for identification; the system was working perfectly, down to its lowest levels.

Rather than following the course of Bishop Kaczmarek's trial, the Episcopate followed the Primate's advice and said Mass for the intention of the defendant. They kept praying, in the faith that God and not man ruled the Church, and that if everything is placed in His hands, He will make possible what is expected of man at each moment. The Primate knew already exactly what God expected of him, but he spoke of it to no one.

At the end of the retreat, the steering committee and then the full Council of Bishops met. After reading the Holy Father's letter on the Saint Stanisław celebration and listening to various reports, the Primate gave his evaluation of present conditions. Events were "ripe," he said; something had reached its fullest development. With remarkable intuition, he said that something was ending, and something new would have to begin. Outlining the various steps that had been taken to protect the Church, he remarked that the more the Episcopate had tried to show its good will, the more the government had sharpened its course. Things had grown worse after the conclusion of the "understanding." Even while the government talked with the Episcopate, it had been throwing religion out of the schools, liquidating the Catholic press, and creating pseudo-Catholic groups. Concessions were regarded as weakness. The Primate's talks with Mazur had led to the decree. Instructions to the press by the Episcopate had gone hand in hand with the suppression of that press. For themselves, Poland's rulers had created a vision of a Church subjugated entirely to politics: for them, the Church was the Vatican, and the bishops were the agents and spies of the West.

The Primate stressed that he was trying to speak the truth, as the pseudo-Catholics would not. He thought that the Church was strong enough for coexistence with a communist state. Now, however, the trial of Bishop Kaczmarek was being directed against the Vatican, the Episcopate, and all branches of the Church. The Primate stated decisively that the Vatican had never given him any instructions that interfered in internal Polish politics. One of the witnesses at Bishop Kaczmarek's trial had spoken of the Pope's alleged hostility toward Poland during discussions with the Primate about the Western Lands —a fiction, the Primate said. He called on the bishops as witnesses that the Episcopate had never concerned itself with the economic or political affairs of the state. Curial departments had confined themselves to religious matters and had not repeated the prewar activities of Catholic Action.

Perhaps because he was ready to make a historic statement, the Primate spoke about the ineffectuality of the Episcopate's efforts and about the insufficient protection of priests from government officials, which he said was a sign of cowardice in the clergy and a sign that the sense of what was fit and dignified had sometimes been lost. In contrast, he outlined the positive principles that ought to shine through the church administration. The Church should be led with its totality in mind, and not only according to the needs of particular dioceses. The Primate advised a faithful adherence to canon law. The Church wanted no special privileges, he said; it ought to stand together with the Catholic nation, with a society subjected to many sufferings and assaults. Finally came the prophetic words. "I will choose imprisonment over privilege," he said, "because in prison I will be at the side of the most tormented ones. Privilege could be a sign of leaving the Church's proper road of truth and love."

In essence, the Primate was giving his closest colleagues instructions on how to carry on, should he have to leave them. Although he had a keen feeling for the situation, he acted as if things were going ahead as usual, following the established course. The Episcopate listened to a wide range of reports on church activities, including aid for expelled bishops and imprisoned priests. When the meeting had concluded, the Primate went back to his normal duties. The trial of Bishop Kaczmarek had been given a distinct anti-Vatican character; Kaczmarek himself was a pretext. Yet on September 22, 1953, the court sentenced him to twelve years in prison.

Meanwhile, the Primate preached to a large congregation in the parish of the Sacred Heart of Jesus, in the Praga section of Warsaw; on Sunday, September 20, he was back at the same church, where large numbers of children and youth received communion. On still another occasion, he spoke to an assembly of mothers and girls on the role of women in the Church. Seven thousand men came to High Mass, and afterward the Primate met with children and young people in their various religious groups, then, with Bishop Baraniak, spent more than two and a half hours confirming over fourteen hundred children.

This visit to an overflowing model parish was an act in confirmation of correct church policy, but the road ahead was full of snares that must have intruded upon the subconscious, in spite of a long and joyful day.

Before all great historic shocks there seem to be moments of quiet peace, when events stop moving, as if holding their breath in anticipation of the inevitable (though it could have been avoided if people were better and wiser). Such was the atmosphere of the next four days. Unfortunately, we know little of the Primate's thoughts the day before his imprisonment, except that he had said that the situation was "ripe" and the time had come to await its development. Bolesław Piasecki came, to recommend that the Primate condemn Bishop Kaczmarek on the basis of his forced confession. The Primate could not bring himself to tell Piasecki what he thought of such advice, so the latter carried away the entirely mistaken impression that he had convinced the Cardinal. Stefan Wyszyński's last "political" move before his arrest was to send the authorities a letter protesting the show trial of Bishop Kaczmarek.

For two years, Wyszyński had taken into account the possibility of his being arrested; he had sensed the growing pressure on the Church, and the logic of a Stalinist system that aimed at creating a desert of ideas, thus assuring Marxism a monopoly of dogma. The main force opposing such aims was the Church and, as its symbol, the Primate.

Finally, the dramatic day arrived. Several people witnessed the arrest of the Primate; though some have since died, they left records of the exact course of events. We shall follow these eyewitness accounts, for they have much to say about the Primate's composure, resolution, dignity, and God's peace—and about the deceit of those who came to take him away.

* * *

Friday, September 25, was the feast of Ladysław of Gielniów, patron of Warsaw. At seven in the morning, the Primate said Mass and addressed the students in the seminary chapel. That evening he preached at Saint Anne's and blessed the faithful with the relics of Ladysław. There was a large crowd of the faithful, but they were quiet, and the tension was palpable. Students and "women of the Gospels"* detained the Primate when he left the rectory of the academic church. He spoke briefly: "Say the Rosary. You know Michelangelo's *Last Judgment?* God's angel pulls man out of the abyss on a rosary. Say the Rosary for my intention." Those were his words of farewell.

The Primate went to Rector Kamiński's for a brief supper. When he left at 9:30, people were waiting in front of the church. Some started shouting, but others, fearing to create a provocation, hushed them. When the Primate got to his residence on Miodowa Street, the staff turned out the lights and retired for the evening. The Cardinal went to his room on the second floor. Half an hour later, Father Goździewicz, who worked in the secretariat, knocked. He said that some people had brought a letter from Minister Bida to Bishop Baraniak and were demanding that the gate be opened. Surprised, the Primate answered, "At this hour? Please tell them that any letters from Minister Bida are to be forwarded to the secretary of the Episcopate, Bishop Choromański. This visit puzzles me, because Minister Bida knows perfectly well to whom letters are to be directed." Feeling a presentiment, he got up, dressed, and went from room to room turning on the lights, first on his floor and then on the ground floor. Earlier he had alerted his staff to light up the house if anything happened, saying, "Let Warsaw know what goes on at the Primate's."

Several people were now hammering at the entrance. The Primate went downstairs again and ordered that the door be opened. He knew very well what the visit was about. At this moment, Bishop Baraniak walked in, "led" from the garden by a group of people who crowded into the Hall of the Popes. "These gentlemen were about to fire," said the bishop.

"It's a pity they didn't," the Primate said. "If they had, we would have known it was a break-in; as it is, we do not know what to think of this nocturnal intrusion." One of the "gentle-

---

*An allusion to the women who are mentioned in Saint John's Gospel as waiting on Christ.

men" explained that they had come on official business and were surprised that no one had opened the door. "Our office hours are during the day, and then both the gates and the doors are open," the Primate said. "The residence is not open now."

"But the government has a right to confer with its citizens whenever it wants," one of the gentlemen said.

The Primate replied that the government also had a duty to behave decently toward its citizens, then went into the yard to look for the porter; none of the priests was about. At this moment the dog, Baca, running in the yard, attacked and wounded one of the plainclothesmen who were shadowing the Primate. The Primate returned to the foyer to take care of the man who had been bitten. Once Sister Maksencja, the sister superior, had fetched some iodine, the Primate personally gave first aid to the victim and assured him that the dog was not rabid.

The moral significance of the Primate's dressing the wound of the policeman who had come to arrest him needs to be emphasized. It was a dramatic moment. The calm man who was being arrested did not know whether he was only going to prison or was destined to lose his life. His gesture toward the injured policeman was dazzling. Finally, it is worth noting that in the account I am relating, the secret-police officers are called "gentlemen"—because that is how the Primate referred to them.

The men from the gate came in, and everyone went to the Hall of the Popes. One of the newcomers lodged an official protest that the door had not been opened to the state authorities. "I still do not know whether I am looking at representatives of the authorities or at a break-in," said the Primate. "Since we are living here in this desolation among ruins and rubble,* we never admit anyone at night. All the more so when the gentlemen at the door start by lying."

Finally, everything became clear. One of the "gentlemen"

---

*The Cardinal here was alluding to damage done during the Second World War, the effects of which were still evident in 1953.

took off his coat, pulled a letter from his briefcase, opened it, and handed the Primate a document citing a government decision made the previous day. In accordance with this decision, the Primate was to be removed from the city immediately. He was not to carry out any duties connected with the posts he had been holding. He was asked to acknowledge this and sign the paper.

"I cannot acknowledge a decision for which I see no legal basis," he said. "Nor can I submit to a decision reached in this way. Have not representatives of the government, like Mr. Mazur and President Bierut, held many discussions with me? They know how to convey their claims to me." Emphasizing that the decision would be harmful to Poland's image and would draw foreign propaganda attacks upon the country, he explained that he would not voluntarily leave his residence.

The official asked him at least to sign the letter, to indicate that he had read it. The Primate wrote, "I have read this."

Next he went upstairs, accompanied by several "gentlemen." The house was full of people, gathered on the ground floor and outside the chapel upstairs. In his private apartment, the Primate was ordered to gather what he needed. "I have no intention of taking anything," he said. To their further attempts at persuasion the Primate kept protesting against the nocturnal intrusion. When the sister superior joined in the urgings that he gather his things, he answered, "Sister, I will take nothing. I came to this house poor and I will leave it poor. Sister, you took the vows of poverty and you know what they mean."

The "gentlemen" were growing nervous, and one of them brought a suitcase into the bedroom. At that point, Bishop Baraniak was led in. "Who is in charge?" someone asked.

"I do not know whom you are taking away," the Primate replied. "Bishop Baraniak is always in charge during my absence." Then he raised his voice and said, "I tell the bishop that I regard what he is witnessing as an act of violence. I ask that no one take up my defense. In case of a trial I want no lawyer. I will defend myself."

Bishop Baraniak was led away. The Primate spent a long time in his study, arranging his books. At the request of the "gentlemen," everyone went into the reception room, where the Cardinal put his papers in order and signed several documents that his secretary had prepared. They brought him his coat and hat. In 1960, speaking to priests who had been inmates of Dachau, the Primate recalled the coat:

> When I became Bishop of Lublin, a friend of Bishop Kozal [killed in Dachau] came to me with his coat and hat and said, "I give you these because they might prove useful." Two years before my imprisonment I already knew what was waiting for me; therefore, like a prudent man, I ordered myself some heavy boots and got my overcoat ready. I thought everything should happen according to plan, exactly, with my full understanding of the facts. So it turned out. When certain "gentlemen" came for me, I had enough presence of mind to put on the boots I had been keeping ready for two years. With the coat, however, it turned out differently. I was supposed to have a warmer one, but my guests became brutal at the last minute and would not allow me to enter the chapel for a farewell. The sister handed me a coat, and only in the car did I see that it was Bishop Kozal's coat. So it did prove useful! I was very glad of the discovery. I had found an intercessor. I prayed to him a lot, so that I would be able to fulfill honestly the task that God had set for me.

The Primate also took his breviary and his rosary. They returned to the study. When the "gentlemen" asked if he had taken everything, he once more protested against the violence being done to him, saying that he would take nothing else.

Everyone went downstairs. The Primate went into the chapel for a moment and then glanced at the picture of the Black Madonna of Częstochowa that was hanging above the entrance to the Hall of the Popes. In the foyer he again stopped to protest what was being done, then got into the car with three "gentlemen." It was past midnight. From the windows of the building across the street, people could see the car containing the Primate turn into Długa Street, where six other cars joined it. All the cars had their windows smeared with mud.

Thus was the Primate of Poland arrested. He protested from beginning to end, and he was unwittingly handed the coat that had come from the murdered Bishop Kozal.

The next day, news of what had happened spread throughout Warsaw and the rest of the country. Indeed, the whole world was electrified. The Stalinist system was visiting an insane act of lawlessness on the first prince of the Roman Catholic Church to conclude an agreement with a communist government.

After the arrest, the Primate was driven northwest, passing by night through Nowy Dwór and Dobrzyń to Grudziądz. A Capuchin monastery in Rywałd, already familiar to the Primate, turned out to be their goal. The prisoner was assigned a cell on the first floor, whose windows had been covered with tissue paper so he could not look outside. "Do you think," he asked, "that tissue will hide the Primate of Poland from the world? The world will see those windows; the world is interested in the fate of every cardinal."

"Exaggeration," replied the gentleman in a typical secret policeman's coat, which looked like oilcloth. He promised the Primate a chance to talk with the authorities—a promise that was of course broken.

"In the room into which I was led," the Primate recalled, "a picture was hanging over the bed with the inscription 'Our Lady of Rywałd, comfort the distressed.' That first friendly voice was the cause of great joy."

The Primate's first thoughts in prison, about which his acquaintances learned only after years, were amazing:

Is this not what I was threatened with so many times? *Pro nomine Jesu contumelias pati* (to suffer abuse for the name of Jesus). I was beginning to fear that I would have no part in this honor that befell all my seminary classmates. They all went through the concentration camps and prison. The majority gave their lives there, and some returned as invalids. One died after a stay in a Polish prison. Thus, the prediction made in the spring of 1920 by Father Antoni Bogdański, professor of liturgy and director of the minor seminary in Włocławek, was fulfilled in part. During one of his lectures on liturgy, this unforgettable man said, "There will come a time when you pass through torments that a man of our time cannot even imagine. Many priests will have nails driven into their tonsures, many will pass through prison. . . ."

Stefan Wyszyński came of spiritual age at a particular time in Europe; the shocks of war and ideology were hanging over his generation. Only against this background can we understand his calm reflection, at his moment of imprisonment, upon the dire warnings given years earlier by his spiritual guides. Stefan Wyszyński took quite literally these words by men he so trusted.

"Most priests and bishops with whom I have worked," he reflected, "have passed through prison. There would have been something incomplete about me if I had never tasted prison. Therefore, something fitting is taking place. I should not hold a grudge against anyone. Christ called Judas 'friend.' "

Brought up with such spiritual attitudes, the Primate considered his guards and prison supervisors as "helping me in the fulfillment of an act whose inevitability had been obvious to everyone for some time. I must appreciate everything that happens to me at the hands of these people."

Meanwhile, the Primate was being guarded by twenty plainclothesmen. Someone kept watch all night at the door of his cell. Since they would not allow him to say Mass in the nearby church, the Primate asked that at least he be provided with the instruments necessary for saying Mass. Liturgical equipment arrived after five days—not from the local church but from the residence on Miodowa Street. Warsaw's approval had certainly been necessary. Although the Primate was supposed to have a chapel at his disposal, there was not even a good table in his cell, so he said Mass on a rickety desk, in total solitude. At the same desk, he ate and worked. Without lights, he spent the evenings reciting the Rosary. He prayed for both of his archdioceses, for the bishops, for his friends, and for his domestic staff. On the walls of his cell he "erected" the Stations of the Cross—marking them with a pencil.

By chance, a newspaper that one of the guards had been reading fell into his hands. The Primate read the accusations printed against him on the night of his arrest in a *Trybuna Ludu* article by General Edward Ochab. The title indicated that the article was a justification of the move: "Who Is Impeding the Normalization of Church-State Relations?" Ochab was writing as secretary of the National Committee of the National Front, which gave his statement all the more weight. Among other things, it said:

> Kaczmarek's confession and the whole course of events show beyond any doubt that for the head of the Episcopate, Primate Wyszyński, signing the understanding was only a maneuver intended to deceive the government and public opinion, while on the contrary the understanding was treated as a screen behind which to conceal the enemies of the people and the nation in their political activities against the People's State.
>
> In accordance with the wishes of the Roman Curia, Primate Wyszyński did everything so as not to allow the stabilization of the church administration in the Recovered Lands.
>
> First of all, it is Primate Wyszyński who bears the responsibility for sabotaging and breaking the principles of the understanding, and for actually helping the West German Teutonic Knights and the Anglo-American enemies of our nation to defame People's Poland and make it appear odious. The repeated warnings of the government and of society did not mitigate the rash adventurousness of this Vatican alumnus.

The man who not only had risked the unprecedented understanding between an Episcopate and a communist government but also had done all he could for three years to save the agreement was meeting such accusations, formulated in such a way. He had just contributed in an important way to stabilizing the church administration in the Western Lands. The perfidy of the Stalinists led to an absurdity. No one could possibly believe Ochab's article, but no one would ever officially disown his words, either.

After a while, the prisoner was allowed to receive books from home. Reading offered an escape from oppressive thoughts. It was paradoxical that one of the first books the Primate received was Father Eugeniusz Dąbrowski's *Story of Paul of Tarsus*, published by Pax. The book brought consolation to the prisoner and inspired him to imitate Paul. As we know, the author was a well-known biblical scholar who had spoken out against the activity of the Episcopate and the Primate during a so-called demonstration of the clergy in December 1952. Now the Primate was grateful for the book. "Thus the cause of Christ has lasted for almost two thousand years, and for this cause people are behind bars even today. The cause is not obsolete. It is actual, fresh, and stirring."

In the meantime, on October 11, a new joy reached the Primate in his cloistered seclusion. On the feast of the Motherhood of the Most Blessed Virgin Mary, the Primate could hear the people singing in the nearby church. It was fortifying: he knew that the Polish Church was enduring.

Unexpectedly, he was moved the next evening to a new place, Stoczek near Lidzbark, in Warmia. The authorities were afraid to keep him in one location for long: the Stalinist terror was continuing, and the person of the Primate could cause unrest among people who wanted to help him, the most revered man in the country; despite his complete isolation, it was impossible to keep the whereabouts of Stefan Wyszyński secret for long. In Stoczek he found himself in a dilapidated former monastery. The house stood among trees, some of which had been cut down to facilitate observation by the secret police from a nearby one-story house. The trees near the fence had been wrapped with barbed wire, and spotlights illuminated the perimeter from outside. These were only a few of the measures taken to isolate the prisoner. After the Primate's liberation, many of the faithful came to see his place of confinement, with horror. The building was damp and painfully cold; water stood on the stone floors. In the winter, sheets of ice covered the walls. Wyszyński was provided with two companions, a priest and a nun both sentenced to several years' imprisonment. The priest had been transferred from the well-known prison in Rawicz, and the nun from one in Grudziądz. At the beginning, they were afraid that the Primate would not confide in them, but the fate they all shared inspired trust over time. The Primate had two small rooms and an improvised chapel on the second floor. On the same floor, the priest and the nun each had a room. Under constant observation, and checked on each morning by the chief of the guards, the Primate calculated that it took thirty people to "protect" him.

He rose at five, said prayers and meditated with the other two prisoners, then devoted the rest of his time to reading intensively the books allowed him. During this period he wrote his father, "For a long while I have wanted to find the time for neglected reading. I would put away piles of unread books—for later. Today I can read more; that is some sort of gain. I have read much already. Lacking the materials for academic work, I cannot work with the pen. . . ." However, he was writing anyway, creating *The Liturgical Year*, reflections on each day of the year.

The place was so primitive that snow was shoveled—by the prisoners—with a plank. The garden was also tended without tools. The only way to erect a cross was to tie two sticks together with barbed wire. Prayer was the one consolation.

There was not a particle of exaltation among the prisoner's emotions, but, rather, a trusting peace, despite his own uncertain fate and the widening threats against the whole Polish Church: under Stalinism, it appeared, literally everything was possible.

On December 8, 1953, after two and a half months of imprisonment, the Primate made an act of spiritual dedication to the Mother of God. He had spent three weeks preparing for the act. He gave himself in submission to Christ through the hands of His "Most Perfect Mother." The act was above all an acceptance of any fate that Divine Providence might assign, a concept to which the Primate returned often in his pastoral program. In prison, it was a heroic ideal. But the Primate, never disheartened, always tried to think as if he had believed from the first that he would be saved and freed. He said later, "I decided to honor the first parish that I would be able to create with the title 'Divine Motherhood of Mary.' " The act of dedication in submission to Mary might surprise or arouse skepticism in some, but the idea of Mary as an intermediary with God is an old one in Catholicism, with a great tradition, even if today it is often forgotten. Naturally, religiosity reflects its epoch and cultural conditioning. The Primate remembered the "social" origins of his religious act:

> The house was illuminated all night, and some of the lights burned during the day. The courtyard and the road likewise. Army sentries stood guard around the fence. In the corridors of the ground floor and upstairs the "gentlemen," officers of the secret police, kept watch. The isolation from the world was total. Only the road to the Mother of God was open.

In the winter, cold tormented the prisoner; the heating stoves in the ruined old house were falling apart. "I could not get my legs warm even at night," the Primate later recalled. "My hands puffed up. My eyes swelled. I had pains in the region of my kidneys." Only militia doctors, however, were admitted to the sick man. He was not allowed to go for a cure. Those who governed the state were avenging themselves on the spiritual leader of the nation. But they did allow the Primate, for his first Christmas in prison, to receive a parcel from his closest friends, containing a manger.

Besides worrying about his own fate and sufferings, the Primate felt responsible for the Church. He tried, even from prison, to re-establish a dialogue with the state authorities. However, all the effort produced was the unfeeling answer of the guard: "I will present the matter to my superior." Of those who had imprisoned him, Franciszek Mazur's part was surprising, because the vice-marshal had known the Primate's attitudes on church-state affairs better than anyone. The Primate also thought that Bierut ought to be more aware of his responsibility for citizens' rights. But the mechanism of the system was relentless. Its leaders themselves were not free, and human considerations were the last thing they could pay attention to in their political calculations. Nevertheless, the Primate wrote, "I would be incapable of feeling the least unfriendliness toward these people. I could not be unpleasant toward them. It seems to me that I am in the right to keep loving, that I am a Christian and the child of my Church, which teaches me to return brotherly feelings even to those who want to regard me as unfriendly."

On July 2, 1954, still in Stoczek, the Primate sent a wide-ranging letter to the government, discussing the accusations in the decree of September 25, 1953—though, despite many requests, he still did not have a copy of this document. His letter, which ran to several pages, recapitulated all his efforts to conclude and carry out the 1950 understanding. It went unanswered, and may actually have contributed to harsher conditions for the prisoner, who started being denied permission to write to his family and acquaintances. Not all of the letters he did write reached their destinations. Certain sentences were cut out of his letters to his father, which his father never looked at in any case: a messenger would read them aloud to him, without witnesses.

A new "stage" began on October 3, 1954, when a government decision about "a change of climatic conditions" was conveyed to the Primate. After the previous refusals of medical care, this decision was a dismal irony.

* * *

The transfer of the Primate from Stoczek to Prudnik Śląski on October 6, 1954, was linked to the political situation in the party; anyone who thought humanitarian considerations came into play was mistaken. Clear signs of de-Stalinization, of a political thaw, and of the divisions thus created in the party were beginning to appear. The authorities had known for a long time that the cold, damp house at Stoczek was downright dangerous to the Cardinal, but they maintained their uncompromising inflexibility, as if they wanted to undermine the frail health of their troublesome prisoner once and for all. Then everything changed suddenly; Cardinal Wyszyński was moved from the damp, icy hole in Warmia to the Opole region, farther south, literally at the other end of Poland. The mountain residence there at least assured the minimal conditions for a man with weak lungs, endangered by rheumatism, and close to exhaustion.

His fellow prisoners, the priest and the nun, were taken from Stoczek first; the Primate followed several hours later. Their reunion on the airplane cheered them, for they had been sure they were being separated. After landing somewhere near the Neisse, the prisoners had to stay put until dark so that nobody would see them.

In Prudnik, the Primate was placed in a former convent of the Franciscan Sisters that stood on a tree-covered hill. Signs of its hurried and unfinished remodeling were visible. The obligatory high fence topped with barbed wire had been erected. Lights were set in the woods to illuminate the area, and there were strange "technical devices" everywhere. It looked like a new concentration camp, as the Primate did not fail to tell the chief of his guards at a convenient moment. There were as yet no paths for walking in the neglected garden, but their time would come as the political thaw progressed.

A few days after the transfer, the Primate renewed his demand for access to the decree ordering his imprisonment. This was still a dialogue with the deaf, but the "change in climate" would encompass even this touchy matter before long. Settling down in the new conditions, the Primate returned to his established routine. He continued working on *The Liturgical Year;* though this task was complicated by the lack of any theological materials beyond a missal, a breviary, and a Bible, he proceeded on the basis of his earlier studies and pastoral experience. In any case, this work was his greatest psychological support, offering him respite from his worries. On February 2, 1955, he wrote to his father, "I fill my time so tightly so that there will be none left over for pointless thoughts."

At this time, the Primate's correspondence with his family was more regular. But Stanisław Wyszyński's five requests to the Council of Ministers to be allowed to visit his son were all denied, as was the Primate's petition to see his father at a time of grave illness, when, in February 1955, Stanisław suffered a partial stroke. And, despite the Primate's protests, his father still had to endure having his son's letters read aloud to him, and not in their entirety. Eventually, the Primate decided it would be better not to write at all than to have his father thus humiliated.

Shortly after arriving in Prudnik, the Primate had sent a letter to the head of the Council of Ministers asking for the "revocation of extraordinary sanctions against me and permission for me to return to my home" on the grounds of damage to health sustained at Stoczek. Now, in connection with his father's illness, he wrote another letter: "I ask the Council of Ministers to enable me to see my father, so that I can satisfy his requests, the needs of my own heart, and the duties that every son has toward his father." The thaw had not yet progressed enough for such a letter to be answered. Therefore, the Primate decided to stop sending letters and requests to the authorities.

Nevertheless, he did demand medical tests, because the consequences of his stay at Stoczek were becoming more and more apparent to him. The same militia doctors who had examined him before returned. In their opinion, his general health had not worsened, but, since he was at the brink of exhaustion, it was decided to take him to the police hospital in Opole at the end of 1954 for clinical tests. The secrecy surrounding this trip was a circus. The whole operation took place late at night, and was stage-managed so that nobody could see the Primate in the secret-police building. The police appreciated his influence on the public enough to fear the leak of any information on his health.

The tests came out surprisingly well, according to the militia doctors—who would not share the precise results with the patient. Officially, he was in blooming health, but in fact he was experiencing pain in his head and legs, along with general weakness and other disorders. Still, his sensitive organism had borne the Stoczek "deep freeze" well. Now, after the transfer, he managed not to take to his bed, enjoyed some activity, worked constantly, and did not think about his distresses. The problem during Christmastime provided an index of his spiritual attitudes: should he offer to break his *opłatek*, the Christmas wafer, with his guards? It was hard to foresee their reactions. The distance was still impenetrable.

His reading of Henryk Sienkiewicz's *The Deluge* at this period was very important. Its description of the miraculous defense of Jasna Góra against the Swedes impressed itself deeply on his consciousness as 1955, the three hundredth anniversary of the miracle, was beginning.

Prisoners can feel the ineffable signs of a relaxation of political tensions extremely quickly. At Easter there came more letters—from his father, brother, and two sisters—than usual. The Primate became aware that the net of isolation was loosening at the very time that these political changes began, according to subsequent historians.

The Primate was still ready to offer God his freedom and even his life, but the slow changes continued. On his name day, he received more parcels. On August 6, 1955, the prison superintendent offered the Primate access to the press. Wyszyński asked for *Trybuna Ludu,* but for the moment he received only the illustrated magazine *The Capital.** Anyone who has been in prison knows, however, what access to even such marginal publications means.

A real sensation occurred on Sunday, August 7, when the government decided to break its long silence, speaking through the mouth of a secret-police official from central head-quarters rather than in writing. The man proposed a belated, not especially encouraging answer to the Primate's earlier petitions: The government saw no possibility of a return to Warsaw and church functions, but it proposed moving the Primate to a mutually agreeable convent. He would not be entitled to leave or to fulfill his public role, and he would also have to commit himself not to sanction any petitions and to guarantee that there would be no demonstrations calling for his complete freedom. He was also told that the September 1953 decision in his case was irreversible.

Cardinal Wyszyński said, first of all, that he was not familiar with the precise content of the decision of the Council of Ministers, or with any legal basis for such a decision. His interlocutor read him article 6 of the Decree on Appointments to Spiritual Offices of February 1953, which covered dismissal from ecclesiastical posts by the state authorities. The Primate protested that the article could not apply: it did not provide for penalties and he had been condemned to prison. Since this legal discussion with the policeman did not arouse any great hopes, the Primate proposed taking several hours to think the matter over. At three in the afternoon he gave his reply, which was of course negative; he did not intend to exchange forced imprisonment for voluntary imprisonment. He also warned the police official that his pseudo-freedom in isolation would lead to conflicts with the authorities, would upset any convent he stayed in, and would cause social problems. He would not agree to give up his free-

---

The Capital: a weekly dedicated to the history of Warsaw, published by the Friends of the History of Warsaw, a special organization with this one purpose. It is described as "marginal" in the sense of specialized, not general.

dom, home, and work for this sort of "voluntary servitude."

Despite its unacceptability, the very fact that a proposal had been made showed that the issue of the Primate was still alive, in the party and government as well as in society. Personal freedom (relative, at that) could not tempt a man who felt responsible to his Church and nation. The Primate stayed in prison, and the government found itself still at an impasse. It is worth mentioning, by the way, that while all his guards referred to the Primate as "Father," the policeman from Warsaw called him "Cardinal."

The number of periodicals available to the prisoner increased, and he concluded from reading them that the struggle against the Church was continuing, religion had been removed from the schools, and the Stalinist juggernaut had not yet been stopped. But changes were evident, both in the press and in the behavior of his guards, who had begun to talk of imminent release, had become very polite, and quickly answered requests for hosts and altar wine, which had earlier been brought only after long delays. Still, the Primate and his two fellow prisoners decided not to change their own behavior or routines.

In Prudnik the Primate finished his sketches for *The Liturgical Year* and part of his *Letter to New Priests*, as well as several minor religious works. Immersed as he was in prayer and intensive work, the Primate was surprised by one new decision of the authorities. On October 28, at 5:30 P.M., an official appeared and handed the Primate a document:

Bureau of Religious Affairs
Warsaw
October 27, 1955

Decree

I declare that the Government of the Polish People's Republic has allowed Archbishop Stefan Wyszyński to change his place of residence and to relocate to the convent of the Sisters of Nazareth in Komańcza, Province of Sanok, without the right to leave this new place of residence.

In case any attempts are made to exploit contacts for actions against the government, the guilty parties will suffer the consequences.

The ban, contained in government decree no. 700, of September 24, 1955, on performing any functions related to formerly held church positions and the ban on public appearances, is still in effect.

> Director of the Bureau of
> Religious Affairs
> Marian Zygmanowski

This document, written in dreadful Polish and constituting a new act of lawlessness, nevertheless brought about an improvement in the Cardinal's living conditions. The initiative had come from the Episcopate; though the Primate was inclined to be distrustful, the official emissary showed him the request by Bishop Klepacz, on behalf of all the bishops, that the Primate be moved to Komańcza. Wyszyński agreed, emphasizing that the government was doing as it liked and that he had neither known of nor requested the action. Now he would be able to meet representatives of the Episcopate and his family, and to move freely about—but not outside—the small, isolated town of Komańcza. The thaw was proceeding, and an increasingly rebellious society was demanding freedom for the Cardinal as well as changes in the system.

Bolesław Piasecki announced publicly that the Primate was interned in a convent. The authorities would have preferred to forget about the period of actual imprisonment, but such was impossible. In the meantime, it was important for the Primate not to make any deals as the price of his partial freedom; he knew that he belonged before the altar and with his flocks in Warsaw and Gniezno.

Before the trip, which was to take place the next day, the Primate inquired about his fellow prisoners and took time to say his farewells to them, religious and full of Christian love; Father Stanisław Skorodecki and Sister Leonia Graczyk were to be amnestied. The first day of "freedom" was to fall during the Rosary Month of Mary and on her feast day—the common prayers of an unusual trio of prisoners were thus being answered.

On October 29, the Primate was transferred under escort from Prudnik to Komańcza, in a laborious journey by way of Katowice, Cracow, Tarnów, Jasło, and Sanok which lasted from six in the morning to half past three in the afternoon. The Sisters of Nazareth had been preparing for a guest since morning, but the state authorities had not given them precise information. The Primate waited a long time in front of the convent before the sister superior appeared and invited him in. He was given a real room instead of a cell. At five in the afternoon, the government representative announced that he was transferring care of the Primate to the Episcopate. The militia withdrew, and further supervision took place discreetly, from a distance.

Now the Primate could breathe easily at last, in a room of his own and without guards. The Sisters of Nazareth and their chaplain, along with the local parish priest, greeted him with open hearts. Now he could receive letters, friends, and newspapers from all over the country and have contact with the Episcopate. Komańcza was as far as possible from Warsaw, near the Czechoslovak border, but healthful and, given its mountain air, suited to a man with weak lungs. The internee was not limited by camp walls and barbed wire, though he of course could not leave town and, specifically because of his presence, Komańcza was added to the restricted border zone, which meant that visits required permits from the central authorities in Warsaw. The controls were severe and meticulous. Even Sister Maksencja, the superior at the residence in Warsaw, was turned back at Sanok when she tried to deliver needed underwear and personal effects to the Primate without having obtained the required documents. The permits were difficult to get and had strictly delineated periods of validity. Thus the Primate's sister Janina Jurkiewicz was practically ordered away from the Easter dinner table and told to leave for home.

The day after he arrived at Komańcza, the Primate learned

that on the day of his arrest, his co-worker Bishop Baraniak had also been imprisoned. The latter was treated with horrible cruelty during his confinement in the Mokotów district prison in Warsaw. A physically frail man, he showed great spiritual strength and steadfastness, and impressed his fellow prisoners with his example of what a bishop should be. This was a moral necessity after Bishop Kaczmarek's earlier capitulation under the influence of blackmail and, possibly, drugs.

On October 31, the Primate received a telegram from Bishop Klepacz, who was serving as head of the Council of Bishops: "I am coming with Zygmunt [Bishop Choromański] and your father for a private visit Wednesday, November 2, at around three in the afternoon." Because of the Primate's delicacy and discretion, little is known of this first visit, but it was moving for both sides. They all cried like children, particularly Bishop Klepacz. The bishops told the Primate of everything that had happened during his absence. They did not know how he would judge their decisions, but the Primate understood everything and showed exceptional tenderness; later he always defended the decisions they had made. He was also grateful for their efforts to win his freedom, or at least ease the terms of his confinement. The Primate realized that, even though he was still in isolation, he was now under their care.

Still, that first meeting was difficult. Now the Primate could familiarize himself with all four of the documents published after his arrest (soon after being imprisoned, he had found a scrap of newspaper, but still had not seen the whole of the documents). The fact that they had been published simultaneously (on the same newspaper page) testified to the government's refined perfidy. The first document was a communiqué from the Presidium of the Government on the prohibition of "Archbishop Stefan Wyszyński from carrying out the functions connected with his former church positions." The communiqué was legally compromising, since the government could not remove the Primate from positions to which the Pope had appointed him. Because the communiqué cited the hostile activities of the Primate and alluded to the show trial of Bishop Kaczmarek as an example, it must have been received by public opinion with indignation and disgust. Beside it was placed a declaration that had been forced out of the Episcopate under the threat of further arrests and the dismemberment of the hierarchy. To disorient public opinion, the "request" of the bishops that the Primate be allowed to reside in a monastery was placed beneath the declaration—the authorities wanted to shift responsibility for the Primate's imprisonment in a "monastery"—which in fact had been a forsaken, damp little building—onto the Episcopate. Third, the newspaper announced that the bishops had chosen Bishop Michał Klepacz of Łódź as the head of the Episcopate. The final document was a statement by Vice-Premier Józef Cyrankiewicz that the government acknowledged the September 28 announcement of the Episcopate and stood by the terms of the "understanding" of April 14, 1950. This was Stalinist political artistry: to cite an agreement while breaking it.

It is easy to imagine Cardinal Wyszyński's feelings as he read these documents, though of course he understood that the bishops had been coerced, acting under pressure of blackmail and trying to look after the Church, not themselves. He also knew what would have happened had the government's demands been rejected. More than the arrest of additional bishops was at stake—the Church would have lost practically its whole leadership. The compromise forced upon the bishops had put the Primate on a pedestal as a man who had sacrificed himself for the whole Church. His understanding of the bishops' situation gave him authority as a statesman.

After his guests left, the Primate set about catching up on back issues of newspapers. There were some heavy blows, perhaps the most stunning being the account of Bishop Kaczmarek's trial, in which various means had been used to extract accusations against the Primate, the Episcopate, and the Pope. The tragedy of the show trial gave new meaning to the Primate's imprisonment. Now it was clearer how much his sacrifice had meant to the Church, to his moral reputation and authority in society.

With disgust the Primate read the speech of Piasecki, who wanted to monopolize the organized clergy and Catholic activities for his own political gain. The Primate was also incensed by a statement from Father Eugeniusz Dąbrowski that implied that between 1946 and 1953 the Church had done nothing at all in the Western Lands. With concern, he read of the oath of loyalty to the Polish People's Republic that had been forced upon the Episcopate.

A bit later, more joyful reading came. A *Trybuna Ludu* article from March 1956 that attacked the "cult of personality" fostered reflections on the quick "twilight" of the gods made by human hands.

On the night of March 13, 1956, the Primate dreamed very distinctly of President Bolesław Bierut. The two men were on the streets of Lublin, but conversing as they had in Belvedere Palace. When they reached an intersection, the Primate wanted to say something of importance regarding church-state affairs, but he lost sight of the president. The signal changed, and as the Primate crossed along the pedestrian stripes, he spotted Bierut jaywalking diagonally across the intersection. In his dream the Primate thought, "Have they even appropriated the right to circumvent the rules of the road?" Then, worried that Bierut had disappeared, he woke up. He soon forgot the strange dream, but later the same day the radio announced news that shook the Cardinal: "Yesterday evening, Bolesław Bierut died in Moscow." The dream must mean more to parapsychologists than to historians, but the next day the Primate prayed for Bierut and thought about him a great deal. Posterity will associate the name of Bolesław Bierut with wrongs done both to the Church and to the nation; he died excommunicated, sentenced by the Holy See along with others responsible for imprisoning Cardinal Wyszyński. The Primate prayed for God's mercy on the deceased and wrote, "Everyone may forget him soon. They may disown him, as today they are disowning Stalin—but I will not do that. So my Christianity demands."

The lengthening stay in Komańcza was beginning to weigh

upon the Primate. Each day he felt his isolation and his absence from his two archdioceses more. The thaw developing in the country did not include the Church. The government wanted to block the realization of a program at Jasna Góra to commemorate the three hundredth anniversary of the miraculous defense against the Swedes and of the vows of King Jan II Kazimierz. The Primate was commemorating the anniversary with the program of submission on which he had embarked.

When the authorities realized that the Primate was exercising a spiritual influence on the Church even from his confinement, they drastically limited the issuance of permits to visit Komańcza. Many priests and well-known colleagues of the Primate were turned down. In large part, these restrictions resulted from the unauthorized publication of a letter that the Primate had sent to the general of the Pauline Fathers in Częstochowa.

On April 20, Bishop Choromański traveled to Komańcza with Father Goździewicz and Father Bronisław Dąbrowski (Bishop Klepacz could not come because he was recovering from an operation). The Primate advised these emissaries from the Episcopate to reactivate the Mixed Commission and to send the government a memorandum about church affairs in general, including the suggestion that Bishops Kaczmarek, Baraniak, and Adamski be released. Close observation of developments in the country showed that change was inevitable. Even the Catholic legislators connected with Pax were finding courage: all five had spoken bravely in the Sejm and voted against a law on abortion.

On May 2, 1956, the Primate was brought a letter from Bishop Choromański relating that the steering committee and Bishop Klepacz had filed with the marshal of the Sejm a petition on freeing the Primate, and the marshal had informed the Episcopate that the matter was being referred to the prosecutor general. The Primate remarked in his prison diary that the appeal should be sent to the state authorities, and ought not to be confined only to himself. The transfer of the matter to the prosecutor showed that, despite the growing social tension, the party leadership did not realize the gravity of the situation and did not want to correct old mistakes. But a general social movement was sweeping the country, the party was engaged in factional battles, and everything indicated that a crisis was inevitable.

In these decisive months, the Eight played a significant role. They had already organized a Family of Families, a group of hundreds of families who were praying for the Primate, guided by Maria Wantowska.* At Jasna Góra, Masses were being said continually for the imprisoned Cardinal. There were also nocturnal adorations and numbers of pilgrimages. Each day a representative of the group set out on a pilgrimage to Częstochowa. Maria Okońska "locked herself up" in Jasna Góra as a voluntary prisoner of the Virgin Mary for the intention of the Primate's freedom, so that she could spend all her time praying for him. Indeed, to this day, a representative of the Eight is always spending a year of voluntary "imprisonment" at Jasna Góra, praying for the freedom of the Primate and the Church in Poland.

The police discovered that Maria Okońska's stay at Jasna Góra was also connected with the pilgrimages and Marian actions for the three hundredth anniversary of the miraculous defense and the vows of King Jan II Kazimierz. Therefore, in February 1956, the security command in Katowice ordered her to leave the monastery within three days. Father Alojzy Wrzalik, superior general of the Paulines, refused, saying, "I am still in charge here, and not the secret police. As long as the Primate has not returned to freedom, the lady may stay here." Not daring an act of violence on the grounds of the sanctuary, the police backed down.

Nineteen fifty-five had been the anniversary of the defense against the Swedes, and 1956 of Jan Kazimierz's vows. Jasna Góra was the scene of continuing Marian activity, including lectures, exhibitions, pilgrimages, and the publishing of appeals to the public. On July 2, 1656, the sanctuary had been named

---

*A member of the Primatial Institute.

the Bright Mountain of Victory. Now people were praying that it would again protect Poland and its Church.

Maria Okońska and Janina Michalska* obtained permits and visited Komańcza on March 25, 1956, which was the Feast of the Annunciation as well as the anniversary of Stefan Wyszyński's consecration as bishop. On that day, the Primate disclosed his Marian program, telling the two women that on December 8, 1953, while imprisoned in Stoczek, after deep reflection, he had made his act of submission to the Blessed Virgin for the freedom of the Church and Poland.

The Primate's main idea was to defend the faith of the nation against militant atheism by means of the power of the Virgin Mary. Having dedicated himself personally in submission to her motherhood for the sake of the Church and the nation, he had slowly been forming the idea that the tormented homeland ought to dedicate itself in submission to Mary, as a national community, for the freedom of its own Church and of the Church throughout the world. This act was to be implemented by the Episcopate in 1966, the thousandth anniversary of Polish Christianity. Placing themselves in the hands of the Most Perfect Mother and Her Divine Son, the nation and the Church would beg that the country be freed from unwanted, imposed political submission. The Primate also wanted this great act of national dedication to bring aid to the universal Church and the family of man. Poland, itself endangered and fighting every day for its own freedom of conscience and religion, was to help the whole world.

Such an act was completely unheard of. There were individual acts of dedication to Mary (for example, those of Saint Louis Maria Grignon de Montfort and Saint Maksymilian Maria Kolbe), but never had an entire nation dedicated itself for the whole Church.

There is a connection here with Poland's historical role as the rampart of European Christianity. Once this had been a matter of arms, as when King Jan III Sobieski saved Vienna

---

*One of the leading members of the Primatial Institute.

from the Turks. Now it was a rampart in a moral sense, a rampart of European culture grown from the soil of Greco-Roman and Christian tradition.

The conception also contained the echoes and traditions of Polish romanticism, and even messianism. Each nation has a feeling for its historic role and fulfills it within the framework of God's plan. The Primate's idea was influenced not only by the events of three centuries earlier, when the Swedish invasion broke at the foot of Jasna Góra, and not only by the particular tradition of Poland's Christian mission, but also by the direct threat of totalitarianism against the national faith and culture.

Personal or national dedication to the Virgin Mary can, of course, only be understood on a supernatural plane, in the order of grace. Thus, it is the biographer's task to present the conceptions and program, but not the theological justifications behind them. The program was obviously a controversial one. Still, one cannot help adding that, by a "strange coincidence," the current situation of Poland is far different from that of the rest of the Eastern bloc, that Poland resisted Stalinism, and that the clash with political atheism resulted in such a spiritual renewal and fortification that Poland was even able to give the world a pope.

It was a long road to the completion of the national act of dedication to Mary, which the Primate intended to conclude in the Millennial Year of 1966. In 1956, the Primate decided to begin preparing the nation. He wanted first of all to focus the eyes of all Poles on the Bright Mountain of Victory, and to build in them the faith that, through the fundamentals of faith and the aid of Mary, everything could be restored. He wanted all Poles to renew Jan Kazimierz's vows in a form adapted to present times, as a great spiritual work and moral renewal for the thousandth anniversary of Polish Christianity.

On May 16, 1956, in Komańcza, the Primate wrote the vows. This document, although planned, was created suddenly, obeying an inner command, between five and seven in the morning, before Mass. The Primate had stated, while reading

Sienkiewicz's *Deluge* during his imprisonment in Prudnik, that "the history of a nation sometimes repeats itself." "I was, after all, imprisoned near the place where Jan Kazimierz and Primate Leszczyński conferred about how to save Poland from the waves of peril." Fascinated by the story of the Swedish invasion and its defeat, the Primate said later:

The thought of renewing the Vows of Kazimierz on their three hundredth anniversary sprang up in my spirit there in Prudnik, not far from Głogówek, where three hundred years ago the king and the Primate thought about how to free the nation from its twin subjugations: to foreign power and to social misery. When, later in my imprisonment, I followed almost the same track, from Prudnik to the southeast [to Komańcza], to the mountains, I went with the thought: There must be new Vows of Renewal! And it was precisely there that they sprang up, in the southeast, among the mountains. They were written and transferred from there to Jasna Góra. . . . The Polish nation was entering an interesting period; we were approaching the Millennium of our Christianity with quick steps. In 1966, we would cross a high mountain pass: a thousand years would become history, and before the eyes of a young nation would open the prospect of a new thousand years of following the cross, reading the Gospels, living in grace, invigorating itself with the Body of Christ, embracing everything with evangelical love.

Knowing that new vows would be needed, the Primate nevertheless held himself back from writing them while in prison. Superior General Alojzy Wrzalik of the Paulines and Jerzy Tomziński, Prior of Częstochowa, asked for the text. The Cardinal was convinced only by the argument that Saint Paul had written Epistles while in prison. Constant thinking about the matter gave birth within the Primate's mind and heart to the idea of the Great Novena of the Millennium, which he finally formulated between August 15 and 29, 1956.

Just as during a normal novena we ask God for some favor, so during the Great Novena, through nine years of prayer and profound moral works, the Polish nation was to renew itself spiritually and ask God, through Mary, for the victory of faith and freedom of the Church. Each year of the Great Novena was to have as its theme a promise from the Jasna Góra vows. On August 29, the Primate presented the program for the Great Novena to Bishops Klepacz and Choromański.

In a letter to Superior General Wrzalik on May 22, the Primate wrote that he, as head of the Church, should read the vows at Jasna Góra, but that he was resigning the honor for the greater glory of Mary, Queen of Poland. He asked that in his place Bishop Michał Klepacz lead the public recitation of the vows and, should that prove impossible, that the father general read them. The Primate was thinking, of course, about the possibility of intervention by the authorities. If the father general's lips were sealed, then the duty should fall to the prior, next to any of the priests, and finally to any of the brothers at Częstochowa. Because of the possibility of interference, the text of the vows was transmitted in great secrecy to the superior general of the Paulines, who made Bishop Klepacz aware of them. The secrecy was so great that not even the Episcopate saw the text before the morning of August 26, when they were to be read publicly. Some impatient bishops asked to see the text on the eve of the reading, but the secrecy was justified. Approximately a million people—more, according to foreign reports—had made the pilgrimage to Jasna Góra from all over the country. They were to take vows in behalf of the whole nation, and the authorities would have given anything to stop them. But the Church had learned about secret-police methods by now. Four people were locked in the Royal Chambers at Jasna Góra to type up the text so that in the morning copies could be handed to bishops, the clergy, and some groups of the faithful.

The Primate was kept informed of the preparations at Częstochowa. It was decided that he would pronounce the vows ten minutes before they were pronounced at Jasna Góra. (Later it turned out that both actually took place at the same time.) In his last place of confinement, Komańcza, Cardinal Wyszyński stood before the picture of the Madonna of Częstochowa and recited the act of dedication at about the same time as Bishop Klepacz at Jasna Góra. The Primate then said his second Mass of the day. In one celebration, a million people took part; in the other, only the isolated cardinal, who had arranged the event that attracted a million believers.

In a country ruled by the communists these words were recited:

Queen of Poland! Today we renew the vows of our ancestors and acknowledge You as our Patron and as Queen of the Polish Nation.

As well as we ourselves, all the Polish land and all the People invite Your particular protection and defense. . . .

We promise to do everything within our power that Poland truly be the Kingdom of You and Your Son, given under Your control in our personal, family, professional, and social lives. . . .

We promise to strengthen the Kingship of Your Son Jesus Christ within the family, to preserve respect for the Name of God, to graft the spirit of the Gospels and love of You in the hearts of children, to preserve the laws of God, and the traditions of Christianity and the homeland.

We promise You that we will raise young generations in the faith of Christ, guard them from godlessness and moral degradation, and surround them with tender family care.

The text is integral, and fragments cannot do it justice. But above all it must be judged by the situation in the country and the reaction of society. At the end of a period in which the destruction of the Church and religion had been attempted, a million people stood before the monastery at Jasna Góra, repeating loudly and full of emotion after each of the verses read by the bishop: "Queen of Poland, we promise!" The scene was incredible, astounding, and difficult for anyone who did not experience it to imagine. After Mass the next morning, the Primate was radiant in a way he had not been during those last years of struggle and imprisonment.

It was indeed an extraordinary event by any standard. In the twilight of the Stalinist era, the nation, represented by the Episcopate and a million pilgrims, pledged itself to Mary, while the communist authorities stood by helpless. The Primate could calmly tell his friends, "Children, the Mother of God has won." And in two months the Primate would be freed.

Not only all Poles, but also the party, the government, and the world understood what had happened. Polish Catholicism had reached one of its greatest heights. We can imagine those million animated, fervent pilgrims in a country ruled under an atheistic program, after years of attacks upon a Church whose head was still imprisoned. Three days after the taking of the vows, the Primate wrote in a letter to the general of the Pauline Fathers, "God has again shown what power is needed for the sake of uniting and regenerating the nation." Cardinal Wyszyński had no doubt that the power was Mary. His program, controversial to many, was proved in the hearts of the people. In the *Appeal to the Clergy*, written during his confinement in Komańcza, he wrote words that showed how the vows were at the root of his pastoral concepts: "We must . . . be fully aware of what happened at Jasna Góra and of what is going to happen in our parishes in May of the coming year, and of what we are aiming at: the fundamental transformation of the national spirit before the Millennium." The plan for the spiritual and ideological offensive had been prepared, and there was nothing for the authorities to do except to free its author as quickly as possible. Society had been demanding as much for months, multiplying the appeals and petitions to the authorities. When October 1956 brought a political crisis, social peace depended on fulfilling the demand that the Primate be released. Two ministers arrived in Komańcza to ask Stefan Cardinal Wyszyński to return promptly to Warsaw.

4

Release and
New Attacks (1956-1963)

On October 26, 1956, there appeared in Komańcza two emissaries from the new first secretary of the communist PZPR,
Władysław Gomułka, who had also spent the Stalinist era in
confinement. These messengers—the deputy party chief,
Zenon Kliszko, and the soon-to-be-named minister of Education, Władysław Bieńkowski—asked Cardinal Wyszyński to
return to Warsaw and resume all of his church posts. In view
of the need to "pacify" society, they insisted on haste. The
Primate wanted social peace and longed to avoid bloodshed,
but he could not imagine agreeing to his own release unless at
least the worst injuries that had been done to the Church were
rectified. Now it was the party's turn to play petitioner, while
the Cardinal set conditions: he wanted church freedom first,
and his own freedom afterward.

After these initial discussions, the envoys went to town to
confer by telephone with their leader. They returned for dinner—superseding the sisters' wishes for an elaborate dinner,

the Cardinal had insisted on having everyday fare. The talks went on during the meal, and the Primate sized up his interlocutors accurately. Bieńkowski was good-humored and open; soon he would be the new government's most popular member, then its *enfant terrible*, and finally a party dissident. Kliszko struck Wyszyński as narrow-minded, a first impression that the future would confirm.

After dinner the two guests left for Warsaw to find out Gomułka's decision on the Cardinal's proposals. The Primate felt that good things were happening in the country, and he would support them if they included the position on Catholicism that Gomułka had taken at the Eighth Plenum of the Central Committee. Specifically, Cardinal Wyszyński wanted the repeal of the February 1953 decree on church appointments, the re-establishment of the government-Episcopate Mixed Commission, the freeing of the unjustly sentenced Bishop Kaczmarek, and the return of all bishops who had been forced out of their dioceses—especially the return of Bishop Adamski and his auxiliaries to Silesia. The government representatives had expressed doubts about Adamski, but the Cardinal was unbending on the point. He also demanded the reinstatement of the Gniezno auxiliaries and the restoring of the canonical diocesan administrations in Wrocław, Opole, Gorzów, Olsztyn, and Gdańsk, the reactivation of the Catholic press, and— he only requested this final point, not insisting—action in the matter of a concordat with the Holy See. His interlocutors had regarded the latter issue as premature.

Kliszko returned to Komańcza the next day with news that the Primate's conditions had been accepted. Cardinal Wyszyński could go home. He wanted to travel by way of Częstochowa to thank the Blessed Virgin there, but Kliszko again insisted on haste. Great hopes had been awakened, and the country was tense; the Primate's return would realize one of the hopes. Since there was no choice, he went straight to Warsaw and was at home on Miodowa Street on the 28th.

Cheering and singing, Warsavians gathered at the Primate's palace. Over and over again, Wyszyński stepped onto his balcony to greet them, thank them for their love and loyalty, and appeal for calm. His very presence in Warsaw was an inducement to levelheadedness. The welcoming took on a religious character, and ended with the singing of the Jasna Góra appeal: "Mary, Queen of Poland, I stand with You remembering, on guard."

The Vatican radio announcement of Cardinal Wyszyński's return, made at eight that evening, touched world opinion deeply. The new Polish leadership had made points with the Western governments on whose economic aid it was counting, as well as with its own people. Most important, the Primate's circumspection—he eschewed all expressions of triumph—allowed Poland to avoid bloodshed. From the moment of his return, Wyszyński was counseling calm to the literally hundreds of people he received, while shoring up their faith and eagerness to serve their Church and country. On the 29th, he met the lay activists who would later form the Znak movement. To all, he advised moderation and calm in face of a situation that was not yet clear.

No one knew how things would turn out. But, as he had been when he became primate in 1948, the Cardinal was ready to talk with the government and look for a *modus vivendi*. It is easy, once again, to contrast his line with that of Cardinal Mindszenty. The Hungarian, arrested in 1948, was released on the same day as Wyszyński—by rebels, rather than by the communists. Justifiably, Mindszenty demanded the invalidation of the understanding that had been forced on his Church in 1950, and the invalidation of his own illegal trial and sentencing. But Mindszenty went further and made it clear that he would never reconcile himself to a communist Hungary. When Soviet tanks crushed the uprising, he had to ask for political asylum in the American embassy on November 4. In 1962 he turned down a government proposal that he emigrate, and in 1964 he rejected a similar initiative from the visiting Cardinal König of Vienna. Nevertheless, the Vatican and the Hungarian government signed a mutual agreement on September 14, 1964, expanding the concord five years later.

Mindszenty opposed the whole process and ignored König's repeated pleas that he leave Budapest. Only on the direct orders of the Pope did Mindszenty finally emigrate, on September 28, 1971. After managing to block the appointment of a new primate of Hungary and creating a scandal by refusing to live in Rome, Cardinal Mindszenty died in Vienna in 1975.

Poland came close to the fate of Hungary, but avoided the catastrophe. During the famous Eighth Plenum of the Central Committee, on October 19–21, Khrushchev and the Soviet leadership flew to Warsaw to intervene while Red Army tanks moved toward the Polish capital. At least three factors prevented a military solution: the Soviets were also facing the Suez crisis and the Hungarian uprising; the Polish party faction championing reform controlled both the media and the Polish armed forces (whose planes could bomb tank columns —the Russians faced the prospect of a war, not just a revolt); finally, the Poles acted realistically despite their reputation as romantics. Society wanted change, but within the limits of the system and the established ties to the Soviet Union. The last war, and especially the tragedy of the Warsaw Uprising, were still fresh memories. Force had already been used, in June, against the workers of Poznań, before the political upheaval began. Furthermore, the new party leadership contained a balance between advocates and enemies of democratization. Gomulka embodied the spirit of popular revolt without himself proposing far-reaching changes. Most important, however, was the fact that on returning to Warsaw, Cardinal Wyszyński helped to keep the situation under control. The party never thanked him for his help—but, then, he had acted for the sake of Poland, not for the sake of its rulers.

* * *

Cardinal Wyszyński's existence after his release can only be described as toil beyond human strength. He was at everyone's disposal. I can cite only a fraction of his work. In Warsaw he held discussions with scores of priests and lay people before celebrating Mass for the seminarians on October 31. On November 2 he made the postponed visit to Częstochowa. After thanking "my Mother" and conferring with the Pauline Fathers over the future of his Marian program, he had to return to Warsaw. There, the Episcopate-government forum, now called the Joint Commission, was preparing for a November 8 session. He visited Lublin, his first episcopal see, and his beloved KUL, on November 11. On the 14th he was in Gniezno to repair some of the administrative damage of the last years. Monsignor Bross was let go and Bishop Bernacki reinstated as vicar general, while Bishop Baraniak, fresh from prison, became dean of the archepiscopal chapter.

Because "October" had reanimated such great hopes, the Primate found himself pursued daily by politicians seeking the Church's moral support. Generally, Wyszyński listened attentively, counseled prudence and consideration, but refrained from making political suggestions. In November he received not only people like Jerzy Zawieyski of Znak (a group full of possibilities, since it was more cultural than political), but also the prewar Piłsudskiite Wacław Bitner, the conservative Stanisław Cat Mackiewicz, the Christian Democrats Konstanty Turowski and Chmara, and Professor Dobrzański, who wanted to revive the National Party. Most of these visitors warned Wyszyński about Pax and Piasecki; most of these visitors' plans soon evaporated, a testimony to the number of illusions born in the flush of October.

At Joint Commission meetings on November 20, 26, and 27, the government suggested that religious education be treated as an optional school subject for pupils whose parents requested it.

On November 23, Cardinal Wyszyński saw representatives of *Tygodnik Powszechny*, which had resumed publication. Without dictating a decision, he enjoined them to think carefully about their plans for entering the Sejm. He also received a delegation from Nowa Huta, the vast steel-mill city being built outside Cracow, where the people were beginning their struggle, which was to last for decades, to build themselves a church.

There was also upsetting news: the government wanted to send its Catholic activist Jan Frankowski to Rome for "consultations" without informing the Episcopate. Naturally, this plan came to nothing. On the other hand, Archbishop Baziak returned to Cracow, and the bishops designated for the Western Lands were able to take over their dioceses. The Joint Commission decided on December 4 to settle church personnel matters in the spirit of the prewar concordat and to lift the limitations on the "imprimatur" in religious publishing houses. On December 8 the commission issued a "little understanding" in which the government stressed its "readiness to eliminate the obstacles to the principle of free religious life that had appeared in the past." The Church agreed to changes "intended to consolidate the rule of law, justice, peaceful coexistence, the raising of social morality, and the correction of wrongs." The Episcopate was meeting public expectations and not making political concessions. The "little understanding" settled six specific issues: (1) it nullified the notorious February 1953 decree on filling church vacancies; (2) it guaranteed optional religious education in the schools; (3) it extended religious care to hospital patients; (4) it established a prison chaplaincy; (5) it allowed the religious and priests ejected from the Western Lands in 1953 to return, while permitting the emigration of sisters who did not regard themselves as Poles (i.e., German sisters); (6) it permitted the five bishops nominated by the Holy See to enter their dioceses in the Western Lands. The last point, on which the Stalinists had constructed their charges against Cardinal Wyszyński, represented a special triumph. Gomułka had reversed this absurd contradiction of Polish national interests. Placing legitimate Polish bishops in the recovered dioceses was essential from a pastoral view, and it would finally be recognized legally by the Vatican in 1972, after the Polish–West German peace treaty.

The "little understanding" left some urgent church questions unsettled, but it resolved those on which Wyszyński had refused to yield in 1953, and for which he had gone to prison. The Cardinal could feel satisfied, and he refrained from pressing more demands while the situation in the country was still uncertain. The fact that the government dragged its heels in releasing the communiqué provided another reason not to strive immediately for even better terms.

On the day of the communiqué, the Primate ordained twenty priests—his first administration of that sacrament since his release. He learned with joy that the first issue of the reborn *Przewodnik Katolicki* (Catholic Guide) had appeared in Poznań. Two days later he received Jerzy Zawieyski and the group of young Catholics, mainly former Pax activists, who were founding the monthly *Więź* (The Bond).

When the Episcopate met on December 14, it was already possible to sum up the Church's gains and the general situation. Splits in the party, the calls for "a Polish road to socialism," and the emigration of many Jews even while other Jews were some of the leading party liberals, were worrisome symptoms of wider, international phenomena. Still, the bishops allowed themselves a tempered optimism. The government's stand on Caritas, which had been illegally stripped from the Church, was still unclear. Lay Catholic alignments seemed interesting but still fluid: Znak was emerging, while Pax had split and Frankowski had set up what would become the Christian Social Association. The bishops were more interested in the reactivation of purely religious associations like the Marian Society of Landowners than in political groups, but they had no great hopes in this regard.

On December 21 Bishop Splett, the German ordinary of Gdańsk, who had been imprisoned and was now returning to Germany, came to see Cardinal Wyszyński. Splett showed no bitterness; he was even grateful for the concern the Polish bishops had shown. He understood that they had been able to do little, and was cheered by the intensity of Polish religious life. It was a decidedly friendly farewell. But all was not so rosy: at a Joint Commission meeting on the same day, the government reneged on one of the December 8 promises and demanded control over the *nihil obstat* and the right to approve nominations for vicar general and dean (a right that had earlier been limited to the posts of bishop ordinary and parish pastors). The Episcopate said no firmly and the government backed off. Still, the action showed that some officials still hoped to influence the Church through administrative pressures.

A sensation occurred on Christmas Eve: the Polish radio broadcast a message that the Primate had recorded two days earlier. The party was still weak, the country restless, and the government wished to profit from Cardinal Wyszyński's authority. More good news came on December 29, with the official rehabilitation of Bishop Kaczmarek and the party's repudiation of his show trial. Still, the Primate spent an uneasy New Year's Day in Gniezno. He knew how uncertain the country's situation remained; 1957 would be a year of endless journeys and meetings with masses of the faithful.

Fresh trouble broke out at the January 7 meeting of the Joint Commission. The government demanded that parents' requests for their children to receive religious instruction at school be written, and any sort of written document always gave the authorities a lever for future pressure. The government was also trying, contrary to earlier agreements, to send army chaplains into the hospitals. At Wyszyński's request, the Church's representatives protested against anti-Catholic slanders in the press. The controllers of the press, having led the October upheavals, now seemed anxious to re-establish their Marxist orthodoxy by baiting the Church.

In a surprise meeting early in January, Bolesław Piasecki—an opponent of the October changes—met with Gomułka and managed to preserve Pax. As a counterweight, the authorities were backing the Frankowski group, publishers of *Hejnał Mariacki* (Marian Bugle-Call) for Polonia* and, just starting up, *Za i Przeciw* (For and Against). In the meantime, church publishers were being allotted no more paper than they had before

---

*"Polonia" is a popular term used to identify communities of Poles and persons of Polish ancestry living abroad, e.g. American Polonia, Canadian Polonia, New York Polonia, etc.

October of the previous year. Jerzy Zawieyski brought Cardinal Wyszyński two requests from Bieńkowski on January 12, asking the Primate to meet with now Premier Cyrankiewicz. Zawieyski overcame Wyszyński's reservations, based on memories of Cyrankiewicz's Stalinist activities, by calling the meeting vital to social peace. At the meeting, which took place in the Council of Ministers' building two days later, Cyrankiewicz made awkward explanations of his earlier role but chiefly emphasized the threat to the party from conservatives who were linked to . . . He left the statement suggestively unfinished. Cyrankiewicz lamented the spread of anti-Semitism. Cardinal Wyszyński replied that the phenomenon was inherent in the party and related to its power struggle; he pointed out the damage being done to Poland's reputation abroad by anti-Semitic statements in the press. Mostly, however, Cyrankiewicz wanted the Episcopate to encourage people to vote in the upcoming elections. The party feared that the Stalinists would try to cross the names of the leading candidates off the ballot. Without refusing to help, the Primate insisted on a definitive renunciation of the February 1953 decree and upon the return of Bishop Kaczmarek to his diocese. The premier said that statutes overturning the 1953 decree were at the printers at that very moment and that the other matters would be taken care of.

The government was running scared. While negotiating with the Church, it also permitted public accusations that, for instance, religious children were intolerant of their atheist schoolmates. Such charges indicated strong opposition within the party to the return of religious instruction. Wyszyński agreed to a pre-election* request to schedule their January 20 services so that the faithful would have time for their civic obligations; at the same time, he criticized the authorities for not keeping their promises about the religious press and publishing.

Just before the elections, Father Lemparty, the president of

---

*That is, the election of members to the Polish Sejm (Parliament).

Caritas, and others were sent to the Primate with a proposal to return the charitable organization to the Church. But an unknown hand blocked the move to correct an old wrong.

Cardinal Wyszyński voted on January 20, but by agreement with the Electoral Commission, he appeared at a different polling place from the one where foreign reporters were expecting him. Most people, aware of the threat from the Stalinists, did not cross out the leading candidates who were representatives of the October ideals.

The rehabilitated Bishop Kaczmarek had still not been allowed back into Kielce when, at a meeting of the Joint Commission on March 21, the government made the astounding suggestion that the Episcopate issue a statement on Kaczmarek's activities in 1945–48.* The bishops refused so decisively that the prosecutor allowed Kaczmarek back into his old diocese on April 4. On the other hand, there was no action on the suggestion that Caritas might be returned. On April 5, Jerzy Hagmayer of Pax proposed to Wyszyński that the charitable organization be split; he received a blistering answer to the effect that Caritas belonged to the Church and the Church alone. On the same day, the writer Zofia Kossak Szczucka (Szatkowska) came to call, having just returned from emigration. She showed clear allegiance to Pax, her publisher in Poland. The next day the Primate asked Jerzy Zawieyski, now representing Znak in the Sejm and the Council of State, to intercede with Minister Bieńkowski on the issue of releasing gifts from abroad, mainly intended for repatriates [from the Soviet Union], from customs. The people, said Wyszyński, were visibly poor—and he added that unless Caritas were restored by the time of his planned visit to Rome, there would be nowhere to send the needed Western aid; such a state of affairs would make the authorities look bad. Zawieyski replied

---

*Bishop Kaczmarek had been imprisoned for "maintaining contact with the underground" (i.e., with the still-active anticommunist partisans) during this period. Kaczmarek had earned the eternal enmity of the Polish party by preaching against communism during the Nazi occupation; as long as he remained there, Kielce was the site of the most virulent church-state struggles.

that the Primate ought to help the government to get the Wawel tapestries* back from Canada; Wyszyński parried by saying that first the authorities should return the treasures of Gniezno Cathedral and other church valuables that had been stolen by the Nazis, then confiscated by the government at the end of the war. After domestic matters were settled, the Cardinal said, he would worry about international ones.

On April 11, the Primate read to the Council of Bishops a letter from Monsignor Del'Acqua, through which Pope Pius expressed his joy at the freeing of the bishops and went on to admonish them to keep fighting until they had obtained all the Church's rights—a noble call, but worlds away from Polish realities! The Primate welcomed Bishop Kaczmarek to his first meeting of the Episcopate in six years. As far as relations with the state permitted, Wyszyński wanted to shift the bishops' attention from political to religious problems. Realizing the Jasna Góra vows were the key, the bishops voted to send a copy of the icon of the Virgin on a tour of all the dioceses.

It was difficult to stick to pastoral matters when, at a Joint Commission meeting the next day, Minister Jerzy Sztachelski, new head of the Bureau of Religious Affairs, spoke of a "religious war" in the countryside. People were fighting to erect churches despite official foot-dragging over the construction permits. Party in-fighting continued to resonate in administrative relations with the Church.

At the government's request and as a preliminary to his trip to Rome, Cardinal Wyszyński held a meeting with Gomułka and Cyrankiewicz on May 1 that lasted until half past midnight. After a general discussion of mutual relations, Gomułka, sensing the tension that was still rampant in the country, proposed an outright concordat. "It turned out that we are going to have to live with one another for a long, long time yet," Gomułka said, "so we might as well have our relations defined perma-

---

*Priceless wall tapestries from the 17th century, executed in Belgium and depicting biblical subjects, which had hung in the Wawel Castle in Krakow. After the beginning of the war in 1939 they were secretly transported by the then Polish government to Canada for safekeeping.

nently. Of course, Poland is People's Poland, and that is the Poland that would conclude the concordat."

The Primate decided to discuss the offer at the Vatican. Obviously, the government wanted an official communiqué on the idea, but Wyszyński was afraid that a public step could harm later efforts. The party had, as usual, acted on the spur of the moment.

Before leaving for Rome, Wyszyński began the second stage of the pastoral program he had laid out in Komańcza. The Jasna Góra vows had been repeated around the country the previous August. Now, on May 5 (the first Sunday after May 3, Feast of Mary, Queen of Poland), the vows were taken again. The third step would be to "work, until 1966, at realizing the promises, in preparation for the Millennium." In other words: a Great Thousand Years' Novena.

On May 5, Cardinal Wyszyński himself led the vows at a pontifical High Mass in Warsaw. Reports came in from all over the country that the faithful had repeated the vows in their parishes, in an atmosphere of special exultation. Those who said—then and later—that Poles went to church as a political protest did not realize the inspirational power of the Primate's program. In every parish, believers personally promised Mary to live in grace, raise their children religiously, and keep their faith in God and the Church. Simple, accessible, at once personal and communal—embracing the whole country—these vows made a great moral and religious impact. Despite the disorganization of life and work—that fostered moral desolation—and certainly did not make it easy to keep the vows—the very act of promising was a lightning flash of brightness and optimism in a society ground down by recent terror and present poverty. It is impossible to understand Poland's packed churches and strong Catholicism over the last quarter-century without understanding the religious meaning of the Jasna Góra vows.

In preparation for his trip, Cardinal Wyszyński received from the Prior of Jasna Góra a copy of the Virgin's face from the icon, to present to the Pope, and a copy of the whole icon which would be brought back and exhibited around Poland after being blessed by the Holy Father.

Accompanied by Bishops Choromański, Klepacz, and Baraniak and by Monsignor Padacz, Cardinal Wyszyński set out at 9:15 A.M. on May 6. There was such a crowd at the Warsaw railroad station that he feared an accident, but the journey turned into a triumphal procession. Another crowd waited at Warsaw West, and at the Ursus stop the whole factory, including its band, had turned out with flowers in hand. The train stopped for a moment and then moved on as the workers cheered, women cried, and children stretched out their hands. There were similar demonstrations in Żyrardów, Skierniewice, and Koluszki. Bishop Goliński and the Pauline prior were standing on the platform at Częstochowa, along with an assembly of the faithful. The Primate joined a group of women in reciting the Rosary aloud.

Archbishop König, who was waiting with his car at Hochenau on the Austrian border, acted as gracious host for a day in Vienna. On the morning of May 8, the parish priest of Tarvisio welcomed Cardinal Wyszyński to Italy, and the archbishop and municipal officials of Udino welcomed him there. At the Venice station, Wyszyński had coffee with Patriarch Giovanni Roncalli, the future John XXIII, and some state officials. Local bishops greeted him as his train rolled through Padua, Rovigo, Ferrara, Bologna, Florence, and Arezzo. At Rome, the Primate did not think he would emerge from the tumult of Termini Station. Polish Ambassador Jan Druto, representatives of the Vatican Secretariat of State, and Father Walerian Meysztowicz of the government-in-exile's delegation to the Vatican received him there. On May 9 he began meetings at the Curia, with countless members of Polonia, and with Monsignor Samore from the Secretariat of State. Wyszyński presented the agreement on filling church posts which had been concluded the previous December as a lesser evil than the 1953 decree. They also discussed general church matters and the actions of the Polish Episcopate during Wyszyński's imprisonment.

On May 14 Cardinal Wyszyński—first alone and then with the bishops who had accompanied him—was received by Pope Pius XII. After a forty-five minute session alone with the tired, wan pontiff, Wyszyński called in his bishops; now he stood before the Pope with Bishop Baraniak, who had suffered the sharpest torments of Stalinist imprisonment, and Bishops Choromański and Klepacz, who had run the Polish Church in the absence of its leader. The scene moved almost everyone to tears. The Holy Father was warm and kind; besides, the visit was a symbol of the way Cardinal Wyszyński stood by not only those who had shared his imprisonment, but also those who had been forced into a compromise in the meantime. His stand demonstrated political wisdom as well as magnanimity.

On May 18, Stefan Wyszyński received the Cardinal's dignities that he had been unable to don in 1952. The Holy Father bestowed the biretta, hat, ring, and a title connected with the Church of Santa Maria in Trastevere. Then he kissed the Cardinal on both cheeks.

The meetings at the Vatican showed that the Holy See was well informed about the difficulties being caused by Piasecki, Pax, and priests like Lagosz, Piskorz, Lemparty, Radosz, Keller, Huet, and others. Had such characters known their reputation in Rome, they would have regretted their efforts to gain power in the Church with the aid of the *brachium saeculare* (secular power). Without Wyszyński's softening influence, there might have been at least two canonical trials—the Primate feared that such moves would only increase tensions in the country. On the other hand, he secured all his intended nominations, including that of Bishop Antoni Baraniak as Metropolitan of Poznań.

On May 26, at the beatification of the Blessed Eugenia Smet, Cardinal Wyszyński made his first public appearance in the company of other cardinals. They showed great affection, and the congregation cheered and chanted his name. When he saw the Pope again, Wyszyński told him, "Holy Father, I have come to know the feeling of freedom. What I experienced in the basilica makes me understand what a great grace is freedom."

On June 1, Cardinal Wyszyński discussed Gomułka's suggestion of a concordat with Monsignors Samore and Poggi. On the 13th there was a long talk with the Pope, frank, wideranging, difficult, but full of warmth. Communism looks far different from the inside and from the outside; Pius XII averred that he would like Wyszyński, whom he regarded as proved by suffering, to serve as his eyes and ears in Warsaw. The Primate urged, in turn, that the Vatican's animosity toward communism not fall upon the nation that had remained Catholic. The two men also discussed the concordat, the status of Poland in the *Annuario Pontificio,** and the fact that the Secretariat of State still regarded the bishops in the Western Lands as vicars general of Wyszyński. It was too early to expect changes. Cardinal Wyszyński also reported on preparations for the Millennium. After this unusually businesslike half-hour discussion, the Pope spoke to the Polish bishops— haltingly, for he had been deeply moved during his talk with the Primate. Before leaving, the Pope told Wyszyński, "I am moved, because it is indeed difficult, as you said, to think that anyone would regard Poland as a communist country. We know that Poland is a Catholic country. That touched me deeply. I could not speak. Pardon me."

Visits, farewells, correspondence, and instructions to Polish priests abroad filled the next days. On June 17, 1957, Cardinal Wyszyński started back toward Warsaw and that world that is so difficult to appraise from the outside. He carried with him Pope Pius's trust, as well as the copy of the Black Madonna that the pontiff had blessed and that would soon begin its travels around Poland.

The return trip was another triumph, with church dignitaries waiting at nearly every stop. The warmest greeting came from Patriarch Roncalli, who took Wyszyński for a gondola

---

*An official Vatican publication which annually publishes information about the Roman Catholic Church in the whole world, including official lists of countries, dioceses, cardinals, bishops, congregations, etc.

ride and told him that the two cardinals were brothers. A warm friendship bound them.

It is hard to judge the results of the journey, but perhaps the greatest was this: to the many Westerners fascinated by the "iron curtain," the Primate remarked that the iron curtain runs not through a part of the world, but through the hearts of individual people. In Italy and France, he told them, there were millions of communists—and in Poland perhaps a few hundred thousand.

During the Corpus Christi celebration on June 20, Cardinal Wyszyński placed the copy of the Madonna in Saint Anne's Church in Warsaw and announced its coming peregrination. On June 26 the Joint Commission discussed the creation of new parishes, the registration of religious, church insurance, and the return of Caritas and the cathedral treasures. The government representatives hinted that they were under heavy pressure from the party apparatus on religious matters. By the next meeting, on July 1, there had still been no progress on Caritas. Kliszko, unable to understand that they were talking about an international organization that could not be split into church and state components, remarked that the bishops were rejecting a compromise. Minister Sztachelski seemed most interested in how the Vatican would treat Poland in the *Annuario Pontificio*. The government side had grown more polemical. Kliszko said that the Church was developing combative tendencies and looking to go on the offensive. Yet the "offensive" was strictly religious, and the government had neither moderated its laicizing campaign nor backed down from the unacceptable idea of an ideologically Marxist state. As he carried out the religious program he had developed in Komańcza, Wyszyński was always looking for a compromise.

The Great Millennial Novena had begun with the recitation of the Jasna Góra vows in May. On August 26, as the Primate again led the vows, the copy of the Black Madonna began its peregrination from Częstochowa. There were approximately a million people there, nearly as many as the year before. After evening services, the Primate preached for an hour on the theme of the first year of the novena: "Fidelity to God, the cross, the Gospel, the Church, and its pastors."

In Gniezno on April 23, the Primate had described the Great Novena as intended "to create a living monument, more lasting than bronze—our Christian life. . . . We are plucking and peeling the mask from the face of our beloved mother temple, the Primate's basilica, to reach her original and unextinguished spirit . . . which will be a flaming banner for you." He told the faithful that the cathedral should be returned to its Gothic form

> so that you can have a Gothic look, like this church, so that you can act with a strengthened will and an open heart. We are soaking off the skin and washing away the old acid so that we can become a new leaven.
>
> That is the meaning of renewing this church, which is an element—perhaps not the most important, but a significant one—in preparing the city, the diocese, and Poland for its Millennium of Christianity. It is a symbol. But it is also a torch! A real, flaming torch! . . . The nation must strengthen itself to support the additions that the new centuries will build onto an excellent Christian culture. . . .
>
> And therefore I have lighted this torch for you!

That torch of faith had to be lighted in an ideologically materialist state; this is perhaps the simplest, but also the most truthful, interpretation of the Primate's program.

For this very reason the first year of the Great Novena was dedicated to faithfulness. Since the Millennium would also mark the state's thousandth anniversary, it could have been an occasion for state and Church to draw together; it turned out to be the opposite.

The Episcopal session of September 16–17, 1957, noted that political stabilization within the party was being accompanied by the first signs of a return to the policy of atheization. The authorities were trying to draw people away from church with attractive Sunday activities and contesting the Church's part in distributing aid to the needy. Yet the majority of such aid from abroad was addressed to the Primate himself. Unable to rely on setting the "patriotic priests" back in motion, the authorities tried to derail the work of the parishes by stirring up local conflicts. The bishops also noted the rise of secular schools that did not offer religious instruction. All this might have been explained to some degree by pressure on Gomułka from the party apparatus. But Gomułka himself wanted to limit church influence, though, for the time being, the party was moving cautiously.

Among pastoral problems, the bishops had to reconcile themselves to the government's *fait accompli* in creating an Academy of Catholic Theology in Warsaw from the disbanded Warsaw and Cracow university theology departments. They also discussed academic chaplaincies, the program for the second year of the Great Novena, charity, and the pastoral care of priests and women.

The general situation became more worrisome. At a Joint Commission meeting in late September, Kliszko and Sztachelski again accused the Church of having hatched its pastoral "offensive" during the bishops' visit to Rome, though it was actually conceived much earlier. The government regarded the Millennium program as meddling in social matters. From this moment, the authorities began personal attacks on bishops, and especially on the Primate. The return of previously confiscated church institutions did not take place. Nor did a delegation from Częstochowa win approval to reactivate the weekly *Niedziela* (Sunday) when it appealed at the Central Committee building on October 5.

At the beginning of the new academic year, the Primate celebrated Mass and preached to a large congregation at Saint Anne's in Warsaw, despite the student demonstrations going on in town against the closing of the democratic-leftist party journal *Po Prostu* (Forthrightly). Characteristically, the leadership—wanting as usual to borrow his authority—proposed a meeting with the Primate at exactly this moment. He put them off, citing unsettled church business. Not until October 18 did representatives of the new Znak lay movement inform the Primate that there had been a split in *For and Against*, the magazine that had broken away from Pax. On September 28 Jan Frankowski had dismissed the whole editorial staff and obtained the sole right to publish it. Before the broken the Znak group had not realized that Frankowski wanted to edge back to the old Pax game of pressuring the Church. When they found out that he had such intentions, they told him that they wanted to publish a Catholic magazine, but not a religious one —they did not want to meddle in church politics. For their efforts, they were accused of erecting an opposition front that ran all the way from the Primate to the communists in *Po Prostu*. Among those who left *Za i Przeciw*, Konstanty Łubieński, Anna Morawska, and Andrzej Micewski maintained contact with the Catholic world and later with Znak. Former Christian Democrats and W. J. Grabski of Pax had represented Znak to the Primate in an unfavorable light, as had some obvious informers. The Primate stuck to his custom of keeping a distance from politicians and their views, especially since those views usually reflected their own interests more than anything else. This distance was in evidence when the Cardinal sent only Father Roman Mieliński of Poznań to represent Poland at a Catholic press congress in Vienna. Later, he would learn how much the *Tygodnik Powszechny* group had been hurt by their exclusion.

The situation in the country was fluid, but the "iron fists," hostile to the Church, seemed to be gaining the upper hand in the government. Gomułka's own position remained a riddle, but the liquidation of *Po Prostu* and expulsion from the party of its editor, Eligiusz Lasota, were expressive.

An impasse in repatriating Poles from the Soviet Union was another bad sign; the Church had been helping repatriates as much as it could. In mid-November the authorities revoked permission for foreign gifts addressed care of the Primate to enter Poland duty free. At the same time the government joined the offensive by organizing an atheist movement under the name, the Association of Atheists and Freethinkers. It was, like all such party performances, a façade for attacks on the Church.

At a meeting on November 19–20, the Episcopate decided that, although it should not shy away from previously proposed meetings with the government, neither should it take the initiative. The bishops also discussed new, fictional Catholic publishing houses like *Augustinum*, set up to avoid the Vatican ban on priests' publishing with Pax. Fears of new attacks on the Church were so strong that the bishops discussed ways they could prevent the obligatory *ad limina** visits to Rome from creating the false impression abroad that the Church in Poland was free. Pressures on the Polish party from the Eastern bloc seemed to explain a lot.

The atheist movement was running secular schools and making use of intellectuals, such as Professor Tadeusz Kotarbiński, who opposed "fideism." Worst of all, the party press was trying to advance laicization by promoting a spirit of indifferentism. Although this tactic showed despair over Marxism's chances with the public, it could lead to the worst moral consequences. More feverish atheism lay behind the promotion of the Society of the Friends of Children (which organized schools without religious studies) to the status of a public welfare agency and the opening of a Center for Religious Studies within the Polish Academy of Sciences. Despite all of this, the bishops discerned the fruits of the Great Novena in growing popular piety.

During 1957, the Polish radio refused to broadcast the Primate's appeal for harvest prayers or to transmit religious programs for those not well enough to go to church. Thus, when

---

*Literally: to the threshold of the Apostles. A term used to designate the old tradition of regular visits to the Holy City and the tombs of SS. Peter and Paul expected of bishops, on the occasion of which a visit to the Supreme Pontiff would afford an opportunity to render a report on the state of the bishop's diocese. The rule now requires a visit every five years.

the radio asked him to record a Christmas message (to give the impression that the situation was the same as the previous year), his answer was negative.

The year's last meeting of the Joint Commission, on December 27, 1957, was a polemical session. The government complained about the ideological drift of sermons, especially the Primate's. Invoking political and even international considerations, the authorities denied reneging on promises made to the Church. The government complained about the clergy's attitude toward the authorities, and the bishops in turn complained about official attitudes toward the clergy and about the atheist press, especially *Argumenty* (Arguments). Zenon Kliszko revealed all the official anxieties by accusing Wyszyński of "messianic tendencies" and attacking the Millennium program. The year thus ended under distinct pressure, although relative courtesy was maintained. For Cardinal Wyszyński it had been above all a year of intensive work. He had spoken publicly 676 times, traveled widely (especially in the Western Lands), greeted numerous pilgrimages to Częstochowa by academics, doctors, and lawyers, and begun the peregrination of the copy of the Black Madonna that was a part of the Great Novena. The Church had not only stood firm— it had moved ahead, and into people's hearts. The Primate had personally confirmed thousands of children and met, talked with, and blessed millions of believers. This direct contact was far from insignificant among the mainsprings of religiosity, for an aura of steadfastness—and of triumph over imprisonment— surrounded the Cardinal. Thanks to him, the Episcopate was morally unified.

Despite strictures, the year had ended with undeniable success. The clergy did encounter difficulties in filling positions and creating new parishes. After the "Polish October," the pre-October harassment had returned, with particular fierceness in the publishing area. But the Primate had used the breathing space of October to erect the Millennium program and establish permanent, direct contact with the people, evoking a great increase in religiosity. The government could not turn back the clock, and the echoes of October would reverberate for twenty years.

Recognizing the Primate's stature, the authorities sought contact with him. After much beseeching, he met Gomułka and Premier Cyrankiewicz at the Council of Ministers building on January 11, 1958. This conference ran nearly eleven hours, breaking all previous records, from 5:00 P.M. until 3:45 the next morning. Although it abounded in polemics from both sides, the marathon had a happy ending, when Gomułka seized on Wyszyński's final suggestion that, despite all the skirmishing, they start afresh next time. The Cardinal regarded Gomułka as a man devoted to his ideas, a stubborn enemy of religion even though he took the Church's influence into political account. The first secretary attacked the Millennium program, among other things, but without the rabidity that would emerge in later years.

We have an account of this meeting in the still-unpublished diary of Jerzy Zawieyski, who, as a member of the Council of State, was in a position to hear both sides' accounts. Zawieyski writes that when Gomułka (as usual) began shouting, the Primate asked him to lower his voice and calmed him down. More amusing was the reprimand that Wyszyński administered to Cyrankiewicz. When the premier tried to make an accusation, the Primate turned on him with more or less the following words, according to Zawieyski:

> I did not come here as an accused person or to accuse anyone of anything. I came here to present facts. I do have an unsettled account with you, sir [referring to Cyrankiewicz's Stalinist role and involvement in the Primate's arrest]. The fact that I haven't brought up personal grievances does not mean that I've forgotten them. If you want to return to accusations, I will first of all accuse you and Mr. Ochab and demand a public rehabilitation, which will disgrace you in the eyes of Poland and the world.

Cyrankiewicz had no choice but to sit quietly and take it.

Zawieyski's account indicates that Gomułka was most disturbed by the hanging of crucifixes on schoolroom walls. "They irritate the nonbelieving young people," he shouted. Wyszyński replied that since at most 10 percent of the children were atheistic, and at least 80 percent were Catholic, he would defend the crucifixes in the schools. As usual, Wyszyński took the occasion to deliver a lecture on Catholic social teaching and the nonessential nature of the link between socialism and atheism, which they listened to patiently. Zawieyski lists the main points of discussion as: (1) the campaign against religion in the schools; (2) discrimination against Catholics in the bureaucracy; (3) the new version of the decree on filling church offices; (4) difficulties in creating new parishes; (5) the establishment of state schools without religious instruction; (6) the lack of Catholic youth associations; (7) the limitations on religious publishing; (8) the abuse of censorship; (9) the absence of the Church from Polish radio; (10) charity and the imposition of customs duty on aid sent to the Primate from abroad; (11) the unreturned church treasures; and (12) travel abroad for clergy on foreign scholarships.

The list speaks for itself. Wyszyński received promises that American gifts would be released from customs and some Catholic journals and publishing houses would be allowed to operate. On the other hand, his Millennium program and public appearances came under attack. At the end, Gomułka asked about the previous offer of a concordat. Wyszyński gave an account of his discussions of the matter at the Vatican, remarking that his efforts had not been aided by the refusal to return Caritas, the censorship of his speeches, or the repetition in the Polish press of Western reports that he had been received coldly at Rome. Gomułka appreciated the account and, despite the antireligious slant of his leadership, the meeting ended civilly. This eleven-hour debate testified to the excellent mental and physical condition of both sides!

The meeting had concrete, although limited, results. The

gifts from abroad cleared customs duty-free, church valuables were returned, and priests began receiving permission to study abroad. On February 2 the press reported changes in the *Annuario Pontificio*, which at last stated that "Breslavia" (Wrocław) is "in Polonia" (in Poland)—a result of the Primate's Vatican discussions.

The February 12–13 meeting of the Episcopate dealt mainly with pastoral matters, including the organization of the second year of the Great Novena on the theme "Living in a State of Sanctifying Grace."

On March 2 the Primate held a long discussion with Zawieyski, Turowicz, Gołubiew, Stomma, and Woźniakowski of Znak. Wyszyński had a difference of opinion with Zawieyski's article "The Road of the Catechumen" in *Znak* and with the socialist accent in *Więź*. In the absence of other Catholic magazines—the Primate had been unable to win approval for reviving *Jasna Góra*—he felt that *Znak* should reflect the general attitude of the Church rather than a one-sided view of Catholicism.

These ideological nuances on the church side would not have been so important had not the party shifted to a harder line. At a March 4 meeting of the Joint Commission, the authorities not only refused to return Caritas but also denied the Church permission to distribute the gifts it had received from abroad in the Primate's name. Instead, the authorities wanted to create a distribution commission on which the Church would have only a representative. Kliszko called the Primate's high reputation in the West "an attempt to peel Poland away from the socialist camp." The government preferred buying foodstuffs on credit to receiving them free from the Church—another ideological error, and the result of general Eastern-bloc policies.

During 1958, Cardinal Wyszyński felt several times that he might be arrested again. Nevertheless, he went calmly about his work, as he had in 1953. Arrest was not, it turned out, in the cards: Gomułka could not allow himself such a step because of the international reverberations. For the moment the two alternatives—coexistence or nuclear catastrophe—opened a new historical epoch. The Church simply had to defend itself, regardless of world fluctuations.

At its next meeting, on April 11–12, the Episcopate decided to fight for the existence of the Cracow and Warsaw theology departments. The bishops also worked on a pastoral program for the professions and the schedule for the peregrination of the copy of the Jasna Góra icon.

Three days later the government refused the Church's request that a seminary be built on the grounds of the Marian Fathers' house in Bielany, outside Warsaw, where the authorities had located the Academy of Catholic Theology. For all intents and purposes, the government stopped issuing permits to build churches. Wyszyński did what he could. On April 20 he welcomed a nurses' pilgrimage to Częstochowa; there were eleven thousand pilgrims despite administrative pressures.

At a May 3 meeting of Catholic editors in Jasna Góra, the Cardinal appealed to all of them to join the Great Novena program. Polish writers met there the next day, and the Primate told them, "Each word must be born of the Immaculate. That is a personal obligation for all who are called to the service of the word." He went on:

We have witnessed the service of words to falsehood. Thus we have gained respect for the objective value of the word. Today we all hunger for and seek a harmony, an absence of discord between the inner life and the spoken word. Perhaps it is the good fortune of contemporary man to understand that the false word will not save him. The word must be truly eternal. It must be born in an unblemished nursery, in an internal, spiritual cleanliness, if it is to be able to persuade, to conquer, to conciliate, to nourish.

Later that day he said, "In the present, unusually difficult situation of our country, we must be a buttress and a strength, a light and a comfort, a support and a help to all who are suffering, afflicted, and vacillating. This is a difficult demand," he told the writers, "but what an important one! We do not yet know what proofs and evidences of love God will demand from us in the harsh situation in which the nation lives and struggles on!"

Continuing its harassment, the government announced on May 10 a 1.5-million-złoty customs fee on the gifts from abroad. At the same time it created a distribution committee including Jan Frankowski and his aide Kazimierz Dziembowski—the confiscation of Caritas all over again.

On June 3, Zofia Kossak Szczucka, who had fallen under the influence of the writer Jan Dobraczyński and Pax, tried to convince the Primate to create a "Millennial library" within that organization, in which she would take part along with Grabski, Dobraczyński, and Skierski. The answer was a categorical no, but the initiative itself had been significant. Seeing Znak's restraint in following Wyszyński's program, Pax wanted to insinuate itself into the Millennium.

Wyszyński preached about the Church's needs, calmly but decisively, to the June 5 Corpus Christi procession in Warsaw. "The freedom to build churches has always been an important part of true religious freedom," he said, and yet in Warsaw alone there were twelve parishes without churches. At least another twenty-five new parishes were needed in the expanding city. On June 18, the Episcopate decided to send Premier Cyrankiewicz a letter outlining the Church's main difficulties. The letter came back on July 15—twenty-four hours after Cyrankiewicz had received it—along with a letter from the premier that accused the bishops of trying to create a religious state within the Polish state. A confrontation was clearly approaching. *Życie Warszawy* and other papers were attacking the Church in language that recalled Stalin's day.

Nevertheless, pastoral work went on. The end of June saw a conference on the role of the Primatial Institute for the Implementation of the National Vows in ministering to the professions. On July 3, five thousand teachers took part in a pilgrimage to Częstochowa despite official discouragement. Next the party tried to get to the Primate by sending "engaged" Catholics to plead for a moderation of the "Catholic activism" of the Millennium. On July 3, Sejm delegates Zawieyski and Stomma begged Wyszyński "to rescue Gomułka." But Wyszyński remembered how Piasecki had tried to restrain him in the Stalinist era by sketching the bleakest possible scenarios. The Znak leaders had different motivations, they could not persuade Wyszyński to change his program, either. Zawieyski passed on an explanation from Minister Bieńkowski in which the latter said he had espoused "indifferentism" only to prevent the application of administrative pressure against the Church. But the Church would rather contend with such pressure than submit to the demoralization of society through indifferentism.

July was the crucial point in the confrontation. The Gomułka leadership showed its true face—not only its own traits, but also its excessive tendency to give in to outside pressure. The Primatial Institute at Jasna Góra was raided on the 21st, the doors kicked in and a great quantity of papers seized. Three days later the Primate delivered a sharp protest to the prosecutor general, reminding him that Church texts could be reproduced in his Institute without the censor's permission. The prosecutor's own communiqué, issued at the end of the month, diverged from the truth and set up false charges. Absurdly, it cited a *prewar* prayer book that contained prayers in connection with the Miracle of the Vistula, the 1920 Polish victory over the Russian Army. Still this raid marked a turning point.

The tense month of July also contained some bright spots. Understanding Cardinal Wyszyński's desire to have a full roster of bishops in case of state interference in personnel matters, Monsignor Filipiak came from Rome on July 24 with nominations for new auxiliary bishops, including Karol Wojtyła and Jerzy Stroba.

The Joint Commission held a stormy meeting on the last day of the month, with Kliszko and Sztachelski demanding that religious instruction be given only after the conclusion of other school lessons, for no more than one hour a week, and without the participation of male religious. In effect, the authorities were breaking the "little understanding" of December 1956, as well as preparing for the complete elimination of religious instruction.

Kliszko next turned to an attack on the Millennium program calling it "the Hispanicization of Poland."* The raid on the Primatial Institute, Radio Free Europe (once again a hot topic), and the "patriotic priests" all came up. Kliszko uttered a clear threat that church activities must be limited. "If we don't do it," he said, "someone else will."

"What does that mean?" Bishop Choromański asked. "Who?"

"I don't know," Kliszko answered. But whether it had been an idle threat or a suggestion of foreign intervention, the bishops had to stand firm on religious education; thus "the war of the schools" was declared. The government mistakenly saw the hand of the Vatican in the Millennium program, still believing that the Primate had set his course after returning from Rome. They did not yet know that his idea of the Great Thousand Years' Novena had been born in prison. On other issues, it was established that the Church could reproduce only administrative materials without censorship. The documents confiscated from the Primatial Institute would be returned, but henceforth they would be subject to censorship. Out of social considerations, the bishops agreed that the gifts sent to the Primate by Polish-Americans would be transferred to the Cracow Committee for the Relief of Flood Victims. On nothing else did they yield.

The Jasna Góra raid had so stirred up public opinion that the prosecutor general had to issue a special communiqué accusing the Primatial Institute of "distributing numerous publications throughout the country over a long period of time." The communiqué justified the raid on the grounds of "antistate

---

*The phrase "Hispanicization of Poland" expressed a fear on the part of Polish authorities that the Episcopate would create during the Polish Millennium Novena the same spirit of devotion to Mary as Spain did after the Fatima apparitions.

materials, directed against the present political system," although it gave no examples of such materials. One person was arrested and several others had cases opened against them for obstructing the prosecutor. The communiqué explained nothing.

Nevertheless, the party press began sounding the alarm about clericalism. In one issue, *Polityka* published an article titled "Religion or Politics?" and another, an outright attack on Jasna Góra as "The Factory of Delusions," over the significant-looking initials "W.G." Neither of these diatribes had much to say about what had happened at Jasna Góra. The first cited a fragment of a publication, considered offensive to the state, about the poor health of Polish youth (which was an obvious fact, a result of the generally recognized economic breakdown). The second article is worth citing as an example of what party liberals, or at least the Gomułka group, were publishing:

> The clergy are satisfied. Their efforts are bearing fruit. The crowds that come here are a manifestation of the Church's strength. It doesn't matter that the prayers of the faithful are not answered. The Factory of Delusions is piling up political capital. For whom? The answer can be found in the illegally printed brochures that the prosecutor's office confiscated.
>
> The clergy are satisfied. Its allies are ignorance, backwardness, hard times, and the eternal human pursuit of happiness. The dispensers of delusions do not want to answer for the fortunes of so afflicted a nation. It is not they who have taken responsibility for the difficulties of establishing social justice. Their road leads in other directions.

The appearance of more such aggressive articles led the Primate to the unusual step of ordering expiatory prayers. Shocked, the party tried to pressure Wyszyński to reverse his decision through a letter from one of the Catholic Sejm delegates. But the government did not limit itself to the press campaign. In the wake of the Jasna Góra raid came one of the most painful post-October decisions. The Ministry of Education issued a circular barring religious from teaching religion. Considering the limited number of priests available for catechization, the ban put a question mark over religious education in the schools.

The Primate's reaction was dignified and strong. On August 26, at Jasna Góra, with more than 300,000 of the faithful and a thousand priests, he read the vows for the third time and then said, "The Church is like a stone lying in a mountain brook. Sometimes it is washed by a little stream of water, and then again a flood rolls over it. Yet it lies peacefully, the water flows on, subsides, and the stone is still there. Our present predicament demands silence and prayer."

When the Episcopate debated the situation on September 5, it decided not to risk the escalation of tension that a public proclamation could bring on. Instead, special meetings would be held to inform the clergy about church-state relations. The steering committee decided that, instead of sending a memorandum to the government, it would use the secretary of the Episcopate and Minister Sztachelski as intermediaries in appealing to Cyrankiewicz. It was also at this meeting that the bishops learned that crucifixes were being removed from classroom walls throughout the country.

Although the Episcopate exercised restraint, First Secretary Gomułka treated a September 24 assembly of party activists to an emotional attack on the bishops for not supporting the communist state despite the ancient principle that "every power comes from God." Gomułka went on to the grotesque threat that "we will not allow a limited part of the church hierarchy, under the influence of Vatican circles hostile to People's Poland and intent upon goals that have nothing in common with the religious mission of the Church, to undermine the rule of law and the sociopolitical structure of our country."

The party remained amazingly misinformed about Vatican influence on the Episcopate's program: in fact, the Holy See had never sent any political instructions to the Polish bishops. But Gomułka's attempt to divide the bishops and clergy into "good and bad" was a classic tactic all during his reign. He wove a legend of the undermining of law and the system by the Episcopate in order to limit the Church exclusively to the sphere of worship, and to control even that domain through, for instance, the censorship of religious texts.

Gomułka's rage against the Vatican ended in an unexpected way when Pope Pius XII died on October 9, 1958. The new pontificate would give the communists a chance to withdraw from their anti-Vatican position and move toward coexistence. In Poland it would mean the hardening of prejudices and an intensification of the struggle with the Primate. Stefan Wyszyński felt the death of Pius XII keenly. His remarks and writings reveal gratitude to Pius for his trust and for leaving the management of the Polish Church to those who knew its problems from their own experience.

Wyszyński left for Rome on October 17, and along the way he was greeted with enthusiasm and affection almost as great as on his previous journey. The conclave opened on October 25 and, after eleven ballots, on October 28, elected Cardinal Wyszyński's friend the Patriarch of Venice, Cardinal Roncalli, as Pope John XXIII.

On November 4, the day of his inauguration, the new pope told the Primate, "Częstochowa, Częstochowa. Make sure that they say a lot of prayers for me before the Black Madonna."

Wyszyński's hectic stay lasted into December. During it, a rumor started, based on remarks by one of the Catholic Sejm delegates who had come to Rome, to the effect that the Holy See—or, specifically, Cardinal Tisserant—would regard "a program of quiet work" as preferable to Wyszyński's energetic Great Novena. Tisserant later detached himself entirely from any such statement, blaming the mistake on his interlocutor's poor French, but the affair must have been painful for Cardinal Wyszyński.

Compensation came in a November 14 audience in which

John XXIII expressed complete confidence in Wyszyński's tactics and stressed that he, the Pope, perfectly understood the Primate's difficult situation. Wyszyński brought up the matter of creating dioceses in the Western Lands, pointing out the absurdity of his being the ordinary of no fewer than six dioceses, four of them in the Western Lands. (Gomułka would repay with a fresh attack this effort to enhance Polish control.) At Wyszyński's next audience, on November 29, John approved his nominations of bishops, saying, "We don't want to give any instructions; we trust you and don't want to hinder you. From experience we know that the work is going very well." Next the Pope received Polish churchmen and spoke to them entirely in the spirit of the Primate's program. In reply, Wyszyński said of the "risky" program of the Millennium, "If the Polish Church suffers, it will be the Primate's fault and not the Holy Father's."

On December 29, Wyszyński was back in Warsaw, reporting to the steering committee on his trip to Rome. In the Episcopal session the next day, the bishops decided to begin trying to make their *ad limina* visits to Rome, but cautiously, so as not to create a false impression abroad that they enjoyed full freedom of movement. Even this decision was later exploited: the charge was made that Wyszyński did not let his bishops go to the Vatican. But the authors of such intrigues did not realize their futility in the face of Wyszyński's strong position at the Vatican. The new pope and the new spirit in the Holy See strengthened this position.

* * *

Nineteen fifty-eight had been critical for church-state relations. Less than two years after the hopeful October, the government had returned to an open struggle against the Church. The Primate reacted by intensifying his strictly pastoral activities.

The Primate was incessantly concerned that Polish dioceses be fully supplied with bishops "just in case." At the beginning of 1959, the Archdiocese of Warsaw obtained, on Wyszyński's suggestion, a third auxiliary in the person of Reverend Dr. Jerzy Modzelewski.

Efforts were under way to exploit Wyszyński's Millennium program for political purposes. One such initiative was the January 15 visit to the Primate by a trio of writers, Zofia Kossak Szczucka, W. J. Grabski, and Jan Dobraczyński, who published with Pax. They defended their organization by saying it included five thousand fervent Catholics, but the Primate preferred to discuss things on a factual basis. This trio, set up by Pax in Łódź, had obtained a license for the Augustinum publishing house while the Primate and the Church were denied permission to print their magazine, *Jasna Góra*. Pax was monopolizing Catholic publishing. The Primate informed his visitors that in October 1956 the government had offered Pax to the Church but that he had turned down the offer because he did not want to "steal what had already been stolen." Pax flourished, he said, on the wrongs done to other publishers and small-scale producers of devotional items. The Primate also had to remind them about Pax's role in the government's blocking of gifts from abroad, and about Pax's occupation of the Inco factory in Bielany, which in fact belonged to the archdiocese. Piasecki's emissaries went away empty-handed.

Although the Church could not dispose of the foreign gifts, the Primate transferred them to the Ministry of Labor and Welfare on condition that church paraphernalia be returned to the Primate's office. The ministry responded by confiscating copies of the New Testament found among parcels from the Vatican. Still the Primate retained his good will. At the end of January he received Professor Marian Zdziechowski and later gave him a letter for Cardinal Leger of Montreal about returning the Wawel tapestries to Poland.

In March 1959, first Gomułka and then Cyrankiewicz used the Third Party Congress as a forum for sharp attacks on the Church. This seemed strange, since it was precisely at that congress that Gomułka clipped both of the party's proverbial wings and established his own complete control. An intransigent attitude toward the Church seemed to be part of the price for a unified leadership. There could be no doubt that the "October" mood had been left behind for good. Gomułka said:

> We warn the church hierarchy against violating the laws and regulations of the state, which they are again doing. We advise them that provoking the people's authority will do them no good, and that they ought to stop trying. (Applause.) Once again we say we don't want war with the Church. But the Church must be only a Church; it must limit itself to matters of faith and stay in the sanctuary.
>
> The Middle Ages were the time of the Church's superiority over the state. Now the Church must adapt to progress and give up the hopeless idea of a battle with socialism.

Cyrankiewicz repeated the theme:

> Why is it that the church hierarchy does not want to limit itself to matters of faith and, respecting the division of Church and state, give up the battle against socialism? . . . A part of the hierarchy . . . wants to maintain in as many people as possible . . . the feeling that our system is impermanent. . . . This attempt to create antisocialist feelings . . . is an attempt to weaken Poland as an element of the socialist camp.

In fact, the government wanted to limit the Church to matters of worship and lock it in the sacristy. It refused the Church any influence on morality, individual or social. The bishops were hardly thinking of breaking laws or of the "impermanence" of the system, but its own lack of popular support made the party nervous and accusatory. Indeed, the bishops were engaged in their proper functions—worship, moral, social, and educational—rather than political.

At its February 17–18 meeting, the Episcopate noted that the Gomułka regime was switching from a program of ideological and moral indifferentism to one of social laicization; the Bureau of Religious Affairs had stopped issuing construction permits and was treating the Church *per non est*. The bishops discussed pastoral matters and the need for a campaign against alcoholism. They also staked out the second year of the Great Novena under the theme "A Nation Faithful to Grace." Father Bronisław Dąbrowski noted that the government had backtracked on an earlier agreement about school retreats and was now limiting them to Holy Week.

The government was still trying to pressure Cardinal Wyszyński through Catholic Sejm delegates. At the beginning of March, Stomma and Zawieyski stopped by to repeat Kliszko's ridiculous charge that the Primate had brought an enormous sum in dollars from abroad. During the conversation they realized that they had been sent as a provocation, to intimidate the Cardinal. Could Kliszko, knowing the past, have thought he would succeed?

At its April meeting, the steering committee decided to send the government a letter protesting the irresponsible congress speeches of Gomułka, Cyrankiewicz, and Interior Minister Wicha. They considered Cyrankiewicz's the most offensive— the premier had been true to his Stalinist self. Besides hostile speeches, the government was making some illegal and troublesome political decisions. Thus the Primate learned on April 14 about the new tax assessments of church institutions. These were so draconian that within a few months all church property, seminary buildings, curias, bishops' residences, and rectories would have to be sold off to pay the bill. The government, feeling itself isolated from the people in comparison with the Church's moral influence over society, was losing touch and acting according to hate rather than political considerations.

Everyone in attendance at the April 14 Episcopal meeting signed a letter of protest against the attacks on the Church at the party congress. At the same meeting, a Vatican Council Committee was established under Bishop Baraniak.

In April, Znak sent the government a memorandum on the Church's situation. Gomułka told Zawieyski that it had been written by Wyszyński—who in fact had not seen the document until three days after it was sent. Despite his reservations, the memorandum changed Cardinal Wyszyński's view of Znak, showing him how greatly the new group differed from Pax. He was still worried that Znak would heed official calls for "quiet, peaceful work"—a program he rejected—but now he trusted the group.

On May 3, the Feast of Mary, Queen of Poland, the Jasna Góra vows were repeated around the country for the third time, and the third year of the Great Novena began under the slogan "In Defense of Spiritual and Physical Life." This "Year of Life" was particularly controversial in the eyes of the party, which advocated sexual freedom and liberalized abortion. The Church asked Mary with particular fervor to keep young people from becoming depraved and to protect the lives of the unborn from assault. In return, the press emphasized more and more forcefully the idea of life without God. An article about Russia in *Nowa Kultura*, by the former Pax Sejm delegate Dominik Horodyński, presenting Russia as a country "Without an Icon," was particularly painful to the Primate. At that moment the whole world was reading *Doctor Zhivago* and its beautiful hymn to the Virgin Mary. Pasternak knew his country's fate, and also knew that it did not want to live without an icon. Horodyński, who had been the only Sejm delegate to call for Cardinal Wyszyński's release in 1956, had now yielded entirely to ideological conventions. The impotence of some intellectuals against the system was becoming more apparent.

Besides exorbitant taxation, the authorities were using the weapon of drafting four straight seminary classes. The Bureau of Religious Affairs would not discuss the matter. In April the government also announced that church property in the Western Lands belonged to the state.

As a consolation, the students' pilgrimage to Częstochowa

was unusually successful, providing Cardinal Wyszyński with a chance to talk individually with many of the six thousand pilgrims. But the battle for the hearts of the young people continued everywhere. The authorities stocked towns hosting pilgrimages and church fairs with alcohol. But by winning them over to the truth, the Church managed to steer young people clear of the threat. May 12 saw special pastoral discussions and a conference of writers, addressed by Bishop Wojtyła, take place at Jasna Góra.

At the Corpus Christi procession in Warsaw on May 29, the Primate raised two points of contention: the sacrilegious razing of the Chapel of the Blessed Virgin on Grójecki Street, and the Primate's inability to address the large crowd effectively since the megaphones had been seized. Next Wyszyński was surprised to hear that his remarks had been broadcast on Western radio stations; he was sure that the government would accuse him of supplying the texts to the West. Tape recorders, however, existed even in Poland; reporters had used them. On Corpus Christi evening, Wyszyński received Gomułka's thirty-page reply to the Episcopate's last message which, as of old, shifted the blame to the bishops. The Primate saw that each of them received a copy, and they generally regarded it as a brutal letter. A few days later Bishop Choromański presented Wyszyński with a government demand that Bishop Kaczmarek be removed from Kielce. Apparently the government, always looking for new pressures to apply, did not know that only the Vatican can remove a bishop.

Before the June 16–17 Episcopal meeting, Bishop Klepacz had a lengthy discussion with Kliszko, who had written to request the talks. Kliszko took offense at the Episcopate's letter to the government and accused the bishops of wanting neither to acknowledge the good things that were happening in Poland nor to condemn the bad. Then Kliszko tried to explain Gomułka's lengthy epistle, apparently fearing that it would evoke a sharp response. Klepacz replied that the government tolerated only a narrow variant of religion, restricting it to matters of worship, and did not understand that the Church had been morally and socially active for two thousand years. This discussion confirmed that the government mistakenly believed the Vatican was dictating the actions of the Polish Church. Kliszko explained the appropriation of church property in the Western Lands simply: "It was German property." Real understanding could hardly come as long as the government demanded support for an "October" that had long been betrayed. A clearer point was the news that seminarians would not necessarily be drafted, although Kliszko would not say so unequivocally. On the recommendation of the steering committee, the Episcopate decided not to answer Gomułka's tough letter, hoping that the Kliszko-Klepacz meeting might have created a new chance for dialogue. The Episcopate decisively rejected the call to remove Bishop Kaczmarek as outside its competence and in the belief that the Holy See would never agree anyway. "If they impute wrongs to Bishop Kaczmarek, ours are no less," added the Primate in an expression of solidarity with the Ordinary of Kielce. Kliszko met with Klepacz again before the end of the Episcopal session and told him that if the bishops refrained from making a strong declaration, the government would be accommodating in the matter of taxes and the conscription of seminarians. The government kept getting itself entangled needlessly in extreme demands; when, time after time, the bishops refused to change their stance, the government kept having to back down—but the tense and unfriendly atmosphere remained. The party had no clear church-state policy.

On June 27, four thousand teachers made it to Częstochowa for a pilgrimage, in spite of official obstacles. Wyszyński remained at the shrine, leading priests' retreats. He was there on June 30 when sentences were announced in connection with the raid on the Primatial Institute. The last phase of the trial had been hushed up for political reasons, raising the question of why the whole affair had ever been launched. All the sentences were suspended.

The next Episcopal meeting, at Jasna Góra on September 4, discussed the laicizing offensive of the Association of Atheists and Freethinkers. The bishops saw a letter John XXIII had sent that greatly strengthened Bishop Kaczmarek's position. Finally, it was announced that the government had withdrawn the absurd February tax regulations and substituted new, milder ones.

While the Primate continued visits around the country, the government did not sit idly by. On October 20, as he was resting in Krynica, Wyszyński learned that the authorities, ever inventive, had decreed that seminaries fell under the provisions of a law on private schools—passed in 1932! On the same day Wyszyński learned that the police had tried to "kidnap" his aide, Father Goździewicz, on the street on the afternoon of the 17th. When the victim shouted for help, a crowd gathered; Goździewicz escaped in the confusion. The police had without doubt been intent on blackmailing such a close associate of the Primate. Priests in general were being harassed increasingly; in Katowice they were seeing their watches taken off their wrists to satisfy the tax collectors.

When the Episcopate met on November 17, it discussed the initiation of *ad limina* visits to Rome, the reactivation of the "patriotic priests," and Bishop Kaczmarek's endurance in Kielce despite the efforts to drive him out. Tactics that had been abandoned elsewhere were still being tried in Kielce, including the drafting of forty-two seminarians. Everywhere, and especially in the Western Lands, where the Church was so important to the national interest, tax assessments were still unrealistically high. The Episcopate spent a great deal of time discussing the fears of some lay circles that devotion to Mary was obscuring devotion to Christ. Such doubts also touched the Great Novena program, and Wyszyński accused the doubters of following foreign fashions and undervaluing the religiosity of their homeland. In view of the systematic expulsion of religious teaching from the schools, it was decided to set up catechetical centers, though still fighting to keep religion in the schools.

The three bishops who made a "trial" *ad limina* visit (Archbishop Baziak and Bishops Barda and Zakrzewski) underwent

unusually harsh and thorough customs searches on their return; they were the only three searched from their car on the
train. At the same time, Znak and other sources hinted at the
possibility of another high-level meeting. Wyszyński was in no
hurry. At the very end of the year the "patriotic priests" went
back into full operation, under the aegis of Caritas. Thus the
government concluded 1959 by sending out new feelers about
a session with Gomułka—while the most compromised Stalinist tactics were being revived. Cardinal Wyszyński felt that
it had been a particularly bad year for public morals, as reflected in the higher number of abortions, the increase in
drunkenness, depravation, and atheism among young people,
and sabotage at work—a form of social self-defense against an
irrational economy. A defective system was striking at the basis
of national morality.

On January 11, 1960, Wyszyński and Gomułka sat down for
a four-hour meeting. Instead of arguing with the irascible first
secretary, Wyszyński presented the Church's positive suggestions. He made Gomułka understand that no one wanted a
replay of the Hungarian tragedy, and that the Church was
receiving no political instructions from the Vatican. He particularly stressed this last point, which had caused so much misunderstanding and so many unjustified attacks by the party.
Next the Primate explained his view of party policy and reminded Gomułka about who had negotiated the Catholic
Church's first understanding with a communist government.
He also drew Gomułka's attention to the Church's role in
preserving social peace in October 1956. Finally, he asked that
the Joint Commission meet again to look for a way out of the
multiple conflicts. The Primate proposed that the subjects of
the application of the 1932 law to seminaries and the excessive
taxes be discussed. Wyszyński went on to speak of wider
demographic and political problems, including the issues associated with the abortion laws: the Cardinal maintained that
with the proper economic policies, Poland could sustain twice
as great a population as it had at the time.

In reply, Gomułka stressed Soviet power and the fact that

Poland's international position could not change. Although he said he appreciated what the Primate had done in 1956, he accused the Church of having stopped helping the authorities. Gomułka claimed that neither Stalin nor Khrushchev opposed Polish sovereignty, but that the latter was as intent as the former on preserving Eastern-bloc unity. His reasoning seemed to imply a difference between the official propaganda and his own private concerns about sovereignty.

By his own standards, at least, Gomułka remained calm. He insisted that Bishop Kaczmarek be sent on a vacation, and the Primate had to explain in elementary terms that the Holy See would never agree to the removal of a bishop who had been imprisoned and then rehabilitated. In turn, Gomułka complained about political overtones and allusions to China in Kaczmarek's sermons, and about the Church's having contact with and passing news to foreigners. Wyszyński patiently stated that if the country were run well, the Western press would be unable to print scandalous stories about Poland. Mainly, however, they talked about church help for the state. Wyszyński did not say the Church would not help but he pointed out, without specifying them, that the Church had suffered many wrongs. For instance, it was difficult to assist the fight against alcoholism when church temperance societies were banned and the censor confiscated church appeals. The two also disagreed on how much of a Catholic press Poland needed. Then Gomułka came right out and asked for help in the villages, and the Primate replied that such help would be possible if the government stated publicly that the farmers' circles would not lead to collectivization. These talks, which touched on many other subjects as well, concluded in a good atmosphere as Gomułka agreed that the Joint Commission should go back to work.

The Episcopate met on January 12 and 13. Archbishop Baziak and Bishops Barda and Zakrzewski reported on their *ad limina* visit to Rome, and it was decided that Bishops Kominek, Jop, and others would lead the next *ad limina* excursions. Discussions in the Vatican had shown the universal Church's great concern over the moral attitudes of youth, impaired in the West by prosperity and in Poland by poverty. Nor had the Holy See sent any instructions to the Polish Church. *Sub secreto*, Cardinal Wyszyński informed the other bishops about the meeting with Gomułka. Bishop Kaczmarek reported that his priests were being forbidden to read his pastoral letters and that there had been unsuccessful attempts to organize a plebiscite against him. The Episcopate's newest anxiety came from a letter that Minister Sztachelski had sent to Bishop Choromański, announcing state inspections of the seminaries. The bishops protested, decided to be on hand themselves if the visits took place, and informed members of the prospective control commission that the regulations of the Holy See for seminaries obtained. Things looked bleak, though it was too early to tell what would come of the Cardinal's discussion with Gomułka.

There was no visible easing of tension over the next weeks. The government still seemed determined to oust Bishop Kaczmarek, and the Episcopate firmly opposed an action that could set the most dangerous sort of precedent.

Furthermore, despite the Primate's warnings, the government went ahead and inspected seminaries on the basis of the 1932 law. In Warsaw, Wyszyński sent Bishop Modzelewski to attend the inspection of the Metropolitan Seminary, on February 12. Although Modzelewski told the inspectors that the "inspection of the Metropolitan Seminary is absolutely unprecedented in the history of the Church," the inspectors went so far into internal church matters as to ask the seminarians about their vocations and decisions to enter the religious life.

Cardinal Wyszyński presented the facts to the Znak group among the Sejm delegation, to keep it from being misled by the government. In this crisis Znak stood up—the Primate learned on February 20 that the group had boycotted a meeting of the National Front because Aleksander Zawadzki, chairman of the Council of State, had received a delegation of "patriotic priests." This new form of organized diversion within the Church would occupy much of the Primate's attention in the coming months and years.

As a result of the meeting with Gomułka, the Joint Commission reconvened on March 14. The government defended the activity of the "patriotic priests" as a *sine qua non* for good church-state relations. Instead of discussing Bishop Kaczmarek or the seminary issue, the parties discussed the situation in the Western Lands, where a sense of Polishness was fading in consequence of limitations on church activities.

Characterizing the state's "supervision" of seminaries and the status of religion in the schools as the most critical issues between Church and state, the Primate made them the subject of a March 25 letter to Gomułka. In his reply of April 19, the first secretary defended the government's right to inspect the seminaries. The impasse grew worse. Nothing had come of the Joint Commission meeting; there were plans for further tax increases and for the taking over of church houses; new administrative harassment was in the works. In Nowa Huta a riot broke out when the authorities removed a cross from the building site of the planned church, the construction of which had been promised in writing by Gomułka. This was the main subject of a tense Joint Commission session on May 10, but Kliszko acted boorishly toward the church representatives and nothing was settled. Cardinal Wyszyński had to soothe the bishops when they returned dejectedly from the meeting.

As always, pastoral work continued despite the problems. The young academics' pilgrimage to Częstochowa in May was a success, and four thousand girls took part in a pilgrimage to Niepokolanów even though the authorities made an illegal attempt to ban the trip. The Primate preached to them about Father Kolbe's* example in sacrificing himself for a world without wars and concentration camps. In revenge for the pilgrimage, the authorities began confiscating the cloister

---

*Saint Maksymilian Kolbe, a Polish Conventual Franciscan priest, who volunteered to die in place of a fellow prisoner, Franciszek Gajowniczek, who had been condemned to death and pleaded for his life, at the German concentration camp at Auschwitz (Oświęcim). He died on August 14, 1941, was beatified by Pope Paul VI in 1971, and canonized a saint by Pope John Paul II in 1982.

grounds at Niepokolanów. A struggle erupted at Zielona Góra in June, when the authorities confiscated the Catholic House. A militia officer climbed a ladder to remove the cross from the building, but someone pulled away the ladder and the officer was killed when he fell, breaking his back.

In the company of many bishops, Cardinal Wyszyński officiated on June 9 at the consecration of the newly rebuilt Cathedral of Saint John in Warsaw. This was a day of great personal joy for him, after years of hard work to raise the edifice from the ruins. Crowds of the faithful joined the architects and professors who had supervised the reconstruction; the only ones invited who stayed away were the state officials.

When the Episcopate next met, on June 21–22, it stated that the violent events in Nowa Huta and Zielona Góra had impressed upon the authorities the need for an easing of tension. Thus the bishops again refrained from making any public protest. Their brothers who had been to Rome on *ad limina* visits reported that the Vatican was well informed about Polish events and that Pope John had again expressed full confidence in the Primate and reaffirmed that Polish church policy should be set by the Episcopate. On the issue of Bishop Kaczmarek, the Vatican had stated that it was interested in appointing bishops, not removing them, and that it would not acknowledge government decrees on church personnel decisions.

The bishops declared that, despite reports in the Polish press, there was no undue German influence at the Vatican, and that the German bishops had in fact signed the request that Father Kolbe be beatified. On the issue of the seminary inspections, the bishops decided not to yield to official attempts at prying into the internal life of church institutions. During the Primate's summer vacation, the inspectors of the seminaries confiscated "banned" prewar and émigré books from seminary libraries.

Cardinal Wyszyński read aloud a telegram from Pope John and led the recitation of the Jasna Góra vows in Częstochowa on August 26. He also spoke out against criticism of the pilgrims in the local press.

In accordance with an earlier decision of the Episcopate, state inspectors were not admitted to the Metropolitan Seminary in Warsaw at the beginning of November. Cardinal Wyszyński replied to the threats of the local Bureau of Religious Affairs authorities with a letter stating that since the matter of seminary inspections had been placed on the Joint Commission agenda, it fell outside the competence of local authorities. The limits of the bishops' flexibility were being approached.

At about the same time, Minister Sztachelski awkwardly admitted during a discussion with Bishop Choromański that the government would not participate in further meetings of the Joint Commission, allegedly because of dissatisfaction with the Primate's sermons.

The Episcopate heard reports of further pressures when it met on November 15–17. Local authorities had demanded that Bishop Kominek sign a lease and pay rent for the use of church buildings in the Western Lands—a proposal that the Bishop of Wrocław had naturally rejected. In the face of antireligious actions—there had been more attempts to inspect seminaries and continued organizing of "patriotic priests"—the steering committee decided to prepare instructions for the clergy on the defense of the faith. They approved a letter from Cardinal Wyszyński to Gomułka protesting all these steps. Bishop Jerzy Stroba reported that religious instruction was now available in only 26 percent of the schools, as opposed to 85 percent a year earlier. The authorities seemed set on the complete elimination of religious instruction and had made great strides toward that goal.

While the Episcopate was meeting, news came that the Sejm had passed laws eliminating Epiphany (January 6) and the Assumption (August 15) as public holidays. The Znak delegate Zbigniew Makarczyk had spoken against the legislation, and Jan Frankowski—who earlier had sacked the whole staff of *Za i Przeciw*—of the Christian Social Association had spoken in favor. Frankowski had even urged that Corpus Christi be eliminated as a holiday, following the Belgian example. His speech had outraged Polish Catholics, and the ten Znak delegates had all voted against the laws.

The Episcopate also learned that Czech Religious Affairs functionaries had been on hand during the inspections of the seminaries in order to advise their Polish counterparts, who were "behind the times" in such actions. It was decided to send the authorities yet another protest of the interference in the seminaries. The bishops then discussed the official reaction against the Episcopal secretariat and the Znak parliamentary group that their September letter on religious education had evoked. And the bishops decided to address treasury officials on the unrealistically high levels of taxation against the Church.

When he visited Gniezno soon after this meeting, Cardinal Wyszyński learned that religious instruction was no longer available at a single school in that city, obviously a personal harassment of the Primate. But the news about extracurricular religious instruction was not bad: 80 percent of the Gniezno high-school students were receiving such lessons.

Speaking from the altar during a pontifical High Mass in Warsaw on Christmas, Cardinal Wyszyński preached a sermon that made waves in the country and abroad. He asked the country to respect truth, man, freedom, and finally the primacy of the spiritual over the material. Explaining the sufferings of the Polish Church in these terms, he stated forcefully that it was completely impossible to bring the Polish religious situation into line with that of the other Eastern-bloc countries. He said he hoped that "we are sovereign and do things in the Polish way—and Poland is Catholic."

At the end of the year, Cardinal Wyszyński met with Bishop Karol Wojtyła and made the bishop the unofficial "protector" of the *Tygodnik Powszechny* staff, a role the Episcopate confirmed at its January 12 session. (Later Bishop Wojtyła would become *Tygodnik Powszechny*'s great defender.) At the same time the bishops noted that the authorities were no longer interested in meetings with the Church—in fact, no longer even answered letters from the Church. They decided to forbid the faithful to read the antichurch magazine *Caritas*. The Episcopate also decided that in March, as part of the Millennium program, it would dedicate itself in servitude to Mary. The bishops also decided to investigate the publication of a defamatory attack on Bishop Kaczmarek, *Green Notebook* by Father Leonard Świderski. Immediately after the session, it was learned that, thanks to Cardinal Wyszyński's efforts, the Polish treasures had been returned by Canada. Yet Professor Zbigniew Makarczyk was unable even to persuade the authorities to invite the Primate to the ceremonies marking the return of the treasures. Mean-spirited, the authorities knew well that the treasures would not have been returned except for the Cardinal's international authority.

On February 7 the steering committee held a special session in connection with the continuing attempts to inspect the seminaries, which were still being resisted. The steering committee also decided to continue to ban priests from publishing with Pax. Bishop Choromański apprised Minister Sztachelski of the fact that the bishops were particularly opposed to any interference in the teaching of theology. Sztachelski was most upset about the Primate's firm stand on the Warsaw seminary, but he was powerless, for he knew that forcing a direct confrontation with Cardinal Wyszyński would put the government exactly where it had been during the Stalinist period. In this case, therefore, the Primate was determining the boundaries of the conflict. Sztachelski made an empty threat that there would be "full consequences" for the Primate's Christmas sermon. Wyszyński had again become the government's *bête noire*.

On February 13, Wyszyński received an evasive letter from Gomułka. The next day, Jerzy Zawieyski and Antoni Marylski* brought unsettling news about the Znak parliamentary delegation. In line with the general tenor of events, the party had refused to allow Zbigniew Makarczyk, the most outspoken

---

*Antoni Marylski: Co-founder (with Mother Róża Czapka, a member of the Franciscan Sisters of the Suffering Christ) of the Institute for the Blind at Laski, near Warsaw. At 70, he was ordained a priest by Cardinal Wyszyński.

Sejm member on religious questions, to stand for "re-election." Zawieyski expressed doubts about remaining on the Council of State and in the Sejm, although it was clear that he really wanted to do so. The Znak group was to be cut from ten to five delegates, one of whom was to be the leftist editor of *Więź*, Tadeusz Mazowiecki. Cardinal Wyszyński said that he could not regard the group as representative of the Church, and would maintain a benign indifference.

In the face of growing difficulties and dangers to the Church, the Primate was working on a letter to the faithful about voluntary dedication in servitude to Mary. In this book, we shall return many times to the idea of voluntary submission to the Virgin as a means of liberation from imposed slavery. We do so fully aware of how controversial this idea is, at home and abroad.

As if to emphasize the gathering dark clouds, the Polish National Bank announced on March 4 that the Catholic Church could no longer maintain an account there. Instead, the Church was told to take its business to the Polish Savings Bank, a sign of being regarded as a private institution. The Religious Affairs officials were leaving no stone unturned in their ingenuity. Pax, the government's Caritas, the Jewish Chamber, and the Polish National Church (a Catholic Church with no allegiance to Rome) were, in a piquant touch, allowed to maintain their accounts in the national bank.

The authorities continued to tighten the screws, not only against the Church, but against the nation in general, particularly in the areas of culture and learning. As a result, disillusioned party members and socialists called on the Primate with increasing frequency, desirous of forming some sort of common opposition. The secret police monitored such contacts with great anxiety.

When the next group of bishops tried to make their *ad limina* visits, two of them were refused passports. The Episcopate decided on March 14–15 that none of them would go to Rome until this latest variety of harassment ended. On the 15th, all the bishops dedicated themselves in servitude to Mary as

Cardinal Wyszyński read the vows aloud. Then, together, they blessed Poland. In the face of open conflict and great dangers the Primate led the Church, as he always had, under Mary's guidance.

These grim times were full of sad ironies. In mid-March, Józefa Hennelowa and the Znak editors gave the Primate the twenty-five author's copies of his book *In the Light of a Thousand Years*. On the same day, unfortunately, Gomułka paraded his ignorance in an attack on the Vatican and the "Roman" influence on the Polish Episcopate.

Another strengthening, uplifting moment came on April 13 in the chapel of the Warsaw seminary when, at the conclusion of a pastoral course on the fourth year of the Great Novena (theme: "Family Strength Through God"), Cardinal Wyszyński dedicated the Warsaw clergy to Mary. The priests repeated the vows with enthusiasm, and the deans decided that all the Warsaw clergy would make a pilgrimage to Częstochowa. The government's reply was amazing: on April 18 they held a counter-congress of the clergy in the Warsaw Philharmonic building, which most of those present attended only under secret-police compulsion. Never before had the police entered directly into the struggle against the Marian cult. Sejm "elections" were being held at the same time, and Wyszyński did not take part.

On May 8, Minister Sztachelski called Bishop Choromański in to issue a warning against the upcoming twenty-fifth anniversary academic pilgrimage to Częstochowa on the grounds that the first prewar pilgrimage had been "anticommunist and anti-Jewish." Sztachelski also defended the "patriotic priests." The two discussed Gomułka's anger over Wyszyński's refusal to vote, the Joint Commission deadlock, and the bank affair, on which the authorities had yielded. Nothing new came of the meeting, but at least it was calm—a welcome exception to the recent norm.

Eleven days later came the announcement that Sztachelski was returning to his Stalinist-era post as minister of health. A cultured man, something of a character, Sztachelski had allowed the security apparatus to dictate religious policy, but without him at the head of the Bureau of Religious Affairs, such police influence was bound to increase now. The Church expected nothing good from the change, and the new director of the Bureau of Religious Affairs turned out to be the infamous Żabiński, who had been driven out of the local administration in Kielce in October 1956.

Despite official prohibitions, police visits to students, and the inspection of identity papers on trains, the academic pilgrimage was so large by the time it reached Częstochowa on May 28 that the Primate and other bishops could only stand in amazement. The chaplains had marshaled young people who were mature, trained, and involved. Wyszyński preached for forty-five minutes on the blessings of unity while numerous secret-police agents watched helplessly from the escarpments. Many priests had feared the pilgrimage was too risky, but the Primate had now won another victory.

Despite an earlier ruling that they could be held only in the afternoon, the Corpus Christi observances were allowed to go on all day on June 1. The crowds in Warsaw had never been larger. Wyszyński dedicated the capital and the archdiocese to the Blessed Mother of Częstochowa and ended his talk with the words, "We forgive God's enemies and those who have wronged us." As the crowd shouted back, "We forgive them," men and women alike were weeping loudly. Such moments showed best that a Church endangered by the administration could win only through the most popular, generally accessible forms of religiosity, like devotion to Mary, especially when the Church's troubles were linked to those of an abused and exploited nation. Mary brought comfort, and the road to that comfort had been opened by the Cardinal-Primates August Hlond and Stefan Wyszyński.

At a meeting on June 21, the Episcopate discussed the authorities' disinclination toward dialogue and the moves toward nationalizing church property in the Western Lands, deciding to send a letter protesting the latter action to the Sejm. The government was also trying to undermine the principle of high-level negotiations by pretending that decisions were being made at the local level, even though they patently came from the top.

In the spring of 1961 Wyszyński had met with the editors of *Więź*, whose chief, Mazowiecki, was now in the Sejm. On June 30 the Primate talked at length with the five Znak delegates— Zawieyski, Stomma, *Tygodnik* editor Stefan Kisielewski, Mazowiecki, and Łubieński—and decided that they were poorly informed about the Church's predicament. The delegates told Wyszyński that "the bishops ought not to cause irritation," unaware that it was the government that was causing the bishops irritation. But even though the authorities had succeeded in misinforming the delegates, the latter showed enough good will so that Wyszyński decided to meet them again in August.

Unexpectedly, while the Primate was resting under doctor's orders, the government called a Joint Commission meeting on July 17 in order to try to intimidate and warn the bishops about the Primate's speeches. On July 31, Cardinal Wyszyński learned that Cardinal Tardini, who had once suspected the Polish bishops of being soft on communists, had died. Tardini had believed the world was divided into "two camps"; he could not fit Poland into his image of things and had blocked decisions of Pius XII that would have helped the Polish Church. Accordingly, Gdańsk and Olsztyn still had no resident Polish bishops, for instance. Wyszyński prayed for the deceased. From Rome it was hard to judge events in distant Poland. Monsignor Filipiak arrived on August 20 with a letter in which Pope John expressed his trust and prayers to the Blessed Mother of Częstochowa, to whom he had set up a chapel in Castel Gandolfo, his summer residence. Saying that he looked forward to seeing Wyszyński in Rome, the Pope added that some people had been asking him to create a second Polish cardinal, a matter about which he had some misgivings, considering the current situation of the Church.

In the meantime, with the new school year approaching and religious instruction effectively expelled, the government set conditions for the establishment of extracurricular catechetical centers. There was to be a total of sixteen thousand of these centers, which could be organized only in church buildings and taught only by diocesan priests; the government reserved the right to inspect the facilities. Finally, the government offered to pay the teachers. A few disoriented priests went ahead, signed contracts, and began receiving pay. When they realized what they had done, however, they quickly backed out of the agreements.

On September 1, the Episcopate convened to discuss religious education and the history of dedicating the nation to Mary. The Polish Episcopate had done so on July 27, 1920, when the Bolshevik Mikhail Tukhachevsky was approaching Warsaw with the Red Army. The tradition thus embraced the most perilous moments in the struggle for spiritual and cultural identity. Returning to the subject of catechism, the bishops learned that the authorities were demanding that ethics and ideology be completely excluded, since they "belong to the party." The Episcopate decided to prepare instructions for the faithful and the clergy, and to send a protest to the government. The situation had turned worse, with further threats to the seminaries and the liquidation of the remaining Catholic schools, whose existence had been guaranteed earlier. Then Archbishop Baraniak reported on preparations for the Vatican Council, and Bishops Wojtyła and Stroba on the training of young clergy. When the meeting was over, the bishops went into a retreat, during which, on September 4, they promised that if Mary would preserve the faith of the Polish nation through a thousand years—until 1966—they would offer the nation in servitude to her for the sake of the Holy Church—*coram populo*.

The government increased hostilities as a battle over the control of catechization shaped up. Seminarians were conscripted in Gniezno, prompting an ineffectual appeal from the Cardinal to Minister of Defense Spychalski. Gomułka attacked the Episcopate in an interview for *Le Monde* that was made public in Poland on October 13, 1961. The bishops held an emergency meeting on October 20 to discuss the fact that lay people were being fined for allowing religious instruction to take place in their homes. On November 15 the Episcopate approved a letter to the Sejm on the illegality of government actions toward the Church; undaunted, the Ministry of Education released a new circular on religious education on November 21.

Bishop Zakrzewski, many years a member of the Joint Commission, died on November 26. Those with whom Cardinal Wyszyński had led the Church for the last fifteen years were beginning to depart. Delegate Stomma, who knew of the Primate's criticisms of Znak, appeared at the beginning of December with the idea that the Church should be defended at the "last trench," beyond which retreat was impossible. Cardinal Wyszyński replied that the Church ought to be defended at the first trench, on the level of religious, national, and human rights. The Gomułka leadership's disinformation had been successful with Znak, though the group would move squarely into the opposition once that leadership fell.

Work on the Great Novena continued. Its fifth year, centering on the raising of children ("Family Strength Through God"), had been upsetting to a government bent on monopolizing education. The Episcopal Marian Commission decided that the sixth year (1962–63) would be titled "Youth Faithful to Christ" and the seventh (1963–64) to "Justice and Social Love." This latter theme had to do with the Mystical Body of Christ and the wide range of personal rights and duties incumbent on each of its members.

The year 1961 had been full of sufferings and triumphs for the Church—the dedication of the clergy and of Warsaw and Gniezno to Mary, as well as tyranny through taxation and attempts to bribe priests. As usual, Cardinal Wyszyński saw out the year in Gniezno, and as usual he spent its last day thinking about his spiritual motto, *Soli Deo.*

The Episcopate met in Warsaw on January 10. The main topic was the inspection of seminaries: there had been no answer to the letter of protest sent to the Sejm, and inspectors were in some cases illegally walking in on theology classes. At the same time, however, the limitation of religious education had become an issue in the world press. Also at this meeting, the bishops approved a letter in connection with the opening of the Second Vatican Council.

The next day, Cardinal Wyszyński informed Father Bronisław Dąbrowski that he had been named Auxiliary Bishop of Warsaw (he later became secretary of the Episcopate).

Cardinal Wyszyński decided to go to Rome before the opening (now scheduled for October 12) of the council; he arrived in the Eternal City on February 16 and was received by the Pope the next day. The Rome newspapers commented on this "lightning" reception and recalled that Pius had kept Wyszyński waiting for a week in 1957. But the journalists were mistaken: in 1957, Monsignor Lurico Dante had come to Cardinal Wyszyński on the second day of his visit and offered him the choice of seeing the Pope at once or later, after the state visit by the President of France. The Primate had decided to wait, simply because he thought it bad policy to present the complex Polish matters at a moment when the Pope's attention would be fixed on France. Yet the misunderstanding has been perpetuated even in some histories.

At his audience now, John was unusually warm, speaking sincerely of his trust in Cardinal Wyszyński and of the way some had misunderstood the Primate's long struggle for church freedom. He mentioned Tardini, and explained that the late cardinal had never understood church-state relations outside Rome. The present pope and his secretary of State, Cardinal Cicognani, had wider knowledge and greater respect for Wyszyński. Three days later, at the sitting of the Council Preparatory Commission, John again welcomed Cardinal Wyszyński warmly, and specifically mentioned the dedication of the Polish bishops to Mary. John well understood the controversial idea. While Cardinal Wyszyński was visiting the papal apartments on February 25, John made the extraordinary gesture of beckoning him onto the balcony and appearing with him before the large crowd that had gathered for the Sunday noon *Angelus Domini* blessing. That same day, Cardinal Wyszyński had supper with Cardinal Döpfner, who was making a point of indicating his desire to overcome the tragic past of Polish-German relations, and to work toward a peaceful reconciliation of the two nations. It was a very friendly meeting, and the prelude to further talks between the two cardinals in November, while the council was in session. On March 1, Pope John took a step toward the regulation of church administration in the Western Lands by bestowing the title of honorary archbishop on Bishop Kominek. Ambassador Willman of People's Poland joined other dignitaries in seeing Cardinal Wyszyński off from Rome; when the Primate arrived home on March 11, however, he found that the authorities were persecuting catechetization with new vigor.

Wyszyński informed the bishops of the preparations for the Vatican Council at a March 13–14 Episcopal meeting. It was decided to try to send at least one delegate from each diocese to the council while at the same time—this showed how much caution the tense situation demanded—leaving no diocese without a bishop during the council.

John XXIII's pontificate and the announcement of the council had stirred great interest in the communist world. The Soviets had in fact long been inclined toward mending fences with the Vatican, and they allowed themselves high expectations at the announcement that the council would "open the Church to the world" and at the publication of the encyclical *Mater et Magistra* in May 1961. Khrushchev himself expressed his praise in *Pravda*. A Russian Orthodox archbishop met with Monsignor Willebrands and Cardinal Tisserant in Paris in August 1962, and the churchmen Borovoy and Kotlyarov were allowed to attend the council as observers. Pope John XXIII's appeals to the United States and the Soviet Union, and his intervention in the Cuban missile crisis, which allowed the Russians to save face when they were compelled to withdraw their rockets on October 26, 1962, further advanced détente between Moscow and the Vatican. It hardly seemed surprising when the Russians freed Archbishop Josyf Slipyj from prison* at the beginning of February 1963 and allowed him to go to Rome (though not to his archdiocese: he had to be content with a glimpse of Lwów from the train). The world looked on with amazement as Khrushchev's son-in-law Adzhubey was received by the Pope on March 7, 1963. But the visit was only a testing of the water and led to none of the political developments the press expected. The whole Eastern bloc made an official acknowledgment of the encyclical *Pacem in terris* (April 11, 1963) and its famous differentiation of false doctrinal systems and the actual societies based on them. But the Soviet approach to the Church at this time was a purely propagandistic switch from insistent criticism to portraying Pope John's policies and encyclicals as endorsement of Eastern-bloc policies. There was no true liberalization of church-state relations.

The attitude of the Polish authorities emerged when Bishop Choromański asked the director of the Bureau of Religious Affairs, Żabiński, whether the bishops would receive passports to the council. Żabiński said that not all the bishops deserved passports. Choromański replied that it was not a question of deserving, but of civil rights. In any case, preparations for the council became a new theme in Cardinal Wyszyński's pastoral work.

On Cardinal Wyszyński's initiative, the Episcopate proclaimed a "council vigil." This vigil was at once a means of aiding the council and a way of awakening the national conscience and focusing it on the issues of the universal Church. It also provided a channel for informing the faithful about the progress of the council in a way that would not otherwise have been possible, given the great limitations placed on the media. The vigil involved more than idle waiting—action was necessary in the defense of society against atheism. The four-year

---

*During the occupation of Lithuania, Slipyj, together with all other bishops and priests, was arrested by the Russians.

program was planned on a large scale and carried out impressively. A particular theme accompanied each council session: "A Prayer Vigil for the Intention of the Council," "Council Good Works," "Victory over the Self—for the Victory of the Church," and "Dedicating Parishes in Submission to Mary for the Sake of the Church." Each action began with preparatory vigils and prayers in the individual parishes, continued with a central vigil at Jasna Góra during each council session, and concluded with the dispatch of offertory symbols of the action to Rome. These included council candles, Marian hosts, rosaries, and medallions with the inscription *Pro Victoria Ecclesiae*. The vigil reminded the world of Poland and brought it a special glory.

At a meeting of the Episcopate on June 14, Cardinal Wyszyński revealed the nominations the Pope had given him. Besides the honorary title for Bishop Kominek, Father Jerzy Ablewicz was named Bishop of Tarnów, and Bishop Jan Wosiński became apostolic administrator of Płock. Bishop Bronisław Dąbrowski, well versed both in religious order affairs and in the state laws and policies concerned with religion, joined the steering committee.

The Episcopate also discussed drafting a pastoral letter on laicization, which read, in part:

> It is important to the Polish Church that the laicizing movement is an organized action, intended to hasten the process of secularization. . . . It is a political movement . . . supported and executed by administrative means. It is a pedagogical movement, which aims above all to educate those who teach (parents and teachers) and those who are taught (children and youth). It is a totalitarian movement, because it aims to impose its influence on all aspects of social life, family and personal, to the exclusion of all judgments and appreciations based on religion. It is a movement that leaves no one a choice. Each child and each young person can attend only those schools in which the aspiration to laicization is included in the program.

This same conference issued instructions to priests about dealing with laicization and discussed ministering to young people and to vacationers. Crowds still attended church ceremonies, but there were signs of laicization among the young. A pilgrimage and youth assembly were scheduled for August 26 at Jasna Góra.

The authorities were stepping up their inspections of seminaries; thirty-one seminarians in Katowice who refused to sit for examinations in the presence of the inspectors found themselves called up by the army. Pax and Caritas, the latter now headed by Father Bonifacy Woźny, were continuing their efforts. The Episcopate decided to issue another warning to priests and to maintain the ban on their publishing with Pax.

Hours after the Episcopate session broke up, at three in the morning on June 15, the Church suffered a great loss: Archbishop Baziak died of a heart attack in Warsaw. He had survived communist prison and the loss of the Archdiocese of Lwów, and even though he had been nominated as Archbishop of Cracow while retaining the Lwów see, the decision had never been announced. His funeral took place at Wawel Cathedral in Cracow on June 19, with the Primate's participation. Bishop Karol Wojtyła was named vicar capitular of Cracow.

During July the authorities conducted a religious war against the ministry to vacationing youth. On Sunday, August 12, a letter from the Primate about the persecution of religious orders was read in the churches. Social reaction was overwhelming, and foreign radio stations publicized the issue. In the meantime, the government refused Cardinal König of Vienna a visa, on the grounds that the invitation had not been officially approved. On the 15th, while Cardinal Wyszyński welcomed to Częstochowa a pilgrimage from Warsaw, Director Żabiński warned Bishop Choromański that there was the possibility of a threat of anti-Polish action at the council— either the party had no understanding of the council, or it still hoped to stir up some trouble.

A thousand priests and more than half a million others, many of them young, were present when Cardinal Wyszyński preached and renewed the vows at Jasna Góra on August 26. After a three-day retreat, the Episcopate came into session there on September 14. Wyszyński began by greeting the secret police, who had set up eavesdropping posts near the monastery. The bishops, fighting openly for their freedom, had nothing to hide. They discussed the Great Novena program and decided that, as fruitful as this year's efforts with the youth had been, there was a need for additional diocesan pilgrimages.

Now the Vatican Council was approaching, and the government, realizing that refusal would create an international scandal, gave Cardinal Wyszyński a passport on September 27. They were not equally forthcoming with Bishops Choromański and Kominek, even though the refusal of the Polish Bishop of Wrocław was as scandalous as refusing the Primate would have been. Kliszko invited Bishop Klepacz to discuss the council. The party was so unsure of itself that it feared even far-off Rome.

On October 5 the bishops set out, but it was decided that auxiliaries would not go from dioceses where the ordinaries had been turned down; Auxiliary Bishop Kałwa thus stayed home with Archbishop Kominek. The Holy Father received the Primate the day after his arrival and, in an exceptionally warm meeting, spoke memorable words about "the Western Lands, recovered after centuries." Even though the words did not constitute church policy, they caused an uproar with the West German ambassador and the press.

A firm telegram from Wyszyński to Gomułka finally resulted in a passport for Archbishop Kominek, but Bishop Kaczmarek of Kielce was still refused.

The council provided a stimulating exchange of information between the Polish Church and the Church elsewhere in the world. At the opening, an elderly cardinal approached the Primate, kissed his cape twice, and said, "I kiss martyred Poland." Wyszyński had an interesting talk with Archbishop Seper of Zagreb, in which he learned how much better off the Church was in Yugoslavia than in Poland. There, the government did not interfere in church appointments and religion was taught in the schools. The contrast was especially poignant for the Primate when he received news from home that more seminarians were being drafted in Gniezno. Pope John distinguished Cardinal Wyszyński by naming him a member of the council commission *de negotiis extra ordinem;* in this capacity the Primate suggested sensationally widening Catholic lay participation in the council, which thus far had been limited to lay separated brethren.

Resistance to government interference in the council delegation turned out well for the bishops. Of the thirty-three who applied for passports, twenty-five eventually received them. There had apparently been a change of official tactics after Gomułka's return from Moscow, where the authorities seemed better able to understand the council. The limitation of the council to religious matters actually disappointed the rulers, since it denied them a chance to meddle and to tack their own propaganda on to the results.

At Cardinal Wyszyński's suggestion, the Holy Father received Jerzy Zawieyski in a twenty-minute private audience on November 20. Zawieyski, fresh from a meeting with Gomułka, passed word that the latter thought that Pope John and Khrushchev had prevented a war. Gomułka had also admitted that the Primate was not harming Poland's interests abroad, but he still would not halt the conscription of seminarians.

There was an audience for the Polish bishops on November 25, Pope John's eighty-first birthday. Cardinal Wyszyński stressed the honor of the occasion, which was warm—as always with John—and highly interesting. The Pope told the Polish bishops that he knew there was no need to encourage them to faithfulness in the Church; rather, he wanted to confide in them and share experiences. He said that people should be won over to the Church and never repelled from it. He had never regretted his mildness, he told them. Instead, he reproved himself at times for being too stern. The audience, lasting nearly an hour, gave the Polish bishops a moving, lasting impression of the "Pope of Love."

Back home, meanwhile, the government had returned to its

old tactic of trying to set "the bad primate" against "the good pope" in a "round-up" of priests who had gathered to honor John XXIII at Wrocław.

On December 1, Jerzy Zawieyski, acting as Kliszko's messenger, came to the Primate with the Polish ambassador's apologies for not having greeted Wyszyński at the station in Rome. There were signs of a thaw: the ambassador proposed to call on Wyszyński and to hold a reception for the bishops at the embassy. Wyszyński turned down the reception because of what was going on at home, but agreed to visit with the ambassador. The visit took place on December 7, and Kliszko himself was waiting at the embassy.

Two months earlier the bishops had been having passport troubles, but now Kliszko was complimenting the Holy Father's positions on Polish issues and acknowledging that they flowed from the Primate's own efforts. Wyszyński explained the absurdity of the passport denials and criticized Żabiński's policies. At the same time, he praised the new tendencies in the Marxist philosophy of man, in terms that must have gone over Kliszko's head. The vice-marshal of the Sejm regretted that the Italian press had said that Polish agriculture was on a sixteenth-century level. His interlocutor reminded him in turn that when he, Wyszyński, had been attacked in the West German press following the Pope's remarks on Poland in October, the Polish *Sztandar Młodych* (Standard of Youth) had joined the chorus and called him a medieval obscurantist. *Soldaten Zeitung* had criticized the Primate for inviting Cardinal König and Archbishop Bengsch to Poland, and the government had denied them visas. Kliszko seemed to understand all the complaints and to be holding out the olive branch. The Primate won agreement to his unceasing call for dialogue in the Joint Commission. A few days later, nevertheless, Kliszko was attacking the Polish bishops on the basis of Lenert's book *L'Eglise catholique en Pologne* at a meeting of Italian communists.

On December 12, Cardinal Wyszyński started for home. He spent the end of the year not in Gniezno, as usual, but in Bydgoszcz. On January 2, 1963, he learned that the educational authorities were trying to inspect catechetical centers and demanding reports on the teaching. There was no question of agreeing, since the teaching was being done in church buildings. Archbishop Baraniak had obtained copies of secret instructions to the inspectors in Poznań. Subinspectors were to visit the centers—even those in churches—anonymously, to identify the teachers and the children. Next they were to order that religious not teach, and that the lectures be limited strictly to catechism, excluding church history, dogmatics, and ethics. Since inspections of seminaries and the drafting of seminarians were also continuing, there can be little wonder at Cardinal Wyszyński's decision, confirmed at the Episcopal meeting of January 9–10, to limit contacts with the government to the Joint Commission. For the moment there would be no meeting with Gomułka.

The atheist magazine *Argumenty* attacked the Polish bishops, on January 6 and 13, for failing in their task at the council and espousing a course of "moderate conservatism." At Laski on January 17, the Znak delegates coaxed Wyszyński to meet with Gomułka, blaming the government's hard-line policies on Żabiński and the director of the Central Committee administrative department, Kazimierz Witaszewski. The Znak delegates had made the mistake of paying more attention to intraparty squabbling than to the party's general attitude toward the Church. They particularly surprised the Primate by saying that they were chastised by party officials whenever he made a sharp statement. He needed to protect human rights and the rights of the whole Church, however, and could not trim his sails to serve one group's interests. He decided not to refuse a meeting with Gomułka outright, but to wait for an act of good will toward the Church before accepting.

On February 9, Cardinal Wyszyński went to Zielona Góra, where the icon of the Blessed Virgin of Częstochowa was continuing its tour of the dioceses. It was an embattled tour: every parish priest who hosted the icon was fined, and one was imprisoned. Nevertheless, the clergy judged the visits to have a highly positive spiritual effect. Also in February, the authorities began inspecting rectories and attaching valuables for unpaid taxes and fines in connection with catechization. Cardinal Wyszyński reminded Kliszko by letter of the latter's promise in Rome to reactivate the Joint Commission. There was no answer. At the beginning of March the Cardinal talked with the philosophers Leszek Kołakowski and Jan Strzelecki, who were interested in the council and detached themselves from the Party's religious policy.

At their March 12 meeting, the bishops were leaning toward changing the Church's position on high-level contacts, fearing that they would seem inflexible if they continued to refuse. Cardinal Wyszyński yielded humbly to their arguments and wrote Gomułka a letter. The Episcopate also renewed the act of dedication to Mary and discussed the second part of the "council vigil."

In its May 17 issue, *Argumenty* printed a vicious attack on Cardinal Wyszyński that revealed customs data on currency imported from abroad. The editors did not realize that they were descending to the level of a police journal. On March 31, Kliszko's brusque reply to the call for a Joint Commission meeting arrived—but a week later the Cardinal received a polite request from Gomułka for a meeting. Kliszko must have been in the dark about his boss's plans.

Wyszyński gave a talk about the council to the Warsaw Catholic Intellectuals' Club on April 5. Though he was in general well received, there were some disputatious voices in the audience.

The Cardinal remained critical of Znak yet continued to trust the group in matters of principle. With Pax it was different: that body's *Słowo Powszechne* attacked the Polish bishops on April 14 over their attitude to *Pacem in terris*. Wyszyński had insisted to his bishops that the encyclical covered human rights as well as peace, and the hosannas of the previous October were turning to cries of "Crucify him."

The April Episcopal meeting dealt mainly with church teachings, on which Bishop Karol Wojtyła was one of the main speakers. The Episcopate also worked on a letter about peace and, at the same time, a missive to the government about freedom of conscience.

Cardinal Wyszyński and First Secretary Gomułka met on April 26. That same day, *Słowo Powszechne* put forward the recognition of socialism as a condition for smooth church-state relations, and Gomułka took a similar stand during the five-hour talk, using the statements of some lay Catholics to bolster his arguments. Each side accused the other of breaking the 1950 understanding. It came out that the violent antichurch emotions in the party had been awakened by the Primate's refusal to attend the embassy reception in Rome: Frol Kozlov of the Soviet leadership had been invited. But the bishops, after their passport problems, had been in no mood for diplomatic receptions. Interestingly, Gomułka was interested in a concordat or some other kind of agreement with the Vatican. The party chief was thinking of establishing a consulate, and Cardinal Wyszyński of a nunciature of the first class, since Poland was a Catholic country. The limitations on catechization, especially the exclusion of dogmatics and ethics, remained a sticking point. A compromise on the curriculum could have been reached, but the party did not want to yield. Cardinal Wyszyński naturally complained about the lack of church building permits, the conscription of seminarians, the liquidation of Catholic schools, the taxes, and so on. Protesting the official toleration of abortion, he appealed to the *racja stanu:* what could thirty million Poles do against three hundred million Russians and Germans? At the end, Gomułka seemed to agree to a reactivation of the Joint Commission, but it had been a difficult meeting. Still, Cardinal Wyszyński was glad it had taken place, even though it augured nothing hopeful for the future.

Cardinal Franz König of Vienna arrived in Poland on April 30 for a visit that, despite press speculations, had little to do with politics. Deeply impressed, particularly fascinated by Częstochowa, the visitor said that the Polish Church was ahead of the council.

On May 8, Cardinal Wyszyński arrived in Rome; he met

with Cardinal Cicognani and, the day after his arrival, with the gravely ill Pope John. In a frank and personal talk, the pontiff shared his concerns with the Cardinal for an hour and three-quarters. Wyszyński's main purpose in the trip had been to gather materials on the council for his bishops, but he told both the Pope and Cicognani about the vascillations in Warsaw between his own idea of a nunciature and Gomułka's suggestion that a consulate be opened. The press, ever speculative and afflicted with a sort of anti-Eastern complex that biased its depiction of Poland, portrayed the Primate as an opponent of diplomatic relations between Warsaw and the Holy See. To Polish Ambassador Willman, as to everyone he met, the Primate said that a Vatican consulate in Warsaw would not mean very much.

On May 12 Cardinal Wyszyński had another papal audience, first alone and then in the company of his bishops. It was a touching meeting; everyone present could sense the seriousness of the Holy Father's illness. When the bishops wished him good health so that he could finish the council, John said, "My successor is coming and he will finish the council. . . ." Both John and his guests knew it would be their last meeting; saying good-bye was difficult for all.

It is an interesting aside that if Gomułka, at the halfway point in his reign, could have witnessed such scenes and appreciated Cardinal Wyszyński's standing in the Vatican and the universal Church, he might have avoided some of the unforgivable mistakes of the next seven years.

On May 24, Cardinal Wyszyński returned to the unpleasant realities of Warsaw. The hopes of a thaw, the recent visit of Khrushchev's son-in-law to the Pope, meant nothing in Poland; the May 27 meeting of the Joint Commission withered any remaining illusions. The government claimed that all catechetical centers had been registered and more than ten thousand reports from priests about their activities had been submitted. When the bishops protested that these priests had complied only under compulsion, Kliszko insisted that the authorities had given instructions for the registration of catechetical centers and were not going to back down. Teaching of religion by nuns was still forbidden. In short, instead of a thaw there was a declaration of war.

Pope John XXIII died on the evening of June 3. The popularity of the Pope of Good Will and his peace proposals among the communists had, unfortunately, never had an answer on the practical level of church-state relations. Yet because the legacy of his program would eventually ease the mood of belligerent atheism, John's brief pontificate had immense meaning, especially in the East. Its deepest religious sense of course had nothing to do with politics, but the opening of the Church to the world also helped to open, even if against their intentions, closed and ossified ideological systems.

On June 10 the Episcopate looked over the new council materials and discussed the government's claims about catechization. The statistics about registration turned out to be fake, and despite the ban, five thousand nuns were still catechizing. Without them the program would collapse, so the bishops decided to reject the government demand.

That same day, Cardinal Wyszyński set out for Rome and the conclave. When he arrived, Monsignor Capovilla told the Primate that a note on the visit of the Polish bishops had been the last entry John was able to make in his journal. Also before the conclave began, Cardinal Wyszyński addressed the College of Cardinals on the memory of the late pope and received warm applause. It was Cardinal Montini who expressed the Cardinals' thanks—he who became Pope Paul VI on June 21.

Cardinal Wyszyński had an audience with the new pope on July 4 in which he briefly sketched the most important Polish problems, especially those concerning the normalization of dioceses in the Western Lands. As a personal memento, Paul gave Cardinal Wyszyński the ring that Pope John had worn since his eightieth birthday.

The Primate left Rome on July 7. On the trip home he learned that Bishop Zdzisław Goliński of Częstochowa had died and, from Cardinal König, that Gomułka had again attacked Wyszyński and Polish intellectuals. The bishops on the Joint Commission had had another shock from the government: catechism conducted in church buildings was to be treated the same as that conducted outside—there would be inspections, and nuns would be barred from teaching. The Episcopate simply could not agree to inspections within church buildings.

At a stormy Joint Commission meeting on August 5, the government representatives paid no heed to the bishops' protests. The charge that they were "treading on the altar" outraged them, and they threatened to settle matters by their own means. This meant further pressure would be applied to priests. From the outset, the bishops had decided not to compromise, even if some of the priests in outlying areas had caved in. The very sanctity of church buildings was at stake. On other matters as well, the authorities were trying to cause trouble where previously they had been indifferent. For instance, they made desperate efforts to block the annual Warsaw-to-Częstochowa pilgrimage, beginning with the declaration of a smallpox epidemic in Częstochowa and going on to include physical attacks on pilgrims.

The pilgrims from Warsaw arrived, however, sham epidemic or not. From all over Poland, two hundred thousand Catholics came to Jasna Góra on August 26.

The Episcopate met during the Marian feast, and the Primate informed the bishops about his meeting with the new pope and the plans for the council. Rather than back down, it was decided to read a letter confirming the Church's stand on catechization from the pulpits.

On September 16, Cardinal Wyszyński talked with the Znak delegates in the Sejm and with the *Tygodnik Powszechny* editors. Konstanty Łubieński of Znak painted a relatively optimistic picture, but the news from the *Tygodnik* staff disagreed. The editors reported that their circulation was being restricted and that contacts with lay circles abroad were being hindered.

Stefan Kisielewski, perhaps the most politically acute of the *Tygodnik* editors, objected to Lubieński's optimism and said, "Both sides disown us." Those in Znak, however, simply wanted to keep on serving as a kind of bridge between the government and the Episcopate. Still, the meeting ended in a friendly way.

Three days later, Kliszko invited Bishop Klepacz to talk about the approaching second session of the council. In fact, Kliszko mainly wanted to report that the party could not accept the Episcopate's suggestion that church-state relations in Poland be normalized before Warsaw opened relations with the Vatican. He wanted, in effect—and this showed his naïveté —to talk with the Apostolic See over Cardinal Wyszyński's head, without even settling the catechization issue. He said that an Episcopate's letter to the clergy on the situation of the Church showed ill will. He also revealed that Archbishop Kominek would not receive a passport for the second session. (Forty-five of the seventy Polish bishops had requested passports; twenty-two received them.) At Saint John's Church in Warsaw, Cardinal Wyszyński spoke out decisively in favor of the right of all bishops to take part in the council—thereby setting off speculation in the Western press that he himself might be refused a passport.

The Primate arrived in Rome on September 27. Two days later, the day the council session opened, Pope Paul invited Wyszyński to an evening audience. The Pope expressed approval of the remarks Wyszyński had made at Saint John's and lamented the absence of so many Polish bishops. He also decided, on his own, to build a church in Rome to commemorate the Polish Millennium.

The Primate did not know that his three books on the Great Novena and the Millennium were being confiscated—twenty thousand copies of each—when they arrived by train in Warsaw. Cyrankiewicz and Gomułka issued an order at night to seize the whole shipment, and the sixty thousand books were taken to Jeziorna (a paper factory) and shredded.

On October 15, during a speech to the council, Cardinal Wyszyński said that the expression *de Ecclesia sanctificante et vivificante** better lends itself to the contemporary world than the traditional *Ecclesia militans.*†
He also spoke with Cardinal Frings and Bishop Splett in the council hall. Frings suggested that the German and Polish Episcopates submit a joint declaration on the beatification of Father Kolbe. On the evening of October 16, in another audience with Pope Paul, the Polish bishops submitted Bishop Wojtyła's petition on the beatification of Queen Jadwiga. The Holy Father asked Wyszyński to honor his mother tongue by reading his remarks in Polish. Italian text in hand, the pontiff attentively followed the Primate's words. Afterward, he spoke affectionately to his guests.

At the Secretariat of State, Wyszyński was discussing Gomułka's proposals for Vatican-Warsaw relations, the Gdańsk issue, and the vacant bishoprics of Cracow, Płock, and Częstochowa. The Vatican officials stated that they would negotiate with Warsaw only if Cardinal Wyszyński took part. Warsaw, refusing to understand this for many years, merely tried to go over Wyszyński's head, sending numerous suspect emissaries to the Vatican.

From home came news that more seminarians were being conscripted—revenge, but for what? For the Episcopate's letter to the clergy about the situation of the Church, it turned out. Ironically, Cardinal Wyszyński spoke to the College of Cardinals on November 4 on the subject of the seminaries, a speech for which Pope Paul and the other cardinals thanked and congratulated him. Cardinal Cicognani reacted warmly to Cardinal Wyszyński's November 17 *L'Osservatore Romano* article on Pope John XXIII. At the same time, however, certain Warsaw operatives were making trouble for the Primate in the Italian press. On November 19, Cardinal Wyszyński asked Jerzy Turowicz about Stanisław Stomma's *Opinion,* which

---

*Church sanctifying (making holy) and vivifying (giving life).
†Church militant (warring).

was circulating in Rome. The text, written without Wyszyń-ski's knowledge, did not mention that the Polish Episcopate was not opposed to relations between Warsaw and the Vatican, although it set conditions for an agreement. Stomma himself had been in Rome but had not called on the Primate. Turowicz denied having known anything about the initiative. The Italian leftist press, along with some Polish party and Pax figures who were staying in Rome, was accusing Wyszyński of blocking a Warsaw-Vatican pact. There was also an anonymous "memo" going around the council, supposedly about the Marian cult but in fact an attack on the Episcopate's policies —a convergence of circumstances that hardly seemed accidental. At the same time, the rightist *Il Borghese* was attacking the Polish bishops as communist "agents"; the Primate protested to the Italian government about this accusation.

This campaign against the Episcopate and its leader by the Polish authorities coincided with a hardened Soviet line. Konstantin Ilyichev, head of the Soviet party's Ideological Commission, issued a statement on November 25 calling for atheist education. The communists obviously feared the ideological consequences of international coexistence, and of the opening of the Church to the world.

At an audience with Pope Paul on December 2, Cardinal Wyszyński and the Polish bishops renewed their plea for the normalization of church administration in the Western Lands. Pope Paul said that the Vatican wanted to help, but it was not an easy matter. For instance, Bishop Splett, no longer residing in his see, was not reacting to suggestions that he step aside as Bishop of Gdańsk. As a new act of trust, Pope Paul made Cardinal Wyszyński a gift of his personal cardinal's ring.

Cardinal Wyszyński left for home the day after the second session of the council closed. He was ill for nearly a week, but by December 17–18 he was able to take part in an Episcopal meeting. The news from around the country was not good. It seems that in August 1963 the Ministry of the Interior had held a conference in Warsaw at which it was decided to open a new battlefront by stirring up intrigues in individual parishes; only through an act of Providence had the bishops obtained a report on this meeting. The authorities intended to go on negotiating with the Vatican, over the Primate's head, even as they set about disrupting parish life in Poland. The Episcopal Steering Committee decided to prepare a "White Paper" about the wrongs done to the Polish Church.

Jerzy Zawieyski brought Cardinal Wyszyński an explanation of Stanisław Stomma's activities abroad, his unauthorized discussions, in France and Switzerland as well as Rome, about the Warsaw-Vatican negotiations. But Zawieyski's explanations did not satisfy the Primate.

On the same day, the government gave its preliminary approval to the nominations of Bishop Wojtyła as Archbishop of Cracow and Bishops Stefan Bareła and Bogdan Sikorski as Ordinaries of Częstochowa and Płock. There were rumors that Stomma and Aleksander Skarżyński, the assistant director of the Bureau of Religious Affairs, had had to persuade Kliszko to accept the nomination of Wojtyła. Political ideas might have tipped the scale; in any case, Kliszko would later try unsuccessfully to set Wojtyła and Wyszyński at odds.

Before Christmas, three different intermediaries tried to feel the Primate out on the possibility of meeting with Gomułka. Cardinal Wyszyński did not leap at the chance, since Gomułka had not come forward himself and the Church was still being treated shabbily.

On December 30 the leaders of the Warsaw Catholic Intellectuals' Club, including Zawieyski, Konstanty Łubieński, and Ludwik Dembiński, told Cardinal Wyszyński that they were dissociating themselves from the meddling that had taken place abroad on the subject of relations with the Vatican. Wyszyński replied that a letter they had sent him had nevertheless smacked of the attitudes propagated in *Opinion*. It would have been unfair to blame Stomma alone for the "Vatican mistake." Besides, the Primate was unhappy about an article that Tadeusz Mazowiecki and Andrzej Wielowieyski had printed in *Więź*, written with the aim of winning the party over to agreement with the Church and containing socialist declarations. Cardinal Wyszyński could see no point in acknowledging socialism now that the system had so compromised itself, and it was plain that the authorities were trying to bypass the Polish bishops in dealing with the Vatican. Differing political courses—he wanted to keep resisting, while Znak was ready to compromise—led Cardinal Wyszyński to distance himself from Znak, without breaking off ties altogether.

I think, however, that there was more to the Primate's differences with Znak than the group's tactic of giving ground to the authorities. On a deeper level, Znak, and particularly Jerzy Turowicz, the editor of *Tygodnik Powszechny*, were fascinated by "the renewal of the Church." *Więź*, moreover, was committed to "to socialist development" and wanted, as Tadeusz Breza said in his famous book *Spiżowa Brama* (The Bronze Portal), to "enroll the Church" in a new social order. Cardinal Wyszyński's speech to the College of Cardinals in remembrance of Pope John had facilitated both the continuation of John's work and the election of Pope Paul. But Wyszyński always juxtaposed the trend to renew the Church with Polish realities. At home, the Church needed most of all to be protected. Enrolling it in a "socialist structure" seemed inadvisable to him as long as that structure was one of economic and social irrationalities, and assaults on human freedom. And though *Więź* would always remain a leftist journal, in time its editors did grow disenchanted with the prevailing system.

In a conversation in 1979, Stefan Kisielewski argued that the differences in spiritual climate between Warsaw and Cracow influenced Cardinal Wyszyński's relations with Znak. Whereas Cracow, Znak's focal point, was liberal, intellectual, international, and receptive to Western influence, Warsaw was homespun, national, unleavened, faithful to the Polish tradition. I am not entirely convinced. After all, the conservative Cracow "Stańczycy"* and the Warsaw positivists of the nineteenth century gave way almost simultaneously to the contem-

---

*"Jesters." A conservative political group centered in Cracow before the first World War. They derive their name from Stańczyk, the wise jester in the renaissance court of King Zygmunt Augustus at the zenith of Polish power.

porary currents of Polish ideology, even though Austrian rule in Cracow had been relatively liberal, while the Russians had kept trying to Russify Warsaw, thus evoking a spirit of opposition and faithfulness to the national tradition. History alone cannot explain the differences I am discussing. Both Cardinal Wyszyński and Znak rejected communism, but they worked for change from completely different premises. The Primate drew on Polish tradition and the past, on religious and national identity. Znak was more influenced by Jacques Maritain's humanism and Emmanuel Mounier's personalism. Their desires for freedom were concurrent, but the different starting points had their consequences. Znak was talking to intellectuals, and Cardinal Wyszyński to the whole nation. Znak feared that thinking in national terms could lead to nationalism; it preferred to speak of "society." Yet nationalism had been a historical episode. Without the concept of "the nation," it is impossible to speak of spiritual and cultural identity. Polish society changed, but the Polish nation remained. Cardinal Wyszyński fought for its survival and for its faithfulness to religion and the Church. Worried about Sovietization, everyone talked about spiritual and cultural identity in the seventies, despite the reappearance of nationalism in a communist version at the end of the sixties. I believe that the differences finally disappeared, and when the system began to question its existence, Znak was so intransigent that only Cardinal Wyszyński himself could save the group.

When Pope John Paul II was elected, Leszek Kołakowski rhetorically asked the Polish Church whether it opposed the prevailing system because that system was atheist, or whether it also opposed the system because that system denied the pluralism of contemporary society. Znak would have spontaneously answered that it opposed the system for denying pluralism. Cardinal Wyszyński certainly never asked himself such a question. It was his duty to fight against atheism and bureaucratic Marxism, though there can be no doubt about the democratic and tolerant attitudes of a man who addressed even his persecutors as "brothers." It is a historical fact that the

Church defended not only national and church rights, but also human rights, and even those of people far removed from the Church. So much for a rather theoretical question, which interests us mostly as a symptom of a painful controversy in the Catholic world. No matter how drastic the controversy sometimes seemed, Znak never lost contact with the hierarchy as Pax had done. That is why, in a moment of danger, it could count on the protection of the Church and the Primate.

The year 1963 was coming to an end. Cardinal Wyszyński spent its last day in Gniezno, where he had gone with his close colleague Bishop Bronisław Dąbrowski. It had been a difficult year. The Primate compared it with 1953, when he had been arrested. Then there had been an open fight with the Church; now there were attempts to tear it apart from inside—and not simply through such marginal tactics as the "patriotic priests," but through criticism of the "Marianism of the Primate and the Episcopate." The most painful blow had been the death of a true and close friend, Pope John XXIII. It was heartening, on the other hand, to see how the nation had grown solid in defending its right to God, and how the clergy had survived the trial of repression by taxes. The fact that all of the young seminarians conscripted to the army had served out their time and returned with their vocations intact was a great victory.

5

Great Deeds and
Greatest Struggle (1964-1970)

Over the next seven years, with the struggle for church freedom, spiritual identity, and human rights at its most arduous, Cardinal Wyszyński realized his life's greatest work.

The open church-state conflict of 1963 was to continue until 1966, the year of the Millennium, when it reached its peak. At the beginning of 1964, Cardinal Wyszyński was working hard to prepare the Millennium and Marian programs, and to brace the Church's organization and personnel for even the sharpest confrontation. On January 13 he received a letter from the Vatican secretary of State naming Karol Wojtyła—whom Wyszyński had nominated in a *terno*—as Archbishop of Cracow. A key, long-unsettled personnel question was thus settled, and Cardinal Wyszyński had gained an invaluable, extraordinarily loyal co-worker. "The long and difficult fatherlessness of the archdiocese, following Cardinal Sapieha's passing," said the Primate in a January 17 message, "has ended —successfully, it seems. The rest is in the Hands of the Mediatrix of all graces, Mary, so loved by the new archbishop." Soon afterward, Bishops Stefan Barela and Bogdan Sikorski were confirmed as Ordinaries of Częstochowa and Płock, respectively.

The Episcopate met on February 5–7. Although the impasse in relations between Church and state continued, the government was trying to draw priests into committees preparing to celebrate the twentieth anniversary of the People's Republic. In view of the economic problems and the coming official celebrations, the state eased up slightly on the Church: the authorities gave up the effort to control seminary curricula, but turned around and demanded the right to inspect religious houses. Government representatives, irked by the way that the Primate insisted in his sermons that there was more to *Pacem in terris* than confirmation of communist peace propaganda, attacked Wyszyński at every meeting with other bishops. Neither were the authorities happy with a frank interview that the Primate had given to the French magazine *La Croix*, nor with a storm of rumors that on his last visit to Rome he had received Father Tadeusz Kirche, the chaplain of Radio Free Europe.

Knowing that the economic crisis was motivating a wave of opposition sentiment, the Episcopate decided not to make any fresh overtures to the government. The bishops wanted to stand firm with the nation in its needs and hardships; relations with the authorities went onto the back burner. Continuing pastoral activities in connection with the council and the eighth year of the Great Novena ("Fighting the National Faults and Achieving Christian Values") also occupied the Episcopate's attention.

In the first weeks of the new year, a succession of Znak figures—Antoni Gołubiew, Jacek Woźniakowski, Jerzy Zawieyski, and Jerzy Turowicz—visited the Primate with explanations of the *Opinion* that Stanisław Stomma had circulated in Rome. These talks helped improve relations with Znak, but they did not convince Wyszyński that the group had renounced Stomma's theses. The lay group failed to persuade the Cardinal to publish an answer in *Tygodnik Powszechny;* he preferred private discussions.

At the end of February the Primate prepared a letter to the

premier on the subject of the actions of the secret police in the parishes. According to the plan of Colonel Stanisław Morawski, the official in the Ministry of the Interior who dealt with the Church, the authorities intended to distract parish communities with plots and rumors stirred up by secret agents, hoping to drive a wedge between the clergy and the faithful.

On March 9, Cardinal Cicognani sent word that Bishop Edmund Nowicki had been named to succeed the late Bishop Splett as Ordinary of Gdańsk. After long effort, Gdańsk at last had a Polish ordinary.

The next meeting of the Episcopate, on April 1 and 2, featured a discussion of Father Kazimierz Przybylski's paper on the act of dedication in submission to the Virgin Mary, connected to the plan for the ninth year of the Great Novena ("Under the protection of the Virgin, Queen of Poland"). Bishop Antoni Pawłowski, the principal Marian theologian among the bishops, spoke of the idea of voluntary submission in servitude, and it was decided that in the year of the Millennium the bishops would dedicate the country in servitude to the Mother for the sake of church freedom in Poland and the world. Mary, after all, seemed to have been keeping her part of the "bargain": the faith of Poles had been maintained, and most young people were receiving religious instruction.

On April 14, the Primate received the five Znak delegates, led by Stanisław Stomma. This was an important step in ending the loss of confidence that had followed the Rome incident. The Primate pointed out the changing conditions in the country, the strengthening and deepening of the Church's work, and the way people were growing tired of the administration's atheization campaign.

On April 30 the Primate left for Rome, where he was received with the usual warmth by Vatican officials. On May 5, the day after his arrival, he had a special audience with the Pope at which he expressed his thanks for the decision on Gdańsk and reported that in Poland the bishops were avoiding needless polemics with the government while defending the principles of faith. He also spoke of his conferences in Saint Anne's about

Pacem in terris, remarking that in Poland the Church had become the main defender of human rights. The Holy Father, in turn, told Wyszyński that the bishops' letters to the clergy were a great help to him in understanding Polish affairs.

At a supper with Paul VI on May 17, Wyszyński brought up a subject close to the hearts of all the Polish bishops: the Pope's proclamation of Mary as Mother of the Church and the dedication to her of the Church and the whole world during the third session of the council. Despite reservations expressed from Belgium, the outlook was favorable; an eighth-century codex containing the term *Mater Ecclesiae* had been discovered. It was also during this supper that Wyszyński first shared his idea of a papal visit to Poland for the Millennium. The Holy Father seemed interested, though he joked that perhaps he would not be let out of Poland. It turned out differently—the government would not let him in. The evening ended with warm feelings all around: one of the Pope's secretaries turned out to know Poland very well, and everyone marveled at the pilgrimage on foot, 240 kilometers in nine days, from Warsaw to Częstochowa.

The next evening Wyszyński set out for Warsaw, where, on June 17–18, he informed the Episcopate of his visit and of the plans for the third session of the council. In the sort of tough language that the bishops rarely heard from him, the Primate characterized the affairs of the seminaries and the catechetical centers as so important that no bishop could spare any effort in standing up to the government on them. He distributed copies of his April 29 letter to the premier on the attempts to divide the parish in Wierzbica: the authorities, taking advantage of the priest's mental breakdown, had tried to set up a parish there independent of the Bishop of Sandomierz. Not only did Wyszyński protest in writing; he also visited Wierzbica and talked with the people. In doing so he ran a risk of physical danger, since long lines of militia trucks were running priests' cars off the road, and in Częstochowa there were uneasy prayers for the Primate's safety. But he went to Wierzbica by a side road, and no one dared do anything while he addressed the crowds there. Similar attempts were under way in Gardków, where the police wanted to destroy the existing parish and set up a church, independent of the hierarchy and completely dependent on the state. Wyszyński's personal appearance in Wierzbica put an end to such tactics for the time being, and the bishops thanked their leader for this new act of personal bravery.

Soon, however, the police were again active in Wierzbica, and Wyszyński sent a personal protest to Gomułka. Another antichurch campaign at this time involved efforts to recruit vacationing priests into the service of the secret police. Most cases involved nothing more than psychological pressure, but the circumstances made a restful vacation impossible.

Wyszyński spent the end of June at Jasna Góra, where he met and preached to pilgrims and also received Robert Kennedy and his family, who took communion together. Kennedy knew that the Polish authorities opposed his visit to the Primate, but he did not waver. For his part, Wyszyński broke his usual habit of avoiding foreign politicians and agreed to the meeting, discussions, and a group photograph in the monastery library.

At the beginning of July, the Primate was troubled by articles that appeared in *La France Catholique* and *Le Monde*. A confidential memorandum from the papal nuncio in France, Paolo Bertoli, to the French bishops had come to light, dealing with Pax, and charging that Piasecki's organization took its orders from the secret police and the Bureau of Religious Affairs. It was mistakenly attributed—internal evidence made the error obvious—to Wyszyński. The latter's rest was further disturbed by the knowledge that children in nearby holiday camps were being forbidden to attend Mass, and by the presence of "sad people," secret-police agents who followed him even on vacation.

Nevertheless, the Primate sent a telegram of condolences as soon as he learned of the death of Aleksander Zawadzki, the chairman of the Council of State, on September 7. The Vatican secretary of State, Cardinal Cicognani, also sent condolences in the name of Pope Paul. Both Wyszyński and the Vatican maintained this exemplary correctness toward the communist authorities for the sake of a future easing of tensions. For the time being, however, things did not change. Cardinal König of Vienna, always eager to visit Częstochowa, was again refused a visa.

On August 15 Wyszyński welcomed the traditional pilgrimage from Warsaw, and the next day he and Archbishop Wojtyła took part in the religious ceremonies at Kalwaria Zebrzydowska. It is interesting to compare these two national shrines. Częstochowa has an all-Polish character, while Kalwaria, near Cracow, is local, folk, mountaineer. It links the Marian cult with the sufferings of Christ.

The above-mentioned memorandum of Nuncio Bertoli was answered by Pax in the worst way possible, with an "Open letter to Cardinal Wyszyński," the most aggressive and hostile document ever directed against the Primate. Piasecki went ahead and published it, even though it created a chasm between his group and the Primate. On the one hand, the document proclaimed the ideological neutrality of the socialist state; on the other hand, it attacked Wyszyński in a manner resonant of the most extreme antichurch factions within the party. Neither stroke came to anything: the extremists never managed to break Wyszyński or to get rid of him, and the neutrality of the communist state remained a mirage. The Primate did not let Pax's erratic blow bother him. On August 22, however, he disclosed to Jerzy Zawieyski his pain at the effect such an attack against the bishops and the Great Novena would have in authentic Catholic circles. Zawieyski said that he was worried about the same possibility.

On September 3, after the great Marian feast at Jasna Góra and an exceptional retreat led for the Episcopate by Bishop Kazimierz Kowalski, the Episcopal Steering Committee met to discuss, among other matters, the Polish delegation to the council. It appeared that the authorities were finally realizing the damage done to Poland's reputation by the difficulties bishops encountered in obtaining passports. The Primate sent a letter to the premier about Archbishop Kominek's passport problems, and another one to the faithful about the true state of religious instruction. Archbishop Wojtyła and Bishop Dąbrowski were delegated to define a position on the *Open Letter* from Pax to the Primate.

When the Plenary Session of the Episcopate met the next day, they took a decisive stand against the authorities' threats of further repressions if nuns were not withdrawn from catechetical teaching. They were similarly intransigent in the matters of inspecting seminaries, and taxes. At the end of the session, Archbishop Baraniak read the Primate a letter from the Episcopate in protest against the scurrilities of the Pax document.

Wyszyński went to Cracow from Częstochowa, where he took part with Archbishop Wojtyła in church ceremonies on the six hundredth anniversary of the Jagiellonian University. Together the two drafted a letter to Vice-Marshal Kliszko about the removal of the university's theology department. They discussed the possibility of continuing the theology department's activities within the walls of Cracow's three seminaries.

Permission had still not been granted to build a church in Nowa Huta. Nevertheless, an enormous crowd came to the Cistercian monastery at nearby Mogiła to hear the Primate preach. Before leaving for Rome on September 11, Wyszyński also visited Lublin and Gniezno—a wearing pace for a frail man.

The third session of the Vatican Council opened on September 15, and on that same day the Pope received Cardinal Wyszyński at six in the evening for an hour's private audience, during which Paul heard with great satisfaction about the Polish pastoral activities connected with the council.

At the Pope's suggestion, Wyszyński gave *L'Osservatore Romano* an article about those pastoral activities, but he did not publish the Episcopate's answer (already translated into French) to Pax's *Open Letter:* rather than defend himself, the Primate relied on Divine Providence. At the same time, he refused to cancel the pastoral letter on religious education despite worrisome intervention by the government. The price of his refusal was a new round of libels in the Polish press.

In Russia, a sensational palace revolution toppled Khrushchev on October 16. There was no immediate visible change in church policy among the Eastern-bloc states. A Catholic layman brought word that Gomułka had ruled out bypassing Wyszyński in a Vatican-Warsaw agreement. Yet the Cardinal learned that members of his secretariat were being interrogated by the secret police in his absence. The party was clearly split in its line toward the Church.

Znak, despite its mistakes of the previous year, was now working to bring the Primate into the Warsaw-Vatican discussions, even suggesting an interview over the telephone with *Tygodnik Powszechny*. But the Primate refused, knowing neither the true intentions of the party nor the effects of Khrushchev's removal. On October 30, during a discussion in the council hall with Monsignor Poggi, Wyszyński asked that Zawieyski, as a member of the Council of State, be received in a papal audience. At the same time, he agreed to the publication of the letter of the Polish bishops in reply to the *Open Letter*, since the matter was being discussed continually in the world press. He also pointed out to Poggi that the publication in Poland of defamatory brochures gave the authorities a pretext to represent the Primate as responsible for "unfavorable information" about the country.

On November 1 the Primate received a confidential report that upon reading the pastoral letter concerning the harassment of religious education, Gomułka had ordered, "Do what you've been doing, only quietly, and back off if they put up a fight." Instead of an improvement in the Church's situation, a sharper struggle seemed to lie ahead.

At his next audience with the Polish Council Fathers* on November 4, the Pope thanked all of Poland for its prayers for

---

*The bishops from Poland who participated in the Second Vatican Council (1963–1965). Any bishop who takes part in an ecumenical council is called a "council father."

the council and promised that he himself would proclaim Mary as Mother of the Church. That same day Wyszyński received a letter from the Pope and a beautiful chalice for the Warsaw Cathedral. The Apostolic See was supporting the Primate's program to the fullest extent.

On November 20, Monsignor Poggi informed Wyszyński that he and Archbishop Samoré had met with Zawieyski and explained to him that although the Church was not avoiding discussions, it was necessary to create the proper conditions first. If there were a cessation of attacks on the bishops and the Primate, then there could be discussions—in Rome or in the Vatican, but in any case in contact with the Polish bishops. Zawieyski's mission was of course a test; Gomułka thought he might get some sort of "easy" understanding, like the Hungarian one. Now, however, he would know that it was impossible to go over Wyszyński's head.

On November 21, with great elation of spirit, Stefan Wyszyński heard the Holy Father fulfill his promise and, after the announcement of the dogmatic constitution on the Church, speak of the Virgin Mary and proclaim her as Mother of the Church. The hall reacted with a standing ovation, a general exultation that testified to the unity of the Church, and not to any division into liberal and conservative camps. No one doubted that the proclamation was a personal triumph for the Primate of Poland, the Episcopate, Jasna Góra, the propagators of the Marian cult, and the whole Polish Church. Many of the council fathers offered warm congratulations to Cardinal Wyszyński. That same day, in a private audience, Pope Paul said, "We follow everything that Your Eminence says, we rejoice in your courage, moderation, spiritual maturity, and the great supernatural spirit that guides you."

Paul VI received Jerzy Zawieyski on November 25, 1964, despite many accusations that had been made against Zawieyski in Rome. The meeting of a member of the Council of State of People's Poland with the Pope owed much to the efforts of Cardinal Wyszyński, whom the party organ *Trybuna Ludu* had called an enemy of the country. Zawieyski met with

a warm reception, but his proposals went nowhere. The sus-
pension of attacks on the Polish Church remained a condition
for a Warsaw-Vatican agreement.

On November 29, Cardinal Wyszyński consecrated Władysław Rubin as a bishop and as his delegate for the pastoral care
of Poles abroad. On December 2, when the Cardinal left for
home, Archbishop Del 'Acqua came to the Termini Station
and told him, "I do not see cardinals off, but the Polish one I
must. On behalf of the Holy Father, I wish you a pleasant
return to Poland." Ambassador Willman was also there: the
government was finally beginning to understand Cardinal
Wyszyński's stature in the world.

The Episcopate discussed the whole situation on December
16–18. The public was fatigued and distrustful of the government because of the economic difficulties and the fractiousness
of the party, and the Primate remarked that the Church ought
to listen to the voice of the people. Because there were personal
battles going on within the party, and because all the factions
were morally and ideologically confused, it would be wrong
to be associated with any faction. And there should be no
initiative for discussions in light of the continuing attacks on
the Primate and the bishops. Negotiations could begin only if
the government took the first step.

As for religious instruction, the Episcopate decided to appeal on the basis of the provisions of several international conventions (the Paris convention and the declaration of religious
freedom) that had been ratified by and proclaimed in Poland.
They also adopted a stiff position on the questions of taxes and
the so-called inventory books of church property. Similarly,
the bishops upheld their earlier refusal to allow state inspections of the seminaries. All this recalled the days of the Russian
partitions, when the bishops also resisted an inspectorate of
seminaries.

Most of the meeting was taken up with matters related to the
council: Bishop Bareła of Częstochowa read a report on pastoral activities around the country, and the bishops decided to
issue a pastoral letter on the council on January 24, 1965. A

majority approved the introduction of the Polish language into the liturgy.

Cardinal Wyszyński met with Jerzy Zawieyski a few days later, to discuss the latter's talk with Gomułka. The party chief had remarked that since the Vatican was aware of Warsaw's desire for an agreement, the Vatican ought to take the initiative. When Zawieyski said that he had been able to see the Pope only because of Wyszyński's intervention, Gomułka said, "Always that cardinal." Zawieyski had also talked with Edward Ochab, who had not been informed at all about the writer's mission. Running things autocratically, Gomułka wanted to establish relations between "the Vatican state and the Polish state" rather than to reach an understanding with the Church. After thanking Zawieyski, Gomułka commented that the latter's talk with the Pope had been private, not public. Thus the party washed its hands of the Zawieyski mission: that was how it dealt with intermediaries who wanted to believe that the communists would voluntarily give up their ideological monopoly.

Before Christmas the Primate learned that the secret police had been trying to recruit his barber as an informant; Wyszyński consoled the man. Members of the Cardinal's family were being pressured in various ways. The authorities had a psychosis about the Primate, the sources of which could be found in the party's troubles and the Cardinal's moral victories. Much of the pressure was half intentional, a result of party infighting: the forces vying for power wanted to use Cardinal Wyszyński to provoke Gomułka into a final, irreparable mistake.

The Episcopate could discern no positive developments at its meeting of January 26–27, 1965. Earlier in the month, Wyszyński had met the Znak delegates, Stomma, Zawieyski, Kisielewski, Łubieński, and Mazowiecki, who had been searching fruitlessly for a *modus vivendi*. The bishops could see no prospect of reactivating the Joint Commission, and they were still reluctant to launch new initiatives. There was one positive note: in Cracow, they learned, Archbishop Wojtyła was trying to re-establish the university's theology department. The bishops approved Bishop Choromański's letter to the government, which firmly rejected state inspection of the seminaries; there would be a confrontation if the inspectors tried to enter. The Episcopate was allowing itself to hope, despite all the problems, that Poland's having ratified the international conventions would alleviate the situation.

When inspectors arrived at the Warsaw seminary they were turned away, and on March 5 the Primate sent the premier a letter rejecting on principle such forms of control. That same day, he lectured on the council at the Warsaw Catholic Intellectuals' Club. During this period he was seeing more of the Znak delegates; relations with the group had improved since the tense time of the second council session. Nevertheless, because of the paper's attitude toward the Great Novena and the council, he did not send a congratulatory letter to *Tygodnik Powszechny* on the twentieth anniversary of its founding.

The March meeting of the Episcopate decided on an additional letter, to be signed by all the bishops, concerning the inspection of the seminaries. The government was also to be notified about planned church celebrations during the Millennial Year and about the matter of inviting the Pope to Poland. The last was left for Wyszyński to discuss privately with the premier, since the world was already full of talk about a papal visit to Poland.

In April, among other issues, the bishops discussed the ambiguous release of Cardinal Beran, who had exchanged confinement in Prague for confinement in Rome. The bishops asked themselves whether such a compromise was proper. In any case, it was a course far different from the one steered by Wyszyński in 1955 and 1956. Bishop Choromański reported that Director Żabiński had been succeeded at the Bureau of Religious Affairs by his assistant, Dr. Aleksander Skarżyński. It was hard to deduce anything from the change except that an intelligent man of extreme views was coming into office. The Episcopate adopted Bishop Klepacz's suggestion that the deans write letters in protest against the antichurch campaign in the press. Otherwise, the usual problems were discussed. With the passing of time, the pressure on the Church was not diminishing, even though its effects were the opposite of what the authorities intended.

On April 21 the deans and vice-deans of the Archdiocese of Gniezno wrote a joint letter protesting the blasphemous program of atheization underwritten by the government, the calumnies being directed at the Primate, the banning of church construction, and the refusal to include priests and religious in the state health-insurance plan. The bishops had been defending priests and church institutions—now they found defenders in the ranks of the clergy.

On the second day of the assembly of the deans in Gniezno, Wyszyński presented an assessment of the situation that went right to the point. "Our hopes: (1) that the Church be saved—we have held out for twenty years; (2) that the people in the party be convinced that the struggle with the Church is fruitless; (3) that the Paris convention and the Declaration of Religious Freedom awaken the conscience of the world; (4) that the enemies of the Church (Ilyichev) leave; (5) that the Church endure and have confidence in the future." It would be hard to put things more concisely or accurately. The next day the entire clergy of the Archdiocese of Gniezno dedicated itself in servitude to the Mother of the Church, and similar acts were initiated in all the dioceses of Poland.

On May 5 the Primate left for Rome, and on the 9th he was co-consecrator for Monsignor Poggi as archbishop. On the 10th he discussed the possibility of a papal visit, with Monsignor Del'Acqua, to Poland on May 3, 1966. On the 11th he had an audience, during which the Pope expressed his misgivings about the situation of the Church in Czechoslovakia. Paul VI was also interested in a memorandum on abortion that the Polish Episcopate had written, and told Wyszyński that he himself was preparing an encyclical on the problem. The Primate and the Pope met again on the 20th to discuss the council, about which they shared some concerns. Next they talked about the Millennium and the rumors associated with a papal visit—the Pope was actually being accused of wanting to support a communist regime—and the Holy Father proposed that the decision not be made until the press had quieted down. After the two men had prayed together for the Millennium, the Pope spoke of the troubles he had brought on himself by proclaiming Mary the Mother of the Church. They prayed together again. The Cardinal who was persecuted in his own country was a moral support in the Vatican.

Monsignor Casaroli informed the Primate that Ambassador Willman had established contact with the Vatican about a possible understanding and had begun discussions on the Western Lands. The Vatican answered that such talks were possible only in close consultation with the Primate. If the government actually wanted an agreement with the Vatican it was starting on the wrong foot, since little could be done about the Western Lands in the absence of a treaty between Poland and West Germany. However, the government was more interested in internal matters and the chance of undermining Cardinal Wyszyński, though as usual it failed.

On his return to the country, the Primate learned that the administrative authorities had toughened up and were refusing to confirm the nominations of priests to ecclesiastical positions. As a mark of protest, the Primate did not vote in the elections on May 30 (in any case, the elections were becoming more and more of a farce). Wyszyński threw himself into pastoral work. Nearly every diocese sent him an invitation, and he did not say no to any of them. While he was traveling and speaking to great crowds, the official press attacked him incessantly. Rumors were propagated about a feud between Wyszyński and Cardinal König, even though it was the Polish government that had twice refused König a visa. Similarly, the Primate was accused of not wanting to take part in the twentieth anniversary of the victory over Hitler. The rumor that the Primate opposed the papal visit topped everything; soon the communists fell silent while the Primate went about his apostolic duties.

At the June 22–23 meeting of the Episcopate, the bishops

discussed the inertia of the central authorities and new local harassment. Attacks on bishops enhanced, rather than undercut, their authority. It was decided that as many bishops as possible should take part in the fourth session of the Vatican Council, while observing the principle that at least one bishop should remain behind in each diocese. A special effort would be made to allow those who had not yet taken part to attend the council. It was decided to organize a women's pilgrimage to Częstochowa on August 26, to refuse to allow inspectors into the seminaries, and not to answer personal questionnaires demanding detailed information about priests. The authorities had even tried to interfere in the selection of rectors at KUL and the Academy of Catholic Theology. Eventually compromise candidates—Fathers Wincenty Granat and Józef Iwanicki, respectively—had been chosen.

The party also kept trying to split the bishops, as the Primate learned when Archbishop Wojtyła reported on a discussion he had had with Zenon Kliszko. The vice-marshal had made a special trip to Cracow, dangled the prospect of a permit for building a church in Nowa Huta before the archbishop's eyes, and gone on to speak about the possibilities of a papal visit to Poland during the Millennium and of a trip to America for the Primate. Kliszko opposed both visits. The discussion was ideological, and Kliszko, criticizing Wyszyński, tried fruitlessly to win Wojtyła as an ally. The party's naïveté, driven by the desire for atheization, had passed all previous limits in this attempt to divide the bishops, which was as much a daydream as the efforts to split the Episcopate from the Vatican.

On August 6 the Primate told his visitor, the prominent journalist Cat Mackiewicz, that a declaration on creative freedom issued recently by thirty-four writers was the first sign of dignity among the artistic intelligentsia, who until then had been acting in a pragmatic manner. Aside from the years 1955–56, about which the Primate knew little because of his imprisonment, his intuition was basically right; he knew the writers' declaration signaled the beginning of a revolt by the intellectuals.

The long-prepared women's pilgrimage brought three hundred thousand female participants to the ninth recitation of the Jasna Góra vows on August 26, 1965. Before the vows, the great crowd stood in silence, holding lighted candles in their left hands and holding their right hands over their hearts. The collective nature of the ceremonies had a great strengthening effect.

On September 1 the Episcopate met publicly in Wrocław Cathedral to hear Archbishop Kominek speak on the Church's twenty years in the Western Lands. In his opening remarks, the Primate underlined the fact that the Episcopate was meeting in that place during these days before the thousandth anniversary of Polish Christianity. He said that the present boundaries of Poland included all the dioceses that had been linked to the metropolitan of Gniezno in the year 1000. Such historical arguments were received grudgingly in West Germany: there, the borders were regarded as a result of the Second World War, and rightly so. But in Poland, with its dramatic past, history plays a different role from in the West. Besides, the Germans themselves use historical arguments and will not admit that the interpretations of the Poles proceed from incontrovertible facts. This does not change the fact that Polish mounds and monuments stand beside German ones in the Western Lands or that German culture was present there for six centuries. Let us hope that the Wrocław celebrations, which stirred up such a controversy in 1965, can be seen today in a calm and objective light.

The same session of the Episcopate sent Pope Paul a letter, signed by all present, to inform him officially of the thousandth anniversary of Polish Christianity. After the meeting it turned out that the censor would not permit the publication of an issue of *Nasza Przeszłość* (Our Past) devoted to the twentieth anniversary of the Church in the Western Lands. The displeasure of certain German circles and the displeasure of the Polish communists coincided here.

On September 8, the Feast of the Nativity of the Blessed Virgin, almost all the bishops dedicated their dioceses in servitude to the Mother of the Church, and the ceremonies attracted an unexpectedly large number of the faithful. Spiritual instinct drew them to the side of the Church, leaving the atheist forces deserted. A marked increase in the number of those receiving Holy Communion and of priestly vocations also testified to the change in public attitudes.

The patriotic church celebrations in Wrocław must have rubbed the authorities the wrong way. On September 8 the Primate told Jerzy Zawieyski that seminarians were being conscripted in all dioceses. The Warsaw seminary had been hit with a pair of astronomical tax assessments. Priests were having more passport troubles. The censor had confiscated entire pastoral letters, including those about the Western Lands.

Still, Wyszyński pushed ahead. On September 8 he dedicated the Archdiocese of Warsaw in servitude to Mary before a throng of believers whose serious and dignified mood showed that they understood the act as a spiritual, voluntary, and decided plea for church freedom. The communists understood as well. On the 10th, Bishop Dąbrowski went to the Bureau of Religious Affairs and listened to the exceptions taken in principle to a pastoral letter on the dedications. The Primate offered, in good will, to drop one phrase, particularly disagreeable to the authorities, about "programmed laicization, atheization, and demoralization." While at the office, however, Dąbrowski delivered a sharp protest against the unfair conscriptions, taxes, and denials of passports for bishops wishing to attend the council.

The Primate left for Rome on September 13, the fourth session of the council opened on the 14th, and on the 16th he had an evening audience with Paul VI. Wyszyński informed the Pope about the situation of the Church in the East, to which the Holy Father replied that he regarded the Polish Primate as his representative in that part of Europe. He also proposed an audience with all the representatives of the Polish Episcopate in Rome as a mark of his respect, and invited the Primate to supper.

Wyszyński was occupied also with Bishop Rubin over the

issue of Poles abroad. They planned a visit to America for the
next year, at the invitation of American Polonia, but unfortunately that visit was to be prevented by reasons beyond the
Primate's control.

During the discussion of the council schema on the Church
in the contemporary world on September 20, Cardinal Wyszyński delivered an important address in which he drew attention
to the fact that dialectical materialism had changed the meaning of concepts like freedom, law, justice, and the state in the
"second world." He called for the recognition of this changed
reality in the pronouncements of the council. His address
struck the council fathers as a complete *novum,* practically
incomprehensible. The West was still wrapped up in itself and
its own problems. Calmly and reasonably, the Primate of Poland called on it to open its eyes. Many of the council fathers
later asked him for copies of the speech.

Excursions of Polish priests to the council, organized by the
state authorities without the approval of the Episcopate,
created a very bad impression in the Vatican and even had to
be specially explained to the Holy Father. There were also
large crowds of Polish laity, mainly from Pax and the Christian
Social Association but also from Znak and *Więź.* The Primate
was troubled because many of these lay people presented the
state's partial view of church matters and ignored the facts
made accessible through the documents of the Episcopate.

On October 28 the Pope, with Cardinal Wyszyński as con-
celebrant, held a special Mass in the Basilica for bishops and
cardinals from the Eastern-bloc countries.

On November 4, considering that the council's declaration
on religious freedom would present only a one-sided, Western
view of the matter, the Polish bishops sent a special letter to
the Pope asking that their views be taken into account.

The Pope received all the Polish bishops on November 13,
Saint Stanisław's day. The Primate managed to touch on the
matter of the papal visit to Poland, still a hot subject in the
Italian press, with a delicacy much appreciated by the Holy
Father. He also asked for an apostolic letter to the Polish nation

on the occasion of the Millennium. Finally, he requested trust in the Polish bishops, who had suffered so much, and in the Polish Church, which had been faithful to the Holy See since the times of John XIII and Sylvester II. Paul VI had a prepared Latin text in hand, but first he spoke in Italian on the question of Wyszyński's request for trust. He stressed the fact that his trust had not been shaken: "We trust you, we look upon you in faith, we appreciate your position and your work." Then the Pope went on to read his Latin address, which was concerned entirely with the Millennium. In giving the apostolic blessing, the Pope asked Wyszyński to participate and, abashed, the Primate did so. When he said farewell to the general of the Pauline order, Father Tomziński, Paul remarked that he had been at Jasna Góra once and hoped that it would not be the last time.

This account of the meeting between the Pope and the Polish bishops, based upon Polish sources, differs entirely from that of the distinguished German journalist Hansjakob Stehle. Like the official Warsaw press, Stehle contends that the request for trust was ill-received by the Pope and resulted in the limited success of the council declarations in Poland. Stehle notes that *L'Osservatore Romano* printed only the Pope's remarks. Our account shows, however, that the Pope first spoke to the bishops spontaneously, in Italian, before going on to read the prepared Latin text that was printed in *L'Osservatore;* the Pope's spontaneous reply to the Primate could not be printed because nowhere was it written down. In this case, Stehle proceeded from incomplete sources.

The government emissaries managed to create, in some circles of Western opinion, the impression that Cardinal Wyszyński was a hardened conservative, who together with the rest of the Polish bishops found himself isolated at the council. They pointed to Wyszyński's declaration in favor of traditional religiosity—which was a far more suitable policy than either church renewal or readiness for dialogue in the struggle against state atheism. In fact, the Primate protected the religious and national traditions and the Polish aspiration for national and spiritual identity. Only after many years did some people in the West appreciate this achievement. To categorize the Primate as an opponent of the principal directions of the council is, however, a great mistake. The Polish Episcopate was not isolated at the council; in fact, it shone there to such a degree that thirteen years later one of the Polish council fathers became pope.

The Primate told the council that words like "freedom," "law," and "justice" are always ambiguous under a communist system. But an elementary familiarity with his remarks at the council shows how well he understood its spirit. The communists presented him as a foe of ecumenism, but consider what he wrote in *Tygodnik Powszechny* in 1965:

> Let's not be prosecutors. We should not try to fix the blame for the division of Christianity into Western and Eastern, or for the division of the Western into Protestantism and other reformed groups, because to do so leads nowhere. . . . When ecumenism begins with historical considerations it always leads to irritations and uneasiness, and never to a step forward. Thus we have an understanding: we will not look at the past; rather, we will look elsewhere—to what unites us.

Looking at the new church constitution in the same *Tygodnik* article, Cardinal Wyszyński evinced his persistent desire to correlate the spirit of conciliar renewal with Polish religious traditions and spiritual needs that pervaded not only an elite but an entire nation.

> The whole church constitution is at once Christocentric and Marian. It is as if there are arms to embrace the Family of Man. . . . The Church includes both Christ and His Mother. Both have their appointed tasks. The council, appropriately, has brought Mariology into contact with ecclesiology.
> The Church must be human, which means it must be

sensitive to all its children. For priests, there is a danger of clericalizing the Church. Similarly, intellectuals pose a danger when they want to overintellectualize the Church, so that it would be made up only of philosophers. The Church must minister in a language everyone understands.

He went on to say that the age of apologetics in theology was coming to an end, and that in the new, positive theology the Polish traditions of combining Christocentrism and Marianism would be completely up to date.

This is hardly to say that Wyszyński lost sight even for a moment of the important role of religious tradition in a situation with outside political and spiritual influences. On the contrary, we shall see shortly how great a part those traditions played in leading the Polish Church to a fate different from the fate of other churches in the Eastern bloc. Now, however, when considering the Millennium, it is important to underline not only the faithfulness of Poland to the council, but also Poland's simultaneous, fruitful inspiration of the council and the country's own religious traditions. This specifically Polish combination was appreciated only later, and even then not everywhere. It was insufficiently understood in the period before the Millennium, while the communist government did everything it could to depict the Church, in domestic and foreign opinion, as occupying an extremely "conservative" position. Cardinal Wyszyński did not allow himself to be particularly concerned with the problem just then, because there were too many other urgent matters at hand, especially in the Millennial Year.

The harassment of the Church, mainly through taxes and the conscription of seminarians, continued apace. Numerous attacks on the bishops were printed, especially on the Primate.

The *spiritus movens* of the antichurch press attacks and intrigues was the Polish correspondent in Rome, Ignacy Krasicki. In an article for *Życie Warszawy* entitled "The Cardinal and the Gifts," Krasicki maliciously interpreted one meeting of Polish and Spanish bishops; in the political subtext, Wyszyński was accused of accepting liturgical gifts from the "fascist" Spain of General Franco. The discrediting of the Primate was attempted on every possible occasion. And soon the greatest occasion of all presented itself.

* * *

While in Rome, the Polish bishops sent letters informing all fifty-six national episcopates of the coming Millennium of Christian Poland. The letter to the German bishops contained the famous, historical phrase "We forgive and we ask to be forgiven," which was mentioned in the Roman press on December 2. On the preceding day, Cardinal Wyszyński had held a discussion with Cardinal Döpfner, who expressed some moderate criticism of Wyszyński's Wrocław sermon. Döpfner had been pained by Wyszyński's failure to mention the German contribution to the culture of the Western Lands. The Primate answered that he had not been speaking of the whole history of the region, but only of the year 1000, when Wrocław came under the authority of the Archdiocese of Gniezno. Both men paid tribute to the sufferings of German and Polish migrants. Cardinal Döpfner stressed that there could be no thought of further displacements of people, and he declared for a Europe without borders. This idea found no reflection in the German mass media, which commented on the letter of the Polish bishops purely in a political sense, rather than as an act of Christian reconciliation.

In the first days of December, news reached Rome that the party Central Committee in Warsaw had discussed the possibility of arresting the Primate because of his speech to the council but that this proposal had been voted down. Regardless of such news or rumors, however, the government was plainly preparing for a "decisive" showdown with the Primate. As usual, Stefan Wyszyński went imperturbably about his duties.

At the meeting of the council on December 4, Archbishop

Felici read Wyszyński's message about the Millennium and announced that all the council fathers would be receiving copies of the Black Madonna, Queen of Poland. The announcement was greeted with applause. Later, on what would be called the "Polish day" at the council, many bishops asked the Primate to autograph their copies of the icon. In the afternoon, Wyszyński attended the blessing of the cornerstone of the Church of the Blessed Virgin of Częstochowa, which was being built in the working-class neighborhood of Borgeto di Rustica at Paul VI's initiative. After he and Cardinal Traglia had spoken, the Primate was besieged by the residents of the district, including many mothers and children, who asked for his blessing.

The council was coming to a close. To great enthusiasm, the decree of excommunication of the Eastern Church, which had divided the Church into East and West, was lifted at a public session on December 7. The next day the council ended.

On the 9th, Professor Stefan Świeżawski, the Polish auditor,* informed the Primate of the accusations being prepared against him by the authorities. Świeżawski had learned about them from the editor of the atheist *Argumenty*, Tadeusz Jaroszewski, who would later become the assistant chief ideologue in a period when Marxism was treated as merely a blind for the *status quo*. Now, Jaroszewski was accusing the Primate of inflexibility, rigidity, inaccessibility, and even of tyranny.

The party was upset because Stefan Wyszyński was speaking in the name of the nation. Wyszyński never thought of it that way, even though as Primate he had the moral right to do so. The most perverse charge, that the Primate opposed an agreement with the Vatican, came just when he was doing everything in his power to make Paul's visit to Poland possible. The Primate favored a Warsaw-Vatican agreement, but natu-

---

*The Second Vatican Council, besides bishops and their advisers *(periti)*, allowed a number of "auditors"—"listeners"—to attend, including the laity. They were like an "audience" who, on occasion, could be called upon for information or advice. Stefan Świeżański, the Polish auditor, was Professor of the History of Medieval Philosophy at the Catholic University of Lublin.

rally only if it took into account the rights and needs of the Church. Since the party had no intention of fulfilling such a condition, it raised a hue and cry.

Also on December 9, the Primate took his farewell of the Holy Father, who spoke openly of his desire to travel to Poland. Still, it was a delicate matter that left Paul full of misgivings: would the visit be construed as an approval of communism? "I oppose [communism] with all my spirit," the Pope said, "as I oppose the tormenting of man." Of his own initiative, the Pope told Wyszyński, "There should certainly have been more said against communism at the council, and in strong terms. But that might have hurt you. Believe me, we are cautious not out of fear, but out of love." He added, "I trust you. We will proceed cautiously and deliberately, even though my heart breaks when I see your troubles. I always admire your sincerity and support you in my prayers." So spoke the Pope whom the communist propagandists praised and contrasted with the Primate. As Wyszyński left, the Pope said, "Until we meet in Poland."

The Cardinal was welcomed home more warmly and enthusiastically than ever, as a public response to the press's attacks on the Episcopate, asking in whose name and by what rights the letter asking for forgiveness had been sent to the German bishops. The Gomułka leadership thought it could actually win the sympathy of the people away from the Primate. As usual, however, the party went too far and lost the psychological contest. Anti-German feelings were still strong in Poland, but so were the traditions of freedom and tolerance that favored the idea of Christian reconciliation.

The day after the Primate returned, Bishop Choromański welcomed him to the Warsaw Cathedral with the warmest of words. In thanking him, the Primate made the unexpected gesture of kissing the bishop's hand. This, the Primate remarked, was his way of thanking the elderly bishop for twenty years of continual struggle for church freedom. The faithful understood this unusual and moving scene in the light of the all-out attack being developed against the Church. During the

Primate's sermon, people filled the church and stood in the street outside as far as the eye could see.

At the December 14–16 meeting of the Episcopate, the causes of the new campaign against the Church were analyzed, among which the letter to the German bishops was considered most important. The party had been arguing that the Soviet Union was the sole guarantor of Poland's borders. Now the Western press was full of remarks about the prewar Soviet-German pact made at Poland's expense. The council speeches of Wyszyński and Archbishop Baraniak had upset the authorities. Besides, a great antichurch campaign was in the cards for the Millennial Year, when church ceremonies would marshal the feelings of society. A papal visit would be particularly significant. Thus, the party decided at the end of 1965 to go on the offensive during the next year, and to refuse permission for a visit by Pope Paul, using the Spanish affair and the German letter as pretexts.

On December 18 the weekly *Forum* published inaccurate texts of the letters exchanged by the Polish and German bishops; the text of the Polish bishops' letter contained more than two hundred inaccuracies.

At this time, Rev. Dr. Ignacy Tokarczuk, who would become the bishop most violently attacked by the authorities, was named Ordinary of Przemyśl.

Figures from various political circles—prewar Christian Democratic activists, writers, and journalists, including Stanisław Mackiewicz—visited the Primate to congratulate him on the letter to the German bishops. Such people sharply criticized Jerzy Zawieyski's wavering speech in the Sejm, during which the Znak delegate had been "pained" by the letter. Jerzy Turowicz later straightened things out by standing firmly on the side of the Episcopate during a meeting of the National Front, which produced a violent polemic from Gomułka.

Archbishop Wojtyła had stayed behind in Rome, and when he returned the antichurch campaign was in full swing. At this December 21 meeting with the Primate, the two men frankly discussed the way in which the government, relying on the archbishop's customary great moderation, was trying to set them against each other. But Wojtyła's loyalty was absolute, and any opposition was out of the question. In fact, these efforts by the authorities may well have enhanced the unanimity of views that endured between Wojtyła and Wyszyński. Once again Zenon Kliszko had judged people wrongly and failed.

At Christmas the Primate met with groups of clergy, professionals, and lay people who packed the churches in an expression of solidarity. The government, on the other hand, was organizing "resolutions" against the letter to the German bishops among teachers and schoolchildren. The illegibility of many of the teachers' signatures testified to the shame with which people took part in these coerced actions. The Primate's office also received hundreds of protest letters written in the same hand.

In January 1966, the Primate decided to go to Rome in connection with the opening of the Millennium and the possibility of a papal visit to Poland. At this point an event occurred which stirred up a scandal around the world. The undersecretary of State in the Council of Ministers informed Bishop Choromański on January 7 that the Primate would not receive a passport because he had acted contrary to the interests of the state on his previous trips abroad. In this the Gomułka leadership had committed one of its greatest blunders. The Primate decided not to petition for a reversal of the unprecedented decision, but he asked Bishop Choromański to lodge a sharp protest. When the matter found its way into the foreign press and radio broadcasts, the government had to issue an official communiqué that evoked consternation in public opinion. People now better understood the motives for the attacks on the letter to the German bishops, which had become the pretext for refusing Wyszyński's passport. The Holy Father sent the Primate a sympathetic telegram. A conference of the Warsaw deans protested against the prevention of the Cardinal's participation in the opening of the international celebration of the Millennium. On January 15 the press published the speech

Gomułka had delivered at a session of the National Front dedicated to the thousandth anniversary of the Polish state (which had been established simultaneously with the conversion of King Mieszko in 966). Gomułka blustered that Wyszyński was trying to turn Poland, which had been part of the East for twenty years, westward. He also attacked the letter to the German bishops.

A layman asked Wyszyński, after a Mass, whether it was true, as *Der Spiegel* had written, that the Vatican had inspired the rapprochement between the Polish and German bishops. Absolutely not, the Primate replied. The Holy See had taken no initiative in the matter; it was only certain Western circles that could not understand that the "conservative" Wyszyński had initiated the reconciliation.

The Episcopal Steering Committee met on January 17, cheered by the thought that the Church was winning morally, and on an international scale. They had extended their hands in reconciliation, regardless of the charges of nationalism hurled at them from abroad. There were signs of a retreat in the press: from the early accusations of "treason" Gomułka had shifted the accent to the "Eastern question," which was far from popular in a country belonging to Latin, European civilization. The Primate remarked that the Episcopate should let the government propaganda "exhaust itself" and afterward the bishops could decide what action to take. He endured the unceasing personal attacks in the newspapers with iron nerves. On February 7, *Życie Warszawy* published "An Open Letter to Primate Wyszyński from Henryk Ryszewski"—a schoolmate of Wyszyński's who had accepted help from the Primate's secretariat before letting himself be turned into a tool of defamation.

When the bishops met in February, it was plain that the authorities had lost the battle. Gomułka's speech about allegiance to the East had stifled whatever doubts the people had about the letter to the German bishops. At the same time, bishops returning from abroad reported an increase everywhere in the prestige of the Polish Church and its leader. In

1956 the world had been captivated by the two names, Gomułka and Wyszyński. Now only Wyszyński's carried any authority. Poles living abroad supported the Primate. On January 10
Archbishop Kominek had granted an interview to Hansjakob
Stehle, who had criticized Wyszyński in the past. The German
journalist had become fascinated with the subject of the letter.
There were even reports of ambivalent feelings about the letter
within the party. The attacks on the Church were being attributed to Gomułka's nationalistic enemies, Piasecki, and certain Soviet-oriented figures. In Germany a new history of the
Polish Church was being published, and in Rome a German-
Polish historical institute was being planned. Germans were
beginning to make penitential journeys to Poland, and compensation was finally being paid to Polish priests who had been
imprisoned in the concentration camps.

The bishops approved the text of a letter thanking the Pope
for his Christmas Eve message to Poland and for his presence
on January 13 at the ceremonies in Rome that marked the
beginning of the international Millennium observances. Actually, there was an unexpected benefit from the attacks on the
bishops: on the principle "Leave the priests alone while
fighting the hierarchy," the government had backed off from
its harsh taxation policy. While the government continued to
try to stir up panic to disrupt the preparations for the Millennium, the bishops went calmly about their work.

In the press, the fight went on. *Trybuna Ludu* recalled the
Primate's prewar writings against communism, and *Życie
Warszawy* published an article entitled "Two Cardinals" that
depicted Cardinal Hlond as a patriot and statesman in contrast
to Wyszyński, an enemy of the state. During a sermon in
Warsaw, Wyszyński remembered that at the trial of Bishop
Kaczmarek in 1953, the prosecutor had insisted on an answer
to the question "After all, was Hlond really a Pole?" Now
Wyszyński witnessed with pleasure the rehabilitation of his
predecessor. He would live, of course, to be praised himself by
the communists as a great patriot. One conclusion emerged
from these maneuvers—that the communists would have to

revise their entire postwar policy of church-state relations if they wanted a reconciliation. As another sign that its actions were mere short-term tactics, during the period of attacks on the hierarchy the Bureau of Religious Affairs suddenly declared its approval and support of the hitherto condemned religious orders.

On February 24, Józef Jarosz, painter and the husband of Stefan Wyszyński's sister Stanisława, died. The many condolences testified to the public mood, although a few people avoided the Primate's residence after the funeral.

On March 1, deciding that it was time to take a step toward dialogue, the Primate wrote a letter to Gomułka outlining all their differences. He also wrote to Cyrankiewicz about the Millennium and worked on a brochure for distribution abroad. Visitors from Znak brought news that the government was going to move on from press attacks to a campaign, redolent of 1953, of making trouble for individual bishops. "God's help is still there," the Cardinal told them.

The government continued stubbornly down a blind alley. On March 8 Premier Cyrankiewicz sent the entire Episcopate with the exception of Primate Wyszyński a letter. The bishops, in turn, sent letters to Gomułka, the premier, and the Council of State. They were anxious to maintain contact in view of coming visits by foreign guests—possibly including, they still hoped, the Pope.

On March 19 the head of the Council of State sent an evasive reply to the Primate, saying that church-state matters lay outside his competence. Ochab did allow himself to observe that there were no relations between Warsaw and the Vatican, and that the Pope acknowledged someone else—an allusion to Ambassador Papée (the emissary of the London government-in-exile), who had been granted Vatican residency out of humanitarian considerations.

When the Episcopate met on March 22–23, the bishops expressed their united support of the Primate in the face of the personal attacks that had been made on him. In turn, Stefan Wyszyński stated his readiness to step down from his post if it turned out that his leadership was damaging to the Church. However, as he had already informed the Vatican, he would never leave the country. The bishops judged that the party would not yet allow itself the sort of steps it had taken in 1953, even though they knew it was dangerous to underestimate the acts to which fear could lead. Bishop Jop of Opole observed that anyone in Cardinal Wyszyński's place would have come under the same sort of attack. The party was aiming at the disintegration of the Episcopate, and the Primate was an obstacle to the sort of developments that had taken place in Czechoslovakia and Hungary. During the conference of bishops, the Primate received an abusive letter from Gomułka that the Episcopate could only regard as evidence of mental disturbance. Among other business, the bishops received copies of the remarks by the historian Professor Oscar Halecki, made in Rome on January 13, that aroused such violent responses in the government. They also heard an explanation of the funds from Fulda (the city where the German Episcopate meets)—alleged German aid to Polish bishops but in fact merely the German Episcopate's share of Council expenses. Remarks were made about the government's futile, coquettish approaches to the religious orders in the latest attempt to fracture church unity.

In Gniezno on Holy Saturday, April 9, the official end of the ninth year of the Great Novena and the beginning of the Millennium were celebrated at the Gniezno Cathedral. No one could doubt the influence of the last nine years' work on the social influence, mass appeal, and unity of the Polish Church.

The first of the Millennium celebrations, a seminar on history and pontifical High Mass in the Gniezno Cathedral, took place on April 14. Forty thousand people heard the Primate preach and sang the *Te Deum* while the bells of the cathedral and all the churches in Gniezno rang. The next day, while Archbishop Wojtyła was leading the Episcopate in vespers at the cathedral, the peace was shattered by the crash of artillery —Defense Minister Spychalski was receiving a salute in the nearby Freedom Square, where the authorities were beginning their own, competing celebrations of the thousandth anniversary of the state. Gniezno established a pattern that would continue as the Millennium celebrations wound through the country: citizens broke through police cordons to stream away from the secular observances and toward the sacred ones. Nevertheless, Minister Spychalski delivered himself of an attack on the Church for the benefit of his remaining audience. Because the Church worked to preserve calm, there were no incidents. During the celebrations the icon of the Virgin of Częstochowa, which was to appear in each bishop's cathedral during the Millennial observances, was carried out of Gniezno —fifty thousand people turned out for its farewell—to Poznań. After their meeting, the state authorities made a hasty withdrawal of their own. The Primate and his bishops kept control of the situation, and the day ended in peace and dignity.

In Poznań the next day, the Primate's sermon was accompanied by the rumble of a twenty-five-gun salute from the "competing" state ceremonies. Gomułka had delivered a brutal personal attack on the Primate during his own speech, while Wyszyński (who knew nothing of the first secretary's remarks) spoke shortly afterward in a spirit of Christian restraint. The noticeable migration of auditors in the direction of the cathedral again served to foil the government's speeches. The bishops, who had come to Poznań in session, had no doubt about the outcome of the struggle for hearts and minds on which the government was insisting; as the Primate was saying good-bye to tens of thousands of the faithful, university students hoisted him and the car in which he was riding onto their shoulders.

It was clear by now that the authorities were not going to admit the Pope or any other foreign bishops and guests. On April 21 the Primate received a telegram in which Pope Paul expressed his distress at not being able to attend—to such an extent was the Gomułka regime compromising itself around the world. While the press attacks upon him continued unceasingly, Wyszyński prayed for Gomułka and for an end to the abuse of Poland's interests.

In addition to his own request to visit Poland, Paul had asked Ambassador Willman on April 17 that the Primate be allowed to come to Rome. Four days later, the Holy Father received negative answers on both counts, because of the Primate's alleged actions "unfavorable to the state." Archbishop Samoré protested the characterization. Then, a few days after the Pope failed to obtain his Polish visa, he received Andrei Gromyko. Gomułka seemed to be way off track, as he had been for some years; the Russians, and not the head of the Polish party, established the first contact with the Vatican. Cardinal Wyszyński appraised the situation coldly:

> I have been considering the consequences of the refusal to allow the Pope to come here. There will perhaps be a partial collapse of the Gomułka myth, but not a final collapse, since the world wants peace in Poland at all costs —that hushes the world's conscience in regard to Poland. "It must be all right there," the Western politicians say. Anyone who reveals the truth meets with incredulity. Every flutter of favorable light is fanned into a flame—it's not so bad there after all. These "world" expectations facilitate the work of the "cooperative Catholics" who tour the Western countries shining up Gomułka's image and smearing the Primate, on whom they blame the predicament of the Polish Church. . . .

On May 2 Father Goździewicz telephoned to Jasna Góra to relate news that Pope Paul had honored Cardinal Wyszyński with the title of papal legate for the next day's celebrations. On the morrow, before imparting the apostolic blessing as papal legate, the Primate reminded the faithful that Nuncio Ratti, Archbishop Giovanni Roncalli, and Monsignor Montini had all visited Częstochowa before becoming pope. Bishop Kominek preached during Mass, the Primate led the recitation of the Jasna Góra appeal in the evening, and crowds sang around the monastery long into the night.

The main celebrations of the Polish Millennium began the next day, with the act that dedicated the country in servitude to Mary, the Mother of the Church, for the sake of church freedom in the country and the world. In a breve that he later directed to Wyszyński, Pope Paul called this act a "second christening of Poland."

Not only the Pope, but also cardinals, bishops, and lay people from abroad had been refused admission to Poland. Some groups and individuals had managed to come anonymously, but the Pope's chair was empty, as the Primate's had been in 1956. On the empty chair stood a portrait of Paul VI wreathed in red and white roses. Three hundred thousand people stood below the monastery—and there would have been a million had the national and regional authorities not done all they could to keep people away.

On this extraordinary occasion, the miraculous icon of the Blessed Virgin was carried out of its chapel in procession. The Primate and bishops, priests, religious brothers and sisters, teachers, writers, former concentration-camp prisoners, workers, the Marian Commission of the Episcopate, and the Primate, again with members of the Primatial Institute, bore the Black Madonna in turn. At the end of the procession, Wyszyński placed new gold crowns, gilded with Angevin lilies that recalled the times of Jagiełło, on the heads of the Infant Jesus and His Mother.

Archbishop Karol Wojtyła said the High Mass that followed, and the Primate preached the sermon before performing the act of dedication. Later he said:

> It seemed to me that we had done something greater, something that first demanded faith and that later would bring forth great fruits for the Holy Church in Poland and the world.
>
> In the face of a totalitarian threat to the nation . . . in the face of an atheistic program supported by the PZPR, in the face of biological destruction—a great supernatural current is needed, so that the nation can consciously draw from the Church the divine strength that will fortify its religious and national life. Nowhere else is the union of Church and nation as strong as in Poland, which is in

absolute danger. Our "temporal theology" demands that we dedicate ourselves into the hands of the Holy Mother, so that we may live up to our tasks.

From Jasna Góra the Primate went to Warsaw, and then to Cracow for the Millennium celebrations at the grave of Saint Stanisław. Cracovians had been waiting for hours to see the visitation of the painting of the Madonna, but at the last moment the police diverted the procession from the planned route, disappointing the enormous crowds. When Archbishop Wojtyła protested, the police tried to blame him for the diversion, in an attempt to antagonize the Primate. Finally, hours late, the bishops welcomed the icon into the packed cathedral at Wawel. On the way to their lodgings for the evening, the bishops encountered demonstrators with banners saying "We Don't Forgive," "We Won't Forget," and "Poland Will Never Be a Bulwark for Foreign Interests." The demonstrators did not try to hide the fact that they were acting under compulsion, and when the bishops reached the curia they were greeted by enthusiastic students singing "Long live . . ." and *"Sto lat."* The Primate said Mass in Mariacki Cathedral that evening for a large crowd, many of whom were still irritated from having attended, again under compulsion, a meeting earlier in the day at which Premier Cyrankiewicz had attacked the Germans but, realizing the mood of his audience, had omitted any mention of the Church. At the cathedral the people showed their feelings by singing the last verse of the hymn *"Boże, coś Polskę"* in the version from the times of the partitions: "Lord, return our free country" instead of "Lord, bless our country."

The next day, May 8, saw a procession from Wawel to the Skałka (Church of the Rock) with the relics of Saints Stanisław, Jacek, and Jan Kanty, and the Arm of St. Wojciech, which was carried by the canons of Gniezno.

A handful of Jesuit seminarians and several dozen students were arrested after incidents between police and demonstrators as the icon was leaving Cracow; the party had decided to put up a fight against the peregrination of the painting, though this merely attested to the social and moral importance of what the regime had denounced as primitive religiosity.

After the Pope was refused a visa, Stefan Wyszyński did not even apply for a passport. In Częstochowa he listened to a broadcast of ceremonies he had hoped to attend in Rome. The Holy Father celebrated Mass in Saint Peter's and delivered an excellent sermon to the Poles there. Also from Rome came news of the extent to which the Gomułka leadership and its mentors were losing touch with reality: Archbishop Samoré had had to reject categorically, as insulting, the suggestion by Ambassador Willman that Wyszyński be appointed to a post in the Vatican.

During the rest of May the Primate attended Millennium celebrations in Częstochowa, Piekary Śląskie, and Gdańsk. At the latter site the government offended a large gathering of the faithful by waving banners denouncing the recently deceased Bishop Splett. At the same time, Director Skarżyński of the Bureau of Religious Affairs warned Bishop Choromański that the Primate and the Episcopate were using the Millennium as a cover for antistate activities; the Primate was to be cautioned against organizing illegal demonstrations. The head of the local office of the Bureau of Religious Affairs in Wrocław "offered a cardinal's hat" to Archbishop Kominek in the following manner: Kominek and Wyszyński should both apply for passports to visit America, but only Kominek would be allowed to go. Kominek had thus succeeded Wojtyła as the government's choice to rival the Primate.

In Lublin the pressure by the authorities was so great that the hierarchy was ready to forgo the plans for a procession with the icon of the Blessed Virgin. But the situation went beyond the control of both church and state authorities. Students and young academics, joined by the general populace, organized a procession from the cathedral on their own and carried the icon to KUL, a natural response that caused the Primate to reflect afterward that he would always do well to consider the healthy, spontaneous instincts of the people. The spontaneity of the Lublin procession, however, led to another result as soon as the icon was out of town and on its way back to Częstochowa: The police stopped the motorcade, covered the icon with a tarpaulin, and bound it with rope. Then an escort of militia officers accompanied it the rest of the way.

On the day when the icon was to come to Olsztyn, workers were kept at the factories until seven in the evening and students of the agricultural school were explicitly forbidden to take part in the festivities. In any case, the icon never arrived in Olsztyn: the police stopped it on the road and directed it to Frombork. After the celebrations in that town, the icon was to travel to Warsaw, but a few kilometers outside Frombork, motorized police stopped the motorcade in which the Primate and the icon were riding, seized the painting, and took it away, to what destination no one could guess. Thus Stefan Wyszyński lost the opportunity he had so fervently anticipated of personally welcoming the icon into his archdiocese. The secret police brought the icon to the Warsaw Cathedral, bypassing planned stops in Nowy Dwór and at the parish of Saint Stanisław Kostka in Żoliborz—where, nevertheless, the Primate was warmly greeted and an empty throne stood eloquently at the front of each of the churches during the observances.

The bishops met in session in Warsaw on June 22–23 to consider the preplanned refusal of a passport for the Primate's projected trip to America and the way in which the official press had distorted an interview Archbishop Kominek had granted to foreign journalists. Henceforth only the Primate and the Episcopal Steering Committee would represent the Church's positions abroad. The bishops also decided to send a letter of general protest to the government and to consider the proposal by Znak that an extraordinary church-government commission be set up in the present serious circumstances.

On June 24, fifty-six Polish bishops, along with officials of other church bodies, took part in Millennium celebrations at the Warsaw Cathedral and Saint Anne's Church. When the bishops left Saint Anne's, their way was blocked by a gang of toughs chanting, without much conviction, "We won't forgive." "Brother, that doesn't matter," said the Primate to one of them, who fell silent. Along the way, the bishops met more thugs, one of whom was tussling with a woman. "Be decent, brother," the Primate told him. Sympathetic bystanders told the bishops, "Now you are among friends," when the last of the toughs had been left behind. Back at the cathedral, Bishop Choromański led the Episcopate in a concelebrated Mass. Leaving the church, the bishops were once more blocked by a gang of thugs, who held them up for fifteen minutes. The dignitaries had wanted to walk toward the Palace Square, but since there was a large force of militia assembled there, they turned right, through Świętojańska and Piekarska streets, and ran into a detachment of ORMO—the reserve militia. In the crowded street, men were applauding the bishops and women were crying. "For you, brothers, we have only love," the Primate told the ORMO men who were standing across the street. At last the bishops reached the Primate's residence on Miodowa Street. After blessing the crowd from his balcony, Wyszyński asked the people to go home peacefully. They sang religious songs as they went, however, even on the buses, and there were some scuffles, in one of which a militia commandant was roughed up.

The cathedral was open day and night from the moment of the icon's arrival, and there were crowds of visitors at all hours. On Sunday, June 26, Archbishop Baraniak led the concelebration of Mass and Archbishop Kominek preached. His sermon jarred slightly with the generally prayerful character of the occasion, for it included a sharp protest against the misrepresentation of his remarks in the press. Nevertheless, this sermon again demonstrated the futility of the communists' efforts to set other bishops against the Primate. Cardinal Wyszyński spoke about the nature of pastoral work after the Millennium, and Bishop Modzelewski officially closed the Warsaw observances, also informing the congregation that the icon would remain in Warsaw as long as there was a danger of its being profaned on the way to its next destination, Sandomierz. The faithful responded with fervent applause. It was difficult for the bishops to make their way back to Miodowa

Street, for they met with further harassment: some thugs went so far as to grab Bishop Bronisław Dąbrowski while the militia stood by watching. In the evening, after the faithful had gone home, police hoodlums appeared in front of the Primate's residence to whistle or chant "Wyszyński to Rome" and "Traitor." However, Warsaw showed its faith and wisdom by refraining from large-scale disturbances. The Primate was resilient; he was determined first of all to see the Millennium through, and he paid no attention to the government's spoiling for a fight.

On July 5 the Primate heard news on Radio Free Europe of a new attempt by the authorities to make trouble for him in Rome. They had sent a pair of "tame" Catholics, Professor Maria Wojciechowska from Poznań and the elderly, confused Professor Konrad Górski of Toruń. Vatican officials received one of these emissaries but made it clear that the predicament of the Polish Church ruled out any understanding between Rome and Warsaw. The authorities also deployed the "patriotic priests," Pax, and the Christian Social Association in Wroc ław, where the cornerstone of a monument to Pope John XXIII was dedicated without the knowledge or approval of the Episcopate. Father Professor Mieczysław Żywczyński of the Catholic University of Lublin, a Pax associate, spoke at the ceremony. Gomułka attacked the role of the Church in Polish history during a Sejm session on July 21. The delegates listened mutely, since any dissent would have concluded the public life of the offending delegate and his group.

In the meantime, Millennium festivities took place in Sandomierz, Kielce, and Opole. Obliged to leave the icon behind in Warsaw, the bishops displayed in its place the powerful symbol of an empty frame filled with flowers. The annual Warsaw pilgrimage and a special academics' pilgrimage brought two hundred thousand people to Jasna Góra on August 15. On the 21st, ceremonies were held in Przemyśl, and more than a quarter of a million people repeated the Jasna Góra vows in Częstochowa on the 26th. With religious life in the country reaching a peak, Stefan Wyszyński had realized his major work: the Great Novena and the Sacrum Poloniae Millennium.

Among other business, the bishops decided during a meeting of August 30–September 2 that it was time to bring the icon from Warsaw to Katowice. Considering that the Millennium had gone well, they also determined that they ought to address themselves to the authorities again, and that the atheistic propaganda directed against the young had to be counteracted. Archbishop Wojtyła called for more attention to progressive theology, since Pax was continually invoking Congar, deLubac, and Chenu.* The Primate warned against confusing the "drama of unbelief" and "the machinery of official atheism." Despite the ejection of religious instruction from the schools, four million children and young people—88% of elementary pupils—were being taught at twenty thousand locations; the ten thousand instructors included 1,785 nuns and seven hundred lay people.

When the icon was taken out of Warsaw on September 2, it was seized by the authorities and taken to Częstochowa instead of its intended destination, Katowice. Militia guards took up posts around the monastery to prevent the icon from leaving again; they remained for years and came to be known as "the Swedes," in memory of the seventeenth-century siege. The Paulines received threats that their houses in Częstochowa and Cracow would be confiscated if the icon journeyed forth. The authorities sent a "social" delegation to the Katowice curia carrying banners that read, "We Don't Want the Icon— the Primate's Political Show."

The Primate resisted such tactics, remembering that Satan had been told, "I will put enmity between thee and the woman" and that her seed "shall bruise thy head, and thou shalt bruise his heel."

On September 8 Archbishop Wojtyła informed the Primate that an official had come to warn him against any disturbances

---

*Progressive French priest-theologians. The members of Pax were contrasting the conservative theology of the Polish bishops with the new currents of thinking coming from the pens of the aforementioned.

in the "hardworking region" of Silesia. Wojtyła had replied that, in the first place, the Church was counseling calm, and, in the second, he himself knew what the workers wanted, since he had been one.

On October 3 the Episcopate decided to send all government ministers copies of Cardinal Wyszyński's letter to Premier Cyrankiewicz. That message, written the previous month, had accused the premier of neglecting his duty to consider the Church's complaints seriously. And Archbishop Baraniak complained about interference in Millennium celebrations in Skalmierzyce and Ostrów Wielkopolski as well as in Poznań. The bishops complained about the seizure of the icon in a letter to the Ministry of the Interior. They wanted as many officials as possible to know about the repression of the Church, and eventually their effort bore fruit among some circles of the leadership.

Yet the crude harassment of the head of the Church continued. On the road to Włocławek the Primate's car was stopped repeatedly, and its innocent driver treated roughly and detained. A militia officer even asked to examine the identity papers of the Primate himself, but desisted after receiving a categorical refusal.

Millennium celebrations took place in Wrocław on October 15, and the local authorities heeded Archbishop Kominek's advice not to make trouble in the Western Lands. They did try to set up counter-activities to draw young people away from the religious celebrations, but the young people chose to go to church.

During those festivities, the Council of Bishops met and approved Archbishop Wojtyła's proposed pastoral letter about the council. Together with the Episcopate's publication for clergy, *Post-Council Tasks and the Situation of the Polish Church,* Wojtyła's letter testifies to the scrupulous implementation of council reforms.

During the fall, the Church began to receive signals through confidential channels that the authorities were looking for a way out of the blind alley in church-state relations. At the local level, the old instructions about harassment still seemed to be in effect, although the authorities did not disturb the Millennium celebrations in Gorzów and Szczecin on November 5–6 —certainly because those cities lay in the Western Lands. The celebrations at Płock on November 12 were confined to the church buildings.

On November 19, the last of the twenty-four diocesan celebrations of the Millennium took place in Białystok, with unusual grandeur. At a meeting of the Episcopate on the 21st, Bishop Kazimierz Kowalski remarked that the score for the year was 24–0 in favor of the Church. Earlier, Bishop Choromański had told the steering committee that although local officials were continuing with such actions as verifying the government registration of the typewriters* in monasteries and forbidding parish priests to mention catechization from the pulpit, the higher authorities had been brought to a standstill by the way in which the people had listened to the Church during the Millennium. The party in-fighting seemed sharper all the time, as evidenced by the hubbub over the "Open Letter to the Party" written by Jacek Kuroń and Karol Modzelewski. Young communists were demanding reform and becoming more critical of the leadership, and everyone was talking about the liberal position adopted by Professor Leszek Kołakowski, the only Polish Marxist philosopher of international standing.

On November 22 the Primate received a letter from the secretary of State at the Vatican, Cardinal Cicognani, informing him that Monsignor Casaroli, accompanied by the Polish prelate Andrzej Deskur, would be arriving in Warsaw on the 24th. In view of the refusal to admit the Pope earlier in the year, this news was completely unexpected.

The guests arrived bearing a greeting signed by the Pope. They told Cardinal Wyszyński that "important and responsible" Polish government envoys had been entertained in Rome, but had told the Vatican that the Primate and ten other bishops

*The Polish government passed a law requiring that all typewriters owned and used by the Church or religious orders be registered. From time to time there were inspections to see whether or not the law had been heeded.

would not be given passports. Monsignor Casaroli told Wyszyński that the Holy Father had made it clear to these government representatives that any Warsaw-Vatican pact was unthinkable without Wyszyński's approval.

Wyszyński thought that Casaroli's visit could be useful if it
gave the Monsignor a chance to see for himself that the sort of
agreement that sufficed for Hungary or Czechoslovakia would
not meet Polish needs. Therefore, the Primate asked Casaroli
to stay longer in the country and familiarize himself with
documents that Bishop Bronisław Dąbrowski would show
him. Casaroli agreed, but his next announcement was completely improbable: he said that the Pope wanted to underline
his identification with the Millennium by celebrating Christmas Eve in Jasna Góra. One can imagine the Primate's surprise. Pope Paul had been offended in May by the refusal of
a visa; now, certainly as a result of talks with the government
envoys in Rome, he had decided to make another attempt at
visiting Poland. Cardinal Wyszyński was full of respect for the
Pope's concern about Poland and his desire to see Częstochowa
again, but he spoke his mind. The Pope had been insulted
recently, and Polish Catholics had felt the blow painfully. The
authorities had lost their struggle with the Church over the
Millennium. The public was disgusted by the party's actions,
and a sudden papal visit might be seen as compromising the
Pope's dignity. Wyszyński reminded Casaroli of the difficulties people would have getting to Częstochowa in the winter.
Reconsidering, he made an alternative proposal: that the Pope
should come to Warsaw, where he could meet many more
people in the churches. Then the Primate cautioned that he
had only been thinking out loud, and that he would like to talk
to his guest the next day, after Bishop Dąbrowski had briefed
Casaroli about the situation.

The next day, the Primate reaffirmed his position. He drew
Casaroli's attention to his remarks at the council about the
altered meanings of concepts like law, the state, and freedom
under communism. In the West, laws are fixed; in the East,
they are bent and changed to accommodate the current needs

of the system. He also warned against the sort of minimalism that had been accepted in Yugoslavia. The Primate said that any Vatican-Warsaw agreement ought to be preceded by the dispatch of a special Vatican commission that would spend two or three months acquainting itself with Polish realities. He warned that the authorities might be interested only in a superficial agreement, and that they would certainly raise the question of church administration in the Western Lands, which would be so difficult for the Holy See. He made a penetrating, almost prophetic remark: that the letter from the Polish bishops to the German bishops, so much attacked by the government, had opened the door and prepared the psychological basis for an agreement between Poland and the German Federal Republic. He thought such an agreement was inevitable, since the "China card" was forcing the Soviets to look for possibilities of unification in Europe. He also remarked that, as long as the Polish bishops were unable to travel freely to Rome for *ad limina* visits, talks between the Holy See and the Warsaw government would resemble haggling over a prisoner's skin.

As for the papal visit, the Primate said that the Polish Church was grateful for the idea, whatever the Pope's final decision. Częstochowa, he observed, was more closely related to the Millennium, but Warsaw was a more realistic winter destination. In reply to Monsignor Casaroli's question, Wyszyński said that it would be possible to bring the miraculous icon of the Black Madonna to Warsaw for such an exceptional occasion, even though there was no precedent. Finally, the Primate suggested two dates in the coming year that would be more suitable for a papal visit: the Assumption, on August 15, or the Feast of Our Lady of Częstochowa, on August 26.

The Primate had to go to Częstochowa for two days, to a previously scheduled meeting with the prewar Rebirth organization. He returned to Warsaw on November 28. Having examined the relevant documents, Monsignor Casaroli was full of praise for the way the Polish Church had defended itself against the sort of disintegration that had occurred in the other

Eastern-bloc countries. However, Casaroli also revealed his opinion that a papal visit, if it took place, would be to Częstochowa, and said that he was going to talk to Central Committee member Andrzej Werblan, who turned out to have been the Polish envoy in Rome.

On the evening of the 29th, Casaroli made his call at the Central Committee building. Werblan was polite, surprised to see this guest from the Vatican, and different from the man he had seemed in Rome. As far as a papal visit went, Casaroli had his illusions painfully shattered: "No, we stand by our decision of last May," Werblan said. He tried to shift the blame away from himself by saying that a "visit by the Pope just now would be a sign of approval for the Episcopate's political line." Naturally, Werblan was acting on instructions from Gomułka, who had the last word.

Casaroli returned from the Central Committee building highly disappointed, and the Primate, who had spent several nervous hours waiting for him, said, "It appears that we have judged these gentlemen as better than they are in fact. . . . This is another insult to the Holy Father." Casaroli replied, "I see that things are worse, more dangerous, and more complicated than I had thought." The Primate could only conclude, "The experience tells us at least that in explaining the situation of the Church we should take nothing for granted; this painful experience shows us the truth."

The party had repeated the same major errors it made in the sixties in judging the international psychological response to its actions. It had lost the battle with the Church over the observance of the Millennium, and then had gone on to deny the Pope admission to the country twice in one year. During the debate that must have taken place in the Central Committee building that night, someone, realizing the awkwardness of the party's position vis-à-vis the Vatican, decided to take a tactical step—a step that not only failed to improve, but would even lower Monsignor Casaroli's opinion of the party.

Andrzej Werblan telephoned the Primate's office the next morning and invited Casaroli to a meeting at two in the afternoon. The party had changed its position, but only cosmetically: the Holy Father was to be allowed into Poland, but only if the trip were kept absolutely secret until the last moment— to cut down on the number of the faithful who could attend. There was a second condition thought up by the members of the leadership during their all-night brainstorming, even more unacceptable: the Pope was to visit not Częstochowa but Wrocław, and a representative of the Council of State must take part in all the activities of the visit. Did they want to turn the Pope's visit into an anti-German demonstration? They were not quite so naïve in the Central Committee. Wrocław was simply a condition that would make the visit impossible. Insisting on participation by a member of the Council of State would ensure that the visit, if it occurred, would serve the party's political ends. In the first meeting the party had at least been frank in its refusal; the alternative presented in the second meeting was far worse. But at this time the Gomułka-Kliszko brain trust was in full operation.

Before Casaroli left Warsaw on December 1, the Primate asked that the Pope signal him about his intentions: if Wyszyński received authorization from Rome to deliver an apostolic blessing at the end of the Sacrum Poloniae Millennium, he would know that the Holy Father had rejected Gomułka's conditions.

We can imagine the Primate's mixed feelings in the wake of Casaroli's visit. On the one hand, there was every reason to rejoice in the Holy Father's concern about the Millennium and his determination to visit Poland. On the other, there could only be misgivings about injuries to the prestige of the Holy See and the credulity with which its representative had come to Warsaw.

There could be little doubt that the Pope would refuse to visit under the conditions, so the Primate could only go back to work. On December 7, he sent Bishop Obłąk to Bartoszyce, where seminarians had been drafted into the army. The bishop stunned the local military headquarters by walking in as the oath of induction was being administered to the seminarians.

On the same day, Wyszyński received the distressing news from the Ministry of Higher Education that proceedings destined to close the Jesuit seminary in Warsaw and the Orionist seminary in Zduńska Wola were under way. Soon two more seminaries were subjected to similar proceedings. It was difficult to tell whether the attacks on the seminaries were part of the backlash over the papal visit, or simply retributions for the success of the Millennium.

On December 10, the Vatican radio announced that Pope Paul would celebrate midnight Mass on Christmas Eve at the Basilica of the Madonna dei Fiori in Florence and then return to Rome. This was almost certainly a message to Wyszyński, as was the announcement that the Pope would celebrate the Mass in Florence for the intention of the suffering nations. The next day, the Primate tried to obtain an explicit answer by sending the Pope a telegraph requesting the right to give the apostolic blessing. The 11th was also memorable because *Życie Warszawy* published a report from its New York correspondent about the proclamation of the United Nations Charter on Human Rights, including the enthusiastic remarks of the Polish representatives on the occasion. The Primate realized perfectly well the significance of the charter in the struggle for freedom in Poland. On the 12th, the same paper published a story from Ignacy Krasicki in Rome stating that a normalization of relations between Poland and the Vatican was being hindered by the Holy See's failure to set up new dioceses or name bishops ordinary in the Western Lands. Besides, Krasicki wrote, the Vatican had done nothing to counteract Cardinal Wyszyński's antistate politics. Thus the government formally and publicly ended any hopes of a visit by the Pope, while at the same time insinuating another false charge against the Primate.

Meanwhile, the threat to the seminaries was causing a great deal of consternation. Despite various counsels, the Primate did not yet want to appeal to the United Nations, because he thought the seminary question ought to be settled at home even though it fell under international agreements. Letters to Premier Cyrankiewicz and Minister of Higher Education Professor Henryk Jabłoński seemed appropriate for the time being. On December 13 the bishops ordinary held a special meeting, but on the same day a dangerous threat appeared from another quarter. General Spychalski, the minister of Defense, replied to the bishops' attempt to intervene in the forced atheization of seminarians in the army with a charge that the bishops were gathering information prejudicial to the defense of the nation. The bishops decided to address themselves to the faithful, Zenon Kliszko, and the Holy Father on the seminary question. At the same time they took a certain risk in reaffirming that the authorities would not be admitted to inspect the seminaries.

Pope Paul gave the expected signal that he would not be coming to Poland: Stefan Wyszyński received on December 21 the authorization to give the apostolic blessing at the end of the Millennial Year. The next day, the Primate received the text of a speech given in the Sejm by the Znak delegate Stanisław Stomma. Stomma had defended the Church, spoken of the seminaries, and expressed his disappointment at the fate of the liberalizing program associated with October 1956. Wyszyński appreciated Stomma's action, which signified the pulling together of the Catholic front and deprived the party of an often used pretext for trying to divide the faithful.

After a long break, a meeting of the Joint Commission was called on December 30. The Primate asked the representatives of the Episcopate to bring up the whole range of church issues, though the seminaries and catechization were clearly the most important. Kliszko, however, limited the discussion to the seminaries—and immediately withdrew the threats to close them. It was decided to have another meeting in the near future to establish regulations for the seminaries, and since the Episcopate had not acknowledged the government decrees of 1961 and 1965 that aimed at bringing the seminaries under the Ministry of Higher Education, the Primate convened a special panel, including Bishops Dąbrowski and Tokarczuk and Father Władysław Miziołek, to establish talking points for the next round of negotiations. The decisive refusal to accept the government's plans had plainly been borne out by events. The last day of the year included final Millennium ceremonies in Warsaw. The Primate spoke of the last nine years. Each of the Church's programs had evoked a counteraction from the government. The slogan "Fidelity to the Cross" had been answered by the removal of crucifixes from schoolroom walls. The government had answered the program "in defense of the life of the spirit and the body" with the introduction of liberalized abortion regulations. Actions for the sake of the council had been countered with appeals for social actions, clearly modeled after the Church's programs. Despite all the bitterness and all the attacks, the Primate characterized the last nine years as ones of great accomplishment for the Church and great grace from God. The Great Novena had progressed precisely and in coordination with the council program, and in the council the Pope had proclaimed the Virgin Mary as Mother of the Church. The Primate singled out the Marian Bishops Pawłowski and Kowalski, who had helped formulate the program of dedication to Mary, and Archbishop Wojtyła, who had been the spokesman for the program. Bishops Dąbrowski and Czerniak, along with the Primatial Institute, had also played a great role. Among intellectuals, there had been a certain reserve about the Marian program, but the faithful had been moved, deepened in faith, and engaged on the side of the Church by the program. That was the deciding argument. The spontaneous Mass celebrations of the Millennium had been the crown of the work. It had been a great, but not a final, accomplishment for Stefan Wyszyński.

* * *

New Year's Eve had a serious mood for the Warsavians who attended the midnight Mass at the basilica, celebrated by Bishop Bronisław Dąbrowski and featuring a sermon by Cardinal Wyszyński. At the end, the people sang the "return our free country" version of *"Boże coś Polskę"*—always an alarming sign for the authorities. But the Catholics left peacefully, the Primate's words in their ears:

Beloved priests of the diocese, and God's Catholic Polish people! The Episcopate comes before you with pain in its heart, full of anxiety, its work and its seminaries threatened. The educational authorities have demanded the dismissal of six seminary rectors and announced the closing of four seminaries. We understand that this is the beginning of a wider action intended soon to deprive the Holy Church in Poland of its young priests. We feel a great danger to the Holy Church and its mission, existence, and apostolic work. This is also an attempt to cut off the rights of the Holy See, to whom the seminaries are responsible.

The bishops called on the people to pray for the defense of the seminaries and informed them of their appeals to the authorities about the Church's right to educate priests. They promised to make public the government's response and again asked for prayers. The serious atmosphere was justified. Cardinal Wyszyński's decision to broach the matter publicly brought Gomułka to a standstill: to go forward was to face unpredictable consequences.

With the seminary question on the agenda, the Joint Commission met on January 20, 1967. Bishop Klepacz could not attend for reasons of health, so Bishops Choromański and Dąbrowski represented the Episcopate. The two sides submitted their proposals for regulating the seminaries. The government wanted the right to supervise and inspect the seminaries, to issue regulations based on the inspections, to evaluate the curricula, and to confirm candidates for rectors and professors. The bishops' answer was succinct: supervision was out of the question as a violation of the Holy See's rights—*non possumus!* Kliszko got angry while his partner, Minister Sztachelski, sat impassively. But the government knew well that its demands were unrealistic. Once again a decisive no based upon the rights of the Church was the best answer.

Bishop Klepacz, Ordinary of Łódź and for many years a negotiator with the government, died on January 27. Archbishop Wojtyła preached at the funeral conducted by Cardinal Wyszyński, who also spoke about the deceased's great services in negotiations and in the understanding of 1950. Bishop Klepacz had always been inclined to compromise—not from lack of principles, but because he could see no other way out of the postwar predicament. Wyszyński had always trusted him.

On February 2, Paul VI received Nikolai Podgorny, the head of the Supreme Soviet. Once again the Polish communists were lagging behind the "first socialist country," which had never even been Catholic. The Podgorny visit apparently made some impression on the Gomułka leadership. Monsignor Deskur came to Warsaw on February 11 with the news that the Pope wanted to send a special mission to Poland; after refusing at first, the government had agreed. Despite the almost universal convictions of the world press and of historians, the idea for the special mission had originated not in the Vatican but, as will be recalled, in a suggestion made by Cardinal Wyszyński during Casaroli's surprise visit of the previous fall. Monsignor Casaroli, who together with Deskur would make up the special mission, arrived on February 14 with a letter for Wyszyński from Paul and a special breve in which the Pope made the ingratiating promise that a copy of the Polish act of dedication to the Virgin Mary would be placed near the grave of Saint Peter. Wyszyński invited Casaroli to stay in the old nunciature, where he could be completely independent.

Monsignor Casaroli (he would be made an archbishop on July 4) later stated that the mission to Poland was a mark of sympathy with the Church and a means to gather information, not to negotiate with the government. No action, he told the bishops on February 15, would be taken without the consent of Cardinal Wyszyński and the Episcopate. On February 18 the Italian churchman met with Andrzej Werblan, who denounced the bishops while the Monsignor stated that the government's proposals about the seminaries were unacceptable.

Then Casaroli set out to tour the dioceses. While he was away, on February 25, Bishop Choromański suffered a severe heart attack. The life of one of the great champions of church freedom was coming to an end.

Monsignor Casaroli spent until April 5—except for two weekend trips to Rome—traveling all around Poland, visiting each diocese. The Primate also introduced him to Jerzy Zawieyski of the Council of State and to "government Catholics" like Bolesław Piasecki of Pax. Casaroli came to share Wyszyński's caution about hurrying into an understanding, and he learned that most bishops felt the government would not keep any agreement it concluded. Like the Primate, however, Casaroli believed that the Podgorny visit had changed everything. The Primate wanted to try for an agreement. When Monsignor Casaroli, accompanied by Monsignor Deskur, returned to Rome on April 7, he understood much better what the Primate had been saying in his speech to the council.

In the meantime, Edward Ochab, head of the Polish Council of State, arrived in Rome on April 5. Everyone took it for granted that Ochab would call on the Pope, yet, in another slap in the Vatican's face, he did not. Everything indicated that Gomułka had vetoed the visit because of his failure to divide the Episcopate and the Vatican.

The conference of bishops decided to send Pope Paul a letter of gratitude for the special mission at its meeting on April 12. Archbishop Kominek, just back from Yugoslavia, reported on the agreement that Tito's government had concluded with the Vatican, though this could not be a model for Poland. It gave the Church a certain margin of freedom in filling offices, publishing, and travel abroad, but, at the same time, there was a noticeable lack of contact between the Yugoslavian hierarchy and the masses of workers.

At Jasna Góra, 250,000 people took part in the Feast of the Queen of Poland on May 3. Since the icon had been prevented from visiting Silesia the year before, it was now carried in procession around the ramparts of the monastery by Silesian miners and steelworkers.

During religious observances in Sosnowiec on May 20, there were confrontations between the faithful and gangs of government toughs. Shouts of "Down with the bishops" competed with "Long live the bishops" that day, and during Cardinal Wyszyński's sermon the next day. The Primate said, "Red Sosnowiec is praying, and crying." Indeed, even the men were crying. This demonstrative piety so enraged the rulers that gangs beat up believers in front of many churches.

On May 28 the Holy Father established apostolic administrations in Wrocław, Opole, Gorzów, and Olsztyn. Opole and Gorzów thus became independent units of the church administrative structure. Although the government's reaction could not be foreseen, the Primate was overjoyed by this important step toward normalization in the Western Lands. There was more good news from Rome the next day: Karol Wojtyła, Archbishop of Cracow, was called to the dignity of a cardinalship—as was, on the same day, the Archbishop of Philadelphia, John Krol, a Pole by descent. The day following, Jan Jaroszewicz, apostolic administrator of Kielce, was made bishop of that diocese.

Preparations were being made for de Gaulle's visit to Poland. The French leader, coming as a guest of the government, had scheduled no participation in Masses or even a visit to Częstochowa en route to Katowice. The French ambassador invited Wyszyński to the diplomatic reception for de Gaulle at Wilanów Palace, but since de Gaulle was making no gesture toward the Church or the people, the Primate had to decline. In any case, the outbreak of the Arab-Israeli war forced a postponement of the visit until September, at which time Wyszyński sent de Gaulle a letter and a relief of the Virgin of Częstochowa.

Cardinal Wyszyński, Cardinal Wojtyła, and Bishop Kałwa were chosen to represent Poland at the Synod of Bishops in Rome by a meeting of the Episcopate on June 14. At that same meeting, a letter to Zenon Kliszko was written criticizing the administrative harassment of the Church, the limitations on Corpus Christi processions, the banning of religion at summer camps, the annoyance caused to priests by the secret police, the continuing efforts to set up a renegade parish in Wierzbica, and the brutal police action in Sosnowiec. The bishops also approved a pastoral letter titled "On Atheism," which protested the use of the mass media to enforce a materialistic philosophy of life and the discrimination suffered in their careers by people who would not renounce God. "The spokesmen for such matters maintain that the acknowledgment of God is an obstacle to progress. They say that a person becomes more fully human by becoming less religious. The genocidal crimes of Nazism, fascism, and similar totalitarian systems inspired by atheistic ideology pose an incontrovertible counterargument to such views."

During the summer there were religious celebrations in Łódź and, on the August feasts, in Częstochowa, at which the great numbers of participants made any organized disruption impossible. But in the small town of Licheń near Wrocław, the Primate was greeted by signs reading "We Demand that the Hierarchy Be Loyal to People's Poland." In his sermon, the Primate replied by saying that loyalty had to be reciprocal. A few days later he learned that permission to build the Church of Divine Providence in Warsaw, already granted, had been revoked.

On September 11, Cardinal Wojtyła announced to the Episcopate that he would not attend the Synod of Bishops in Rome if Cardinal Wyszyński were denied a passport. The other bishops adopted a similar stand in solidarity with the Primate. In mid-September, Jerzy Zawieyski informed the Primate that Gomułka had told him the Primate's passport would be denied, but that the government was putting off an announcement in the hope that other bishops would commit themselves to attending the synod in the meantime. The Council of Ministers finally made the decision official on September 28. The next day, the Episcopal Steering Committee reiterated its decision: no other bishop would go to Rome. Cardinal Wojtyła said during the meeting, "The Primate's road was under the protection of Providence before Komańcza [i.e., before his release from prison] and so it is after Komańcza." The authorities tried to pressure the bishops who had obtained passports to attend, but, despite the intervention of various Catholic political groups, they stood firm.

At the end of October, Jerzy Zawieyski reported on his latest meeting with Gomułka, at which the first secretary had seemed despotic and emotional; clearly he was being manipulated by the party factions and behind-the-scenes forces. Meanwhile, Poland's predicament grew worse and worse. Gomułka had accepted an anti-Zionist proclamation which was issued at the trade-union conference on June 19, and thus had opened the way for the anti-Semitic campaign that would soon be unleashed.

The line toward the Church was becoming more irresolute. After seven years of popular demonstrations, permission was finally given to build a church in Nowa Huta. At the same time, however, the Bureau of Religious Affairs began trying to stir up the provincials of religious orders against the bishops in the seminary affair. Activity by Caritas and the "patriotic priests" intensified—a sure sign of a harder line. The secret police began keeping a closer watch on catechetical centers; in a confidential directive, they were ordered to draw up lists not only of the children who attended, but even of the workplaces of the children's parents. Thus action against religious instruction could be augmented by discrimination against parents.

The Primate took time out from his pastoral work to meet the Znak politicians, who judged the situation as dramatic and understood the Church's action. Counseling the defense of basic ethics, the Cardinal stated, "There can be no politics in Poland in the absence of freedom for all the groups that make up the political system." The words turned out to be prophetic; certainly the Znak group would feel the full consequences of them.

At the end of December, Cardinal Wyszyński and Bishop Dąbrowski cooperated on a communiqué in response to a speech against the bishops that Bolesław Piasecki had delivered in the Sejm. Piasecki's speech was characteristic, since the

Party leadership itself was not ready to come out publicly against the Church. It also demonstrated how eager some factions were to win the applause of the nationalistic extremists in the party.

The year 1966 had ended with the triumph of the Millennium and the grave threat to the seminaries; 1967 ended with the preservation of the *status quo*—and, thanks to the work of the Primate, Episcopate, and all the clergy, the seminaries had been saved.

On January fifth, Cardinal Wyszyński—who had once joked that he seemed doomed to spend his whole life in cars—had a road accident on the way home from Gniezno. He had nothing worse than a slight injury near his eye, but had to spend two days resting.

On January 11, the Pax delegates replied to the Episcopate's last censure with an article in *Słowo Powszechne* that attacked the bishops' policies. This drew forth the Episcopate's condemnation of Pax and its works in a letter to all the clergy.

Bishop Rubin told the January meeting of the Episcopate that Pope Paul had praised "the work and ardor of the Polish Church" as something "of great value not only for Poland, but for other parts of the Church as well." It was decided to refer to the Holy See the Bureau of Religious Affairs' new compromise proposal that the inspection of seminaries concern only secular subjects.

The bishops, dissatisfied with the state of morals and manners in the country—a result in large measure of the economic difficulties—approved a pastoral letter "On the Moral Danger to the Nation," which read, in part:

> Proceeding from erroneous doctrines that regard hatred as an engine of progress, they have established the principle *divide et impera*. The campaign for alleged justice, which at the heart of things is pagan hatred, makes war against the Christian spirit of forgiveness and peace. Programmed hatred is a fundamental threat to Christian love. Yet our society is yielding to the pressure. Among

us there is divisiveness, malice, calumny, slander, insult, the spirit of revenge, dissent, even crime—almost every day they outrage public opinion! The brutalization of personal relations creates enmity and mutual ill will.

The words were not exaggerated. The brutalization of relationships and the combative atmosphere against which the bishops cautioned had its roots in the struggle for control of the party as well as in the economic crisis. The warning was another nearly prophetic utterance in the year 1968, during the course of which the struggle for power would lead to the anti-Semitic campaign that besmirched the name of Poland.

Early in February, Cardinal Wyszyński had a visit from the well-known writer and former Znak delegate Stefan Kisielewski, who did not try to hide his apprehensions that the progressive Sovietization of Poland would lead to some sort of general national treason. The spirit of protest had in fact spread from the Church to the intellectual elite. At the end of the month came news that a production of Adam Mickiewicz's play, *Forefathers*, had been closed following a provoked demonstration after the last performance. At a stormy Union of Polish Writers meeting, Kisielewski spoke unflinchingly of the "dictatorship of the ignorant" that was ruling the country. The social unrest spread to Warsaw University on March 8, when the militia and its reserves, the ORMO, brutally suppressed a student demonstration. Students who tried to take shelter in Holy Cross, Capuchin, and Saint Anne's churches were beaten with truncheons. They called the militia "Gestapo." Professor Czesław Bobrowski was struck with a police baton as he addressed the students. Dozens of injured academics lay in Warsaw hospitals. In the next days, student demonstrations occurred all over the country. The state press blamed everything on—Zionism.

Cardinal Wyszyński met with thirty academic chaplains on March 12 to discuss ways of increasing the protection of the students. He remarked, ironically, "It is surprising to find so many thousands of Zionists among the students." Two days later, Stefan Kisielewski was beaten with police truncheons by "unknown assailants." The social opposition that had spread from the Church to the intellectuals was being taken up by young people and writers, and everyone could sense the battles taking place within the party. Gomułka alienated himself entirely in a televised speech on March 19. In the meantime, the Primate had been receiving most of the student leaflets, and he was impressed by their moderation.

On March 20 and 21 the Episcopate approved *Words of the Polish Episcopate on the Painful Events,* which demanded "respect for the basic rights of persons and of society." A letter in defense of young academics was also sent to the government. On May 3 of the same year, the Episcopate was to publish "Words on the March Events," in which the Church demanded

the admission of all members of the nation and all citizens of the state to work for the common good according to their convictions and in harmony with their consciences. No one should be labeled an enemy because of differences of convictions. Trying to make enemies of people who want to serve the good of the nation according to their own distinct convictions is a disservice to social morality and deprives the country of many honorable forces and initiatives that could enrich social life in diverse areas.

At the end of March a protest was also sent to the Ministry of the Interior, whose functionaries had chased students and fired tear gas into many Warsaw churches. Zawieyski passed along the Primate's thoughts that steps taken toward a reconciliation with the youth and a papal visit in September would help the endangered party leadership. Instead, April 9–11 brought the "black Mass"* against the Znak delegates in the

---

*A travesty of the Christian Mass ascribed to reputed worshipers of Satan. Mass of the devil. Here the term is used as a metaphor for the fact that uncharacteristically on this occasion almost all members of the Polish Parliament viciously attacked the members of the Catholic Znak group because they defended the students' demands for greater freedom.

Sejm, who had dared to speak out in favor of the students. Jerzy Zawieyski was dismissed from the Council of State. The Primate regarded the Sejm session as a "theatrical presentation" in which those who were isolated from the people blabbed about the nation, while little "David"—the Znak delegates—won a moral victory. At Saint Joseph's Church, the Primate preached in strong terms about the damage being done to Poland's international reputation.

At the end of May, the Primate told the five Znak delegates that the country needed Catholic politicians less than it needed confessors of the faith. He warned against the growing differences in Znak and said that despite contradictory appraisals of the political situation, the important thing was the moral sense of the delegates' stand in support of the students. He evoked their solidarity in that spirit.

When the Episcopate met on June 27–29 in Gniezno, it noted the escalating pressure against priests by way of taxation (new questionnaires had been sent out) and against catechization—parents were frightened by the prospect of reprisals. Greater efforts at atheization were being made at children's holiday camps. The authorities had also begun to tear down Protestant churches in the Western Lands, and the Episcopate protested to the government.

Cardinal Wyszyński managed to escape to Bachledówka for a vacation in July, and Cardinal Wojtyła visited him there on the 4th. They received materials from the latest meeting of the party Central Committee, where the ideologues Professors Schaff and Żółkiewski had been made scapegoats and the nationalistic wing had come under criticism. Andrzej Werblan was made the new ideologue, under the slogan "Socialistic Patriotism." In one speech, Gomułka had managed to denounce revisionism, Zionism, nationalism, and clericalism. Henryk Szafrański, secretary of the Warsaw party committee, made the sharpest attack on the Church: "What Wyszyński and his well-known anti-Polish and antisocialist platform are all about was shown in the letter to the German bishops. In our region, as all over the country, not only almost all the people but also the majority of the priests oppose his adventurist political aspirations."

The political and ideological disintegration of the party served the interests of extremely demagogical apparatchiks, who wanted to make names and advance themselves. However, the noisy state celebrations marking fifty years of Polish independence, held on July 22, could not change the prevailing conviction that the country was living in a state of dependence, and that Marxism was only a tool of subjugation.

On the way back to Warsaw after his holiday, Cardinal Wyszyński stopped as usual at Jasna Góra, where this year there were large numbers of pilgrims from Czechoslovakia, Hungary, and Yugoslavia. August began peacefully enough, but the easy rhythms of pastoral work were transformed into dramatic tension when, on the 21st, it was announced that Polish soldiers had been sent to occupy Czechoslovakia along with the Red Army. For the Primate, as for most Poles, the news was a heavy, personal blow. As a result, perhaps, there were more pilgrims at Jasna Góra—three hundred thousand of them—on August 26 than there had been for some years.

After the events of March and August, the Znak delegates considered withdrawing from the Sejm, but the Primate advised them not to make a hasty decision: he observed accurately that they would learn more about the party's program later. In mid-September, Bishop Dąbrowski met with Director Skarżyński of the Office of Religious Affairs. They spoke mostly about *ad limina* visits to Rome by the bishops. Skarżyński remarked that all the bishops would receive passports except for Tokarczuk and Kominek, who had engaged themselves in the "Czech affair." When Bishop Dąbrowski asked about a passport for the Primate, Skarżyński replied, "The Primate has not asked for one, but if he did—in my private opinion—he would receive it." He might have been trying to give the impression that the authorities were softening their position toward the Primate after the recent serious events.

On September 15, the bishops sang a *Te Deum* of thanksgiving at Jasna Góra to commemorate the fiftieth anniversary of the recovery of independence, then set out for Opole, where they would hold a session to underline the unity of the Western Lands with Poland. On the way to Opole, however, tragedy struck: Bishop Antoni Pawłowski of Włocławek was killed in a car accident.

During the meeting of the Episcopate, Bishop Dąbrowski reported on the situation of the Church. He noted signs that the authorities were relaxing their contention with the Church and their attempts to interfere in its affairs. The bishops agreed that on the Feast of Christ the King a letter should be read to the faithful about the beginning of a prayer-and-charitable-works action developed by the Episcopate under the title "Social Crusade of Love." The crusade was to be a struggle "to graft brotherly Christian love onto our personal, family, social, professional, and public lives."

On September 24 a priest in the Archdiocese of Gniezno was arrested for failing to pay a tax judgment. The Primate ordered that one of the auxiliary bishops of Gniezno always be saying Mass in the parish of the arrested priest. In the eyes of the parish, the government had suffered a great setback, and its only way out was to release the priest.

At celebrations of the fiftieth anniversary of KUL, on October 19, the Primate spoke about realizing the council reforms. "Before standing *facie ad populum* in front of the altar," he said, "we must first stand *facie ad populum* theologically, ascetically, and sociologically."

The Episcopate decided at its October meeting to send a protest letter about the continued conscription of seminarians and about the fact that the amended penal code now provided for the death sentence in twenty different instances. Cardinal Wojtyła relayed the Pope's thanks for the Episcopate's stand on the encyclical *Humanae vitae*. The commercialization of Western life pained the Pope, who noted that his encyclical had found its most distinct echo in the Third World. Cardinal Wyszyński spoke of the growing "fear of professing faith" in the countryside and stressed the need to fight for "Catholic social and cultural autonomy." The Episcopate decided to inform the faithful about the threats to church institutions in the provinces in the pastoral letters for Christmas and Lent. They would also file protests against requirements that people work on Sundays and holidays.

There were some signs of a thaw. On October 26, after three years, the Primate finally obtained a passport. He left for Rome on November 4. Three days later the Pope greeted him with words that were indeed moving: "We have been waiting to tell you that we are with you, that we are praying, that we have not stopped trusting. In all the works and actions of Your Eminence, we admire your faith and consistent guidance of the Polish Church. We admire and rejoice in your courage. In everything, Christ will be victorious."

Cardinal Wyszyński sketched the general development of religious life in Poland and handed Pope Paul a letter of thanks for *Humanae vitae* signed by Polish physicians, including one hundred professors. A second letter was signed by more than a hundred large Catholic families, some of which had more than a dozen children. The general state of relations between the Holy See and the countries of the Eastern bloc constituted a major theme of the discussions with the Pope.

At dinner on Sunday, October 10, the Holy Father said to Cardinal Wyszyński: "Please tell the bishops, the clergy, religious, families, young people, children—the faithful—that we trust them fully, believing that they are true to the Holy Church, that they are fighting with dignity for the rights of Christ, that we have great respect for their stand, which we observe with admiration as a model for the contemporary world." Next Paul VI gave his guest "a Golden Rose for Jasna Góra," which he had intended to present on May 3, 1966. He said, sadly, "Perhaps not I, but my successor, will take it to Jasna Góra."

On December 7 the Primate shared a farewell dinner with Pope Paul and Archbishop Casaroli. He paid a courtesy call at the Polish embassy on December 9 and reminded Consul

Kazimierz Szablewski of the Holy Father's continuing desire to visit Poland. On his arrival in Warsaw on December 11, he told the faithful in the cathedral the same thing. No one could accuse him of conducting his diplomacy in secret!

On December 26 the Polish Church suffered a great loss, and the Primate was deprived of his closest collaborator over the last twenty years. Bishop Dr. Zygmunt Choromański, the secretary of the Polish Episcopate, died in the hospital. Stefan Wyszyński was deeply affected, speaking of the bishop's faith and the crucial role he had played in two decades of negotiations with the government. The Primate dispatched a message to the faithful and telegrams to all the bishops and to the government. At the funeral on December 29, attended by twenty-seven bishops and Cardinal Wojtyła, there was no government representative to pay respect to Choromański, the leading figure in both the Mixed and Joint Commissions. The Primate, who had spoken at the funeral, spoke again at a memorial service in the cathedral on December 30. Crowds of the faithful, the Znak delegates, and the American ambassador with a group of embassy employees all attended. Even the first, quickly dismissed, postwar Polish premier, Edward Osóbka Morawski, was there. But no one came from the government. Everyone thought the same thing: "They are always callous."

On the last day of 1968, Stefan Wyszyński went to Gniezno with Reverend Dr. Józef Glemp. It had been a year of hard work, much of it spent driving to and from religious ceremonies. Yet the Primate's gift for direct contact with the people was a great part of his character. Many people stated that observances in which he took part had a completely different nature from those at which he was not present. He imparted to the people his fervent charisma, his integrity, and his unshaken faith.

Eight bishops, including such personalities as Bishop Choromański and Bishop Pękala, had passed away during the year, but at the same time Cardinal Wyszyński had consecrated the thirty-second bishop of his primateship. His work was entering a new phase. Nothing indicated that the work would be any easier, but it was clear that the antichurch offensive begun in 1966 was coming to a halt. The unsettled domestic political situation and international peace propaganda were blunting the government's aggressiveness.

* * *

The events of the previous year had increased the Primate's trust in Catholic intellectual organizations. Early in 1969 he met with Jerzy Zawieyski and the leadership of the Catholic Intellectuals' Club, which would henceforth be allowed to participate in the Episcopal commissions. He also received the noted writer and historian Paweł Jasienica (Lech Beynar). In March of the previous year Gomułka, unable to break Jasienica down, had publicly smeared the writer by accusing him of having been a secret-police agent after the war. Wyszyński told Jasienica, "I will express no sympathy, because by doing your duty you have earned the greatest honor: the respect and thanks of society." Such words, coming from the pre-eminent moral authority in Poland, had a great fortifying effect on the writer who, though his torture had been "merely" psychological, was nevertheless approaching a premature death.

A meeting between Bishop Dąbrowski and Director Skarżyński of the Bureau of Religious Affairs reflected the continuing impasse in church-state relations. Skarżyński ducked as many questions as he could, saying, for instance, that grave matters like the continuing threat to the Silesian seminary were merely local affairs. The few questions to which Dąbrowski received concrete answers were minor and truly local.

The meeting of the Episcopate on February 11 took several positive steps: adding to a letter sent earlier by the Primate about the conscription of seminarians it sent the premier a letter about a papal visit. There were reports of larceny and arson against churches. Finally, Bishop Dąbrowski was named to succeed Bishop Choromański as secretary of the Episcopate.

To assuage the anxieties of the clergy, the Primate met in

Warsaw with two hundred priests at the Jesuit House on February 27, answering questions that they submitted anonymously. He covered the council, archdiocesan affairs, politics, and the difficulties of ecumenism in Poland. There was much interest at the time in the creation of priests' councils, and the Cardinal pointed out that the curia and the pastoral department had been functioning collegially since 1949. He also noted the growing numbers of priests returning from the Polish National Church (a Catholic rite that acknowledged no allegiance to Rome).

In March, Bishop Dąbrowski met with Director Skarżyński again and was able to make his interlocutor understand that the bishops would never negotiate the status of the seminaries. Skarżyński also seemed interested in letters complaining of harassment from seminary students who had been conscripted into the army. Furthermore, he said there was no opposition to continuing *ad limina* visits by bishops, and he approved the setting up of the Office of the Secretary of the Episcopate and, more importantly, the Press Bureau of the Episcopate, headed by Father Alojzy Orszulik, SAC,* which had enjoyed an uncertain status since its announcement in the previous year.

Given the signs of a thaw, Cardinal Wyszyński intensified his contacts with Znak through meetings early in March with Antoni Marylski and editor Tadeusz Mazowiecki of *Więź* about Jerzy Turowicz's article "Crisis in the Church." Wyszyński tried to impress on them the fact that they were living on the moral capital of the Church and that the Marxists were exploiting divisions among Catholics.

In the assessment made by the Episcopal Steering Committee at its April 16 session, church-state relations were calm at the center, though harassment was continuing on a local scale. There were worries on other fronts, however: the government had excluded Jerzy Zawieyski from the Znak delegation to the Sejm, the Christian Social Association was more active than ever, and the Western press had stopped writing about the

---

*Societas Apostolatus Catholici, Society of the Catholic Apostolate.

Polish Church—a fact imputed to the disgrace the authorities' anti-Semitic campaign had brought on the country. The political situation seemed to be dominated by a battle within the party between a gerontocracy, imported in large part from Russia after the war, and a native, xenophobic younger generation. Both factions were antirevisionist and antiliberal. From Rome came news that nothing justified hope of a papal visit, and the Western press was spreading rumors that Pope Paul had become deeply pessimistic about the post-council Church.

The Primate's Council for Building Churches in Warsaw met on April 18 to consider the painful situation caused by the authorities' refusal to sanction even a single new church in the capital. On the 20th, the Primate set out for Gniezno, where he learned the next day that Jerzy Zawieyski had suffered a severe stroke. The writer was not to survive his political defeat, though it had been at the same time a great moral victory.

At the beginning of May, the Primate went to Jasna Góra for celebrations of a new pastoral program titled "Credo Pawłowe"—"Paul's Creed." Pope Paul, faced with a turmoil of opposition and controversy in the universal Church, had made his own public profession of faith, which came to be known as Paul's Creed. Now, at the Primate's initiative, the Polish Church had begun a program of prayer and good works intended to stir the conscience and vivify the religiosity of Poland, and to support the Pope. The Creed was repeated after the Jasna Góra vows on May 3, and on June 20 pilgrimages of bishops, clergy, and the faithful converged at Częstochowa from all over the country to pray day and night for the intention of the universal Church.

On May 3 the Episcopate met at Jasna Góra and approved both a letter to Pope Paul and an intensification of prayer actions in his name. Cardinal Wojtyła reported that the Pope had told him in Rome that there was little chance of a visit to Poland. The government's last suggestion, that the Holy Father visit the memorial erected to Pope John XXIII by the "patriotic priests" in Wrocław, had been seen in Rome as a diplomatic gaffe. The invasion of Czechoslovakia also created a certain reserve on the Vatican's part in regard to steps toward the Eastern bloc. The Episcopate also discussed the existence of two catechisms in the country, one produced by the Catechetical Commission and one by the Jesuits. The duplication was a mark of creative energy, but the scarcity of copies of either catechism remained the more important fact.

On May 11 the Primate took part in the massive Saint Stanisław's procession from Wawel to Skałka in Cracow. He remarked, "The people are full of joy. They require a common expression of faith. This is not a demonstration. These people have shown great patience, taking part in a ceremony that lasts for many for five hours."

As will be remembered, Stefan Wyszyński had not taken part in the last Sejm "elections." Now a new vote was at hand, and Kliszko, managing things, had forced a candidate of its own choice upon the Znak group. The Primate decided that once again he would have to stay away from the polls, as a protest against a Sejm now deprived of even illusory representation of society. In general, church-state relations were frozen, as the complete cessation of sacral construction showed. Still, on election day the Primate was followed by secret-police agents as he ordained priests at the seminary and then proceeded to an inspection of the parish in Żabka. People mocked the elections, yet in the face of possible repression—which in most cases had now become merely theoretical—they still voted. The situation was ambiguous, a moral ambush, and the Primate refused to play the game. It was necessary, he said, to live in truth—"Somebody has to."

On June 18, Jerzy Zawieyski's suffering came to a tragic end. A long period of unconsciousness had left him unable to speak and, disoriented, he wandered through the hospital, crying much of the time. On that morning, he bathed, locked himself in his room, and after ten minutes fell to his death from the fourth-floor balcony. His wish to be buried at Laski was fulfilled during a funeral conducted by Bishop Władysław Mizołek and attended by a great crowd, believers and nonbelievers both, who paid tribute to the man who had courageously stood up in the Sejm against Gomułka and the anti-Zionist campaign.

At its June meeting, the Episcopate considered shaping its pastoral program for the coming year in response to drastic problems of behavior among the young. Archbishop Kominek reported that the economic situation in the Western Lands was catastrophic. The bishops also approved a pastoral letter commemorating the thirtieth anniversary of the outbreak of the war, which read in part, "The Polish nation sprang to the defense of world culture against the totalitarian-militaristic moloch. Its action showed the world that freedom is a value worth more than any suffering or sacrifice. Its stand was a warning against the degenerate militarism of its invaders." That last word—because it was plural—caused a panic in the party. The authorities insisted that there had been only one invader of Poland in September 1939.* However, the Primate resisted all pressures for an emendation, and the letter was read as it had been written. Later, it was printed in Paris.

At the end of June, the Cardinal and Bishop Dąbrowski had to send the government a letter protesting a confidential bulletin from the authorities about fighting catechization. It was typical for such a secret directive to come into the hands of the Episcopate.

The annual pilgrimage to Jasna Góra by teachers took place on July 1, and as was the custom, many teachers stayed afterward for private retreats. As usual, the Primate inaugurated the retreats with a private conference in the basilica.

On July 4 he left for his annual holiday, this time in Bachledówka in Podhale. There he learned that the authorities had carried out an attack in Zbrosza Duża, tearing down the church, carrying off the cross and the liturgical instruments, and hauling in the parish priest, Father Czesław Sadłowski, for

---

*Soviet troops had of course entered the Polish Republic on September 17, 1939, and moved up to a line of demarcation previously arranged with their (then) Nazi allies. The official Polish and Soviet histories have always stated that the Red Army was coming "to the aid of the endangered Byelorussian and Ukrainian minorities" of eastern Poland.

interrogation. The despondent parishioners prayed before a roadside cross; Bishops Dąbrowski and Miziołek visited them. At the end of July, Cardinal Wojtyła joined the Primate on holiday and affirmed that, as before, he would not attend the synod in Rome if the Primate was refused a passport.

In Warsaw, the Primate received numerous congratulations as he celebrated his sixty-eighth birthday and the forty-fifth anniversary of his ordination on September 3. He spent the rest of the month busy with the usual August observances.

When the Episcopate met at the end of September, it named Cardinal Wojtyła as its vice-chairman. Much of the session centered on the grave shortage of church buildings and the government's establishment of a new "opposition priests" movement to work in tandem with the old "patriotic priests." At the same time, the authorities had printed up new forms that were to be used to register catechetical centers. The bishops decided that the forms should not be filled out. In Gniezno and Poznań the authorities were again trying to inspect the seminaries—simply, it seemed, because there were always forces in the party eager to stir up trouble.

Cardinal Wyszyński slowly prepared for the trip to Rome; it appeared that he would need an operation while he was there. On the train, on October 8, he met a group of young Jews who were being forced to emigrate. They told him that they had been compelled to give up their studies and subjected to intolerable psychological pressures, but that they hoped to return someday. The Primate expressed his sympathy and encouraged them to return when circumstances allowed. These young people were amiably disposed toward the Church and spoke of "our bishops." One of them was named Wyszyńska —the daughter of a Jewish woman named Bermstein and a Pole named Wyszyński. Such people as she were being forced to leave. The Primate parted sadly with the emigrants, trying with good words to ease the wrong that had been committed in our—and their—country.

In Rome he was greeted by Vatican and Polish-embassy officials before speaking at the opening session of the Synod of

Bishops on October 13. The business of the synod, he said, was not to consider doctrinal problems of collegiality—that had been done by the council. "Rather," he went on, "we need to make a decisive confession of our allegiance to the Holy Father, for which everyone, and especially those living under the yoke of state atheism—are waiting." From the Eastern European point of view, the universality of the Church and the primacy of the Bishop of Rome were a shield that allowed some margin of freedom. Many bishops never realized this when discussing collegiality.

After the session, Cardinal Wyszyński visited Pope Paul and presented him with the copy of the icon of the Virgin of Częstochowa, which the Pope hung in his private apartments, as well as a letter from the Polish bishops calling on the Holy Father to defend the veneration of the Virgin Mary, to establish a Feast of the Mother of the Church, and to put the entire family of man under her protection. The bishops urged that this be done collegially, with all the bishops of the world. The Pope said that he knew about the prayer campaign in Poland called "Paul's Creed" and acknowledged it as "an exception in the world." He added, "You have maintained your unity in faith, unity as an episcopate, and unity with the people, which is not the case everywhere." Paul said that he had appreciated Wyszyński's remarks to the synod.

The Primate received applause when he spoke unambiguously to the Congregation for the Clergy at the Lateran University on October 14: "For forty-four years I have had no doubt about what the priesthood is. It is sent in the name of the Holy Trinity for the purpose of preaching and baptizing." He said that drawing people into community with the Holy Trinity is the essence of the priesthood. He observed that the example of the Eastern countries showed that a decline in priestly vocations was caused not by the obligation of celibacy, but by the deeper crisis springing from practical materialism.

The next day the Primate discussed the situation of the universal Church with such figures as Cardinal Slipyj, Cardinal Danielou, and Bishop Carlo Colombo. They drew two conclusions: that the symptoms of the crisis in the Church require unity in support of papal authority, and that the charisma of the Bishop of Rome's primacy has a spiritual as well as a juridical nature.

On October 28, Cardinal Wyszyński had major surgery. During his recovery in a Rome hospital, between visits from Cardinal Wojtyła, Archbishops Kominek and Casaroli, Bishop Rubin, and others, he worked on the final version of *Letters to My Priests* for Les Editions du Dialogue, Paris. He stayed in Rome after leaving the hospital, and had a warm final meeting with Pope Paul on December 15, two days before he left for Warsaw.

At the end of 1969, little was clear except that the government's policy toward the Church was confused. The year 1970 began in apparent calm, but the country's moral and economic situation was steadily worsening, which the Episcopate could not ignore.

At its January meeting, the Episcopate approved a Polish text for the whole Mass in a continuation of efforts to introduce the vernacular. It was decided to organize the May 3 celebrations around prayers for the faithfulness to the Church of priests, religious, and intellectuals—an intention necessitated by unceasing efforts to split the Church and society into factions. The Episcopate also discussed the continuing deadlock over permission to build new churches or create new parishes. The Warsaw curia decided on January 17 to deal with part of the problem by setting up informal affiliate parishes where regular parishes were forbidden. The material situation of priests was declining to such an extent that the Primate exempted smaller parishes from contributions to the support of the curia.

On January 20 Father Sadłowski of Zbrosza Duża, whose church had been torn down by the authorities, received a sentence of three months' imprisonment for celebrating Mass in a private home.

The Primate's father, Stanisław Wyszyński, died on February 15 at the age of ninety-three. Because his father had always led a modest life, Cardinal Wyszyński avoided any public observances in Warsaw of his passing. With Cardinal Wojtyła and fifteen bishops, the Primate took part in the funeral in the village of Wrociszew, where Stanisław Wyszyński had lived so long and served as church organist.

The government's activities reflected indecision and weakness. Cardinals Marty of Paris and Poma of Bologna were granted permission to visit Poland; Father Sadłowski, though sentenced, had not yet been imprisoned. On the other hand, the local authorities in Łódź were imposing fines on catechetical centers.

In March, the Episcopate discussed a subject that was also arousing much interest in Rome: the Bonn-Moscow negotiations, which would certainly be followed by Bonn-Warsaw talks. It was plain that a peace treaty between Poland and West Germany would allow for the stabilization of the Church in the Western Lands and for the naming of resident bishops ordinary in Wrocław and Olsztyn. Concerning government actions, the bishops noted that the administrative authorities were beginning attacks on Catholic cemeteries.

In early April Poland received a visit from the West German *Bensberger Kreis* group, which had been a pioneer in recognizing the postwar Polish boundaries. The visit, initiated by Delegate Stomma of Znak, took on an ambiguous character through the participation of Pax. The German guests did not know what Pax was like, but when the visit was turned to propaganda purposes by *Słowo Powszechne*, Cardinal Wyszyński had to decide not to receive the group.

On May 3, two thousand seminarians from around the country made pilgrimages to Częstochowa; the Primate also welcomed bishops Tomašzek and Trochta from Czechoslovakia. After preaching, the Primate left that same afternoon to take part in celebrations in Wrocław of the twenty-fifth anniversary of the Polish Church in the Western Lands. The anniversary was an important meeting, especially in view of the approaching Bonn-Moscow rapprochement. The Episcopate met (in the room where they convened, eavesdropping devices had been discovered behind a painting of Saint Peter that was taken down for restoration) and heard the Primate state that further normalization depended on the government's returning church property that had been confiscated in the Western Lands. Bishop Pluta spoke of the need to divide the enormous Gorzów diocese, and Bishop Józef Drzazga of the need to build new churches. The Episcopate noted new censorial restrictions and decided not to acquiesce in the authorities' humiliating practice of summoning bishops for frequent talks.

A great pilgrimage of miners and steelworkers arrived at the shrine of Piekary Śląskie on May 31. Bishop Bednorz spoke to them of the need for new churches, and the Primate wondered publicly about the reasons for the continued anti-Zionist propaganda, since the majority of the Jewish population had emigrated by now.

The June meeting of the Episcopate decided to circulate a pastoral letter in September about the Miracle of the Vistula— the 1920 victory over the Red Army. The bishops were motivated not by anti-Russian feelings, but by the conviction that they could not keep silent about the nation's history. Nevertheless, a stormy reaction ensued. In July, Director Skarżyński demanded the withdrawal of the scheduled pastoral letter and, at Bishop Dąbrowski's request, went so far as to put his demand in writing. Cardinal Wyszyński reasoned that a letter unanimously approved by the bishops had to be kept on the historical record, even if it were not read publicly in all the churches. He summoned a special meeting of the Episcopate for August 1, and then went to Cracow to confer with Cardinal Wojtyła about the situation. When Cardinal Wojtyła wished the Primate a happy birthday, he received a significant response. The Cardinal thanked him and remarked that Cardinal Wojtyła, nineteen years his junior, would certainly have the responsibility of guiding the Polish Church in the future. Everyone in Poland assumed the same, but Providence was to grant Primate Wyszyński a long life and to shape an unexpected destiny for Cardinal Wojtyła in Rome.

In the meantime, the Soviet-German treaty had been concluded. A similar Polish-German agreement seemed to be in the works, so the bishops decided, in view of the delicate international situation, not to have the letter read in the churches. The statement was not, however, formally withdrawn. "The Episcopate had to speak to the nation," the Primate said, "because the bishops had a moral obligation to do so, as sons of Poland. The letter has already served its purpose through the publicity given it by the government."

On August 13, Monsignor Deskur arrived from Rome to relate that the Polish government representatives there had made urgent diplomatic interventions against the letter. The Primate told him, "The Church cannot leave itself open to the charge that it has forgotten the history of the nation in which it lives." The Vatican had no influence over the decision not to read the letter, which had been made earlier in the month.

The next meeting of the Episcopate, on September 2, heard reports of new harassments against priests who were being charged with "building crimes" for the unlicensed restoration or repair of ecclesiastical buildings. The bishops also discussed the new legal code being prepared, which increased various penalties and moved in the direction of a police state. Polish society was worrying at this period about the Soviet-German treaty, which also included references to Poland's borders. Gomułka understood, as did most people, that a separate Polish-German treaty defining the Polish borders was necessary. The Primate emphasized that a settlement of church-state issues in the Western Lands ought to be reached by the Polish Episcopate and the Polish government before the Vatican made its final decision on the question. Director Skarżyński, unfortunately, was displaying a negative attitude in negotiations with Bishop Dąbrowski about the important question of dividing the unmanageably large Gorzów diocese.

The Cardinal left on October 10 for the Vatican, where there was a great deal of interest in the possibility of a Warsaw-Bonn treaty. Archbishop Casaroli and Monsignor Deskur, who greeted Primate Wyszyński, asked if he would like to meet with the Pope immediately or later; Wyszyński decided that he needed more time to prepare for the important discussions. At supper on October 14, Wyszyński and Cardinal Döpfner discussed Eastern matters and the viability of the new Brandt-Scheel government in West Germany. The Primate spoke in historic terms of Catherine the Great, Frederick the Great, the Rapallo Pact, and the Molotov-Ribbentrop Pact—all of which, as he had said in the past, had resulted in the retreat of Catholic influence six hundred kilometers westward over the course of two hundred years. Now, he said, resident Polish ordinaries ought to be named in Wrocław and Olsztyn, and the Gorzów diocese ought to be divided as soon as possible for pastoral reasons. The Polish Church held these positions, regardless of whether the Eastern treaties were ratified in Bonn. What Döpfner thought of these arguments is not known, but Wyszyński presented them fully and honestly to the head of the West German Episcopate.

Discussing these issues with the Primate on October 15, Cardinal Wojtyła and Archbishop Kominek did not hide their opinion that the Polish Church could not afford to return empty-handed from Rome, and therefore ought to present the Holy See with a suggestion that could be realized. That same day the Primate told the Znak delegates Stomma and Mazowiecki that, although he usually tried to negotiate from a "developmental" position rather than from an ultimatum, he was going to have to act radically in this case. Deep in his heart, he felt it was time to assume an inflexible stance. Cardinal Wyszyński ended the day by visiting Archbishop Casaroli and presenting his views with regard to the Western Lands.

Pope Paul must already have been acquainted with Wyszyński's position when he greeted him on October 17, for he began by saying that he was full of good will for Poland even if he could not do everything it needed. The Primate replied that all Poland had been praying on the semicentennial of the Pope's priesthood. He gave his usual sketch of church and general matters in the East, saying that things were slowly evolving, even though the centers of power favored political homogenization. Then, to the Pope's surprise, he suggested that the

Vatican initiate talks with the Polish government, even though the two sides were out of touch at the moment. The two men shared well-known doubts and misgivings about such negotiations, but Wyszyński had an accurate idea of the trends in East-West relations and he thought the time was right for a good-will gesture to Poland from the Vatican. Then, map in hand, he showed the Pope the difference between the Polish borders of 1772 and those of 1970, and what that difference meant to the Church.

Four days later, Archbishop Casaroli said that the Vatican would create no obstacles to the division of the Gorzów diocese if the Polish Episcopate could win its government's approval. As for the question of Olsztyn, Casaroli thought that hasty action might make ratification of the German-Soviet treaty more difficult. Cardinal Wyszyński, however, did not change his position. Casaroli also observed that the Polish Episcopate had changed its mind about talks between the Holy See and the Warsaw authorities. Times had changed, Wyszyński replied, and added that government propaganda was charging him with blocking an agreement between Poland and the Vatican. He added that he had always favored an agreement with the government; it was only capitulation that he had opposed. He asked that *L'Osservatore Romano* print more articles about Polish religious life in the Western Lands.

At the beginning of November, Wyszyński visited Cardinals Lercaro and Poma in Bologna, accompanying them to the nearby house of Maria Teresa Carloni, in Urbania, where Cardinal Beran was staying. He learned a great deal about the Czech primate's fate. To the offer made during his own imprisonment of freedom in exchange for emigration, Cardinal Wyszyński had replied that he "would rather sit in a Polish prison than in Biarritz." He knew that in its efforts to ease the lot of Cardinal Beran, and later of Cardinal Mindszenty, the Vatican had not benefited from his experience or views.

Primate Wyszyński's stand on the dioceses in the Western Lands was so decisive that it initially caught the Vatican off balance. But Archbishop Casaroli realized that Wyszyński was not motivated by questions of personal prestige—the matter at hand was the possibility the issue might serve to discredit the Church before its nation. Casaroli expressed his trust. In return, Wyszyński asked for a letter from the Holy Father to the Polish bishops affirming that the apostolic administrator of Olsztyn was a resident bishop, that the Holy See was studying and ready to resolve in the near future the question of Wrocław, and that there were no objections to a division of the Gorzów diocese if the Polish government agreed to it.

Cardinal Wyszyński and Monsignor Franciszek Mączyński* joined Pope Paul for dinner on November 8. Early on, the Pope told the Primate, "We are both martyrs. . . . We are brothers in suffering." The Holy Father also hinted, engagingly, that there was still a chance of his visiting Poland, perhaps at the beatification of Father Maksymilian Maria Kolbe, planned for the coming year. Paul seemed careworn, however, and complained of bad news from around the world. During dinner the two men talked about the general situation in the East, and afterward the Pope led his guests to his picture of the Blessed Virgin of Częstochowa. "Whenever I go from the dining room to the chapel," he said, "I stop here and say a prayer for the Polish Church." Then Paul returned to his earlier theme, saying that he and Wyszyński were both martyrs, that they both wanted to do good but were both tightly constrained in different ways. The Pope said that he recognized the correctness of the Polish Episcopate's arguments, that he wanted to meet its wishes and stood on its side, but that some of the factors that had to go into his decisions were not apparent. He said, however, that work to meet Wyszynski's requests was under way (in fact, Archbishop Casaroli was at that moment drafting the letter that the Primate had requested). The invocation of Mary as Mother of the Church was being introduced into the litany, according to Paul, but it was not yet possible to establish a Feast

---

*Mączyński: Rector of the Polish Institute in Rome (a residence for Polish priest-students attending Roman universities for advanced degrees), where Cardinal Wyszyński resided when in the Holy City.

of the Mother of the Church or to dedicate the world to her. Cardinal Wyszyński said that he had presented his suggestions so decisively only because he had felt he had no other choice. The Pope understood. "It will not affect our relationship," he said. "That is always full of respect and trust—always friendly toward the Cardinal." The Pope refused to let Cardinal Wyszyński kiss his feet at parting, as was customary, saying, "Let's take our farewells as brothers." As he handed the Primate a chalice for Jasna Góra, he said, "Let it be my forerunner." Archbishop Casaroli came that evening with the letter that the Pope had promised, and three days later he accompanied Cardinal Wyszyński to Termini Station and the homeward-bound train.

On his arrival, the Primate played his cards close to his chest. The Polish and German negotiators were meeting (they initialed an agreement on November 20), and Wyszyński decided not to reveal the Pope's letter until after the conclusion of the international pact that would serve as a basis for the canonical decisions.

Warsaw political circles were stirred up when Piasecki, the leader of Pax, attacked the government leadership. Wyszyński decided that it would be better to steer clear of political issues at such a tense moment and concentrate instead on the general problems that the Episcopate had already raised. Thus he wrote letters to all the government ministers, attaching copies of an earlier letter on the demographic threat to the nation. On November 22, churchgoers heard a letter from the Episcopate about the "Social Crusade of Love—In Defense of Life." The bishops' documents were closely related to the increasing crisis, but they embraced the problems within moral categories.

The Episcopate heard at its November 24–26 meeting that mounting troubles within the party and the state had issued in a new politeness from the Bureau of Religious Affairs, palpable even at the local level. *Sub secreto*, the Primate shared the letter from Paul VI. A commission began work under Archbishop Kominek to demarcate the dioceses in the Western Lands, and a communiqué on its work received Episcopal approval. The

Holy See had promised the final regulation of diocesan affairs in the West and North in a measure commensurate with relations between the interested states.

Public opinion was riveted by the conclusion of the Polish–West German treaty on December 7. Stefan Wyszyński always held back from claiming a direct relationship between the letter of the Polish bishops and the later agreement between the states, but the world press and foreign radio stations made the connection. Most people, unconcerned with nuances, saw the later agreement as merely a repetition of the letter. And the Episcopate's call may indeed have been the more important of the two, since it dealt with the reconciliation of nations.

On December 11, Director Skarżyński politely requested of Bishop Dąbrowski that the pastoral letter about the biological threat to the nation not be read. For the moment, the Primate did not change his decision to distribute the letter.

Two days later, the government drastically raised the prices of essential items. With the Primate in Łódź for the day and the Episcopate not having reached a final decision, Director Skarżyński again asked that the letter be held back, even though he refused to specify the passages that the government regarded as "harmful to the state." To withhold an approved letter for the second time in one year could have a bad psychological effect. The decision was delayed again, in view of the delicate situation.

Just at this time the popular protests, and the authorities' bloody response to them, began in Gdańsk. The conflict spread along the coast and soon became a showdown with the people. There were hundreds of injured and killed. Gomułka said nothing. Cyrankiewicz went on television to announce repressive measures and suggest a threat to Polish sovereignty. He also took personal responsibility for authorizing the militia to use firearms.

The government was now contending with the workers and the Episcopate simultaneously. The Bureau of Religious Affairs tried to exert indirect pressure on the Primate through the Znak delegates. On December 18 Delegate Zabłocki underlined the need for caution in the face of what was happening in Szczecin. The Primate pointed out that the pastoral letter on the biological threat to the nation had been approved on September 4. He also said that the party should roll back the price increases, acknowledging its political and economic mistakes. Nor did he conceal his appraisal of Premier Cyrankiewicz's actions. Still, in spite of the continuing bloodshed and tension, he was inclined, in talking with Bishop Dąbrowski the next day, to postpone the letter.

On the evening of December 20, while he was in Gniezno, the Primate learned that Gomułka, Kliszko, Spychalski, and Jaszczuk* had been dismissed at a Central Committee meeting. One of the saddest pages in Poland's postwar history was being turned. The leadership that had governed Poland for fourteen years, brought it to the brink of the abyss and finally to bloodshed, and committed innumerable wrongs against the Church was making its exit. The Gomułka clique had poisoned the years of the Primate's greatest work, the Great Novena and the Millennium. After consulting with Bishop Dąbrowski in Warsaw on the 22nd, the Primate set a meeting of the Episcopal Steering Committee for the 29th.

A Sejm delegate looking forward to a career in the new order of things informed the Primate on December 23 of changes in the government (aside from those already made in the party) and said that Premier Cyrankiewicz would be transferred to the Council of State. This news hardly reassured the Primate, since Cyrankiewicz's activities stretched back as far as the Stalinist period. It was hard to see how someone with an acknowledged role in the December events avoided straightforward dismissal. But, rather than coming to an honest moral reckoning, the party was making "arrangements" and compromises. The Primate continued to insist on a revocation of the price rises. He also shared the consternation of the workers on the Coast at the inclusion in the new leadership of Stanisław

---

*Bolesław Jaszczuk: a member of the Central Committee of the Polish Communist Party.

Kociołek,* who bore significant responsibility for the events in Gdańsk.

Christmas 1970 signified a major pastoral responsibility for Stefan Wyszyński. During his sermon at the cathedral, he said that even though the party and the government were trying to cover up what was happening on the Coast, it was necessary for someone to take responsibility upon himself—if only to forestall further bloodshed and arrests. The Cardinal's words shook his listeners.

If it were possible, with a feeling of justice and rightness for me to take upon myself the responsibility for all that has happened recently in Poland, I would do so willingly! . . . Because in the nation there must be a sacrificial victim, to ransom the guilt of the nation. And if Christ, the Eternal Priest, took upon his shoulders the burden of man's sins, so in Poland it would have been the duty, if it could have redeemed us, of the Primate of Poland to take everything upon his shoulders! How I would have wanted, had the offer been accepted, to shield everyone from that responsibility, from pain and suffering. Because perhaps I did not call out enough, did not exhort enough, did not warn and plead enough! Even so, it is known that my voice was not always listened to, did not always move consciences and wills, did not always prompt reflection. So, apparently, it had to be.

In the same sermon he addressed "brotherly sympathy . . . to all the families on the Coast, in the port cities of the republic, for whom today's holiday is full of awful pain. We send the

---

*As party first secretary in Gdańsk, he had broadcast an appeal to striking shipyard workers to return to work, promising to negotiate their demands if they did so. At the commuter train stations in front of the yards, workers were met with automatic-weapon fire; many died. It was later reported that Kociołek had not known about the violent greeting and had acted in good faith; in any case, he went on to become Warsaw first secretary, a leading exponent in 1981 of the tendency sometimes called "neo-Stalinism," and, after General Jaruzelski's attack on the latter tendency, ambassador to the Soviet Union in 1982.

blessing of the Holy Father to you, orphaned children and widowed mothers. We send it to you, brothers in hard work, who have lost your comrades in labor, suffering, and the effort to create a common good for our country. . . ."

Although the prevailing system in Poland led to the political camouflaging of what had happened on the Coast, the bloodshed caused political changes that would have great meaning for the Church. The end of the year meant a time of deep reflection on the tragedy, for the Primate as for everyone else. For Stefan Wyszyński, that reflection led to a strengthening of pastoral efforts and a more energetic involvement in the affairs and fortune of the nation.

The Episcopal Steering Committee met on December 29, and naturally it analyzed the course of the "December events." The bishops tried to establish the extent to which the cruel and blind repression resulted from militia actions as opposed to intrigues within the splintered party. Rumors were circulating that bullets of a type banned by the Geneva Convention had been used against the demonstrators, and that the militia—the MO and ORMO units—were given alcohol, or even narcotics, to stimulate their aggressiveness. Some young people had had a soothing effect on tempers, on the other hand: girls gave flowers to tank crews and asked the soldiers not to join in the repressive actions. The army, after all, did not want to open fire. Generally, however, the reports from the Coast were shocking. Much later it appeared that Gomułka's evil spirit in church-state matters and the leader of the fight against the Episcopate, Zenon Kliszko, had been one of the chief stage managers of the bloodbath. The Episcopate decided to postpone the letter on the biological threat to the nation until Lent, by which time it was hoped the political tension would have dissipated.

The Primate spent the last day of the year, as usual, in Gniezno. The fact that people there were still being frightened by nocturnal movements of troops, tanks, and artillery illustrates the political tension. The Primate called from the pulpit for peace and Christian love, but the country remained full of apprehension.

The expiring year had been difficult in view of the controversies over the two pastoral letters.* Administrative harassment, because of the weakness at the top, had been confined mainly to outlying areas. The Church still painfully felt the lack of sacral buildings. In society, however, faith in the transformation or reform of socialism had diminished markedly, despite assurances given by the new authorities. The government's move to create "opposition priests" had come to nothing, while pastoral work and the concentration of energy on Jasna Góra had yielded the expected results. The "gathering of fruits" from the letter to the German bishops had been unexpected: henceforth no one could accuse the bishops of acting "against Polish state interests."

Domestically, in the wake of the bloody suppression of popular demonstrations, the Church and the Primate had played an important role in moderating tensions. Yet Cardinal Wyszyński had withdrawn none of his demands against the state.

---

*The much-delayed pastoral letter on the biological threat to the nation, written in the fall of 1970, was finally read in all the churches on January 28, 1971.

6

Greatness
Acknowledged
(1970-1979)

The Central Committee of the Polish United Workers' Party, the PZPR, elected Edward Gierek as its first secretary on December 20, 1970. The change of leadership was important, though insufficient to put the country at ease. In the first place, the new leadership did not understand the need to revoke Gomułka's drastic raising of prices, and, in the second, it never lived up to the words that Gierek spoke over radio and television on the night of his election:

> In the last weeks, events have occurred that have deeply agitated the whole society and brought the country face to face with great danger. The cities of the Coast have become the scene of workers' demonstrations, riots, and street fighting. People have died. . . . Questions force themselves upon us: Why did such misfortunes occur? Where did this great social conflict originate, and what caused it to explode? . . . The leadership of the party and

the government owes the party and the nation full answers to these questions—that is our duty. The answers will be difficult and self-critical, but they will be clear and honest. . . ."

Unfortunately, the nation has not received these answers yet —not, in my opinion, because Gierek did not want to give them, but because he was restricted by "arrangements" and coalitions within the party, and by influence from outside. Too many truths compromising to the system would have come to light. The government rolled back prices only after a general mutiny by the working class, in which the women textile workers of Łódź played the decisive role.

The people had to be calmed down in order to avoid further bloodshed and a new occupation of Poland. Once again it was Cardinal Wyszyński who took up the task. He met it through sermons, through the proclamations of the Episcopal Steering Committee, and through an official statement submitted at the conference of bishops on January 27, 1971, which the Episcopate approved and published. In part, the Primate stated:

Two months ago, we did not think we would live through such painful trials and experiences. They demand of us exceptional maturity, temperance, and calm. . . .

We confront the important task of being able to walk into the House of our Country, with all its troubles, remembering what Christ said: "And into whatsoever house ye enter, first say, Peace be to this house." . . .

We know that our unity with the Nation places us under a double obligation: to the Country and to the Church. We must fulfill our obligation to the Church in such a way that we are able to assist the Country in difficult circumstances. . . .

Having matters of such an enormous scale before our eyes, we should want nevertheless to establish a hierarchy of values. . . . We cannot forget that we have been sent to lead the Nation to the Gospel. . . . At this moment, our feelings lead us particularly in the direction of our Worker Brothers, who suffered greatly, undertaking a difficult task that has cost them much. They had the courage to lay claim to the equitable rights guaranteed in all of law and nature—the right to a just, fitting existence—because a worker deserves his pay.

But—while we express our full respect and sympathy with our workers, conscious of our gratitude for their work and sacrifices, we see at the same time the whole state of the Country. We must well and accurately define the proportion of rights and obligations in the national community, which always arises from a plurality well put together. . . . Speaking the truth to everyone—as befits bishops—and thus speaking the truth to the nation, to those who guide the nation, and to all layers of society, we always observe the higher principles of the Gospel, and not of politics. . . .

We are not economists, but Christ told his Apostles, "Give ye them to eat"—therefore teach and admonish, so that there will be bread for every mouth. After all, we promised as much in the Jasna Góra vows. We do not want to organize official life, but at the same time, in the name of Christian and human moral principles, we must speak for the common good from the most evangelical, human, and social position, which is always linked to morality. There is an admirable proximity between the morality of the Gospel and social morality, between the Gospel and the labor codex. We can even say that all the labor legislation, no matter what its authorship, that makes up the great socioeconomic struggle of labor in the last century, derives from the spirit of the Gospel.

Conscious that it serves us, we refer to the world of labor: we long on our side to serve labor and to respect its just demands. That is why, at this moment, the Catholic bishops of Poland cannot be indifferent to what is going on.

We must—each according to his competence and in

proportion to his abilities—show our sympathy for people who are suffering, help them as much as we can, and call on the flock that has been entrusted to us to help us to help them. . . .

The Primate called on the rulers to respect law and justice, while leaving no doubt that he was asking the nation for social peace. It was an objective warning to society in a tense situation. The nation obeyed, and the rulers, in a spirit of gratitude, finally began to speak of Cardinal Wyszyński's patriotism, and even of his greatness. After twenty years of bitterness and struggle, the Primate finally enjoyed the respect even of his ideological enemies.

At their January session, the bishops called on the faithful to "preserve order and calm—the values that guarantee our country's independence." The Episcopate also noted certain realistic steps taken by the new leadership. Piotr Jaroszewicz, the premier, had told the Sejm on December 23, 1970, that the government would try to achieve a full normalization of church-state relations. On January 25 he announced his decision on church property in the Western Lands, which was to open negotiations with the Episcopate. A compromise was finally achieved that corrected the injury done to Polish property there during the last quarter-century.

The Episcopate called on January 27 for "Prayers for the Country"; these prayers included

First of all prayers for those who have fallen on the Coast,
For families plunged in sorrow, for widows and orphans
—comfort for their hearts and bread for the orphans,
For those who regarded it as their civic duty to call for the
true rights of working people,
For those who committed the lamented deeds, that God
will forgive them and that we can learn to forgive them,
For those who have accepted at present the responsibility
for order, the domestic peace of the country, and justice
for all—that in the difficult economic and social situation

of the country they will find the correct road to calm and healthy development, faithful to their promises, respecting the basic rights of man and the citizen.

This last intention evoked the objections of the émigré writer Józef Mackiewicz, who could not understand how it was possible to pray for communists. An impulsive anticommunist, he did not want to think in the spirit of the Gospel.

The Episcopate was faithful to that spirit, but it did not give anyone credit before it was earned. While asking for prayers for the rulers, it demanded of them respect for human rights. Long before "human rights" became a slogan in the West and among the lay political opposition in the communist countries, it had been a leading principle of Cardinal Wyszyński's actions. All of his writings attest to this fact, and justice demands that it be underscored.

Finally, the busy January meeting of the Episcopate noted with astonishment that in some dioceses the official attitude toward catechization had not improved; quite the contrary. The bishops decided to oppose such a development in strong terms—some priests had been threatened with legal sanctions for refusing to submit reports on their educational activities.

On March 3, nevertheless, the Primate had his first high-level contact with the government in years, a meeting with Premier Jaroszewicz that raised high hopes. Jaroszewicz judged Gomułka's church-state policy harshly, referred to the Primate's patriotism, and promised that representatives of the Episcopate would take part in all future Polish-Vatican talks. But Bishop Dąbrowski's ongoing discussions with Director Skarżyński— who had not only survived the changes of government but had even been given the rank of undersecretary of State for the purpose of dealing with the Holy See—were not easy. The "arrangements" within the party and pressure from outside made the new policies more apparent than real. However, the social pressures evoked by the December tragedy would make any return to the old church-state line impossible.

Meeting on March 30–April 1, the Episcopate deliberated the process of transferring church property in the Western Lands. The report of Bishop Dąbrowski, who had just returned from Rome, made it clear that diplomatic contacts between Warsaw and the Vatican would soon be established. Speaking from experience, the Primate called for the presence of Episcopal representation—even if informal—in the talks. He thus controlled the talks and prevented the sort of diplomatic minimalism appropriate to a country with a weak Church, but not to Poland.

Cardinal Wojtyła reported on his participation in the *Consilium de laicis* (Consultation on the Laity) and the Congregation *pro Clero* (for the Clergy) in Rome between March 14 and 25; Wojtyła had also met with the Holy Father and the prefects of the various congregations. Pope Paul had said that he had prayed with the Polish Church on February 14, when the Episcopate had declared a day of prayer for the country. Cardinal Wojtyła's stature within the Catholic world was becoming more important all the time; Wojtyła's agreement with the Primate on all matters of principle was as great as it had been before December 1970. The Archbishop of Cracow deliberately stayed a bit in the shadows so that the policy of *divide et impera* could never work against the two cardinals.

Skarżyński and Stefan Staniszewski of the Foreign Ministry arrived in Rome on April 27 and met over the next three days with Archbishop Casaroli and Monsignor Montalvo. Little occurred beyond an exchange of views and initial positions, but the Vatican made the informal presence of the Polish Episcopate clear: Bishop Dąbrowski arrived on the same day as the government representatives and met with Paul VI on May 3.

On the twenty-fifth anniversary of Stefan Wyszyński's consecration as bishop, Karol Wojtyła wrote, in an article published by the Catholic University's *Academic Notes*, that

The Primate of Poland . . . bases his position within the universal Church on his roots in that part of the Christian community to which Providence has linked him in his

pastoral and primatial duties . . . : the Church in Poland.
. . . That Church, united for over a thousand years with
a predominantly Catholic nation, has also learned to exist
and act within a system founded on the atheistic doctrine
of Marxism. It is easy to understand that in such circumstances the very existence and activity of the Church become a fundamental trial of strength. In the contemporary
Church Cardinal Wyszyński is an expression, even a symbol, of the precise historical trial in which the Church
verifies its strength.

Cardinal Wojtyła's act of homage came at an appropriate
time. From Jasna Góra on May 4, the Episcopate issued a
communiqué pointing out that despite the beginning of
negotiations, the Church's difficulties had not ceased: "That
the administrative authorities, and particularly the local ones,
are acting according to the guidelines of the past is shown in
the negative answers to requests from church authorities for
building churches and setting up parishes in new residential
developments."
The same meeting of the Episcopate decided to address the
Sejm about a proposed bill to combat social parasitism. The
pending legislation was meeting widespread criticism, since
"parasitism" could mean almost anything and such a law might
infringe upon human and civic rights. Under the pressure of
public opinion, to which the Church gave voice, the authorities
ended up by discarding the bill.
In the same session, the Episcopate approved a letter to the
faithful on observances for the Mother of the Church, and a
letter on the situation of working people to mark the occasion
of the eightieth anniversary of Leo XIII's encyclical *Rerum
novarum.* In the latter document the bishops wrote of the

right to life and a decent existence . . . the right to the
satisfaction of moral and cultural needs, . . . the right to
witness one's own religion in private and public, the right
to choose one's own vocation, the right to work, to eco-

nomic initiatives, and to justified strikes, the right to gather and assemble freely, the right to emigrate and immigrate, the right to legal protection, to take part in public life, and to make one's own contribution to the public good.

Once again the Church was acting as precursor of the movement for human rights in Poland, as it had been doing since the 1940s.

On June 21, 1971, the Episcopate published in the bulletin of its press office a document of historic importance. The article, titled "The Meaning of Normalization in Church-State Relations," recalled, in a logical and organized way, all the fundamental principles of church-state coexistence. In short, it stated that the Polish Church was a part of the universal Church, fulfilled its mission in obedience to the Pope, and must therefore have an independent legal status different from that of state churches; that the Church played an indispensable role in Polish history, early and recent; that the United Nations Charter on Human Rights included freedom of thought, conscience, and open religious profession; that the Church sought only to advance the country's national morality and development rather than to play the role of a political force; and that the process of normalization demanded that the state acknowledge in legislation and in practice that:

1. The Catholic Church is a legal person in public law and a social organization. . . .
2. The Catholic Church is governed according to its own laws: the principles of the Gospel, moral law, and canon law.
3. The Catholic Church in all its rites should enjoy full freedom of action, in accordance with its mission and calling. . . .

The document betrays the hand of Cardinal Wyszyński in its composition; it contains the positions that he had adopted on the day in 1949 when he became primate and had maintained with realism, no matter who was running the country, ever since. Able to acknowledge the existing system and even its alliances, the Primate nevertheless became unyielding whenever the subject turned to fundamental freedoms. The article stressed that the Episcopate was fighting not just for church freedom, but for the civic freedom and human rights of the entire society. The explicit acknowledgment of the state and its international alliances drew the ire of intransigent people like Józef Mackiewicz, who could not accept the long-term character of decisions imposed on Poland at the end of the Second World War with the complicity of the Western powers.

The government never made a full response to this comprehensive vision of a *modus vivendi*. State policy toward the Church had always been expedient, ad hoc, and respectful of the principle *Cuius regio, eius religio*. Characteristically, and despite the Episcopate's wishes, neither now nor later was the institution of the Joint Commission revived as a step toward normalization.

The bishops' comprehensive document on church-state relations bore the date June 21. Two days later, *Słowo Powszechne* reported that Bolesław Piasecki had met with Pax's "patriotic priests," and also that he had been named to the Council of State. An adjacent story reported that General Mieczysław Moczar had been named president of the Office of Supreme Control and thus had lost the influential post of Central Committee secretary and nominal supervision over church-state relations. These events followed too closely on the Episcopate's statement to be taken as responses. Activity among the "patriotic priests," however, always meant that someone wanted to exacerbate relations with the Episcopate. Piasecki's promotion seemed a similar portent to most people. The concurrent demotion of Moczar, acknowledged as leader of the party "hawks," signaled further tectonic changes in the coalition that had come to power in December 1970. Yet the next months also brought faint signs of a relaxing attitude toward the Church—in short, the party had yet to achieve even a relatively fixed leadership or direction. At the party congress in December 1971, Moczar's old position in the leadership fell to his one-time assistant in the secret police, General Franciszek Szlachcic, who passed for an intelligent man but not for a liberal.

The Episcopate met on June 23–24 in Gorzów diocese, in the Western Lands. The site was no accident. The bishops regarded it as a

> happy circumstance . . . that at this very time the Sejm of the Polish People's Republic has approved legislation by the strength of which the Church recovers the right to own church buildings and monasteries, and to acquire other properties necessary to its pastoral work in the Western Lands and in the north. This facilitates the normalization of church-state relations and corrects wrongs done in the previous period to the Church, which was working here in difficult circumstances for the good of society.

At its September meeting, the Episcopate approved a message, drafted in final form by Cardinal Wojtyła, calling on ninety-three episcopates around the world to establish holidays for the Mother of the Church in their countries, to dedicate their countries to the protection of the Virgin Mary, and above all else to join with the Polish bishops in a collegial request that the Holy Father dedicate the whole Church and all humanity to her. The appeal based itself on the collegial responsibility of all bishops for the fate of Christ's work on earth and for the greatly endangered human race.

Cardinal Wyszyński left for Rome on September 26. He would stay there until November 16, taking part in two events of significance for the universal and the Polish Church: the meeting of the Synod of Bishops from September 30 until November 6, and the beatification of Father Kolbe on October 17.

Back home, meanwhile, Director Aleksander Skarżyński of

the Bureau of Religious Affairs spoke on October 3, during the twenty-fifth anniversary celebrations of Pax. Both the forum and the remarks were remarkable. To honor Pax was of course an unfriendly act toward the Episcopate, and Skarżyński's speech constituted an indirect retort to the Episcopate's position paper of June 21 on church-state normalization. The Episcopate had stated that it had not been able to and would not make choices of a sociopolitical nature. Now, among generalities about church freedom, Skarżyński mentioned the "antagonistic political position in relation to the people's state" of "some representatives of the Polish church authorities." He expected "the Episcopate and all the clergy to understand and respect the patriotic and constitutional demands of our socialist state," although he did not demand that the bishops "press clergy and Catholic lay people directly to adopt progressive, socialist attitudes." Skarżyński added that the government expected the Episcopate "not to bestow distinctions on people who have antagonistic attitudes toward socialism and the people's state."

Skarżyński was trying to play the game of "good bishops, bad bishops," while defending the "patriotic priests" on the grounds that their political involvement did not undermine the religious unity of the Church. Although Skarżyński had criticized and even bravely opposed Gomułka and Kliszko before December, his speech continued old attitudes rather than introducing a new spirit into church-state relations. His criticism of the bishops' rather conciliatory June 21 document left their positive suggestions glaringly unanswered. Then to call for respecting the constitutional interests of the socialist state was to call for recognizing Marxist policies in culture, science, and education—far more than recognizing the existing system. Skarżyński's speech contained some conciliatory shadings, but it cast an uneasy shadow over the future. The author hedged his bets by citing the more optimistic statements of Gierek and Jaroszewicz. In the same month, Skarżyński donned a hurriedly tailored morning coat to represent the Polish government at the beatification of Father Kolbe in Rome. He sat beside Ambassador Habasiński in the first row of the dignitaries' section at Saint Peter's. This section was large enough also to accommodate Karol Popiel, émigré leader of the Christian Democrat Labor Party, Ambassador Papée of the government-in-exile, and Jan Nowak, director of the Polish section of Radio Free Europe and *bête noire* of the party and the police. The government could not complain—the Vatican, rather than the Episcopate, had sent the invitations, and the authorities were still trying to woo the Holy See.

The celebrations for Father Kolbe on October 17 and 18 meshed with the synod session on the formation of priests. It was a great time for the Polish Catholics who had come to Rome from all over the world. Pope Paul told them, after he had completed the beatification, "The spiritual heritage of the beatified leaves room for not a shadow of hesitation or doubt, although today this very Marian piety arouses a certain mistrust. . . . Indeed, the Mother of God derives greatness and privilege from her fulfilling, subordinate tasks in relation to the cosmological, anthropological, redeeming action of Christ himself." The Pope went on to speak of Father Kolbe's sacrifice of his life for the sake of his fellow man in Auschwitz. That evening, the Holy Father shared dinner with Cardinals Wyszyński and Wojtyła and Bishop Rubin.

October 18 was "Polish Day" in Rome. In the audience hall the Primate spoke of the day's meaning and went on to delineate his concept of Polish religiosity. Father Kolbe had followed Christ, he said, "by giving his life in the starvation cell for his fellow prisoner. Father Kolbe is the flower of Polish Catholicism, led to Christ by the Handmaiden of the Lord, whose ideal of service he accepted. This shows that the fullness of Catholic life must draw its strength through Mary, who is present in the ministry of Christ and the Church." He concluded by repeating his plea to the Pope: "That you would be willing again to give the universal Church and all humanity into the Hands of Mary, Mother of the Church—this time together with all the bishops of the world, who are responsible for Christ's Image on this earth."

In reply, the Pope characterized the Primate as "a fervent and courageous pastor" and linked these qualities with his Marian orientation. "In a particular way we now call upon your Blessed Mother of Częstochowa, that she may protect, comfort, and win for you all the graces of Christ, for your material and moral good. We will keep praying to her for your intention." The Pope called Poland to religious and ecclesiastical faith, without omitting these diplomatic words: "Do not suppose that our summons is to delay the economic, social, and cultural development on which you have embarked. On the contrary, we ask you to learn to draw on your faith, on your spiritual and cultural tradition, on your national and civic identity for strength to move forward and shape your abilities to meet the new tasks of today."

An indescribable mood united the Polish community during these Roman celebrations. Nor is it possible to ignore the words of Cardinal Julius Döpfner, head of the West German Council of Bishops. In the Basilica of the Twelve Apostles, on October 19, he said, "Father Kolbe is the martyr of reconciliation. This fact compels us to ask our Polish brothers for forgiveness of all the evils that we, Germans, have committed, and to reiterate our renunciation of all desire for revenge. Political efforts to secure order and peace must find their springs in this spirit of creative reconciliation."

The domestic Polish press, both secular and Catholic, could not help dedicating a good deal of space to these moving ceremonies in which representatives of the government were taking part. The Catholic press in particular tried to convey all the emotion and exultation, and for a while the censor stayed quiet. Then things began to be cut, and even the name of the Blessed Father Kolbe was not safe. Adherents of the principle *Cuius regio, eius religio,* in Poland and elsewhere, must finally have had enough. The return of the church party from Rome to Warsaw at the end of November was thus a fall from heaven back to the realities of earth.

At a December 1–3 meeting, the Episcopate heard Cardinal Wyszyński's remarks on the warmth shown by Pope Paul to the Polish pilgrims and expressed its satisfaction with talks held between representatives of the Polish government and the Holy See. The bishops approved the continuation of such discussions, while thanking the Vatican for having cooperated closely with the Polish Episcopate during the negotiations. Real progress between Warsaw and the Vatican, the bishops said, would have to depend on concrete results in relations between the government and the Episcopate. Within this latter sphere, it was necessary to note continuing problems at the local level. Such a formulation represented a euphemism, since all aspects of church-state relations occurred in one locality or another—especially when it came to building churches. On this last point, there had been no progress.

The next meeting of the Episcopate, on February 9–10, 1972, decided to publicize the lack of building permits by appointing Bishop Bednorz to lead a special Commission on Building Churches. The secretary of the Episcopate had been negotiating incessantly with the authorities, keeping the Episcopate advised and seeking its counsel, but the impasse continued. A transformation of church-state relations would clearly not occur in the immediate wake of the December 1970 events, but not until much later.

The December 1971 party congress at which Szlachcic succeeded Moczar thus meant nothing in terms of relations with the Church. Most of the restrictions from the Gomułka era remained in force. Premier Jaroszewicz told the Sejm on March 29 that the authorities wanted to normalize relations, but this was just talk. The bishops had to keep protesting, calmly but decisively. At their meeting at Jasna Góra on May 5–6, 1972, they expressed their anxieties about the "local" situation and the attitudes of administrators. The Episcopate pointed out that the authorities were planning to base the taxation of church institutions on the very "inventory books" that had been ruled out by a decision of the Ministry of Finance on February 10, 1972. Regulations against the Church were thus being applied in practice despite having been formally rescinded. Obviously, the Finance Ministry was following the dictates of the Bureau of Religious Affairs in such matters, rather than acting independently. The bureau thus seemed actually to be sabotaging the liberalized tax policy toward the Church. This May session of the Episcopate also noted the continuing deadlock over church building.

The West German Bundestag ratified the Polish–West German treaty on June 3, 1972. Two days later, Bishop Bronisław Dąbrowski went to Rome to seek a final decision on church administration in the Western Lands. Pope Paul accorded with the wishes of the Polish bishops as soon as the conclusion of the international pact allowed, and on June 28 he created a permanent ecclesiastical administration in the Western Lands by naming six resident Polish bishops. The government, after years of Homeric struggle, had been somewhat passed over in the Vatican's response to the long-standing efforts of the Polish Primate and Episcopate (the bishops sent their gratitude to the Holy See on June 28).

The papal decision also involved the creation of two new dioceses in the northwest part of the country, and although the government favored the harmonizing of ecclesiastical and state boundaries, it could not have been pleased with an increase in the number of dioceses. The whole arrangement reflected Cardinal Wyszyński's long-term efforts, and enhanced not only pastoral possibilities but also the national interest. This achievement alone would have established Stefan Wyszyński's place in Polish and church history, but it was merely one of his successes. The government press ignored the whole story.

In Poznań, the Episcopate met on September 5–6. Pressure by the authorities against religious education determined that the bishops again address an appeal to parents about the catechetical obligation. The matter required constant reminders from the Episcopate—a sign that little had really changed in the state's attitude. Among other important proclamations, this session issued a letter on patriotism in the spirit of Christianity, to mark the bicentennial of the 1772 partitions of Poland. The bishops also spoke out against the tragic attack on the Munich Olympics, during which there had been a mass murder of

Israeli athletes. In this context the bishops recalled the millions of victims of racist hatred during the Second World War. The Episcopate also approved a pastoral letter about the increase in divorces, to be read on the Feast of the Holy Family.

October brought the government a certain satisfaction, as the Holy See announced that the mission of Ambassador Papée, representing the government-in-exile, had come to an end. Papée had in fact been nothing more than a resident of the Vatican for many years, but the Warsaw government had stipulated the formal closing of his activities as a precondition to normalized relations with the Vatican. Thus one more symbol of the prewar, fully independent Poland passed into history.

At the beginning of November, the Episcopate learned, to its unpleasant surprise, that seminarians were being conscripted again, in violation of a promise made a year earlier by the authorities. In general, 1972 and 1973 contained a hardening rather than a softening of the official line. At its January 24–25, 1973, meeting, the Episcopate had to caution that despite the premier's words about normalizing church-state relations, "the administrative-political authorities in some provinces are attempting to limit further the religious freedom of the faithful, and especially of young academics, but also of the village clergy." While the central government negotiated with the Episcopate, local officials were trying to subject religious instruction to the control of the state educational authorities. Pressures on priests and families were so widespread that the bishops felt impelled to add that

> families have the right to raise their children in accordance with their convictions, and Catholics in accordance with church teaching. It is incumbent upon the state to create the conditions under which families can perform this task. Because of the fundamental rights of the human person, and also because the majority of Polish citizens are Catholics, this basic right cannot be displaced by our political reality.

The Church was speaking out more and more energetically about human and church rights. The Episcopate drew the government's attention to the depravation of youth through the bad influence of certain television programs. At the same time, the bishops appreciated some of the government's social decisions, such as the expansion of health-insurance coverage in the villages, the lengthening of unpaid maternity leaves, and some positive steps in family and pronatalist policy.

Now, as at other times since the war, Cardinal Wyszyński wanted to be objective and just toward the rulers, but the course of events caused greater and greater concern. Nineteen seventy-three saw one of the sharpest church-state conflicts: the government attempted to remove the upbringing of children almost entirely from the influence of families and the Church. To this end the government proposed "consolidated schools," in which the children would remain late in the afternoon. Such schools may well exist in many countries, but their establishment in a state that devotes education to the monopoly of Marxist doctrine would create a mortal danger to religious views and to Polish spiritual and cultural identity. The March 22–23 meeting of the Episcopate thus petitioned the Sejm, asking that the new educational system take into account parents' natural right to raise their children according to their own religious convictions. All-day schools would make not only catechization but also the influence of the family home impossible. Despite the protest, however, the Sejm approved the new educational charter. Things looked dangerous, but as it turned out, the government could not bring off its designs. Neither the buildings for the consolidated schools nor the numbers of buses needed to transport village children existed. Still, the intention of the legislation and its quick approval showed the danger that would have confronted the Church and Catholic families, had economic weakness not tempered monopolistic, materialistic doctrine.

The catastrophic lack of church buildings in new residential settlements formed a second alarming subject of this Episcopal session. Bishops had obtained heaps of letters and petitions asking to have new churches built. In reaction, they defended, in communiqués and from the pulpit, the right to erect churches in all new housing developments. They stated frankly that it was difficult to talk about normalized relations with the state as long as this problem remained unsolved. The official decisions against church construction were leading to a new aggravation as residents in some areas began erecting temporary chapels without permission. The authorities inevitably tried to make whole communities suffer for the anonymous actions of a few.

The Primate and the Episcopate also considered the education of young people and approved a pastoral letter about priestly vocations. To the state authorities they directed a demand that pastoral service be extended to young academics because the Religious Affairs officials had begun exerting political pressure on academic chaplaincies. Finally, the Episcopate directed its secretary to include in the agenda for negotiations about normalizing relations with the state the Church's right to conduct charitable activities.

The Holy See came to its aid whenever the Polish Church found itself in difficulties at home. So it was in 1973, in a most significant way. Following up on his June 1972 decision that normalized the Church in the Western Lands, Pope Paul made Archbishop Bolesław Kominek cardinal on March 5. Bestowing such a dignity on the Archbishop of Wrocław underlined the union of the Church in the Western Lands with the Polish Episcopate; it is hard not to see Cardinal Wyszyński's hand in the nomination. Thus a communist country obtained its third cardinal—a mark of its close links to the universal church and the Holy See. These links gave the Polish Church a worldwide importance. Thanks to them, the Church in Poland, since 1945, had always been much more than an element in domestic communist politics: it had always been united with Catholics everywhere and with the Chair of Peter.

During its meeting in Częstochowa on May 4–5, the Episcopate named Cardinal Wojtyła to head a special commission that would draft a position for the next session of the Synod of Bishops ("The Evangelization of the World"). The Episcopate also felt that a stand on education had to be taken.

> The conference has analyzed the "Positions and Theses of a Report on the State of Education" which reveals tendencies toward the elimination of religious instruction from the schools. . . . In our reality, ignoring the Church in the planned system for educating the younger generation must have a negative impact on the process of education within the family as well as within the school, and will harm the whole nation. . . . The resolution passed by the Sejm on April 12, 1973, must cause distress to the conscience of believers. . . . To build social unity on the basis of an exclusively materialistic outlook, as announced officially by those in power, is contrary to the principles of freedom of conscience, and dangerous. Such a unity is artificial, and transitory. The Church must oppose this legislation: it is obliged, as a moral authority, to defend the rights of parents to bring up their children according to their personal convictions.

Such a clear and unambiguous statement needs no commentary. During the Sejm debate on April 12, Stanisław Stomma, the leader of the Znak Delegates' Circle, had taken a position similar to that of the bishops, mirroring the anxieties of all Catholics; of the afternoon school sessions, Stomma said:

> In practice, this would mean keeping the children outside their homes almost all day, in the same school atmosphere, within the same school walls, surrounded by the same people. A child needs variety, and he finds relaxation in a good family. . . . Believing parents want the religious education of their children to be fully guaranteed. They deserve the complete assurance to which they are entitled socially, and in the constitution.

The Sejm, as we have noted earlier, passed the new educational legislation, and, as we have also noted, the new program fell victim to the lack of material means, but the threat still hung over Poland's Catholic population.

The May session of the Episcopate reflected that the normalization of relations with the state was moving forward sluggishly, the local administrations trying to hinder the work of the Church and still discriminating against believers. The bishops noted that only a dozen or so permits to build churches had come through in the previous year, and the realization of even those permissions had been made difficult.

Church-state relations in 1973 recalled those of Gomułka's last years in power, and not only because the education bill had been rammed through the Sejm over the Episcopate's reservations. The government practically broke off meetings with representatives of the Episcopate. The next round of Vatican-Warsaw talks was also postponed. As always in a difficult moment, Cardinal Wyszyński went about his work. In this way he had weathered every crisis and emerged victorious each time.

The Episcopate was organizing nationwide celebrations for the five hundredth anniversary of the birth of the great astronomer—and canon of Frombork—Copernicus. The government, of course, was organizing its own celebrations (with an anti-church accent, even though foreign visitors were being allowed in for the church observances). Policy had thus changed little in fact since the December 1970 crisis, although a new style was becoming discernible. Nevertheless, Cardinal Wyszyński's sermon set the tone of the celebrations in Frombork.

The bishops issued a communiqué during their session in June, calling for freedom of religious practice for young people in holiday camps, tours, and vacation houses. Violations of this right continued to be notorious.

Relations between the state and the Episcopate, as well as between Warsaw and the Vatican, remained at an impasse. The government had not carried through on anything that had been settled at the previous meetings. Out of an impulse to get things moving again, Archbishop Casaroli met with the foreign minister, Stefan Olszowski, during preliminary discussions in Helsinki of the so-called Conference on European Security and Cooperation. The two men would also meet in November at the Vatican.

Cardinal Wyszyński spent his summer vacation under the psychological pressure of events that were growing more painful to the Church. The old spirit had emerged as the authorities demolished the "barracks-chapels" that people in new residential areas raised. Furthermore, disturbing efforts were still going on to register and supervise catechetical centers, and every day the Primate could see with his own eyes the trouble that children in holiday camps had when they tried to practice their religion. There was no cause for joy—but comfort, as always, came from Rome. Bishop Dąbrowski returned carrying an assurance that the Vatican would hold no talks with the Polish government unless the Episcopate also took part.

The problems posed for religious instruction by the new education laws occupied the Primate's mind and the meeting of the Episcopate on September 13–14. Bishop Dąbrowski reported on the lack of progress in negotiations with the authorities. The bishops adopted a stand on cooperation with the state, saying that "such cooperation will, however, be possible and beneficial to society [only] if there is respect for the right of the Church to carry out its mission freely, and if believers are not discriminated against in public, social, professional, and cultural life because of their religious convictions."

The church leadership repeated such calls again and again, offering to cooperate with the authorities for the good of the society—but never receiving a response. The second half of 1973 brought a twitch in the direction of better relations: there was a perceptible, although insignificant, increase in the number of permits to build new churches. Preparations for the Conference on European Security and Cooperation must have played some role. But some dioceses received not a single permit during this period. In many areas of the country—Warsaw, Szczecin, Łódź, Gdańsk, Częstochowa, Poznań, and the Katowice and Cracow regions—intensive development had increased the population and made the need for new churches especially urgent. The complete ban on church construction under Gomułka had left an additional backlog of need, and the trickle of new permits did little to ease a painfully difficult pastoral problem.

The Episcopate was also concerned about the general moral situation. Divorces were becoming ever more numerous, so the bishops decided to devote more energy to premarital counseling. The Episcopate also set in motion new counseling programs in the face of the spreading plague of alcoholism. The September session dealt as well with preparations in Poland for the approaching Holy Year.

The continuation of his Millennium program lay closest to the Primate's heart. The Millennial Act of Dedication was protection for the nation's faith, an expression of trust in the Mother of the Church, standing guard over the indissoluble union of Christ and His Church. Now, in the face of a new threat to the faith of youth, Cardinal Wyszyński drew on the binding strength of the Act of Dedication. Its text, printed in large format by Polish Americans, was sent from Jasna Góra to all churches as a "shield of faith" for the Polish nation.

Similarly, the activity of the "Auxiliaries of Mary, Mother of the Church" found ever greater understanding among clergy and lay people. I will quote the main obligations of the Auxiliaries of Mary, as formulated by Cardinal Wyszyński: "I will come to the aid of Mary, Mother of the Church. . . . I will come to the aid of Christ's Church. . . . I will come to the aid of each person. . . . I will come to the aid of the country. . . . " The simplicity, comprehensibility, and accessibility of these obligations is striking. The same can be said of Cardinal Wyszyński's formulation of the principles of the Crusade of Social Love, which were propagated throughout the Polish Church.

The simple, almost elementary evangelical precepts hardly seem innovative, but they perfectly characterize Cardinal Wyszyński's homely didacticism—and their plainness was effective in their social context. The fundamental social concepts through which Marxist-Leninist doctrine operates are terms like "class struggle," "enemy," "hatred," "reaction," and "revisionism." In contrast to such concepts there is Cardinal Wyszyński's summons to pray even for those who are unfriendly, to forgive all, to respect each person, and to work hard. The secret of the Primate's social and moral activity may well lie exactly in the simple evangelical attitudes that he preached—and practiced—toward his antagonists in the Stalinist era, as well as in Gomułka's time. These exhortations that we have quoted were composed earlier, during the 1960s, in the most difficult period of Wyszyński's career. Now, with the situation of the Church having seemed to improve somewhat in the second half of 1973, the Primate all the more energetically propagated his program of social love throughout the Polish Church and all its parishes.

However, this program did not indicate any retreat in matters of principle. Thus, when the government made of 1973 a "Year of Polish Science," with a Marxist, atheistic character, Primate Wyszyński responded by calling a Plenary Session of the Episcopate in Cracow on October 19–20, to mark the five hundredth anniversary of the death of Saint John Kanty, who had been a professor at the Jagiellonian University. The Primate wanted to define, during the Year of Polish Science, the contributions made by theology and church teaching to the achievements of Polish scholarship. During their concurrent conference, the Episcopate and its educational committee pointed out once more that the new education laws passed over in silence the right of believers to raise their children according to their conscience. The Episcopate also complained that the government proposal to leave two afternoons a week free was unacceptable because the Church had no means to organize religious education for all pupils in such a limited period. The communiqué also "expected the unpleasant actions and symptoms of illegality in the state administration, as described in a document delivered to the authorities a year ago, to have no place in the future."

The communiqué was decisive in tone, but loyalty forbade the bishops to publicize the full text of the previous paper since the complete truth about the struggle against religion and the Church might have provoked a social outburst. There can be no doubt, however, that the Episcopate's decisive public posture gave the authorities a good deal to think about, especially during preparations for discussions with the Holy See.

Somewhat more than three weeks later, on November 12, Pope Paul VI received the Polish foreign minister, Stefan Olszowski. Olszowski, who was thus correcting Edward Ochab's shameful error of visiting Rome as the Polish head of state without calling at the Vatican, told the press corps that his visit had a "historic character." In fact, it was a preliminary to the negotiations that were to begin in Warsaw in February 1974. Hansjakob Stehle has remarked that Olszowski arrived in Rome without any clear political conceptions. I am of another opinion. I do not know what Minister Olszowski was thinking, but I have no doubts that the religious affairs apparat (represented in Olszowski's party by Colonel Józefa Siemaszkiewicz, recently promoted to counselor in the Foreign Affairs Ministry and assistant director of the administrative division of the party Central Committee) wanted to reach an agreement with the Vatican over the heads of the Polish Episcopate. The Holy Father shattered such illusions—as Stehle relates in his noted *Die Ostpolitik des Vatikans*—by telling Olszowski that "without the agreement of the Episcopate we will decide nothing."

And so it was. Six days after Olszowski's call, Cardinal Wyszyński arrived in Rome for a visit of more than three weeks (November 18–December 10). The Primate must have been satisfied in his talks with the Pope and the Vatican officials: in a sermon after he returned to Warsaw, he defined Olszowski's visit as "an extremely important event." Now, as before, the Primate favored an agreement, but with the well-informed participation of the Polish Episcopate. Olszowski's visit had not only repaired the unforgivable affront committed by Ochab; it had also shattered any delusions that a wedge could be driven between the Episcopate and the Vatican. In this sense, the otherwise difficult year 1973 ended well for the Polish Church. New hope had arisen for negotiations that would be more than tactical maneuvers, that would lead to an agreement—even if a limited one. It remains to ask why such genuine negotiations were possible now, as they had not been earlier. Many commentators find the reason in domestic Polish political changes. In my opinion, preparations for the Conference on European Security and Cooperation were the real reason. The Eastern-bloc countries had to move toward a certain internal liberalization if the West was to be inclined to confirm the postwar European *status quo* at a conference in which the United States and the Soviet Union would be taking part. Thus, although changes in the Polish domestic scene followed upon the opening of talks with the Holy See, they certainly made it easier for the Soviet Union to adapt itself to the new European politics.

* * *

Other Polish bishops ordinary made an *ad limina* visit to Rome at the end of 1973. On January 23–24, 1974, the ordinaries reported to the Episcopate on their visit. The Holy Father, they said, had expressed particular approval of programming pastoral work on a nationwide scale, a practice developed in Poland by the Primate. The Holy Father also sent a special blessing to parents who had their children go to catechism, and to children who attended regularly. Thus the Pope associated himself with the most principled endeavors of the Polish bishops.

The Episcopate issued a communiqué in which Minister Olszowski's visit to the Vatican was interpreted positively:

This is another step on the announced road to the normalization of church-state relations in Poland. In the opinion of the conference of the Episcopate, full normalization must include more than such merely administrative and institutional contents as were involved in the settlement of church property in the west and north of Poland. We are speaking of full normalization. In this concept the Episcopate embraces religious freedom and freedom of profession and worship within the boundaries of the appropriate tasks of Christ's Church, as defined in the Episcopate's memoranda to the government; moreover, the Episcopate sees here a complex of problems related to Catholic culture. The Catholic community desires and expects their resolution, as it desires and expects respect for its present existence and the right to develop. Among the components of normalization the Episcopate includes the moral and social environment of Polish life, as well as its protection against destructive forces that are ruinous to the national morality. Finally, it has in mind a place for all citizens, regardless of their beliefs, in social, professional, economic, and political life, in which they act positively as citizens active in the life of the nation and the state. To this complex of problems belongs the freedom of Catholic association for young people and all of Polish society.

The Episcopate devoted much attention to the continuing difficulties in church building. In the Archdiocese of Cracow, requests for building permits from approximately seventy parishes had been left generally unresolved in 1973. Those bishops to whom the authorities took the most grudging line had the most troubles with building permits. Such was the case with Cardinal Wojtyła, who had not succumbed to the campaign discussed previously in the 1960s to make of him an antagonist to the Primate. In the coming years Cardinal Wojtyła was regarded as the "worst of all."

From time to time a building permit was granted, but then its realization would be blocked. Priests were being fined for saying Mass for children and their parents in teaching chapels far from the nearest church. A priest from the Archdiocese of Białystok had been confined in a psychiatric institution for saying Mass in his own home. Catechization also suffered the usual difficulties. Although negotiations had begun, the actions of the authorities had not changed.

The second round of Polish-Vatican negotiations took place on February 4–6. Archbishop Casaroli, secretary of the Church's Council on Public Affairs, now came to Poland as a guest of the government. To emphasize his trust in the Holy See and his conviction that the negotiations would be conducted in accordance with the interests of the Polish Church as publicly formulated by the Episcopate, the Primate went to Gniezno just before Archbishop Casaroli's arrival.

Cardinal Wyszyński did not want to hinder Archbishop Casaroli in any way during the negotiations. The talks resulted in no sensations; Minister Olszowski was less forthcoming than he had been in Rome. Some commentators even said that he had hardened his position, devoting his attention to European peace and praising Pax—something that always had to be read as a polemic against the Episcopate. The communiqué, however, spoke of institutionalizing relations through "permanent working contacts." After the negotiations, Archbishop Casaroli was the Primate's guest. On February 7 they concelebrated Mass in the Warsaw Cathedral. In his sermon, Cardinal Wyszyński gave voice to his major principles for church-state relations:

> From the beginning there has been true cooperation in Poland between the Church and the Nation—and often cooperation between the Church and the State as well. Of course, the dimensions of the unceasing links between the Church and the Nation are one thing, and the cooperation between the Church and the State another. The nation, after all, is a permanent phenomenon, like the family, from which the nation is born. The proof of this permanence is the fact that, despite the persecutions and the unceasing struggle it has been subjected to in defense of its independence, living on the borders of [various] cultures, languages, faiths, and rites, the nation has neverthe-

less survived until today. The Church, supporting the Polish nation so that it would not be destroyed, has helped it to survive. . . . There have been moments when the state fell silent, and only Christ's Church could speak out in the Polish nation. It never stopped speaking out, not even when, in the time of the partitions, the state was forced into silence. . . . It is the particular merit of the Church never to have abandoned the Polish Nation and never to have stopped working, even in the most difficult situations. We ought to realize this when we speak of establishing correct relations between the Nation and the Church, between the State and the Church in our country.

These remarks deserve consideration because they embody Cardinal Wyszyński's doctrine of Church, nation, and state. The Church and the nation, lying at the crossroads of cultures and spheres of political influence, have been and still are endangered. It is not a matter of nationalism; in the same sermon, Cardinal Wyszyński said, "Christ's command *'Ite, docete* [Go, teach]' is a mission and a message to all peoples and nations of the earth, because God's Church is supranational. It is a message to all nations, and thus also to the Polish nation."
It is difficult to emphasize the universal mission of the Church, as a message to all peoples and nations, more expressively than did the Primate in this and other sermons. He considered the Church to have a special attribute of "engrafting itself . . . into the life and history of a nation so deeply that almost every Catholic country thinks of the Roman Catholic Church as a national Church—as 'Our Church.' " The forces opposed to the contemporary engrafting of the Church into national life accused the Primate of nationalism. In the light of the passages just quoted, this charge appears completely groundless, but it was picked up by certain leftist and liberal circles and put to wide use. Later, however, when they needed his help, the rulers changed the accusation of nationalism into praise of his patriotism, and the liberals came to acknowledge the Primate as the main defender of freedom in postwar Po-

land. The truth was that the Primate always thought in terms of the Church's universal mission but, called to preach the Gospel in a particular country, living in a state of danger, he decided to engraft that mission into the history and life of the nation so that the Church could survive along with the nation and fulfill its mission within the nation.

It was characteristic of the Primate to voice his doctrine of the relation between Church and nation exactly as the first steps were being taken toward regulating the relation between the Holy See and the Polish state. The Cardinal wanted, and managed, to say that the Church's presence in and close links with the nation are most important, while relations with the government are relevant but secondary. This had to do not only with the skepticism toward the incipient negotiations that some Western commentators and communist publicists have imputed to Cardinal Wyszyński. It was a matter of principle with the Primate, and it turned out to be accurate. The Church has survived in Poland because it has engrafted itself deeply into the life of the nation, even though relations between the government and the Episcopate, and between the Polish state and the Apostolic See, have not been formalized to this day. Yet Poland possesses the liveliest Catholicism in Europe and has managed to produce a pope. The Primate's doctrine of the fundamental meaning of church-nation relations has been fully justified: life itself has made his point for him.

In February 1974, Cardinal Wyszyński was absolutely not opposed to negotiations—he never had been and never would be. Those who say that he was seem not too see that it was Cardinal Wyszyński himself who initiated Archbishop Casaroli's first working visit to Poland, who convinced three successive popes—Pius XII, John XXIII, and Paul VI—to apply the method of patient but not unconditional discussions with communist governments, and who first proposed understandings with three successive postwar communist leaderships. In the sermon that we have been citing, Cardinal Wyszyński took a principled, doctrinal stand toward the negotiations:

All Christian people and nations, and even non-Christians, look today toward the Head of the Roman Catholic Church with unusual trust. That is why the Holy Father must take up and lead numerous discussions with the representatives of various peoples and nations, so that the mission of the Church—"Go, teach, baptize"—can be fulfilled calmly, fruitfully, for the redemption of the Family of Man. From this comes the indispensable necessity of establishing and maintaining contacts with nations and with the representatives of the states that rule over those nations.

Leaving no doubts about his support for such discussions, Cardinal Wyszyński circumscribed their goals and directions: "Such is the Holy Father's desire in regard to our country. The indispensable thing is the safeguarding of the Church in each nation, and thus also in the Polish nation, of the possibility of fulfilling the evangelical mission."

At the end of his sermon, Cardinal Wyszyński addressed himself directly to Archbishop Casaroli, speaking in Italian, and expressed appreciation for his labors. Nor did the Primate neglect to mention the Holy Father's fervent desire to visit Poland.

Cardinal Wyszyński did not conduct secret diplomacy. He made his course of action entirely public, and the effort to set him up as an opponent of the understanding with the Vatican was bound to fail. It was not long before the government backed away from such insinuations.

Two days before the joint appearance of Cardinal Wyszyński and Archbishop Casaroli in Warsaw's Saint John's Cathedral, Cardinal Mindszenty was recalled from Vienna to Rome. This event gave rise to much errant speculation, and even to analogies with Polish affairs. Archbishop Casaroli told Cardinal Wyszyński that he had known nothing of the decision, which fell at such an unfortunate moment. Cardinal Wyszyński was upset, but he knew the decision had not been aimed at him. He knew the Pope too well, and their relations were too sincere and friendly for such a thought. A few months earlier, Paul had told Wyszyński in Rome that he would reach no conclusions without consulting the Episcopate. Archbishop Casaroli now repeated the same assurance. Later it became clear that the recall of Cardinal Mindszenty had been sudden and unforeseen, a reaction to the publication of his works.

On March 10 the Polish Church sustained a painful loss in the death of Bolesław Cardinal Kominek, the first Polish metropolitan of Wrocław.

Bishop Dąbrowski, the secretary of the Episcopate, conducted talks in the Vatican Secretariat of State and was received by the Holy Father on March 21. Thus, one could say, the Primate of Poland kept a finger on the pulse of Polish matters in the Vatican's Eastern policy and maintained full control of events.

At its March session, the Episcopate stated that

> the visit of the official delegation from the Apostolic See was an important event both for the Church and for the Polish state. In the establishment of contact between the government and the Holy See, the Episcopate sees appropriate benefits for the Church and for the nation. . . . The Episcopate declares itself in favor of such discussions, which ought to be honest, forthright, and systematic. The Plenary Session expresses its gratitude to the Holy Father for his position that in the composition of relations between the Holy See and Poland, and also between the State and the Church, there shall be no decision made without the participation of the Polish Episcopate. . . . [The Episcopate] similarly desires to conduct discussions with representatives of the government at the appropriate level.

The Primate and the Episcopate spelled things out carefully because they knew well that certain circles in the government wanted to shunt the Polish bishops aside and impose upon the Vatican an understanding after the Hungarian or Yugoslavian model. The Episcopate therefore demanded the settlement of the Church's legal status, complete freedom in fulfilling its religious mission, free catechization, equal civic, social, and professional rights for believers, the unhindered development of Catholic culture, and so on.

At the same time, the Episcopate protested against the spectacular extent to which pastors were being asked to take loyalty oaths upon their appointment to parishes. The bishops demanded that the statute requiring such oaths, dating from the Stalinist era, be repealed. They also reminded priests not to take part in meetings or conferences without the permission of the spiritual authorities—a reminder evoked by the efforts of Pax and the state authorities, yet again, to organize "patriotic priests." Finally, the Episcopate heard a report by Bishop Jerzy Stroba (elected to the steering committee in the late Archbishop Kominek's place) on his talks with Minister of Education Jerzy Kuberski on the rights of young people to religious beliefs. Individual reports from Episcopal commissions were also heard, and Bishop Szczepan Wesoły spoke about the pastoral care of the émigré community, for which new priests in Poland ought to be earmarked. The Episcopate acted in Polish life at home and abroad, without waiting for the uncertainties of political decisions.

A shake-up of the political leadership occurred in 1974: Vice-Minister Skarżyński was recalled from his post in the Bureau of Religious Affairs, and other changes took place behind the scenes. All this had something to do with the departure, foreseen some months earlier, of General Franciszek Szlachcic from among the leaders. On May 29 he was dropped from the Central Committee secretariat, and the next party congress did not choose him for any important post. The new chief of the Bureau of Religious Affairs, holding the rank of vice-minister but soon made a minister, was Kazimierz Kąkol. At the beginning these changes seemed less important than they really were, for it was not yet obvious that significant divisions were opening in an apparat that had previously been united in opposition to Gomułka's nationalism. Kąkol, initially regarded as a lightweight because he lacked his predecessor's great experience, turned out to be more flexible and, to the Episcopate, more palatable. In the party secretariat, Stanisław Kania—always faithful to the party line but also relatively flexible—inherited the responsibility for religious affairs. Ultimately, however, I do not think that the new attitude toward the Church resulted from personnel changes. It was, rather, conditioned by the Soviet Union's European politics and by the beginning of the Polish economic difficulties. Nevertheless, the exit from the scene of men accustomed to autocratic rule meant something—even if the new officials at first practiced the politics of dubious quality and arbitrariness. It must always be remembered that the international communist camp is all of a piece in politics and ideology; its politics in particular countries, though conditioned by local circumstances, submit to principles and decisions made at headquarters.

Cardinal Wyszyński and his church strategy were strong because they proceeded from a conviction of the Church's historical and contemporary union with the nation, and not from political fluctuations. The Primate always tried to choose the most instrumental course, regardless of such oscillations. Thus, the Episcopate dedicated its meeting in Cracow on May 11, 1974, to contemporary trends in and relations between theology and philosophy. Relations with the government intruded even into such strictly theological considerations, however—in the demand that the Cracow theology department, separated from the university during the twilight of Stalinism in 1954, be reactivated.

In Wawel Cathedral the Episcopate and its foreign guests conducted a service to mark the six hundredth anniversary of the Blessed Queen Jadwiga. Afterward, the steering committee met to face its never-changing agenda: the normalization of relations with the government.

The same subject dominated the session of the Episcopate in Warsaw on June 19 and 20. The next round of Warsaw-Vatican talks was under way, and Bishop Dąbrowski reported on his talks with representatives of the Polish authorities and with the Council for Public Affairs of the Church in Rome. The bishops criticized the domestic situation, expressing anxiety over sex-education programs in the schools and the mass media. They also called on parents sending their children to holiday camps to send along declarations stating that they wanted their children to participate in Mass and religious practices. Since the government was beginning to make state awards and prizes to some priests, in what looked like another effort to divide the clergy, the bishops declared firmly in their communiqué that "Priests, called to the service of God's people, should before all else wait for Christ's appreciation of their pastoral and social work. Therefore they should not accept awards and distinctions of a nonreligious nature."

The Vatican Secretariat of State invited Bishop Dąbrowski to Rome during the Polish-Vatican negotiations of July 4–6. Vice-Minister of Foreign Affairs Józef Czyrek was Archbishop Casaroli's interlocutor on this occasion, and the results were mainly formalistic. It was decided that the Polish government would establish a counselor in its Quirinal embassy to look after relations with the Vatican, which in turn would occasionally send the chief of its mission to Warsaw. Both sides were proceeding temperately, and the main opponent of true and full diplomatic relations was not the Primate but the Polish government, conditioned by Eastern-bloc policies toward the Vatican. It was announced in Warsaw on September 25 that Consul Kazimierz Szablewski would lead the government's group in working contacts with the Vatican. When the Episcopate met on September 7–8, it expressed its reservations over the slow tempo of normalization, while also noting with regret that young people were once again being hindered in their religious observances during the summer vacation. Life and formal agreements thus turned out to be different things.

On the second day of this Episcopal session, a celebration took place in Saint James's Cathedral in Szczecin. A *Te Deum* was sung and, in his sermon, Cardinal Wyszyński gave thanks for the gift of Christianization received 850 years earlier by Pomerania. He emphasized the importance of Saint Otto of

Bamberg's mission to Pomerania and Poland, and the value of faith to the nation. As always, he was sticking to the useful level of the national-historical apostolate in the face of the political negotiations. This level strengthened the Church and gave the Primate amazing calm amid the pressures and surprises in which the collision of Church and communism abounded. His calm had other sources as well. On August 3 he had celebrated the fiftieth anniversary of his ordination; twenty-eight of those years he had been a bishop. Bishops, clergy, and faithful took part in a celebratory Mass in the Warsaw Cathedral, and after warm remarks by Bishop Jerzy Modzelewski, the Primate himself spoke:

> I am convinced that the greatest of the priestly virtues is apostolic love. It endures. All the others fade, but love always endures and grows stronger. Yet to serve with love is very difficult, for love has no limits. When a man gives himself to love he knows that he is giving too little, always too little. Love is bottomless and beyond dimension. Used in the best way, it always demands more. "I will show you another way," said the Apostle.
>
> Thus one must serve like Christ. "Greater love hath no man than this, that a man lay down his life for his friends." So did our professors, so did my classmates and the many, many priests to whom God gave the grace of suffering injuries in the Name of Christ.

These words include the essential attitude of the Primate, to which a biographer can add nothing. In this sermon the Cardinal recalled one of his teachers, who told young priests to prepare themselves, because they would live to have spikes driven into their tonsures. Stefan Wyszyński confided that he had always taken the warning seriously, and that even though he did not have to fulfill it in a literal sense, he had always been prepared. How much that attitude had meant during twenty-eight years of struggle as a bishop, through imprisonment and a running battle that had now assumed the elegant form of diplomatic negotiations! The Primate treated nothing lightly; he took to heart everything that affected the Church, but his policy was not a spur-of-the-moment thing—on the contrary, he followed the doctrine of engrafting the Church into the nation, always ready to serve it in love, even to the point of giving his own life. This "line" established him in Poland as an unconquered man whose enemies would soon be seeking his support and help, and not for the first time.

During the next two years, influenced by the growing economic difficulties and later by the establishment of a lay democratic opposition, the attitude of government officials toward Cardinal Wyszyński would undergo a fundamental change. From being the principal enemy, he would become "a great Polish patriot." This change, one must emphasize, was a change of course by the political leadership, and not a change of direction on Cardinal Wyszyński's part. There exist literally thousands of documents—sermons, speeches, declarations—from the seventies as well as from the preceding decades, showing that, regardless of whatever lay or other opposition groups sprang up, Stefan Wyszyński was the main spokesman for freedom and human rights in Poland for more than thirty years. We can cite only a minuscule fraction of them (the official bibliography of Cardinal Wyszyński's published work, through 1979, contains 1,029 items), and shall be content to show that even as the authorities were changing their attitude toward him, Cardinal Wyszyński was equally a consistent adherent of an understanding with the government and an intransigent exponent of freedom.

Beyond statements of the Episcopate that he inspired, the Primate delivered his own appeals to parents and teachers about respect for the religious rights of youth. Speaking to Polish youngsters from England on August 4, 1974, he said:

> If you could come to know the programmed education in our country, programmed without religion and Christian morality, rejecting even the symptoms of free activity in culture—unless for the needs of tourist propaganda, but

not as the creation of a free man—you would then realize how many values in our nation have been brought to a standstill. Man cannot follow the free lines of thought, preference, and desire; he cannot organize his life according to his own aspirations, tastes, and endeavors. The freedom of opinion, the freedom of the press, the freedom of association, the freedom to create culture according to one's own abilities and tastes, the freedom to dispose of one's own time—to a greater or lesser degree these are limited everywhere today. These values are mowed down today like treetops being lopped off by an airplane flying too low over the forest. But to understand contemporary Poland, the Polish Church, and Poland's struggles, you have to know that we are fighting for the freedom of our children, for the freedom to take charge of our own heads and our own hearts. That is most essential.

Cardinal Wyszyński never concealed his feelings about the reigning system of social relations in the country. In his letter for Mercy Week (October 6–13, 1974), along with a call for greater social aid, he stated concisely but eloquently, "We have already been through various recipes for making people happy. Some did it by spreading prosperity, others wanted to do it by taking from the wealthy to feed the needy, but instead they brought fear and dread to everyone. . . ."

Cardinal Wyszyński's sermons on Saint Stanisław, bishop and martyr to an arbitrary king, constitute in themselves a chapter on the value of freedom. From the sermons on that saint's day:

Poland has earned the appellation *Polonia semper fidelis.*
. . . Let us remember that [Saint Stanisław] was killed, but he did not kill. . . . Stanisław fell in another cause, in defense of the moral order, in defense of the moral rights that have meaning for the little ones and for the great ones of the nation, that are obligations for those that govern as

well as for those who are governed. Conflicts can arise between the Church and other groups whenever those groups do not acknowledge the spiritual, supernatural values that the Church offers, or when the supernatural, godly values are destroyed or removed from human life— then, inevitably, conflicts can arise, just as in the time of Saint Stanisław who bravely told those who were in charge: "It is indecent to do this!" [Cracow, May 8, 1966]

Meeting the younger generation that is going forth into the new Poland, we, the Polish bishops, are preaching a Crusade for Social Love and a Crusade for Truth, which is born of that love. Speak truth one to another, even if it costs you much, as it cost Saint Stanisław. . . . He gave his life, like a good shepherd, so that his flock would not be stricken with falsehood. . . . The Church, like a good shepherd, following Christ's example, is sensitive to man and his rights. That is why, the more human dignity is disdained, the more the rights of the human individual are assaulted—in such situations the Church must call out and admonish that, nevertheless, *the most important value on earth is man!*

Therefore: *Kneel down before man!* No matter who it is. Whether it be Peter, or Judas. Thus did Christ, and he has left us his example. [Cracow, May 8, 1971]

Today in our homeland we must defend the working man and his right to a day of rest. [Cracow, May 8, 1974]

In that last sermon, the Primate was thinking of compulsory "volunteer" work and of the miners who had to work Sundays; then he went on to defend faith and God's place in Poland, native culture and national history, and economic freedom. He emphasized the point that "the economy must belong to the nation" and thus must first of all meet the nation's needs, rather than serve international political goals.

Stefan Wyszyński went to Rome on September 24, 1974, for the Synod of Bishops, in the company of Cardinal Wojtyła and

Bishop Jerzy Ablewicz. Received by the Pope, Cardinal Wyszyński listened to a gracious assessment of the Polish delegation's contribution to the synod.

On November 25–27, the Primate led a session of the Episcopate in which the bishops declared themselves in favor of normalizing relations with the state "under the condition that the normalization have a substantive content, and not only an institutional and administrative character." Furthermore, they noted that aside from the questions of church property in the Western Lands and the elimination of the so-called inventory books of church holdings, the government had not accepted or legally settled any church concerns. Despite the change in atmosphere that was beginning in 1974, normalization remained largely theoretical. Demands for complete freedom and the return of the rights stripped from the Church in previous political periods seemed less real within the framework of the existing system and Poland's subjugation. The next meeting of the Episcopate, on January 15–16, 1975, confirmed this by stating in its communiqué that it had been

> pondering the meaning of documents from the last Synod of Bishops, in which the Polish example was approved. ... The Polish Episcopate expresses its conviction that the rights that guarantee freedom of conscience and religion deserve particular attention. The situation of societies or groups of people who have been deprived of these freedoms or who have allowed them to be taken away is fearful. The Polish Episcopate has decided to do everything to make the Church a faithful guardian of those basic rights in our country, and to protect people from the alienation that weighs down the development of national culture.

The bishops also lamented the government's refusal to take up several matters related to normalization, and spoke out against the summoning of priests for "confidential talks," never legally or factually justified, by the secret police. Archbishop Luigi Poggi was about to come to Warsaw as the first Vatican delegate to the Polish government, and the security authorities had nothing better to do than to harass priests.

Bishop Dąbrowski conducted extensive talks in the Vatican Secretariat of State to prepare for Poggi's visit. The latter arrived on February 25 and presented his credentials to the Foreign Ministry. The Episcopate also invited Poggi to visit several dioceses and meet bishops, clergy, and lay people.

Though he had no unrealistic expectations, Cardinal Wyszyński fully supported the Poggi mission. On March 11, 1975, he told the Episcopate:

> According to the Holy Father's wishes, Archbishop Poggi is, in effect, our guest, the guest of the Episcopate. Beyond that, he is also a man who has come for a restful trip—and I emphasize the word *restful*—around the country, so that he can get to know it better. . . . Afterward he will return to Warsaw for discussions. He will probably hold more discussions with the government in mid-March. . . . We have heard the government's proposals, and they contain nothing new. Of course, the press communiqué suggests that the authorities' position is that these are talks on international affairs between the Polish state and the Vatican state, concerned with the developing countries and the threat of hunger and so on. As we have seen, the Polish Press Agency dispatch mentioned that "matters of interest to both sides were discussed," without giving any specifics, but that must include the "church-state" issue in Poland. Since the work of and responsibility for the Holy Church in Poland falls on the shoulders of the Episcopate, we cannot protect ourselves too much from the outcome of these or other negotiations. Nor can we slacken our efforts in the hope that we will find ourselves in some shelter, which by covenant will protect us. Such protection we will probably not obtain. . . . We want the government to realize that the Church has a public, legal nature, so that the government will delineate the

practical consequences in administrative terms and, instead of treating the Church like some sort of ordinary parochial association, take into account its essential character. . . .

Despite his doubts, the Primate thought that the effort had some meaning. He recalled that twenty years earlier, "priests were fined for hanging out the papal flag. Now no one would have the nerve to call priests or bishops to account. . . . Our interlocutors are polite; all they do is impose their own subjects in discussions, which always have an administrative character —the sorts of things that ought to be taken up with the Episcopal secretariat. Of course," he went on, "on these occasions there have been . . . attempts to introduce into the talks . . . the presentation to the Holy See of candidates for vacant bishoprics." He made it clear that the Episcopate would never cede that responsibility to the government. Having unveiled before the Episcopate these deceitful stratagems and shared his doubts about the significance of whatever would result from the negotiations—because there was no common legal language shared by Church and state—the Primate quite expressly defined Archbishop Poggi's status as that of an employee of the Vatican Secretariat of State, and not a representative of the Holy See. Wyszyński said that the bishops received Archbishop Poggi with joy and, despite everything, regarded his visit as a step forward in church-state relations.

Then he returned to his fundamental doctrine in the matter: "There have been situations in which the Church has lost with the government. And we may lose again with this or that government, but *we can never lose with the Nation!* Our sensitivity to what is going on in the soul of the Nation must always be acute." The Primate's speech reflected not only the present situation, but also his principled, long-term strategy for the Polish Church.

Archbishop Poggi's mission had gone well enough for the bishops to state, in their communiqués from this session, that "The Polish Episcopate has received with approval Archbishop Poggi's statement of March 12, 1975, in which he told the bishops that he regarded his mission as a service to the Polish Church and wished to carry it out in unity with the Primate, the Episcopate, the bishops, the clergy, and the faithful," and that there "can be no doubt of the full and complete unity between the Holy Father and the Polish Episcopate."

Any hopes that the negotiations could be used to drive a wedge between the Vatican and the Episcopate thus evaporated, and for this reason the Warsaw-Vatican talks, begun so energetically, proceeded with less and less enthusiasm.

The March conference of the Episcopate discussed the often raised sticking point in negotiations—the civil rights of believers. The bishops stated that "believing people are being relegated to the ranks of second-class citizens." Reassured by his solidarity with the Holy See, Cardinal Wyszyński was carrying on the defense of civil, religious, and moral rights from which neither open diplomacy nor the secret police could deflect him.

This same conference discussed plans for Poles to make pilgrimages to Rome in October, for the Holy Year celebrations. It was obvious that the authorities would have to refrain from administrative attempts to thwart the pilgrims. The bishops also denounced compulsory Sunday labor as contrary to religious freedom and a threat to the family ties and spiritual freedom required for a healthy society.

The Primate traveled to Rome in May; Pope Paul received him on the 22nd. In an Episcopal communiqué, we read that "the Primate, evaluating the significance of the working contacts that had been established between the Holy See and People's Poland, advanced in the name of the Episcopate several suggestions aimed at streamlining the contacts. These were accepted positively by the Holy See." Cardinal Wyszyński was thus taking a *de facto* initiative in negotiations that, paradoxically, had been conceived as a means of going over his head. This is perfectly natural, given the Primate's unswerving conception of an understanding in which recognition of the existing system and its international alliances would depend on the state's respect for the rights of Church, man, and nation. The other side's plan, in the meantime, was without substance and aimed only at shunting the Primate aside. The very inability of a materialistic state to possess any substantive theory of an understanding helped place the initiative in the Primate's hands. Before long, the government would decide that, within the narrow range made possible by the system, it would be better to deal with Cardinal Wyszyński directly.

The June session of the Episcopate noted some improvement in the methods of assessing church property for taxation. Some problems, this showed, could be settled domestically between the authorities and the Episcopate. The government realized that while its subjection made a comprehensive regulation of church-state relations impossible, particular matters could still be settled. It was in 1975 that government circles began to ring with the catch phrase, "We can best settle our Polish matters among ourselves in our own home." To the Primate, the stance was perfectly acceptable, even though he still wished for a comprehensive settlement spelled out from the Holy See. In any case, it was clearly not the Primate who was opposing the new direction.

Still, he did not change his fundamental outlook on matters about which the rulers were sensitive. The Miracle of the Vistula, the victory over the Red Army on the August 15 feast of the Virgin Mary, had its fifty-fifth anniversary in 1975. Stefan Wyszyński did not hesitate to recall:

This Polish land, which we know how to defend, as today's anniversary of the victory of Polish arms on the Vistula testifies, this Polish land is admirably fertile and admirably grateful. . . . We still have an obligation not only to profit from the land, but to love the land as well. There is a marked cause for unease in our nation today: the flight from the villages to the towns, or, as people would sometimes have it, the flight to an easier life. . . . Love for the land of our country demands that we stay on this soil. . . . Do not flee from the villages, do not flee from the farms, stay on them and raise the standards of life. . . . Stay like a tree rooted in the soil of the homeland, so that our nation will not be pushed around within its ethnic borders as a result of underpopulation and insufficient engrafting of itself into the soil of the country.

This particular concentration on a social problem illustrates the Primate's rigid defense of principles at the moment when the authorities had given up open combat against him and had begun trying to win him over. He imparted a similar stance to the entire Episcopate. The bishops thus called on young farmers "to accept the labors and the fruits of their parents in the form of agricultural landholdings, and to treat farmwork as an important service to the society and the nation, appreciating the inheritance of land from their parents as a great treasure." The Primate and his bishops were defending the existing system of private agriculture for reasons of morality, the national interest, and even ethnic cohesion.

The same session of the Episcopate took an important step toward the realization of the Vatican Council's ideas by issuing a proclamation on the creation of parish councils, which reflected the universal responsibility for the Church of all its members. Basing themselves upon the Synod of Bishops' attitude toward the vulnerability of human rights, the Episcopate approved a pastoral program for 1975–76 under the motto "Man in God's Eternal Plan."

The programs of the Episcopate and the Primate had not changed—in fact, they were becoming more distinct. The government, however, preferred not to pay attention. The economic crisis, after all, was looming larger, and there were plans, which the Church knew all about, to write the leading role of the party and the alliance with the Soviet Union into the Polish constitution.

A year and a half had passed since Cardinal Kominek's death, yet no new Archbishop of Wrocław had been named. The government had rejected three candidates, including the Pope's nominee. Instead, the authorities went so far as to submit their own personnel recommendations, which the Episcopate and the Vatican rejected absolutely. Things dragged on so long that, in the communiqué from its September 5–6 session, the Episcopate made its dissatisfaction public. The government's persistence, however unsuccessful, in attempting to influence personnel matters after thirty years resulted from a lack of imagination, but the haggling over this archbishopric in the Western Lands damaged the national interest. Successive government leaderships committed the same mistakes.

The Episcopal communiqués of this period contain somewhat monotonously repeated appeals that the government not hinder catechization, and that parents safeguard their children's right to religious education. Behind the monotony lies the regrettable fact that, despite political changes and direct contact between the government and the Episcopate, the situation of the Church had improved only minimally. Among other particular matters, the drastic increase in abortions, now based on a law that required only "social justification," was particularly worrying, and the Episcopate approved a message to the faithful on protecting the unborn.

One positive change that the better atmosphere in Episcopate-government talks had issued in was that representatives of the Polish dioceses were given permission to take part in the Holy Year celebrations by making pilgrimages led by the Primate. Observances in Rome celebrated the work of Teresa Ledóchowska in developing African missions. Back in Poland, after its November 19–20 meeting, the Episcopate stated that "the Holy See, like the Episcopate, is interested in defining the legal status of the Church in Poland." The bishops went on to say that they could not remain indifferent to the great problems and difficulties facing the nation. "Every contribution to the good of the nation must be appreciated, even though many needs remain to be met. In meeting them, an atmosphere of calm and order, as well as respect for the common good, are indispensable. The conference expresses its conviction that the announced projected changes in the statutes will not be contrary to the principles of democracy or to the will of the great majority of citizens."

What did these words, obscure to the uninitiated, mean? The bishops were giving some credit to the Gierek leadership and calling for calm despite the accumulating economic problems; the Episcopate shared the authorities' hopes that dynamic economic policies could overcome the difficulties. The euphemism "announced projected changes in the statutes" refers to the leadership's intention to bring the Polish constitution into line with the Eastern-bloc norm—formalizing the leading role of the party and the Soviet alliance. While publicly drawing attention to the "principles of democracy," the bishops presented their more crucial reservations in letters to the government that remained secret so as not to inflame an already aroused public opinion.

In October, an Episcopal delegation led by Bishop Bronisław Dąbrowski and including Bishop Szczepan Wesoły and Father Alojzy Orszulik had visited the United States and studied the question of training Polish priests for pastoral work abroad. The Episcopate noted the necessity of reviving the university theology departments in Cracow, Wrocław, and Poznań, and spoke out against the continuing disturbance of seminary studies through the conscription of seminarians, contrary to the 1950 church-state understanding. Only 6 percent of the permits to build churches applied for over the last six years had been granted—yet even this minimal response constituted progress in comparison with the Gomułka era. Normalization, however, remained far off: church publishing houses still had trouble obtaining paper.

In an average year, the Primate delivered six hundred sermons, and all of them dealt in one way or another with the situation of the individual and the nation; indeed, the Primate spoke out against inequality not only in great matters of state, but even in such mundane affairs as health insurance. Addressing Catholic intellectuals in Warsaw's Saint Alexander's Church in 1973, he told of an incident that had occurred in the Archdiocese of Gniezno. "A priest, suffering from tuberculo-

sis, was sent to recuperate in a sanatorium, and then was accused of illegally benefiting from social privileges—even
though he had paid for it all. So the social 'privileges' were not
for him, and God forbid that he should be treated! Why?
Because he is a priest. For this crime, the prosecutor asked for
. . . five years' imprisonment! And throughout the trial, phone
calls were constantly made to find out what to do next, as if
the judges were somewhere else and not in the courtroom. All
of this is documented." In the context of this hardly isolated
incident, the Primate called for the ending of the "terrible
spiritual enslavement to which people are still subjected in
their own free country."

Now the constitution was about to be revised. Even though
the application of law raised many doubts, the letter of the law
—to which appeals could be made in time of need—was important. The projected changes had been under consideration for
some time, and the Primate of Poland devoted three sermon
cycles, delivered at Holy Cross Church in Warsaw in January
1974, 1975, and 1976, to the question. Here I can only note the
problems dealt with in these sermons, which have since been
published in their entirety and are available in the West.

In the first cycle, Cardinal Wyszyński tried, on the basis of
the encyclical *Pacem in terris,* to answer the recurrent contemporary question, What is man in himself? First, the Primate
said, man is *homo Dei*—the man of God, a brother of humanity.
Next, he is *homo oeconomicus* and *homo politicus*—engaged in
socioeconomic and politico-civic life. All human aspirations
and desires, he said, are a heritage from God, and man must
have the freedom to discover and reveal that God-given heritage in his individual and social life. Beyond the general human
rights, man as *homo oeconomicus* must have the right

> to earn his living in a suitable way in his own community
> . . . in his own country . . . [and] each has the right to
> working conditions that do not sap his physical strength
> or leave him prematurely worn out. . . . Man has the right
> to engage in economic activity . . . to be paid according

to the dictates of justice, and to have his family provided for . . . and from the nature of man flows the right to possess private property in such measure as to ensure the freedom and dignity of the human person.

Cardinal Wyszyński spoke against the primacy of materialism and economism and practices that strike at religious and family life, such as Sunday work. All earthly authority, he stressed, has limits and depends on the Creator.

The deliberations of the Synod of Bishops on evangelization formed the basis of the January 1975 sermon cycle, but the Primate did not shy away from the particularly sensitive problems of evangelization in Poland and—where the difficulties were still greater—in the neighboring countries.

Things can reach such extremes that a priest cannot approach the altar because he is not registered. Dressed in everyday clothes, he must watch the peculiar sort of religious observance that is carried out by a "committee." One conducts the Asperges, another prepares the liturgical vestments at the altar, and a third reads the liturgical prayers. The moment of consecration approaches and there is silence and weeping because there is no one to perform the consecration. In fact, there is someone, but he kneels in the pew, forbidden to do anything, forbidden even to admit that he is a priest. Then comes the moment of Holy Communion. From the tabernacle, one of the committee members takes out the ciborium full of consecrated hosts, which were brought beforehand from a dean in a distant town, and distributes them to the faithful.

Such reality, Wyszyński said, was a debasement of the state, which ought to serve the common good. Applying totalitarian political atheism, the state debases itself—there is no other way, he said, to understand things.

In the January 1976 sermon cycle, the Primate informed the faithful that "at the beginning of December [1975] the secretariat of the Polish Episcopate submitted its observations on the 'platform' of the Seventh [Party] Congress. At the same time the Episcopal Steering Committee was meeting in Warsaw to prepare the basic principles which—in the opinion of the church, the Catholic community, and the hierarchy—should be respected in the announced 'slight,' as they call them, changes in the Constitution." The Primate in his sermons, like the Episcopate in its communiqués, viewed the constitutional question in a religious light, for, as the Primate said, "each person, existing for centuries in God's thoughts and plans, is a son of God, God's son." All laws, including the constitution, ought to take into account the fact that man is the highest value in the world. The Cardinal also stressed the fact that the family and nation are the most enduring environments of human development, and that social policy ought thus to support national economic sovereignty rather than derogating it in the name of international aims.

Most Poles recognized the postwar reality in which the Communist Party played a leading role and the state allied itself with the Soviet Union, but the entrenchment of these realities in the law of the land aroused social resistance. Basing his remarks on Catholic ethics, the Primate gave clear expression to that opposition:

The just right of the Nation is above all the right to preserve its national and territorial individuality. . . . Our nation has the right to preserve its own native culture and national independence within the borders of the country, the right to preserve its own national or state life and existence. The right of education in the spirit of the national culture, so important for the formation of the national culture, also belongs to the proper rights of the Nation. . . .

Without wandering from the social-ethics sphere into the political, Cardinal Wyszyński expressed society's opposition to

constitutional changes that would limit our national independence, sovereignty, and native culture, which had developed
from Greco-Roman, Christian foundations. Cardinal Wyszyński demanded a "feeling of freedom and openness in life" for
citizens. He defended "the undying right of coalition, or association," and demanded that the state "make allowance for
social pluralism."

Finally, he touched directly on the constitution:

> We were a little troubled by the formulation in the pro-
> jected constitutional amendments that indicates a strict
> dependence of civil rights on the fulfilling of obligations
> toward the country (article 57, projected constitution).
> We know that there can be many different understand-
> ings of obligations. There are people of the best will for
> whom it is difficult even to define, let alone to carry out,
> obligations. Yet they do not thereby forfeit the fundamen-
> tal human rights.

The Primate was alluding here to the mentally ill and retarded.

But such obligations could also be given an ideological interpretation. Thus the Cardinal demanded "that the state not
impose some 'state' ideology upon citizens" and that it "desist
from official atheization and atheistic or laicizing programs in
schools and everywhere. It should also desist from the appraisal
of people according to whether they believe or not: if they
believe they can sit at the back, and if they do not believe they
can go to the head of the class."

He went on to the constitutional enshrinement of the alliance with the Soviet Union. "There is one more weighty
proposition. The political community—taking into account
national realities, the culture of its own nation, and its cultural
and political sovereignty—cannot enter into pacts or assume
international commitments that would be detrimental to the
national culture and to economic sovereignty." He said what
needed to be said, and in a memorandum to the government

that the bishops did not publicize immediately, the bishops said more. The government made significant concessions. The principle of the party's leading role was left theoretical, in reference to society rather than to the state, its application undefined. Similarly, the principle of alliance with the Soviet Union ended up being expressed much more generally than in the original propositions or in the other Eastern-bloc constitutions. Finally, the government withdrew completely from the linking of civil rights with civic obligations.

The Church and the energetic protests of public opinion had won a joint victory in the softened constitutional changes, but there can be no doubt that the Church played the decisive role. While recognizing the Church's great social influence, the government noted the moderation of its leading representatives. Cardinal Wyszyński clearly stated in his sermons that Poland needed more long years of social peace. He was correct in preaching calm: seven major fires had broken out in Warsaw between September 21 and 29, 1975, burning down (among other things) a new metal bridge over the Vistula and a large downtown department store, and opinion linked the blazes with the Seventh Party Congress. The country was tense. Thus, the Episcopate did not make public at once its November 25 statement of reservations about the constitutional changes that had been announced at the Congress. On January 9, 1976, the bishops sent a letter on the constitution to Henryk Jabłoński, leader of the Sejm extraordinary commission that was preparing the amendments. On January 26 they sent Jabłoński an appendix to the earlier letter. The most famous letter on the constitution, containing the signatures of 101 lay intellectuals, bore the date January 31, 1976. The Church's protests had led the way, though the moderation of the Primate's public statements, and the fact that the protests were kept secret for a certain time, made the Episcopate's efforts all the more effective. Cardinal Wyszyński had directed the strategy and composed the most important statements. From the time of the controversy over the constitution, Wyszyński not only retained undiminished authority within Polish society, he also won over the governing circles, who faced mushrooming economic difficulties.

Thus, even Poland's communist rulers began to say that Cardinal Wyszyński was a great man and a great patriot. All this came about without any compromise on essential matters by the Cardinal.

In the secret memoranda to the government, Wyszyński had been able to speak out on the constitution much more sharply than the lay intellectuals could in their public statements—and the rulers, with their Eastern cult of secrecy in public life, respected him all the more because he had not published the Episcopate's statements. Not until June 1976 did the Episcopate's letters become public—and then only in an Italian translation. For a certain period, therefore, the authorities could pretend that the Church had been restrained in its criticism of the constitution. The lay democratic opposition that had sprung up at the time of the constitution controversy struck fear into the authorities, who resorted to the tactic of dividing their enemies. Therefore, even when the Church and the lay opposition said the same thing, offense was taken only at the statements of the latter group. Some people feared that the Church would lose prestige in such a situation, but they were mistaken. Everyone knew that Cardinal Wyszyński and the Episcopate were defending the same human and national moral rights that the lay opposition championed. The Church, without forfeiting its authority, became an instrument of social peace between the government and public opinion, which was splintered. Both the Church and its leader kept speaking the truth, more and more often bitter, to the government.

Stanisław Stomma of Znak cast the lone abstaining vote when the Sejm approved the watered-down constitutional changes on February 10, 1976. His dissent marked the end of the authentic Znak representation in the Sejm. In a complete reversal of the pattern of the sixties, the government now made peace with the Episcopate while opening an attack on true lay

Catholic groups and the democratic opposition with which Znak was in strong sympathy. The tactic would fail, of course, since the Episcopate extended its protection to the laity.

* * *

As a part of the discussion of pastoral matters at the February 1976 conference of the Episcopate, the bishops compared the moral attitudes of young people in Poland and the West. Even taking into account the relative influences of civilization, the bishops decided that the advantage lay on the Polish side. They also selected the delegation to attend the Eucharistic Congress in Philadelphia August 1–8, with Karol Wojtyła at its head.

On April 23, Archbishop Luigi Poggi arrived for what would prove to be inconclusive talks with the government. Poggi attended a session of the Episcopate on April 29, where expressions of unity and support were exchanged. The Episcopate also considered, in relation to the program for the next synod, the problem of official efforts to woo youth away from Catholic ethical principles. The bishops also noted the roadblocks still being laid in the way of pastoral work by local administrators and the need to extend health insurance to the villages.

Most significantly, however, the Episcopate answered the government's attacks on Znak with a public statement of support for and cooperation with the laity. The bishops responded to official wooing of Polonia by stating that it regarded Poles, wherever they lived, as part of the church family, as well as of the national family.

At its June session, the Episcopate felt obliged to address the marshal of the Sejm in connection with a proposed bill on acquiring and developing agricultural land that would have been injurious to private farmers and a cause of further depopulation of the villages, a danger against which Cardinal Wyszyński had been warning for many years. The bishops also complained about chronic violations of the freedom of conscience guaranteed by the constitution. High-school graduates were being discouraged from choosing the religious life, students in the seminaries were being harassed, and young people were being vigorously distracted from participation in pilgrimages.

Meanwhile, the gravest of Poland's postwar economic crises was deepening. On June 24, Premier Jaroszewicz announced to the new Sejm (chosen on March 21, and with the true Znak delegation replaced by a progovernment group using the same name) some drastic price increases. The Sejm accepted the increases without protest, but the people reacted. Violent disorder broke out in Radom, and in Ursus near Warsaw; the wildcat strikes spreading across the country almost amounted to the extent of a general stoppage. Within twenty-four hours, Premier Jaroszewicz revoked the price increases that he had announced, and the government found itself in an extraordinarily difficult situation.

Together with the secretary of the Episcopate, Cardinal Wyszyński interceded by means of a letter to the government in behalf of those touched by repression, calling for economic rationality adjusted to the needs of the nation. The letter was not publicized: Wyszyński wanted to nudge the rulers toward economic change without intensifying the social agitation.

During Archbishop Poggi's spring visit to Poland, he had been handed a letter addressed to the Holy Father from Pax, the Christian Social Association, and the (slightly more progovernment) group now known as Neo-Znak, requesting that Primate Wyszyński, despite his approaching seventy-fifth birthday, continue to hold office. The government representative in Rome, Szablewski, made an identical request. In the face of the Primate's restraint in a dramatic politico-economic situation, the authorities tried to strengthen their own tottering credibility by demonstrating good relations with Wyszyński. On September 3—as the press announced—Premier Jaroszewicz sent flowers and birthday greetings to the Cardinal. It was clear that Wyszyński—although, in accordance with the rulings of the council he expressed his willingness to step down

—would remain at his post. This was because the Pope believed in the continuing effectiveness of his work, because the whole Polish Church felt the same, because he was in excellent physical condition, but not because the government wished it. As a prince of the Church and the spiritual leader of his nation, he was irreplaceable. It was no accident that, during the birthday celebrations, Bishop Bronisław Dąbrowski called Cardinal Wyszyński "the father of his country," and stated that even his former enemies now regarded him as the only real authority in the country. In his reply to Dąbrowski, Wyszyński said:

> I felt good when they wrote bad things about me. But ever since they started writing good things, I've been wondering about the way I am living. . . . If, my dear friends, you ask, "What next?" I answer *sicut erat in principio et nunc et semper* [as it was in the beginning, is now, and ever shall be], but I will not say "amen," since that is not up to me. If you think that anything can change after thirty years of work, after a man turns seventy-five, you are mistaken. Bishop Dąbrowski said that "our experience teaches us that at least we are following an established course of action." We did not have to change. Others had to understand better the road along which the Polish Episcopate, supported by the power of the Holy Spirit and following the Handmaiden of the Lord, is leading the Church.

In these same remarks he touched upon his main directions in shaping Polish religiosity.

> Our example is the Handmaiden of the Lord. God called upon her to give the Son of God to the world, and He accepted the character of a servant. From the beginning, some people regarded our attitudes toward her as a sort of weakness—the weakness of our Polish religiosity, and particularly my weakness. The so-called Marianism of the Polish Church, its Episcopate, and its primate has been reproached by the press at home and abroad. In my opin-

ion, the Church would not be Catholic if it were not Marian. Why did the Lord God begin with Mary of Nazareth? There were other fine people to whom He could have sent His Annunciation, were there not? And yet He sent it to her. . . .

Western observers are becoming aware of the historical roots of the Marian piety that the Cardinal was speaking of. One of them, the West German Brigitte Waterkott, later said in a radio broadcast (Saarlandischer Rundfunk, May 27, 1979):

> It would be a complete misunderstanding to treat Polish Marian devotion as exclusively a matter of feelings. . . . The Polish Church affirms the interpretation of its national history, which finds its peak in the idea of the Polish nation's special calling in relation to the universal Church, to Europe, and to the World, in devotion to the Blessed Virgin of Jasna Góra. . . . Częstochowa is the central point of a historical image of messianic lineaments. . . . When the nation, after the partitions, came together before the altar of the Virgin, the external unity of the state was succeeded by an internal, mystical one.

Brigitte Waterkott points out the historical roots; from another point of view, I will add that under a totalitarian ideological system it is Marian piety that accounts for the extensive influence of Catholicism in Polish social life, and also for the cultural pluralism of our country.

A turning point in the government's attitude toward the Primate seemed to occur on his seventy-fifth birthday; it was not, unfortunately, a disinterested change of attitude. In June 1976 the police had repressed the workers of Ursus and Radom, and after being awakened by the constitution affair, public opinion would not now accept such repression. In September 1976, KOR (Komitet Obrony Robotników)—the Committee for Defense of the Workers—came into being with the intention of providing legal and material aid to arrested and repressed workers and their families. This was the beginning of a wider opposition movement that, as it spread, expressed different orientations and divided into factions. Conscious that the whole society was in opposition, the government sought support from the Church. Cardinal Wyszyński had no illusions about the government's motives, but from the year 1976 he operated from premises altered by the flow of events. He feared the escalation of social tensions and the sort of bloodshed that had occurred on the Coast in 1970. His greatest worry was that such disturbances might bring on armed Soviet intervention, as in Hungary in 1956 and Czechoslovakia in 1968. Therefore, the bishops stated during the September 8–9 session of the Episcopate:

At present, the good of the country demands internal order and calm. The conference realizes that the state authorities ought to respect civil rights fully and carry on an authentic dialogue with society. The Plenary Session of the Episcopate calls on the highest state authorities to desist from all repression of workers who took part in protests against the excessive increases in the price of foodstuffs in June. The workers who took part in those protests should have their rights restored, along with their social and career positions. There should be compensation for wrongs done, and an amnesty for those who were sentenced.

Taking into account the country's present economic difficulties, all citizens have an obligation to contribute to the easing of those difficulties. For this reason the conference appeals to all strata of society, not only to maintain social order but also to redouble their efforts and honest labor, and even to be prepared to make sacrifices for the sake of the common good. Honest labor is a moral obligation, and knowing how to make sacrifices is a Christian virtue. The condition for honest work and sacrifice is trust in the authorities, who earn that trust by true concern and effort for the good of all citizens. Only joint endeavor can triumph over the difficulties facing our country.

This Episcopate statement was very carefully balanced; in calling for an end to repression and the restoration of workers' rights, the bishops anticipated KOR's struggle of the coming months. At the same time, while calling on the workers to increase their efforts and maintain order, the Episcopate also reminded the authorities that everything depended on proper concern for all citizens. His thirty years' experience allowed Cardinal Wyszyński to formulate propositions that were at once morally unequivocal and capable of being accepted by a leadership constrained by its dependence on the socialist camp. The Primate had achieved a position of moral superiority. As early as July he had come forward in a letter to the government, and now, through the Episcopate, he delineated the course that the entire opposition would accept, by calling simultaneously for work and calm. As mentioned earlier, the government rulers began taking his protests and demands into account while concentrating on combating the lay opposition —a clever tactic, but one which solved no real problems. The country was sliding into an ever-deeper economic crisis, pushed along by an irrational economic system, excessive investments, shortages of raw materials, and other consequences of economic dependence. By 1979 there were an $18-billion debt, drastic price increases and market shortages, power blackouts and transportation breakdowns. In the dramatic year of 1976, this had not yet been foreseen.

The Episcopate meanwhile kept sight of other problems: the right to religious education, official efforts to replace the sacraments of marriage and baptism with state ceremonies, the growing number of divorces. A day of prayer for the defense of faith was declared in all parishes, and the bishops decided to deliver all possible help to families, who were threatened not only by the economic crisis but also by alcoholism and the breakdown of traditional ties as migration from the villages continued.

Not only in private letters and through Episcopal communiqués, but also through pastoral letters, Cardinal Wyszyński continued to speak out. In a letter for Mercy Week (October 3–9, 1976), he wrote forthrightly but with restraint:

> Despite optimistic propaganda, our domestic life is painfully disturbed by the multiplication of human sufferings in matters great and small. It is not enough to recognize these everyday evils. There must be a social will to right wrongs. There must be a brave acknowledgment of the disappointments, failures, and mistakes that have led to daily torment.

After discussing the government's mistakes and the lack of necessary goods, the Primate went on to write of the destruction of villages and suburbs.

> Whole family settlements, where families hitherto lived, where thanks to their work and their savings they ensured themselves, on their own, a place to live, are now falling victim to the pickax. Today, plans for developing the cities take no account of the fact that the pickaxes and bulldozers strike at human hearts and destroy without mercy the work of years. So it is in the family settlements that surround the capital and other developing cities. . . . If it is impossible to control the concrete wave of building skyscraper-prisons, it is necessary to think of the people who are forced out of the warmth of modest family homes, of children deprived of gardens and packed into confining dwellings, of the infirm who lose what they had dreamed of all their lives. It is necessary to seek these people out, become close to them, hasten to cheer them up; especially pastors, visiting the office buildings and the endless apartment projects, ministering sensitively to the afflicted.

Despite his continuing, uncompromising moral and social service, even though he was healthy and active, Wyszyński decided, as a matter of principle, to travel to Rome and put his future at the disposition of the Holy Father. On October 29 he presented himself to Paul and was handed a letter inviting him to continue fulfilling all his church offices—which he would in fact do until the day of his death.

Back home, the Episcopate was ready to speak out again on the moral aspects of the national crisis. On November 18, a little more than two weeks after the Primate's return from Rome, the bishops issued a communiqué that took the important step of calling for an amnesty: "Since June of this year, when society was shocked by what occurred in many workplaces, the Episcopate has continually appealed to the state authorities to apply an amnesty toward those workers who demanded an equitable living standard, and for the return of all the social entitlements which they have lost." This public message, read from the pulpits in all churches, came after the Episcopate's earlier, confidential appeals had gone unanswered. Now everyone could see that Cardinal Wyszyński's policy of addressing the government through the agreeable medium of unpublished memoranda had its limits. If the government would not react, it would have to deal with a public statement of the Episcopate's concurrence with the goals of the lay political opposition. On the matter of amnesty, however, the government would not bend until the pressure of domestic and international opinion became insufferable, in the summer of 1977. The leaders' inability to reach a compromise at the right moment hurt themselves and society.

The Episcopate also voiced its concern at the continuing roadblocks to religious education, at revisions in the school program that would dilute Poland's Christian heritage in literature and history classes, and at the fact that in all of 1976 the authorities had permitted the building of only a dozen or so churches and fewer than a dozen each of chapels and catechetical centers. Sixteen of the twenty-seven Polish dioceses had received no building permits at all. Like the continuing problems of Catholic publishing houses, this virtual ban on church construction stood in sharp contrast to earlier promises.

In his Christmas message, Cardinal Wyszyński concluded 1976 by reminding the faithful of the need to respect the rights of workers. When he said that the Church would support any social changes that brought true progress, he left it up to Poland's rulers to contemplate the degree to which they had squandered society's trust. "Even amid the greatest confusion," he wrote, "someone must calmly look far into the nation's future, like the helmsman of a ship, so that the nation can be led through the rolling waves to God's peace." There was no doubt that the Primate was ready to take that heavy responsibility onto his own shoulders.

Little hope remained for a church-state "normalization." On September 15, 1976, the publication in *La Documentation Catholique* of a secret speech that Minister Kąkol had delivered to party journalists in May caused an international sensation and evoked much pessimism. Kąkol's policy of adherence to Marxist doctrine in church-state matters was expected, but his frankness in laying out the tactics of the so-called new course came as a shock. As long as the government could not keep the people away from church, he said, it would cultivate Catholics well disposed toward the party and use them to head off church attacks on the authorities. The government's tactics against lay Catholics, including the attempt in January 1977 to transfer control of a certain business firm (owned by *Więź* and the Catholic Intellectuals' Club of Warsaw) from authentic lay circles to the progovernment Neo-Znak group, was even more disturbing.

At its February 8–10 session, the Episcopate came to the defense of the lay groups with a statement that "The steering committee will endeavor to increase the possibilities for lay Catholics to work in apostolic groups. It records its judgment that the few Catholic publishing houses and periodicals active in Poland, as well as active lay Catholic circles, are part of the Church's assets. Limiting their activity is a limitation of the Church's freedom of action." The statement had to do with

Znak and *Tygodnik Powszechny*, and above all with *Więź* and the Catholic Intellectuals' Club in Warsaw. The Episcopate's claim of ownership and an accompanying letter to Minister Kąkol prevented the transfer of property, despite some trumped-up legal actions in the case. Thanks to the Episcopate's protection, all these groups exist and are active today.

This meeting of the Episcopate chose Bishop Bronisław Dąbrowski as its secretary for another five-year term, thanking him for his skillful work in a position that involved constant contact with the bishops ordinary of all the dioceses as well as the state authorities. The Episcopate struck a new accent by drawing attention to the declining birthrate and diminishing viability of marriages, signs of a moral decline related not only to laicization but also to difficult socioeconomic conditions. The Episcopate approved a letter from Cardinal Wyszyński and Bishop Dąbrowski to the government on this problem.

Soon after the Episcopal session, Cardinal Wyszyński fell ill. He underwent successful gall-bladder surgery on February 22, and was back at work in several weeks. On May 3 he would be able to take part in the Feast of the Queen of Poland at Częstochowa, and soon he would be traveling around the country in a burst of activity motivated by the continuing social tensions. Repressive measures against those who had participated in the June 1976 protests were still being applied, and the actions of the opposition in defense of the workers were increasing. New opposition factions and groups were springing up, among them SKS (Studencki Komitet Samoobrony, the Student Self-Defense Committee), which became active first in Cracow, Wrocław, and Poznań, and then in other university cities. The mobilization of academic youth was an important phenomenon. To the right of KOR, ROPCiO (Ruch Obrony Praw Człowieka i Obywatela, the Movement for the Defense of Human and Civil Rights), established itself and then went through several internal convulsions and divisions before stabilizing. The government thus faced a confrontation with new opposition groups and a growing student movement; reaching for an understanding with the Church seemed to be the best possible tactic. However, this tactic met the opposition of anonymous groups within the party, which began to circulate a faked twenty-page sermon, ostensibly from Cardinal Wyszyński's January Holy Cross cycles, in which the Primate was presented as expressing support for the system and policies of People's Poland. This distasteful forgery apparently caused real shock in the party leadership, which took the unprecedented step of allowing the Episcopal secretariat to publish a correction in *Życie Warszawy* on February 24, 1977.

On March 4, in the midst of this complicated situation, Archbishop Poggi arrived for his third visit as head of the Vatican's task force to establish contact with the Polish government. The fact that only middle-level officials—assistant directors of the Bureau of Religious Affairs and the Ministry of the Interior—greeted Poggi at the airport reflected the lack of expectations concerning the talks.

The authorities' policy of good behavior resulted in some principled but propitiatory moves from the Primate, including a statement in the Lenten pastoral letter that "the majority of our economic failures result from our concluding, on the example of other nations, that we ought to live comfortably but not do anything." The moral decline caused by a faulty economic system and erroneous decisions justified Wyszyński's words, but public opinion attributed the difficulties to fundamental defects in the economic and political structure. Cardinal Wyszyński's remarks received a primarily political interpretation: he seemed to be counseling calm and hard work through fear of a Soviet intervention if the social tension continued. His primary motivation was to urge the nation to stick to the Jasna Góra vows, yet the people received the letter in a political sense, the government made propaganda use of it, and *Słowo Powszechne* even reprinted it without its author's approval.

The developing political opposition, which had been counting on support from the Church, was uneasy. The Primate was to step forward with such support in May, but in the meantime the authorities kept trying to neutralize the Church so that they could deal with the opposition. Cardinal Wyszyński, wanting to maintain a position of moral superiority, certainly could not allow the Church to be used for political ends, and therefore defended, as he had done and would continue to do, all who had been wronged or subjected to repression. His perspective differed from that of some opposition activists who had until recently been engaged in the party. Such people were living out a final disenchantment with the communist system. Cardinal Wyszyński had always regarded that system as alien, but in terms of church-state relations he regarded the Gierek leadership as preferable to that of Gomułka. At the same time, however, although differences of experience led to different judgments and tactics, the fundamental principles of freedom that the Cardinal had been expressing for thirty years now figured unquestionably among the guiding slogans of the political opposition.

The body of Stanisław Pyjas, a student who had been associated with the democratic opposition, was discovered in Cracow on May 7. Pyjas's death led to a boycott of the student Juvenalia festival and to a demonstration of public mourning in which KOR activists took part. The Cracow students were convinced that he had died at the hands of the secret police. The government, categorically denying that Pyjas had been murdered, presented the counter-explanation that the student had been intoxicated and died accidentally. Unsettled by the protest actions, the authorities arrested the KOR leaders in late May. In reply, the opposition initiated a seven-day hunger strike by some dozen protesters in Saint Martin's Church in Warsaw. *Trybuna Ludu,* the central party organ, greeted the hunger strike with an article by Dominik Horodyński under the provocative title "Political Exhibitionism." The Pyjas affair became known around the world, and under the pressure of Polish and foreign opinion, as well as of the Church, the government announced an amnesty for the Ursus and Radom workers and the KOR activists before July 22, the national holiday.

Cardinal Wyszyński had spoken out against police repression at the ceremonies on Saint Stanisław's day in Cracow on May 8, the day after the discovery of Pyjas's body. "Just as it was necessary in Saint Stanisław's time to admonish King Bolesław, the leader of Poland," he said, "so today it is necessary to admonish unceasingly that the citizen has the right to justice and love in his homeland. When that right is respected, only then, can social peace come about. There is no other way! The most efficient police apparatus is unable to establish social peace unless we are all guided by justice united with Christian love."

At its May meeting, the Episcopate noted an increase in pressure for atheization among the people. The steering committee spoke out in defense of Znak, which the authorities were trying to liquidate because of its apparent sympathy with the opposition. The bishops also called attention to the divergence "between the honorable remarks in the declarations of the highest state officials, and the practices of local authorities, who continue to impede the Church's pastoral and catechetical work." Significantly, although not for the first time, the Episcopate interceded with the government in behalf of industrial workers—specifically, miners and steelworkers, who were pulling stretches of twenty-one consecutive workdays, including Sundays. And a statement about farm policy reflected Cardinal Wyszyński's well-known views: "Healthy villages are a necessary condition for the sufficiency and defensibility of the country, for the health of the nation, and for demographic correctness."

Interestingly, the communiqué from this Episcopal session also mentioned the dissemination in Poland of anonymous publications attacking the Church. The bishops associated them with certain ex-priests, but the pamphlets were clearly inspired by party apparatchiks opposed to détente with the Church.

The bishops ordinary—whose sessions had become an important part of church leadership—met on June 16, six days after Archbishop Poggi had returned to Rome from his second

Warsaw mission of the year. The bishops could say nothing more encouraging about the Warsaw-Vatican talks than that they were being carried out in close cooperation with the Polish Episcopate. The ordinaries noted the disparity between government declarations and practices and proposed that either the local authorities were disobedient, or the central authorities were double-dealing, a suggestion reinforced by Minister Kąkol's talk with journalists during the previous summer.

Cardinal Wyszyński worked incessantly throughout May and June, visiting one or even two parishes a day. On June 9, during the Corpus Christi procession, he carried the Blessed Sacrament under a scorching sun for three hours. On July 1 he went on a working vacation, composing pastoral letters and a speech he would deliver in Rome that fall; he told friends that he had "perhaps never before been able to write more easily, or wanted more to do so." He also spent a good deal of this vacation worrying about internal conflicts among the Pauline Fathers who staffed his beloved Jasna Góra.

Back in Warsaw in August, the Cardinal was conducting a meeting of the metropolitan curia on the morning of the 13th when he learned that Archbishop Antoni Baraniak had died in Poznań. It was a great blow: Stefan Wyszyński had lost his closest friend, his former secretary, the man who had been arrested with him in 1953. Over the next four days, in observances at Niepokolanów, Częstochowa, and Opole, the Cardinal looked gaunt and sallow. After consecrating Bishop Alfons Nossol in Opole on the 18th, he returned to Gniezno at one in the morning and set out the next day for Archbishop Baraniak's funeral in Poznań. There he preached the farewell to his favorite bishop in a slow but careful voice, and his complexion was so obviously yellow that it did not take a physician to note the signs of jaundice. That evening he was in good form as he gave an interview for American television in Gniezno, but in Warsaw the next day his physician diagnosed the jaundice, suspecting that it was infectious. Fortunately this diagnosis was incorrect, but on the 31st a council of doctors, lamenting the loss of twelve days' treatment, confirmed that the Primate was suffering from obstructive jaundice. The Primate bore the illness well, although he regretted having to interrupt his work, and especially missing the August 26 celebrations in Częstochowa for the first time in twenty years.

On September 5, Cardinal Wyszyński underwent isotope tests; the next day his consulting physicians told him that he ought to enter a clinic for further tests and, probably, surgery. He chose the Banach Street clinic, directed by Professor Łapiński, and was admitted on September 8, after turning all diocesan business over to his assistants.

On Sunday the 11th, Cardinal Wojtyła led the entire Episcopate in prayers for the Primate during a service in Gietrzwałd. The Primate knew full well that he was gravely ill. He made his confession. During the three-hour operation, the surgeons noted increased inflammation. They considered the surgery a success, but the fate of the patient was uncertain. The Polish bishops called for prayers, thousands of letters and telegrams arrived at the clinic, and Marian Śliwiński, the minister of Health, put the entire Polish health service at the disposal of the Primate and also offered to transport him abroad for care. (Cardinal Wyszyński thanked the minister, but preferred to remain in Poland.) The 18th was the most critical day, when it became clear that the operation had not produced the desired results.

On the 20th, Cardinal Wojtyła and Bishop Dąbrowski issued a communiqué dedicating all Rosaries said during October for the intention of the Primate and establishing the first Sunday of that month as a national day of prayer. Yet before their announcement, on the 19th, all signs indicated that a miracle had occurred. There was a crisis that evening, and the next day came news from the clinic that the level of bilirubin in Cardinal Wyszyński's blood had fallen by half. On Thursday he felt better for the first time, and on the same day the results of a biopsy revealed that there was no malignancy. Slowly the patient began to recover. Even the physicians began to speak of divine intervention. One of the professors told me, "In human terms, there was no way he could survive." By the 25th he felt well enough to think about going to Rome, and on October 1 he was allowed to return home. All of Catholic Poland breathed with relief, and the planned prayers of supplication were changed to prayers of thanksgiving.

While Cardinal Wyszyński began his short convalescence, his pastoral letter for Mercy Week, which he had composed during the summer, was read. Though the letter was deeply religious, it also noted that "Not only war, but also social and political transformation, can cause great human unhappiness. In such situations sympathetic love in adversity, flowing from and to God, supernatural in its extent, is indispensable. . . ." The letter also spoke of the victims of "ideological reform": "It is exactly here that one can find people deprived of the means to live, often because they had 'the courage to think independently.' " Next, Cardinal Wyszyński wrote of the suffering of parents "whose children are atheized by school programs, or even demoralized by the experience of education." State policies caused human suffering, he wrote, because

> We know how to undertake great economic plans, we know how to erect great public edifices, we know how to produce exports for all corners of the globe. But we do not think about the fact that people must eat every day, that there must be decent food stores and easy access to bread, meat, and milk without the loss of hours of time, health, or strength. The prodigious sight of long lines where women stand for whole hours, some of them with children in their arms, those filthy stores in which harassed clerks shoo away angry customers—all this demands prompt change.

Before writing these words, Cardinal Wyszyński visited the food stores himself—not to shop, but to find out personally how his flock was living.

In this same letter, the Primate wrote of the inefficiently organized labor, which destroyed the workers' health and strength; of the difficulties posed to family life by excessive work; of juvenile delinquency, the crime of abortion, and the destructive scope of alcoholism. He also wrote, with particular significance:

> God's mercy is today much needed in our baptized nation, which has been drawn away from God's love and sometimes doubts that there is still justice among the nations of this world. Not everyone has the courage to remind the nation about the right to God, to love, to freedom of conscience, to history, to culture and to our heritage. Not everyone feels obliged to defend these endangered values of our Christian national culture, which are being ground in the Godless mill of dialectical materialism. . . . But it is not permissible to remain silent when our native culture, with its literature and art, with its proven Christian morality and its union with the Roman Church and the values of the Gospels, is being shoved aside in the new plans for educating the younger generation. Our national dignity demands that we oppose the arrogance that treats everything Polish with contempt, for the sake of alien imports.

Cardinal Wyszyński slowly recovered during October, and on the 22nd he affirmed in a pastoral letter that he wanted "to attribute this successful convalescence directly to the Virgin Mary of Jasna Góra, around whom were gathered the prayers of living faith and insistent appeals for the sake of her servant and slave."

Little more than a week later, the newspapers carried the following unexpected dispatch: "On October 29 the first secretary of the PZPR, Edward Gierek, received the leader of the conference of bishops, the Primate of Poland, Cardinal Stefan Wyszyński, at the Sejm building. During the discussion there was an exchange of views about the most important matters of the nation and the Church, which have significant meaning for the unity of Poles in the successful building of the Polish People's Republic."

It was Cardinal Wyszyński's assessment of the situation in

the country that led him to begin his return to work with his first meeting with Gierek since the latter took power in 1970. Significantly, the communiqué described the two men as exchanging views on national issues first, and on church matters second. The Primate had obviously followed the deepening economic, social, and political crisis even during his illness, and had decided then to make his views known to Gierek. For Gierek, the meeting was a chance to gain much-needed prestige, which was why much of the lay opposition greeted it with skepticism. But the Cardinal knew what he was doing. For one thing, Gierek was due to visit the Pope in Rome at the end of November, and for him to do so without ever having met with the Primate would have been highly irregular.

We can assume the nature of Cardinal Wyszyński's presentation to Gierek on the basis of the fall pastoral letters. Although the Primate, acting with discretion, never divulged the exact course of the discussion, he did comment on its subject at a meeting with the faithful in the Warsaw Cathedral basilica on November 6:

> Speaking of my obligations, there is one more that I must mention. After many years of consideration, I have recognized that in particularly difficult situations the Primate of Poland must also keep the requirements of the Polish *racja stanu* before his eyes. Thus, in accepting the duties assigned to me by the Church—the sees of Gniezno and Warsaw—I also accepted a moral and civic duty to undertake appropriate discussions on the requirements of Polish state interests. You know what I am talking about, so I need say no more. As I said, this is a dictate of my conscience, as a bishop and as a Pole, in the hope that the good Lord will bring forth the blessed fruit that our homeland so needs.

In light of these words, there can be no doubt that the Primate and the first secretary had discussed the crisis in which the country—not through its own fault, but because of its leaders' erroneous policies—found itself. The discussion was necessary, even if it brought no immediate results. So many propositions for improving the country that came forward in the late seventies led to nothing—and yet going on record was for Cardinal Wyszyński the fulfillment of a moral obligation to the nation that he had for years been expressing by calling for changes in economic and social policy.

Wyszyński arrived in Rome on November 8 and saw the Pope in the company of the other Polish bishops on November 12. He also had a private audience with the Holy Father, to discuss relations with the Warsaw government and stress the need for establishing the legal status of the Polish Church.

On November 18, Cardinal Wyszyński went to the Grotto of Ferrata for a short rest and there suffered another attack of jaundice. His Polish physicians prescribed medication that brought about sufficient improvement for him to attend a reception given on November 29 by Edward Gierek for Giulio Andreotti of Italy. A still-sallow complexion could not keep him away from this diplomatic function, which brought together around one table Andreotti; leading Christian Democrats including Aldo Moro; the Italian communist chief, Enrico Berlinguer; Gierek and Central Committee Secretary Stanisław Kania; the Primate himself and Bishop Dąbrowski; and finally Archbishop Casaroli and other Vatican dignitaries. The world press spoke of a "historic compromise," but Cardinal Wyszyński certainly did not share their optimism. Keeping up his relations with politicians and diplomats as well as with Vatican representatives, he hoped at the most for some small accomplishment in the upcoming talks between Gierek and Pope Paul. Although the Cardinal did not speak to the journalists who crowded around him after the reception, he could not conceal an air of sadness and dejection caused by the situation at home.

The Pope received Gierek on December 1, 1977. The Polish Press Agency dispatch betrayed the fact that, although the atmosphere had been cordial, nothing concrete had been achieved: the meeting was "a continuation of Polish activity in

the international arena in the name of détente and peace.
..." The agency also spoke of the "consistent development of
ever-better relations between our country and the Holy See,
and between Church and state. . . ." As we know, such improved relations remained in the realm of wishes, and the
grand expectations created around the "extraordinary gathering" two days earlier issued in no "historic compromise." The
Primate did know that the spectacular Roman meetings would
inhibit the government from any energetic antichurch actions.
For its part, the government was able to exploit the meetings,
and especially the Primate's presence at the reception for Andreotti, for propaganda purposes. The weak authorities made
as much media capital as possible of the meetings, and the
propaganda occasioned a reaction from *Tygodnik Powszechny*,
which printed abridged versions of the speeches exchanged
during Gierek's visit with the Holy Father. The abbreviations
so pained the authorities that *Słowo Powszechne* printed a blistering accusation that *Tygodnik Powszechny* had censored the
Pope. On December 21, an unknown assailant beat up Father
Andrzej Bardecki, a church assistant to the *Tygodnik Powszechny* editorial staff who was generally acknowledged to have
made the abridgements. The possibility that he was beaten in
a diversionary action against Gierek's church-state policy cannot be excluded.

Regardless of these incidents, Gierek's visit was of the highest importance. The assurances exchanged in Rome had imposed on Polish government policy toward the Church limits
that could be crossed only at the risk of a reaction from both
the Vatican and world opinion. On December 5, Pope Paul
received Cardinal Wyszyński and informed him about the talks
with Gierek. Far from being left out of the Warsaw-Vatican
negotiations, the Primate was placed in a strengthened and
perhaps even commanding position. Never again would anyone in Warsaw think of going over the Primate's head.

At home, the crisis showed no signs of improvement. The
opposition movement continued to develop. In late September
and early October 1977, KOR set for itself the task of perma-

nently representing the interests of society under a new name, Committee for Social Self-Defense–KOR *(Komitet Samoobrony Społecznej)* (KSS-KOR). At the end of 1977, TKN (Towarzystwo Kursów Naukowych, the Association for Academic Courses) came into being as the sponsor of the "flying university" courses that recalled by their name the analogical independent teaching efforts during the nineteenth-century partitions. Concerned about this widening opposition, the authorities tried to create the best possible impression of relations with the Church.

Cardinal Wyszyński returned to this complicated situation on December 12, and the Episcopate met two days later. Beginning by expressing their thanks for the Primate's recovery and their appreciation of all those who had prayed for him, the bishops went on to talk about relations with the government. They made the "eternal" statement that "the permanent safety of these relations should be founded on an acknowledgment of the legal nature of the Church (such as it had before the war) and by appropriate bilateral agreements. The cooperation of Church and state for the good of the nation deserves a permanent basis."

The Episcopate learned of Pope Paul's approval of Cardinal Wyszyński's program; there thus existed full concord between the Episcopate and the Vatican, even if "normalization" with the state had not proceeded. The Episcopate nevertheless expressed its support for, as the bishops termed it, the discussions between the Primate and Edward Gierek, and between the delegates of the Polish People's Republic and the Holy Father. The party would shortly complain that this formulation had cheated Gierek of recognition as the Pope's interlocutor.

The Episcopate addressed the authorities over the fining of priests who had led, and property owners who had acted as hosts to, the Catholic Oasis camping-pastoral program. Such repression contradicted the propaganda about "normalization." The bishops also complained about the continuing exclusion of priests and sisters employed by church institutions from social security—the clergy, in fact, was now the only group not covered—and about the imposition on all youth organizations of an antireligious viewpoint contrary to the beliefs of most of the members. Great, therefore, was the gap between spectacular meetings or phraseology about normalization and the reality of everyday practice.

Well aware of this gap, the Primate used his Epiphany sermon, on January 6, 1978, to state three main requirements for church-state relations: legal status for the Church, the establishment of Catholic associations, and authentic Catholic publishing and press institutions. After the Rome spectacular, the government felt obliged to permit publication of this sermon in the January 12 edition of *Tygodnik Powszechny,* which led to the widespread conviction that the Church and the state would soon conclude an accord on the basis of the three conditions. In fact, however, the permission to publish the sermon meant nothing of the sort; after a few weeks of hope, the representatives of the Episcopate were given to understand in talks with the government that the Church would have to fulfill its mission through the three channels it had always enjoyed—the pulpit, the confessional, and the catechism. After seven years of negotiations, the Church was back where it had started. Thus it had to return to Cardinal Wyszyński's dictum of engrafting itself into the nation, at least as long as the state was too weak to allow itself even the most minimal and limited of accords with the Church.

The political and economic crisis that had surfaced so dramatically in 1976 continued to engross Cardinal Wyszyński's attention. In an answer, dated February 2, to a letter from Bishop Herbert Bednorz on the predicament of Silesian miners, Cardinal Wyszyński wrote that "today the question moves significantly away from the level of 'capitalism-proletariat' to another level, not foreseen by Karl Marx—the establishment of 'neocapitalism' in a collective economy, exercised by a communist state in the name of the primacy of export production over the workingman." In this lengthy letter, the Primate recalled having spoken in his Epiphany sermon of "saving not economics and production but, rather, man." He recalled the Church's postwar concern about labor and related that when, after the "December revolution," it had been proposed that "he benefit from the government's difficult situation by advancing the Church's program," he had replied then that "the Polish Episcopate is not in the habit of taking advantage of situations. Let the government meet the demands of the shipyard workers." The Primate revealed in his letter to Bednorz that in his first meeting with Premier Jaroszewicz, in March 1971, he had brought up the matter of labor law, which left the workers without legal protection in a socialist state, and had also charged that unions had been reduced to the spokesmen of the "monopolist employer—the state." Wyszyński also recalled how he and Bishop Dąbrowski had demanded amnesty and the restoration of rights for the workers arrested in the 1976 "Ursus-Radom revolution," and how such protests had led to an amnesty and a relaxation of the official line. The Primate told Bishop Bednorz that even though he could not reveal the course of his recent talk with Gierek, he could say that the rights and difficult predicament of workers had been on the agenda. The Primate also said that he had spoken against "voluntary" public-service work on Sundays and holidays, claiming that even the party members who usually took part in such work had the right to a day of rest. The Cardinal had also warned against the reckless introduction of the four-shift system in mining, which was not only a burden to the miners but also a hindrance to their religious practice. At the same time, he mentioned the need to warn the workers against "an excessive desire to make money."

Cardinal Wyszyński expressed another characteristic side of his convictions in a letter that he wrote at this time to Izrael Zyngman, the author of *Janusz Korczak Among the Orphans.* The Cardinal went beyond thanks for the book, which had arrived during the time of his illness, to give witness to his position on the Jewish question. There had been efforts to cast a shadow on that position, both by the communists during the struggle with "Zionism," and by people afflicted with psychological complexes based on their own involvement in this most intricate problem of the human history of our time. Cardinal Wyszyński wrote:

The pedagogical contribution of Janusz Korczak, who suffered in Treblinka, is so important that it should never be forgotten. It is part of that great affliction of the Family of Man in various nations, which can serve as an aid in the education of the generations to come. Janusz Korczak's voluntary choice of death in Treblinka is the most perfect example of how to give one's life for one's brother, especially for children sentenced to annihilation, to whom he dedicated his whole life and from whom he did not want to part.

. . . I want . . . to add that these accounts of Janusz Korczak among the orphans have greatly enriched my image of existence in the Warsaw ghetto, which I observed for several months through the wall along Elektoralna Street. The accounts contained in the book remain in my considerations of the occupation era, of the fighting in the ghetto, and of the Warsaw Uprising.

If you will allow me, I will conclude these thoughts with the words of Władysław Szlengel, the poet of the Warsaw ghetto, as quoted at the end of the book: "Janusz Korczak died so that we too could have our Westerplatte."* I am of the opinion that there is a great truth, indispensable to the spiritual development of each nation, contained in those words. I remember a conversation I had before the war, in a train from Bydgoszcz to Warsaw. A young Jewish woman was lamenting what was going on in Bydgoszcz. Sympathizing with her, I explained my own viewpoint. For the full spiritual development of the ancient Nation of Israel, I told her, which had performed such a great service in transmitting to mankind the idea

---

*This small promontory at the mouth of the Vistula just north of Gdańsk symbolizes the Polish military heroism of 1939; the small army outpost there came under heavy artillery bombardment on September 1, 1939, and withstood an unceasing barrage for more than a week before the handful of survivors capitulated to the Germans.

of the One Living God, it was necessary to recover an independent state that could serve as the cradle for the future of Israel. It would be best if that state centered on Jerusalem.

Today, as I observe the reborn State of Israel with great interest, I think that the People of God are following the right course of development. And when that road is difficult, I think that help in overcoming these difficulties will come not only from the Old Testament exodus from Egypt and the house of bondage, and not only from surviving the Assyrian and Babylonian captivities, not only from the burdensome war of the Maccabees against the Hellenes, but also from the heavy sacrifices of the Nation of the Lord in the uprising in the Warsaw ghetto and the terrible losses of your Nation.

We are in agreement that both the Polish Nation and the Nation of Israel needed their own "Westerplatte" in this new era of history. This common history is shared by both of these nations, which share centuries of history on Polish land. I think that from the moment of those horrible sufferings and sacrifices there has been a fuller understanding of the new history. . . .

I know that the building of a free State of Israel is linked with considerable difficulties, efforts, and sacrifices, but only through such difficulties can the nation work out its own character and its own ambitions. Therefore I am heartened that your nation has its own homeland, and on the ancient site of the House of David. I state my hope that the building will endure.

This letter attests to the Polish affirmation of Israel's status as nation and state in a sad period when, because of international considerations, diplomatic relations between Israel and Poland were broken in the most distasteful circumstances.* Cardinal

---

*All of the communist countries except Rumania were ordered to break off relations with Israel after the 1967 Arab-Israeli war; the action was particularly distasteful in the Polish case—among other reasons, because it coincided with the party's

Wyszyński shouldered the responsibility of expressing Polish honor and dignity and Polish respect for the most historically afflicted of nations.

The existing improvement in church-state relations was brought to an end in Cardinal Wyszyński's eyes when Henryk Jabłoński, head of the Council of State, accepted the leadership of the progovernment Caritas, which sponsored the "patriotic priests." There could have been no more effective way of worsening the climate of mutual relations. Caritas had begun to distribute abroad a misleading brochure about its activities, so in 1977 and 1978 the Episcopate issued unexpectedly decisive rebuttals in the form of a clarification by the Episcopal secretariat on March 8, 1977, and an Episcopal letter to the clergy on June 15, 1978. An appendix to this letter recounted the shameful history of the seizure of the Church's Caritas, and the state authorities' establishment of their own organization under the same name. The church leadership was further upset when the authorities tried to pressure elderly clergy by offering them social security through the Caritas pension fund. The Episcopate's pronouncements were thus decisive and deflated the propaganda, channeled through such semi-respectable journals as *Polityka* and the Pax press, about progress in church-state normalization.

At its March 1978 meeting, the Episcopate took steps to protect active social groups by reminding the authorities that "citizens long to work for the good of the country, they want to gather their strength in service to the nation, but this requires the appropriate social and political conditions, which will liberate the energies of the citizens." The Episcopate was calling on the government not only to trust the citizens more fully, but also to honor the civil rights guaranteed by the constitution and by international documents that Poland had signed. The Episcopate's statement was, objectively, an important support for the democratic opposition.

In conjunction with Cardinal Wojtyła's report on the first

"anti-Zionist" campaign.

five years of the Episcopate's Council on Learning, the bishops expressed their disapproval of "all circumstances that hinder the human spirit in the free creation of cultural values." The killing effect of censorship on scientific, artistic, and religious creativity was stressed. The bishops said that "The Church will support any initiative that attempts to present culture, the productions of the human spirit, or the history of the nation in an authentic form, because the nation has the right to the objective truth about itself"—clear support for TKN and the "flying university." A few months later, Cardinal Wyszyński would share this support in a more direct way.

The 1970s saw a great increase in the importance and authority of Cardinal Karol Wojtyła within both the Polish and the universal Church. During the Primate's illness, Cardinal Wojtyła had acted as his replacement and showed him great affection. Pope Paul took account of the opinions of the metropolitan of Cracow and even asked him to lead a papal retreat at the Vatican. Cardinal Wojtyła's influence within the Polish Episcopate, as well as the tact and skill with which he coordinated his own efforts with the unfailing leadership of Cardinal Wyszyński, were obvious. Unfortunately, the authorities tried to suggest significant differences between the two cardinals, portraying the Primate as more conciliatory and Cardinal Wojtyła as confrontational and likely to follow the directions of opposition circles. The March Episcopal communiqué, of course, had shown that all the bishops believed that grass-roots social initiatives were necessary to a country that existed in permanent crisis. The authorities, however, would not face this reality and tried to harass Cardinal Wojtyła in matters of appearance and administration. For instance, these days they always gave Cardinal Wyszyński a diplomatic passport for his trips to Rome, but now denied one to Cardinal Wojtyła. Thus the authorities managed to mislead some of the public, especially the people who regarded the Church as a political instrument, but this had no effect within the Episcopate. Despite the difference of nineteen years in the age of the two men, they showed a remarkable unity of thought and actions. It is worth remembering that during Gomułka's time the authorities had flirted with Cardinal Wojtyła—without results.

At the May 4–5 meeting of the Episcopate, Cardinal Wyszyński noted that his three conditions for church-state normalization, as defined in January, had not been met; he said forthrightly that normalization "is still not a fact, but . . . we are in its opening stage." These words contradicted official propaganda and the statements of progovernment Catholics; the bishops renewed their demand that the status of the Church be affirmed in law. At the same time, the bishops stated their opposition to all outside interference in academic pastoral work, and to all attempts at defining it as nonchurch activity. They emphasized the inclusion of not only theology, philosophy, and Catholic social teaching, but also many elements of history, literature, and culture within the competence of the academic chaplaincy. This was their response to government actions against conducting lectures on the premises of academic chapels. And they established an independent student movement in reaction to official attempts to cram all youth into one Marxist organization. Here the government had fallen into its own snare. In its communiqué the Episcopate spoke of Catholic educational institutions in Lublin, Warsaw, Cracow, Wrocław, and Poznań, even though the government did not acknowledge the existence of the latter three. The bishops also called for the establishment of seminaries in the two newly created dioceses in the Western Lands and of the Catholic Temperance Society in response to the spread of alcoholism— an initiative the government would not even discuss.

Archbishop Poggi's next official visit to Warsaw, from May 23 to June 6, led to nothing significant. The government proclaimed the Society for Spreading Lay Culture a "public welfare agency," thus ignoring proposals from the Vatican and the Episcopate.

At its June meeting, the Episcopate again called for the vacationing children's right to worship God, and protested the harassment of the Oasis summer-retreat movement. It also called for freedom for Catholic culture. There is no way to avoid the conclusion that by this point the government had given up on anything beyond the appearance of a desire for normalization. For a man who had lived through as many unpleasant experiences as Cardinal Wyszyński, however, it must have seemed that, despite the open conflict, things could have been worse. After all, the Primate had always thought in terms of the nation, and not in terms of a pact with the government. The Primate spoke unceasingly to the nation, voicing his concern for its growing everyday difficulties. At the celebrations on Saint Stanisław's day in Cracow on May 8 he spoke, in a long sermon, of "the biological destruction of man and his strength" through the authorities' demands for increased production to make up for economic mistakes. "The organization of labor," he said, "does not take account of man, but only of economic plans that become more and more demanding and lead to permanent exhaustion. An exhausted man has no joy in life, nothing matters to him, he has no hope of improving his lot, not even religious life attracts him, because he is always weary and wants to do nothing but sleep away like a mindless creature—until it is time for work." These words reflect the state of a large part of Polish society and explain the behavior, often passive, at which zealous reformers who were out of touch with real life often marveled. Spoken before tens of thousands of people, such words also constituted a great accusation against the rulers.

Despite Cardinal Wyszyński's uncompromising position on matters of principle, his sober realism and understanding of the government's predicament combined to make some achievements possible. Thus, when he preached at the groundbreaking ceremonies for the Church of the Conversion of Saint Paul on May 27, the Primate could report that more than a dozen new churches were under construction in Warsaw. He said, "It is useless to do battle with the faith of a nation, with its desire to profess God."

In May and June the Primate carried out an important exchange of letters with Minister Kąkol of the Bureau of Religious Affairs. In the initial letter, Minister Kąkol accused the academic chaplaincies of antistate activity. In reply, Cardinal Wyszyński said that the authorities defined "political life" in such a way that "the citizen is almost completely excluded from his rights in that arena." The Primate had decided, he wrote, that the time had come "to defend those essential rights." In defending the "flying universities," he said that none of the texts of lectures given there that he had seen contained anything illegal or hostile to the state. "The 'flying university' programs are modest attempts to supply the lacunae in public education, to uncover facts about the past era that have been wrapped in silence, to rectify the frequently erroneous presentation of obvious facts in school and university teaching. Such are not grounds for accusations of activity hostile to the state—every intelligent person has the right to such things." Cardinal Wyszyński advised Minister Kąkol that he would do better to "look for the enemies of the socialist state" among the cowardly, silent ones. The Cardinal condemned police harassment of the TKN courses and their participants, and in an unusually forthright way he spoke of the damage being done to Poland on the international level by the system of rule applied by the party and government. This can only be interpreted as a warning to the authorities about the danger of foreign intervention should they provoke society to an explosion.

There was perhaps no church, national, or social problem that Cardinal Wyszyński failed to address in his public appearances or in his correspondence with the government. Thus he acquired an authority unknown to the spiritual leaders of other countries. This authority flowed, as I have tried to show, from three main sources: his unusual, unswerving faith; his flexibility and benevolent interest in public life; and his philosophy of engrafting the Church into the nation through an active, loving presence in its history, for better or for worse. These three sources form the psychological and intellectual profile of Cardinal Wyszyński that will be recalled by many generations of Poles.

Great changes came over the universal Church at this time.

Although Pope Paul VI had been ill for a long time, his death on August 6, 1978, was a great shock to the Polish Church. The Episcopate issued a statement characterizing him as "a great and valiant pope." Both Polish cardinals went to Rome for the funeral, and the government sent its condolences to Cardinal Jean Villot, the prosecretary of State. Before leaving, Cardinal Wyszyński remarked during a sermon in Warsaw that this pope had been unable to make his longed-for visit to Poland, but had established Polish dioceses in the Western Lands and, on the initiative of the Polish Episcopate, had proclaimed Mary as Mother of the Church.

On August 26, the Feast of Our Lady of Częstochowa, the conclave chose Albino Luciani, the metropolitan of Venice, who took the name John Paul I. Happy with the choice of "the smiling pope," Cardinal Wyszyński returned home and plunged back into pastoral work. Unexpectedly, the new Pope died after thirty-three days. The Primate tried in a memorial service at the Warsaw Cathedral to explain how the man chosen by the cardinals could die so quickly. "Not the highest of human callings," he said, "no office or dignity, not even the most elevated, most perfectly harmonized with the will of the Creator, can guarantee man a longer presence on earth." Leaving so soon for a second conclave, he said, was "a great lesson for the whole world." So it was. The great and small were given an occasion to consider their dependence on the will of God.

During the short pontificate of John Paul I, Cardinal Wyszyński and a delegation of the Polish Episcopate had spent five days in West Germany, a visit that amounted to an event of global significance. It constituted a reply to the visit made earlier to Poland by the late Cardinal Julius Döpfner, the head of the West German conference of bishops, Jösef Hoffner, and many other German bishops. The great significance of these visits derived from the brave, pioneering letter of the Polish Episcopate in 1965, which had told the German bishops "we forgive and ask to be forgiven." The campaign of hatred organized by the Gomułka regime had only underlined the significance of that letter. Now the Polish delegation could take another step in the direction of Christian unity between the Polish and the German nations. The international press spoke of Cardinal Wyszyński's triumphal journey through Germany and closely followed his actions and words. Speaking of the ills of the past, the Primate showed great tact and moderation, though commentators focused on his words about the common European values that the two nations shared. At his arrival in Fulda on September 20, he recalled the discussions he had had with Cardinal Döpfner during the council: "Many times we hoped that the day would come when we could—as had been done in the past, as we are doing today—build a Europe of Christ, a Christian Europe. All the more because we have worked for centuries in Central Europe to establish here the Kingdom of Christ, which is the kingdom of truth, of justice, and of love, the kingdom of peace and grace." The next day he said that the meeting of the two Episcopates "will not be a sensation for the politicians; for them it might even be an outrage. But for the Christian world it can be a salvation and the beginning of a road to the evangelical rebirth of Europe. . . ." Speaking to German Catholics in Cologne Cathedral on September 22, Cardinal Wyszyński said, "Europe must realize once again that she is a new Bethlehem— of the world, of peoples and nations for whom the King and Prince of Peace, the one Saviour of the Family of Man, came into the world."

It is necessary to read these texts in full to realize how subtly Cardinal Wyszyński wove together the European warp with the woof of Polish-German reconciliation. The Primate thought of Europe's shared Christian roots, of its spiritual unity which could and should lead to the reconciliation of the European nations and to the common cultivation of our cultural values and our Christian value system. The Primate spoke of peace, but also of spiritual unity; politicians might choose to emphasize one of these threads, but truth demanded that they pay attention to both. By relating these two levels, the Polish visit to Germany became a success and a significant event. An important foundation was laid in 1978, on which more may be built in the future.

Shortly after the visit to Germany, the Polish Episcopate convened in sadness over the death of two popes, calling for prayers for both of their intentions. The bishops pointed out the lamentable discrimination that was still taking place after Warsaw's diplomatic gestures toward the Vatican. Fines were being levied against those who housed Oasis participants; people arranging local visits of the Jasna Góra icon were being interrogated; those who took part in religious celebrations were being demoted or dismissed from work. Despite the 1950 understanding, the Episcopate protested, seminarians were still being conscripted and, once in the army, dissuaded from their vocations. Finally, the bishops noted that lay people "are a part of the Church and play an active role in its mission." Appealing to the council resolutions, they stated categorically:

> The state authorities cannot refuse the right of lay Catholic associations to establish and maintain their own, diverse activity in conjunction with the hierarchy, to publish, and to possess the property that is needed to accomplish these goals. The administrative means held in the hands of the state must not be used to direct the activity of, oppose, or subjugate one more association for political ends. The members of these associations cannot allow themselves to be used to such purposes.

This statement was crucial to the defense of Znak, whose property had been placed *de facto* under the control of delegate Zabłocki's ODiSS (Ośrodek Dokumentacji Studiów Społecznych, the Center for Social Documentation and Studies). Zabłocki had already wrongly appropriated the name of Znak. Now, when he asked a representative of the Episcopate whether the bishops' statement referred to him, he received an affirmative reply. This compelled him to stop short of assuming final control of the Znak holdings, even though he had begun legal action to that very end. The fact that only the intervention of the Episcopate brought about this half-solution is sad, but the whole affair showed nevertheless that no church-state normalization was thinkable in Poland without the recognition of the laity's right to authentic, morally and politically independent action. Making the authorities realize this was an unquestionable success for the Episcopate and its leader's patient tactics.

* * *

Cardinal Wyszyński never said that he had foreseen the result of the second conclave in which he found himself during such a short period in 1978. On the contrary, having taken part in three previous conclaves, and knowing well the currents that moved the College of Cardinals, he thought that tradition would be respected in the election of another Italian pope. What is more, he regarded such an outcome as fitting: not only did he think the Romans should have an Italian bishop, but he also feared the consequences of violating a 455-year-old tradition. Similarly, Cardinal Wojtyła thought that the tradition would be maintained for a time, even though it would eventually fall, as the Church continued to universalize itself—and even though he was aware of how highly he himself was regarded within the College of Cardinals. As the Primate revealed, Cardinal Wojtyła's thoughts were still wrapped up in the affairs of the Archdiocese of Cracow as he left for the conclave, carrying only the minimum personal belongings and traveling, as always, on the passport of an ordinary Polish citizen.

Cardinal Wyszyński later recalled that the cardinals had entered this second conclave humbly, since Providence had so quickly struck down their previous choice. Now they were cautious about looking ahead, and absorbed more than ever before in prayers for the cooperation of the Holy Spirit. While the journalists diverted themselves with horoscopes and predictions, the cardinals gathered in a mood of great concentration and pressure.

About the choice of a Pole, the metropolitan of Cracow, Karol Cardinal Wojtyła, on the eighth ballot, Cardinal Wyszyński said, "We understood still more deeply that God, and particularly the power of the Holy Spirit, are at work in the Church. If people doubt that there are signs and miracles in the world today, I say to them, 'If anything is a miracle, what happened in the Sistine Chapel on October 16 is one.' "

Neither Cardinal Wyszyński nor—as his own testimony showed—the Pope himself had any doubts about who had worked the miracle. As the Primate disclosed, "When I approached John Paul II to pay my first homage, he and I almost simultaneously pronounced the name of Our Lady of Jasna Góra: this was her work. So we believed, and so we decidedly still believe."

The ceremonies that inaugurated the pontificate of John Paul II were broadcast and commented upon around the world, so I will confine myself to the particulars that touched the Primate of Poland. At the moment of the cardinals' homage, the new pope gave a sign of his respect for the Primate. Before the eyes of the world, they played out a heart-rending scene as they fell into a brotherly embrace. The attentive observer could see not only that the Primate kissed the Pope's ring, but also that the Pope kissed the Primate's hands. A similar scene occurred the next day when the Pope greeted the Poles who had come to Rome. After Wyszyński's speech, in which he remarked about the dear price that the new pope was paying in leaving his homeland in obedience to the summons "Go forth and teach all the nations," and in which he promised permanent prayers for the intention of the Pope in Poland's Marian sanctuaries, Cardinal Wyszyński fell to his knees. Instantly, the Pope did the same, and the two men held each other in a long, long embrace. Everyone in the hall wept. During this meeting Pope John Paul spoke the words that I quoted in the introduction:

In the Chair of Peter there would not be a Polish pope who today, full of the fear of God but also full of confidence, begins a new pontificate, if it had not been for your faith, which never withdrew before imprisonment and suffering, your heroic hope, your unceasing belief in the Mother of the Church, if there had not been Jasna Góra and that whole period in the history of the Church in our homeland that is linked to your ministrations as bishop and primate.

Henryk Jabłoński, the chairman of the Council of State of the Polish People's Republic, took part in the inauguration and was received the next day in a private papal audience. From the moment of Cardinal Wojtyła's election, everyone had been asking whether and when he would again see his homeland. As early as October 23 Minister Kąkol of the Bureau of Religious Affairs stated:

There have been many misunderstandings and much disinformation about this matter. Thus an official clarification is called for. Everyone knows that the Pope is at the same time the head of the Church and the head of state of the Vatican. Our attitude toward the entrusting of this highest church dignity to Cardinal Wojtyła is one of contentment and gratification. If the Pope comes to Poland, it is a matter of certainty that he will be warmly welcomed by the state authorities as well as by the people. The choice of the date and the duration of the journey are obviously conditioned by circumstances having a mutual and many-faceted nature. You yourselves know that this is the case with all important visits.

Many clever statesmen must have labored over the phrasing of this brief note, which was printed in *Słowo Powszechne*. Within the ongoing miracle, however, Kąkol's words did their job. Despite months of negotiations about specifics, it was clear that the Pope would visit Poland in 1979, and that what had been absolutely unthinkable even a few months before would now come to pass.

Cardinal Wyszyński found himself besieged after the election by people who wanted to peer into the secrets of the conclave. Others recognized the event as recompense for all the Polish Church's sufferings, and as recognition. Recognition for the Primate, as well. No other Polish primate had done as much. The Primate later recalled that he had heard many saying, "Poland has earned this by its example of how to defend God and the laws of Christ, how to defend the faith and to keep one's head up despite sufferings and persecution." Such voices meant all the more because there had been other, painful, notes in the past. At the Polish Institute in Rome, Wyszyński said:

> In the postcouncil period, as we recall, the Polish Church suffered the greatest attacks. It was written, all over the European press and particularly in France and Germany, that the Church was not implementing the council, was not progressive. The Episcopate was constantly attacked for being conservative and antiprogressive, for delaying the council reforms of the liturgy. As it turns out, however, the Polish Church has its merits. This was the argument in the Sistine, which calmed all the electors. Since Poland has preserved its religiosity and church unity, it is obvious that the whole world needs such methods, such work, and such pastoral style.

Eight days after Cardinal Wyszyński returned to Warsaw on October 29, he preached about the election in the Warsaw Cathedral.

> The greatest accusation is that after all the Polish Church is Marian. Right after the election of John Paul II, someone wrote, "He has already spoken twice about the Blessed Virgin, so this will be a Marian, and thus certainly a conservative, papacy." . . . And I reply: God began

saving the world with the Virgin from Nazareth. He put her by the manger in Bethlehem, under the cross on Calvary, he wanted her to be in the Pentecostal Upper Room. If that is not enough, the last council pronounced that Mary is present in the mystery of Christ and the Church. The Polish bishops forcefully requested that Pope Paul VI name her Mother of the Church, and so he did. . . .

Cardinal Wyszyński gave his thoughts their fullest expression on the election later, at a "Christmas Eve Wigilia" supper for priests on December 23.

It is hard to speak about the great mystery through which this came to pass. On December 8 it was twenty-five years since, at Stoczek in Warmia, I understood the meaning of Our Lady within the Polish Church as a unifying force, a force that could mobilize and move Poles in each great and proper matter. That is when I gave myself up in servitude to the Most Blessed Mother. When, later, I began to speak of devoting Poland into her servitude, outspoken but pusillanimous brothers said, "The Primate is making a blunder here." Now it has turned out differently. . . . From the beginning of the so-called defeat, it has been necessary to stake everything on Mary.

I had some difficult moments at the conclave. Losing such an excellent co-worker as Cardinal Wojtyła costs me a great deal. You would have to know the mystery of our cooperation and interaction for yourself to understand that. But just when I was full of pain and tears, the new pope began to speak about the Most Blessed Mother—from his position. Then they wrote in the press that he will be a Marian pope because he has already spoken about her twice. But you add up the number of times he has spoken of her since then! Truly, he believes that victory in the universal Church, when it comes, will be her victory.

Immediately upon his return home, the Primate threw himself into the vortex of work. He spoke often of the "Polish pope," but his hands were full of current church matters; his second-in-command in the Episcopate, the head of the Scientific Council, of the Commission for Academic Affairs, and of the Commission for the Pastoral Care of the Laity had been taken to Rome.

The state authorities, shocked by the election, were now endowing Cardinal Wyszyński with extraordinary attention, such as full diplomatic protocol at arrivals and departures. On November 12, the thirtieth anniversary of Wyszyński's appointment as Archbishop of Gniezno and Warsaw, Minister Kąkol sent congratulations in the name of the People's Republic. In Warsaw, more than a dozen churches were under construction at last.

John Paul II sent his thanks to the Episcopate and its leader when the bishops met in session on November 28–29. The new pope particularly stressed the importance of the areas for which he had held the Episcopal portfolios, the lay and academic apostolates. They were, he wrote, "important sectors of the front in the spiritual battle that the Polish Church is leading under the protection of the Mother of the Church and Seat of Wisdom." He also asked the bishops for their prayers.

Lamenting that Catholic publishing houses were receiving less paper and of a poorer quality than a year earlier, and that catechisms and liturgical texts were in short supply, the bishops sent the government a request that printing runs be increased and that censorship be limited in connection with the widespread interest in the Holy Father's activities. The requests went unanswered. The Episcopate also stated its continuing interest "in the difficult position of working people, especially in mining, metalworking, and collectivized agriculture." The Episcopate reminded the faithful that the nine hundredth anniversary of the martyrdom of Saint Stanisław at the hands of the Polish king would fall in the coming year; most Catholics knew that Pope John Paul II wanted to come to Poland for that anniversary.

Cardinal Wojtyła's election to the papacy was hardly an isolated success for the Polish Church, which was stronger than ever at the end of 1978, with 19,913 priests (15,219 diocesan and 4,694 religious). There were 569 priests ordained in 1978, and 5,325 students in the seminaries. The papal visit gave rise to a jump in the number of vocations in the coming year—Poland enjoyed the highest ratio of callings to population in the world. Despite discrimination against believers, the churches were full and participation in the sacraments had increased. Morality often fell short of Catholic principles, but declining living standards, the growth of social inequality, corruption, and other effects of drastic economic mistakes and a faulty system conditioned these moral shortcomings to a large degree.

With a papal visit taken for granted, all eyes turned to Cardinal Wyszyński and his task of negotiating its particulars. Without relenting in his pastoral work, Wyszyński himself considered the nature of the visit. He also delivered dozens of talks on the new pontiff, excerpts of which were published in a book, *The Polish Pope from Cracow*, that was sent to priests at Christmas.

Bolesław Piasecki, the head of Pax, died in Warsaw on January 1, 1979. Mortally ill for two years, Piasecki had dragged himself from his deathbed to address his followers in an act of personal heroism in October. Until the end he maintained his ideological struggle with Cardinal Wyszyński. Earlier in 1978, Piasecki had formulated the theory of a government by two socialist parties, one Marxist and the other Catholic, that would rule in coalition or by turn. The system was to remain collectivized, and no other orientations would be permitted. Piasecki had even suggested his system to the Soviets as the one way of overcoming the dissident movement. The communists had allowed Piasecki to nourish such abstractions as recompense for his unending struggle with the Church, while Piasecki had gone on demonstrating his usefulness as an alternative to the political opposition. Piasecki had been unable to disentangle himself from his past, and in the end his ideas ossified and strayed from the practicable. He died a tragic figure. When he learned of Piasecki's death, Cardinal Wyszyński made it known that he would say a Mass for the intention of the deceased. He could do nothing more, though the public did not understand and may have been scandalized. Piasecki's dramatic life demonstrates the risks of playing politics in a totalitarian state, especially in opposition to popular feelings and to the Church. Despite a burial with the honors of a member of the Council of State, Piasecki's failure, in contrast to the Primate's acknowledged authority, was obvious.

Cardinal Wyszyński held his second meeting with First Secretary Gierek on January 24. The ensuing joint communiqué spoke of "a continued exchange of views on the most important affairs of the nation and the Church, which are important in the establishment of appropriate relations and cooperation between Church and state for the sake of national unity in the task of forming the success of the Polish People's Republic and strengthening its position in the world." The talks represented an undoubted success for Gierek, beset as he was by economic and political troubles. Similarly, public opinion interpreted the communiqué as beneficial to the government. It must be noted, however, that matters of the nation were mentioned first. We know what the Primate must have said. It was not the first time he had laid aside all considerations of prestige and propaganda in order to fulfill the moral duty of warning the government. This was certainly the main theme of the meeting. In addition, there was significant improvement in the general atmosphere which was so necessary for the forthcoming visit of the Pope in little more than four months. Thus, Wyszyński opened the doors to Poland for Pope John Paul II.

In the heated, rumor-laden atmosphere that followed the meeting with Gierek, Cardinal Wyszyński reached the thirtieth anniversary of his archepiscopal service, on February 6. The Pope sent a telegram:

On the day of the thirtieth anniversary of Your Eminence's call to the Primacy, I join with all God's people in our homeland in prayers for this Venerable Jubilee. . . . Jesus

Christ, the Pastor Prince, has allowed the Primate to take part in his mysteries, and particularly in the mystery of suffering, in the course of these years. In Saint Paul's words: "For you have been given the favor on Christ's behalf—not only to believe in him but also to suffer for him." With the Apostle of the Nations, respected Primate, you too can say that "my experiences have turned out rather for the advancement of the gospel . . . because a greater number of the brethren in the Lord, gaining courage from my chains, have dared to speak the word of God more freely and without fear." (Phil. 1:29 & 12–14)

Bishop Jerzy Modzelewski preached during the celebrations in the cathedral and recalled the words of Saint Peter:

"Better for us to obey God than men." (Acts 5:29) Clearly this expresses the divine truth taught by Wyszyński that atheism and laicization are contrary to God's will, human dignity, and the Polish *racja stanu*. His proclamations and writings proclaiming the Good News brought this home to many. For such attitudes he suffered physical and moral torments. For several years he lost even his personal freedom. . . . He appeared among us as a herald and forerunner of God's hope. He showed this in a special way as he survived the tragic days of Warsaw and the Coast. In hours so difficult for the nation he appealed for moderation, patience, and trust in God, fulfilling the words of Saint Paul: "For we work and are reviled for this reason, that we hope in the Living God." (1 Tim. 4:10)

Cardinal Wyszyński's answer was short. He said only that he had tried to remain true to his motto: *Soli Deo—Per Mariam.*

Jan Nowak, the former director of Radio Free Europe, wrote in March 1979, "Personally I regard the Primate as a leader in the once-in-a-thousand-years category, but not even a man endowed with the greatest courage, will, and understanding would be able to accomplish anything without the strong support of the masses." Cardinal Wyszyński enjoyed such mass support because he came forward under the banner of basic church, national, and human rights, in behalf of Polish spiritual and cultural identity, rather than under the flag of a political party. As far back as the memory reaches, it encounters no Polish statesman, prince of the Church, or spiritual leader who enjoyed such unquestioned national authority.

When it convened on February 7–8, the Episcopate expressed its approval of Cardinal Wyszyński's meeting with Gierek while reminding the authorities that "socioeconomic progress is impossible without simultaneous respect for the standards of social morality and for freedom." It also reaffirmed the meaning of the laity to the Church and chose Archbishop Franciszek Macharski, successor to Cardinal Wojtyła in Cracow, as leader of the Commission for the Pastoral Care of the Laity.

Intensive negotiations with the government, conducted in the atmosphere created by the talks between Wyszyński and Gierek, led to the publication in the Polish press (on March 3) of a communiqué by the secretary of the Episcopate stating that "The Primate of Poland, Stefan Cardinal Wyszyński, sent Pope John Paul II an official letter in the name of the Episcopate on February 22, expressing gratitude for his readiness to visit Poland and our Church." In the name of the Episcopate and the people, the Primate invited the Holy Father to make the visit in the near future. At the same time, a Polish Press Agency communiqué expressed how satisfied the Council of State and the authorities were with the invitation. June 2–10 was set for the event, during which the Pope was to visit Warsaw, Gniezno, Częstochowa, and Cracow.

Everyone knew that the communiqués reflected a compromise. The Pope had wanted to come in May for the observances in honor of Saint Stanisław, but the government was sensitive to the implications of a martyr who had died because he unhesitatingly spoke the truth to the authorities. It had also been on Saint Stanisław's day, May 8, 1953, that Cardinal Wyszyński and the Polish bishops presented the government with the famous *non possumus* letter. On successive Stanisław days, the Primate had forced the communist authorities to pay attention to their mistakes and society's discontents. Thus the authorities had categorically refused a papal visit in May. An impasse threatened until the Pope offered to come in June— and then switched the celebrations for Saint Stanisław so that he could take part in them. The visit could take place after all, in the fine weather of June. The Pope and the head of state, Jabłoński, exchanged confirmatory letters of courtesy in early March.

When the bishops next met, on March 21–22, they stated that "The visit of Christ's Vicar, the head of the Catholic Church, to Poland, united for the last thousand years with Christian culture and the See of Peter, is an event of exceptional religious and supernatural meaning in the history of our nation. The fact that the Vicar of Christ is a son of the Polish land emphasizes the visit's extraordinary character." The bishops called on the faithful to prepare with prayers, and voiced their hope that the visit would lead to further normalization of church-state relations. The bishops did not mention the most striking aspect of the visit—that it would be taking place in a communist country. This was possible only because of Cardinal Wyszyński's patient tactics of defending the nation's rights while remaining ready to negotiate with the authorities. His tactics were bearing fruit not only in Poland but also, to a certain degree, in other communist-ruled countries. But the bishops did have to add to their statement reminders about the right of young people to practice religion on vacation, and about the need for more church buildings and catechetical centers.

The details of the Pope's visit had not yet been settled. The authorities wanted to keep the greatest possible degree of control for themselves, for political purposes. Despite the doubts of many Catholics, Cardinal Wyszyński adopted an attitude that was as brave as it was effective. Namely, he ceded to the authorities control over construction—as, for instance, of the huge cross beneath which the Pope would celebrate Mass in Warsaw—and even of media services, in the belief that it was the Pope himself who would give the visit its special character. The outcome showed that the Primate was not mistaken, even though there was much anxiety about allowing the Interpress Agency,* with its political coloration, to handle the press coverage. Cardinal Wyszyński nevertheless stated calmly that he was happy to see the "Red brothers" building crosses. And in fact the Church had to limit its press activities, since it hardly possessed the telephones, telexes, and other technical means needed for anything beyond Catholic journalism.

The Primate busied himself in the meantime with other church business, addressing an April 2 session of the Academy of Catholic Theology and filling vacant bishoprics. Pope John Paul's successor as metropolitan of Cracow, Archbishop Macharski, had been named in record time, and the nominations of Bishop Stroba in Poznań and Bishop Walenty Majdański in Szczecin, both important to the Church, came through quickly. When Cardinal Wyszyński consecrated his former Gniezno chaplain, Monsignor Józef Glemp, as Bishop of Warmia on April 21, he had filled the last vacant diocesan see and provided for the future beyond the term of life that he could expect for himself.

Following the death of Cardinal Villot, Pope John Paul II named Archbishop Agostino Casaroli as prosecretary of State. Cardinal Wyszyński could feel satisfied: besides having a Polish pope, the Vatican now found its foreign affairs in the hands of a man who knew Polish issues through his own experience.

Two months after the official announcement of the Pope's visit, particulars of the trip had yet to be established. Obviously there were difficulties. The Western press reported that the authorities would not agree to the Pope's wish to visit the tomb of Saint Jadwiga in Trzebnica or to meet with Silesian workers at Piekary. The Episcopate finally divulged the Pope's schedule on May 8. While formally meeting the authorities' demands

---

*A government publishing agency which provides official information about Poland to foreigners, publishes books and periodicals in foreign languages for distribution outside of Poland, and makes official contacts with foreign organizations and individuals.

by omitting Trzebnica and Piekary, the schedule contained opportunities for workers to meet the Pope in Częstochowa, and for young people to do so in Warsaw, Gniezno, and Cracow. The Episcopal communiqué spoke of the significance of the visit's taking place in the anniversary year of Saint Stanisław's martyrdom. Thanks, then, to Cardinal Wyszyński's patience and flexibility, the wolf went away satisfied and the flock was intact. It must be said, however, that there was a great deal of anxiety and impatience among Catholic opinion in the two months before the fixing of the schedule. It had been Cardinal Wyszyński's impressive calm and distance from minor matters that allowed things to conclude well.

The Primate, eager to discuss the upcoming trip with the Pope, went to Rome late in May. It was a visit of intensive work, fitting together the mosaic of a coherent pastoral and social-moral program. In a letter to the faithful on May 23, Wyszyński spoke of the joy with which the Holy Father was preparing for his visit, appealed to society for "mutual aid," and expressed the hope that the authorities would "do everything possible to mobilize train and bus transportation to Warsaw, Gniezno, Częstochowa, Cracow, Oświęcim [Auschwitz], and other places that the Holy Father wants to visit." The authorities answered this appeal selectively: everything was formally in order, but tickets to Częstochowa were not being sold in some train stations. This is not, however, to deny the government credit for its decisive contribution to organizing the visit.

On May 27, Cardinal Wyszyński's letter welcoming the Pope to Warsaw was read at Sunday Masses in the capital. "This heroic and tolerant Warsaw has always remained a Catholic city," the Primate wrote, "never deserting the Church despite attempts to give it a different coloration. Warsaw, a bridgehead between Roman Catholic Europe and the far-ranging expeditions of the missionaries, has created the fabric of national and religious culture." In the light of these words, it was not surprising that John Paul II addressed himself to other Slavs, beyond the Polish borders, who draw their cultural essence from the same spring of Christianity as we. On May 26, the Pope announced his first consistory. Franciszek Macharski and Władysław Rubin joined thirteen other new cardinals, and Poland again had three princes of the Church, as it had had before the death of Cardinals Filipiak and Kominek.

On May 29, four days before the Pope's arrival, Cardinal Wyszyński went to the Sejm building for another meeting with Edward Gierek. Their joint communiqué sounded hopeful:

> Cardinal Wyszyński stated that there is a strengthening conviction of the importance of the Church's religious and moral work in Poland. The Episcopate desires that the Pope be received everywhere with joy and dignity and that his meetings be accompanied by order, courtesy, and seriousness commensurate with this exceptional visit. The Primate of Poland thanked the central and local authorities for their help and efforts in preparing for the Pope's visit.
>
> The conviction was expressed that the visit of Pope John Paul II will bring about new impulses for church-state cooperation and for the further development of relations between Poland and the Holy See, in service of the unity of Poles in the realization of the national goal: the welfare of the country, the Polish People's Republic.

The hopes voiced in the communiqué were not to be realized. Beyond the decision to admit the Pope, which had obviously been made in close consultation with the Soviets, the Polish authorities would apparently proceed no further in matters of substance. Nevertheless, the visit was a national event that imparted a feeling of dignity, straightened the Poles' moral and ideological backbone, and consolidated allegiance to the Church and religious tradition. This would not have been possible had the Primate not negotiated the visit, although it was naturally the Pope's charismatic spiritual unity with great crowds that decided matters.

The Pope's visit, which took place between June 2 and 10, has such a rich literature of its own—unfortunately richer in foreign languages than in Polish—that we will consider it only from the perspective of Cardinal Wyszyński's life. This encompasses the postwar history of the Polish Church, since Cardinal Wyszyński had given himself wholly to the service of Church and nation. He had no time even to read and study Catholic sociology; his service as a bishop had become his whole life. He survived all phases of the postwar struggle against the Church because supernatural forces animated him —and because nature had given him a nervous system of improbable resilience, allowing him to spend the morning taking part in dramatic scenes under great pressure, to spend the afternoon meeting with ordinary people, and always to find a common language with them. The Primate had an unshakable, childlike faith that others could only envy. Yet he had a lively flexibility—based not on political speculations but on a knowledge of social life and its needs. He was able, despite the communist government and system, to maintain the links between Church and nation, and this was the basis of all he accomplished.

For almost a quarter of his term as Primate, until the end of 1970, Cardinal Wyszyński was presented by the communists as an extreme conservative in theological as well as social and political matters. All communist fellow travelers, a large part of the liberal left in the West, and even a considerable number of Catholics as radical as they were disoriented, bought this characterization—and some were *bought* for the sake of it. In view of the facts that have been presented here about the systematic struggle conducted against the Church by an atheistic state, there is no need to reply to this characterization. Every council reform was introduced into the Polish Church, albeit incrementally and, in each case, after the faithful had been prepared so that they would understand the changes. It was, rather, his resistance to the limitation and destruction of the Church, to the forced atheization of the nation, and to the violation of human rights that was referred to as "Wyszyński's conservatism."

Cardinal Wyszyński founded his conception of religion and his methods of opposing atheism on tradition and history. He knew how well these qualities united Poland and hindered its Sovietization and the deprivation of its proper spirit, its cultural identity. An attitude of defensiveness, resistance, even pugnacity, conditioned by constant struggle, created perhaps a certain reserve on the Cardinal's part toward new theological tendencies. Also, the Primate was so Polish, so wrapped up heart and soul in the Polish part of the universal Church, that he was less receptive to the conditions reigning in other parts of the Church. He certainly did not cherish any excessive hopes about what was happening to the Church in the West. It is not easy to assess objectively the outcome of the de-Christianization and increasing practical materialism there, but it was precisely the crisis of the Church in the West that moved Wyszyński, more than once during the council and the Synod of Bishops, to emphasize the union of the Polish Church with the Holy See and its obedience and doctrinal faithfulness to the Vicar of Christ.

No one even generally familiar with Cardinal Wyszyński's socioeconomic views can doubt that, in Western terms, he would have to be regarded as a rather radical, progressive exponent of Christian social teaching—one who questions with equal acerbity the social system based on dialectical materialism and the unlimited capitalism that has grown out of individualistic liberalism. I would go so far as to say that the Cardinal was at times too harsh toward capitalism, since he always thought of it in terms of what he had known in his youth. He knew, however, that the secret power of Freemasonry* and the complete predominance of capital over labor

---

*The Masonic movement, particularly strong in nineteenth- and early-twentieth-century Poland (as in Russia), was associated with capitalist development, liberalism, and opposition to the Church. The actual degree of its prevalence remains a subject

lay largely in the past, and that the contemporary West was evolving in the direction of the welfare state, the open society, and true social and political entitlements for its citizens. His anxieties about Western practical materialism were nevertheless well founded.

Finally, Cardinal Wyszyński was accused of being anticommunist and hostile to the left. A dignitary of the Catholic Church naturally cannot be an enthusiast of communism, and the Primate knew its weaknesses and errors better than others, not only as an authority on Catholic social teachings but also as a man who had guided his Church through thirty-five years of communist rule, with all its multiplying absurdities. These absurdities were such that virtually every few years there was bloodshed and powerful social unrest, and each time Cardinal Wyszyński was asked to calm the nation in order to avert greater disasters. The man who had before him this theoretical knowledge and these practical experiences proposed an accord with each successive communist leadership, in spite of everything. The communists did not accept these propositions sincerely, and whenever they concluded an agreement, it was only a matter of time before they violated and broke it. Then some more time would pass, and, for the good of Poland, Cardinal Wyszyński would again have to save the communists from themselves and from the catastrophes into which they had led the country. Can all of this be termed conservatism and reaction? I think that we are dealing here, rather, with absolute fidelity to the Church's social teachings combined with unswerving adherence to the virtue of moderation, which is the chief of all other values.

I also doubt that there is another church figure or national spiritual leader in the world who, in the dramatic circumstances that confronted Cardinal Wyszyński, would have remained as faithful to his own doctrine while, at the same time, being so flexible that his enemies in authority would call on

---

of historical uncertainty, but now and then a reference to the evils of masonry can still be heard in a village sermon.

him for help—and not be refused. As long as the nation was in question, he never refused. Nor was he sparing, in such dramatic moments, of the words of truth, to which the rulers had to listen patiently.

Thus, does it make any sense at all to speak of Cardinal Wyszyński as a conservative? Had he lived in the West, I suggest, he would have passed for a social radical—although he would certainly have been no exponent of the theology of revolution, or of the general theory of revolution as a means to a better society.

In this context we can ask: to what degree were the Primate's character and program evident in Pope John Paul II's pilgrimage to Poland? When Cardinal Wyszyński mentioned Pope Pius XII at the Pope's first meeting with the faithful in Victory Square in Warsaw on June 2, the older members of the assembly recalled Father Stefan Wyszyński's defense of that pope after the war. The authorities, championing their materialistic system, had been trying then to discredit Pius in the eyes of Polish society. Now, almost thirty-five years later, Cardinal Wyszyński reminded his listeners of what Pius XII had told the Polish colony in Rome on November 15, 1944—in the aftermath of the Warsaw Uprising:

A torment by fire? No! We should, rather, speak of a crucible, in which gold of the highest assay is purified and ennobled. And however deeply we feel pity at the sight of this tremendous suffering, we are even more deeply seized by a feeling of awe, which enjoins us to bow our heads before the fortitude of the fighters and the victims. These victims and these fighters have shown the world the heights to which a heroism born of and maintained by such noble sentiments of honor and strong Christian faith can rise.

During this same celebration, Pope John Paul II spoke of Pope Paul's fervent desire to visit Poland, a desire so strong "that it outgrew the limits of his pontificate and—in a way that strains the human understanding—is being realized today." It was impossible, listening to those words, not to think of Cardinal Wyszyński's years of efforts, and of Monsignor Casaroli's visit at the end of 1966, when he tried to negotiate a Christmas visit to Jasna Góra by the Pope. Cardinal Wyszyński had been subjected to incredible pressures then, only to see the authorities finally reject Paul's proposition, which had been so full of love for Poland but so difficult to bring about.

When John Paul II said, ". . . Christ cannot be excluded from the history of man anywhere on earth, no matter what the latitude or longitude," I thought of Cardinal Wyszyński's hundreds of remarks on the subject and his annual reminders that children and young people have a right to worship God. When the Pope recalled his presence at the *Te Deum* of thanksgiving sung at Gniezno on the thousandth anniversary of Poland's Christianization and repeated that thanksgiving, the Primate of Poland must have thought of his own major life's work. It must have been the same when the Pope spoke to all Slavs, for Cardinal Wyszyński's feelings of responsibility had never been limited, formally or in fact, to the territory of present-day Poland.

The apogee of spiritual consonance for the Pope and the Cardinal came at Częstochowa on June 4. Cardinal Wyszyński welcomed the pontiff by speaking of Our Lady's defense of the nation, but his words were more than a conventional welcome. He spoke again of the hope that the whole Family of Man would be dedicated to the Virgin, and the Pope replied by speaking of his desire to realize the Primate's wish on the scale of the universal Church.

I particularly want to repeat and renew the Millennial Jasna Góra vows of May 3, 1966, in which to you, Mother of God, and to your maternal love, the Polish bishops gave themselves for the freedom of the Church, not only in their own country but throughout the world. A few years later, on September 5, 1971, they dedicated to you, Mother of the Church, all humanity, all the nations and peoples of the contemporary world, their kin in faith, in language, in the shared fate of history, enlarging their trust to those farthest boundaries of love—as your heart demands: the heart of a mother, who reaches out to each and all, everywhere and always.

Today, the first pilgrim pope at Jasna Góra, I want to renew that whole heritage of trust, submission, and hope that has been so magnanimously laid up here by my brothers among the bishops and by my countrymen.

And that is why I entrust to you, Mother of the Church, all the workings of the Church, all its missions and all its service in the perspective of the second thousand years of Christianity that are now ending on earth.

To the Primate and the Pope, these were more than mere words. Both men were aware that their Marian vision would encounter the opposition and the doubts of elitist church circles, particularly in the West. They believed equally in the importance of Mary's mediation for church freedom around the world, and they wanted to entrust everything to her.

Late the next evening, June 5, the Pope and the Primate met with people particularly close to them. Undisguised happiness emanated from the Primate's face. He said, speaking not without a certain pathos to his former co-worker, now the Pope, that he could not dare to ask anything more since the Holy Father had fulfilled his most heartfelt longing. John Paul was deeply moved, even though he tried good-humoredly to deflect the Cardinal's thanks with a quip. He must have known that on the previous day he had spoken words that would tip the scales of his pontificate, that established a program that was not only brave but also controversial. The very intonation with which he uttered the words had, however, testified to his deep conviction of this program's rightness. Not for nothing had he observed the Primate's program and actions for the twenty years he was a bishop. These two men, whom politicians of various stripes had tried to set at odds, thought and believed almost as one.

For Cardinal Wyszyński, the Pope's Marian statements must have been the high point of the visit. Called as a young man to the highest church dignity in his country, Cardinal Wyszyński had then been thrown into prison, where he entrusted everything to Mary. Not only did he recover his freedom; in spite of the ruling system, he managed to defend the Church's social and moral power. Then he lived to see the miracle of the Polish pope, which was an extraordinary force in strengthening the position of the Church throughout the Eastern bloc. It strengthened this position enough to produce a second miracle, with the Cardinal's active, forceful participation—the visit of the Roman Pope to a communist country. The Cardinal's attitude toward Mary had "checked out." It is understandable that he wanted the same thing for the Church in the other communist countries, and everywhere not completely free.

We could enumerate other examples of remarks by the Pope that reflect Cardinal Wyszyński's ideas. For example, when he spoke to the Episcopate on June 6, the Pope took a stand identical to the Cardinal's on church-state matters, relying on the engrafting of the Church into the nation and working toward an accord with the state on the condition that church rights were guaranteed.

Not only was the system of the church hierarchy written into the nation's history in the year 1000, but at the same time the history of the nation was providentially embedded in the structure of the Polish Church, which we owe to the Gniezno Congress [when the legate of Pope Sylvester II and Emperor Otto III established the metropolitan see at Gniezno, embracing the dioceses of Cracow, Wrocław, and Kołobrzeg]. This fact becomes apparent at various times in Polish history, especially at the most trying times. Then, lacking its own, native state structure, the overwhelmingly Catholic society found support in the hierarchical system of the Church. This helped it to survive the times of partition and occupation, to maintain and even to deepen the consciousness of its identity. This might seem an "atypical" situation to foreigners. Nonetheless, it has an unequivocal eloquence for Poles. It is simply part of the truth about the history of their own country.

Elsewhere, the Pope said that "true dialogue [with the rulers] must signify the complete respect of the convictions of believers, the complete security of their civil rights, and normal conditions of activity for the Church as a religious community to which the great majority of Poles belong." Even in Poland, therefore, the Pope spoke of the full normalization of church-state relations—but only on the conditions that Cardinal Wyszyński had always set. Unity with the nation thus remained the main premise. The Primate could hardly have dreamed that his program would find such support from the Apostolic See.

At his farewell to the Polish people on the Cracow Błonia, the Pope appealed to his countrymen and placed them under an obligation:

> As I depart, I ask you to accept once again all that spiritual heritage that is called "Poland" with faith, hope, and love —such love as Christ imparts to us at baptism—
>
> That you never despair, never grow weary, never become discouraged,
>
> That those roots from which we grow are never severed.
>
> I ask you:
>
> That you keep your faith despite each of your weaknesses, that you always seek spiritual strength in Him, where so many generations of our mothers and fathers have found it,
>
> That you never abandon Him,
>
> That you never lose that freedom of the spirit for which He has liberated man,
>
> That you never spurn that love that is greatest, that is

expressed by the cross, without which human life has no roots and no meaning.

I ask this of you

Through the remembrance and the powerful intercession of the Mother of God of Jasna Góra and all her sanctuaries on Polish soil;

Through the remembrance of Saint Wojciech, who died for Christ on the Baltic;

Through the remembrance of Saint Stanisław, who fell beneath the sword of the king on Skałka.

This I ask of you. Amen.

This fervent appeal to Poles, perhaps fully understandable only to those who know the history of our country well, set a great obligation before the present and future generations of our country. This appeal to keep the faith of the fathers, to maintain Christian culture in Poland, to preserve spiritual identity, is also an obligation for the Holy See and the Pope to support the Polish nation in its strivings against materialism and to preserve Christian piety. Thus Cardinal Wyszyński achieved more than he supposed. Was it possible to imagine that a Polish pope would come to communist Poland and beseech his countrymen to maintain their faith and national culture? A year—even a week—beforehand, everyone thought it impossible. I repeat: the Pope's words set a mutual obligation, binding on Polish society and also the Vatican, that will endure as long as Poland finds itself in its present situation. In the Pope's trip, Cardinal Wyszyński could see the reflection of his own work and his own spiritual presence.

We can say of Cardinal Wyszyński that Divine Providence prepared for few as much as it gave to him. All future generations of Poles will speak his name with reverence.

7

Irreplaceable to the End (1979-1981)

The Papal pilgrimage to Poland had lent great splendor to the Primate, but Wyszyński was not the sort of man to rest content with what had been accomplished. New, serious, and even dramatic problems were emerging; tempestuous events were approaching in Poland.

At the same time, Cardinal Wyszyński was realizing his next pastoral program, the preparations for celebrating the six hundredth anniversary of the arrival of the miraculous icon of Our Lady in Częstochowa. The program had begun in 1976, and each year had its own theme: reflections on the history of Jasna Góra and its radiant unifying power (1976); the recollection of the national vows, which were repeated at Jasna Góra and in all parishes on August 26 (1977); recollection of the Millennial dedication of Poland to Our Lady (1978); a return to the idea of the Helpers of the Mother of the Church (1979); the fulfillment of the papal program formulated during his visit (1980). The Primate called for the placing of crucifixes in all family homes. The sixth year, 1981, would be devoted to direct preparations for the jubilee in the form of examination of conscience, confession, and Holy Communion, to allow the faithful to celebrate the jubilee in a state of sanctifying grace. The Primate was not personally to see the program through to its end, but there was never any doubt that the anniversary would be celebrated according to his will.

On August 3, his birthday, the Primate reminded a gathering of priests:

When the Pope spoke to the young people from the balcony of the primate's residence in Gniezno, people from his entourage said, "Poland is a nation of great civility. This is obvious to the whole world from the behavior of young people and the crowds with which we have been meeting." This is largely due to the hard work and great efforts of the Church. Even though we are inclined as a nation to enthusiasm, we never lose our realism and feeling for facts. At a given moment, we know what we can do, what we cannot do, and what will have to wait.

Cardinal Wyszyński also discussed the misgivings among the people over the authorities' part in preparing for the papal visit, which had even included the building of the great cross in Warsaw. To such doubts, the Primate replied, "Are you afraid because our communist brothers built the cross in Victory Square? That is what it comes down to. Thanks be to God, they built it."

The papal visit increased devotion and strengthened people's moral attitudes. Thirty-eight thousand people made the 268th annual pilgrimage on foot from Warsaw to Częstochowa in August. This included four hundred priests and many students, including nine hundred from Italy. "As the Holy Father said on June 4, we owe everything to her. Her, too, we thank today, remembering 1920, when, through the Most Blessed Mother's support, Poland was able to preserve its freedom," Cardinal Wyszyński said at Jasna Góra on August 15, during a sermon titled "Time Is Love." His words were so poignant that the prayerful masses gathered around the monastery chanted "Time is love, time is love!"

Cardinal Wyszyński kept referring to the way the Pope's visit went on illuminating Polish realities. In his Mercy Week letter of October 1979, he wrote:

A good teacher leads his whole life in such a way that his enemies have nothing to accuse him of. Wanting to condemn Christ to death, they had to rely on lies. So it is today: the accusations against Christ and His Church are based mainly on lies and slanders, and even though the Church is run by people, it receives such strength from the light of the Holy Spirit that through the centuries it has been protected from evil and has constantly awakened in people a desire to rescue peoples and nations from the adversities of evil and sin.

The Primate added that during the Pope's visit, "throughout the nation the number of criminal offenses diminished to an unprecedented degree. The consumption of alcohol decreased by 25 to 35 percent. An atmosphere of religious dignity, seriousness, and sublimity reigned among great masses of people."

Besides pastoral work, the Primate had to carry out the normal tasks of governing the Church and regulating its relations with the state. The session of the Episcopate on December 13–14, 1979, made a sharply critical assessment of the socioeconomic situation, stressing the disorganization of life, the moral crisis, economic shortfalls, corruption, alcoholism, and all the other symptoms of social and moral evil. They also criticized the policy of advancing people on the basis of servility to official ideology, regardless of their competence. The bishops demanded full observance of the law. Each successive Episcopal communiqué now contained more admonishments and clearer warnings of the impending crisis.

Unexpectedly, a sharp and lamentable new wrangle between Church and state broke out just before Christmas, on

December 23. The government announced plans to cut the Jasna Góra monastery off from the city of Częstochowa by constructing an expressway. Not only would this hinder the access of pilgrims, but it would also threaten the priceless architecture of the cloisters with vibrations from traffic. It is hard to tell whether the plans came from the top, or whether they represented some local or other official's reaction to the state's recent levelheaded relations with the Church. Cardinal Wyszyński sent a team of bishops, led by Cardinal Macharski, to make an on-site inspection. After receiving their report, he replied by telegram in terms of unusual sharpness, calling the plans "barbarism for which there are no adequate words of indignation." He made his position public, and it was repeated by the international media. This influenced a change of plans. However, the affair dragged on for some time before it was satisfactorily resolved. On Christmas Eve, at his usual meeting with the priests of Warsaw, the Primate preached on the subject "A Voice of Truth for the Day." This sermon was notable because the Primate used it to reveal the existence of thirty volumes of his daily notes, called *pro memoria*, which will be an invaluable source for future biographers as well as for historians of the postwar Polish Church. The sermon also contained a new protest against the Częstochowa expressway. One after another, the Primate's protests had to be taken into account by the government in the midst of crisis.

Poland's predicament was growing worse, literally by the week, and perhaps even by the day. On January 6, the second anniversary of his famous Epiphany sermon, Cardinal Wyszyński joined sharp criticism of the situation in the country to his earlier statement of principles for the existence and activity of the Polish Church. This criticism, founded on moral premises, admonished the rulers that the current economic and social conditions could not go on indefinitely without, sooner or later, ending in catastrophe. It is frankly incredible that such warnings—also formulated, as we have seen, in personal discussions with the highest officials—brought no result and were ignored.

Nor did Cardinal Wyszyński confine his anxieties to strictly Polish matters. During the Jasna Góra appeal on January 10, moved by the signs of international tension, he called for peace and disarmament: he thought of obtaining grace not only for his own country, but for the whole world, through the intercession of Mary and the Son of God.

The Polish Church and its leader continued making pastoral capital of the Pope's visit. They published a document titled "The Polish Bishops Call for Responsibility and Prayers for the Brother Nations" on March 31, 1980. This document took up one of the Pope's major themes from the previous June— that we live among brother [Slavic] nations that also long for Christianity but have less access to its values than we enjoy.

Nothing was changing in the country except that the economy was deteriorating while political pressure increased tangibly. The next Episcopal conference, on May 6–7, again pointed to disturbing phenomena in social, cultural, economic, and political life. The Episcopate went beyond issuing warnings and advanced its own proposals for profound social and economic reform—proposals that corresponded to those being made by the lay opposition, reflecting the convictions of engineers, economists, technicians, and the whole Polish intelligentsia. Now, too, one could say that the voice of the Church was the voice of the nation. Unfortunately, that voice, like the voice of the nation, went unheeded. The nation was more and more the object, rather than the subject, of social life. Man was disregarded. It is therefore not surprising that the Episcopate again emphasized the growing problems when it met at Saint Anne's Mountain on June 27–28, days before the great social upheaval began. While pointing out society's woes, the bishops also complained of the "lack of fundamental progress in the normalization of relations between Church and state." The failure to resolve the most important social, economic, and church problems was about to lead to a deep convulsion.

We have mentioned the signs of improved relations with the state during the Gierek era. At the same time, there were upsetting facts to which the Episcopate had to react categorically. Thus, the Episcopate sent a letter to Premier Edward Babiuch on April 27, stating, among other things:

> Given the systematic limitation and prohibition of religious profession and practice and the attempts by state institutes to educate the young, including Catholics, in a spirit of lay ethics, and even contrary to human moral principles, the Polish Episcopate states that the educational program as carried out by state institutions is contrary to the laws of the Polish People's Republic, and particularly to article 80 of the constitution. . . . The creation of numerous occasions for the demoralization of youth must be condemned by any system of ethics in the civilized world as a danger to the spiritual development of young people.

The conditions prevalent in summer holiday camps justified such assertions. The Episcopate knew of incidents in which children who went to Mass or prayed were sentenced to kneel for two hours with their hands held above their heads. Activities were organized so as to leave the children no time to say their prayers. Children who prayed were ridiculed. Counselors and older youths drank alcohol together. Sexual freedom was allowed to go to great lengths. Worst of all were incidents of counselors' luring young girls to evening assignations.

There were other points of contention. On December 21, 1979, the Bureau of Religious Affairs had received a list of long-unsettled matters from the hierarchy. These had to do in large part with the persistent refusal to enlarge the print run of *Tygodnik Powszechny* and to reactivate the monthly *Rosary Circle*. There was also the matter of illegal and unjustified censoring of religious and theological texts. The bishops wanted to start a Polish edition of the theological review *Communio* and to settle the issue of the publications of the Catholic University of Lublin. Nor had the Libella property, most of which belonged to the Catholic Intellectuals' Club and the magazine *Więź,* been settled. Seminarians were still being drafted in some dioceses, Catholic lay activists were being refused passports, requests to build churches were being neglected, and cemetery property, such as the North Cemetery in Warsaw, was still in question. Once again the bishops protested against the four-shift system of labor in the coal mines. The world knows all about the Church's refusal to allow an expressway adjacent to the Jasna Góra monastery, but it is less well known that the bishops had to make similar interventions to prevent the erection of highways near the Gniezno and Łódź cathedrals.

Despite all these problems, Cardinal Wyszyński continued to work normally. On June 30 he invited a delegation of the German conference of bishops, who repaid the Polish bishops' visit of 1978. The German bishops arrived in September 1980.

* * *

The often repeated warnings and appeals of the Church, society, intellectuals, and experts had had no effect, so the inevitable happened: a powerful convulsion of social protest. It found expression in the wave of strikes that ended with the signing, on August 31, 1980, of the so-called social contract between workers and the government in Gdańsk, Szczecin, and Jastrzęb. This "social contract" provided for the establishment of independent, self-governing trade unions and acknowledged the right to strike. It dealt with such general matters as cultural freedom, humanistic studies, church freedom and access to the mass media, and the limitation of illegal censorship—in a word, with all of national life. Before the conclusion of the agreement and the consequent easing of tension, however, there were, according to informed parties, at least two moments when events seemed to be slipping out of Polish hands and to be in danger of provoking action from outside. The first such moment came during the strike in Lublin,* when the east-west rail lines were blocked in several places around the country. Fortunately, railroad workers managed to clear the tracks. The second dangerous moment came at the end of the strike on the Coast, when the workers won. In the last days of the strike the situation was very grave, and there was justified speculation that intervention might occur.

Before preaching his August 26 sermon in Częstochowa, Cardinal Wyszyński met first with Central Committee Secretary Stanisław Kania and then, at Kania's request, with party leader Gierek. The Cardinal told Kania that perhaps he owed Gierek the meeting, to give him "the comfort he needs." Wyszyński had already composed his sermon, however, and the two meetings had no influence on it. This controversial sermon was therefore not delivered under pressure, but as a result of the Primate's own concern about the threats to Poland. In it, he called for "national and civic maturity." At the same time, he pointed out that "atheizing propaganda has shaken the unity and cultural strength of our thousand-year-old nation." He developed this theme fully, charging that materialistic and atheistic monism, by rejecting the Christian roots of Polish national culture, had broken down the dynamics of society and labor and helped to bring on the crisis. This whole section was cut from the sermon when it was broadcast on television, an omission that gave rise to misunderstandings. The Primate had spoken of the evil social consequences of atheism, and called on society to overcome those consequences. Among other things, he appealed to the pilgrims to work. Some took this mistakenly as an appeal to the striking workers. The cuts and distortions of the sermon as televised increased the misunderstanding and anxiety. It must be pointed out that on the same day the Episcopal Steering Com-

---

*In July 1980, before labor stoppages began on the Coast, a regional strike, later settled by the local authorities, broke out in Lublin.

mittee, meeting under Cardinal Wyszyński's leadership, approved a communiqué that had been drafted some days earlier. This communiqué, which was in Cardinal Wyszyński's possession as he preached, stated that respect for the indispensable national rights, including the right to form labor unions, was a condition for social peace. The Episcopate based this assertion on remarks about the freedom of the labor movement from the Second Vatican Council. Juxtaposing the sermon and the communiqué leaves no doubts about the Church's true position, which favored the new phenomonon of free labor unions. At the same time, in view of Poland's international situation, the Episcopate appealed to society for prudence and social peace so as not to provoke outside interference.

Events moved quickly in the country. Obviously, the two months of social agitation and strikes would have to lead not only to changes at the highest levels of government but also, after the signing of the August agreements, to fundamental transformations of social, economic, and political life. It was not necessary to wait long.

The night meeting of the Sixth Plenum of the Central Committee on September 6 dismissed Edward Gierek as first secretary and named Stanisław Kania as his replacement. The highest party body also made other personnel changes, and continued to do so at its subsequent meetings.

Three days later, on the 9th, the Episcopal Steering Committee met at Jasna Góra to assess developments and their influence upon the Church's tasks. The committee again analyzed the causes of the crisis, expressed its support for the new labor unions, and called for the social peace that was required if Poles were to be left to settle their own problems. Unfortunately, the changes in the country were not happening quickly enough. Grateful for the Church's concern about social peace, the authorities were inclined toward a certain liberalization with regard to the Church. On September 24, 1980, the Joint Commission of Church and government representatives met—after not convening at all during the 1970s, despite that decade's improvements in church-state climate. Now the state authorities wanted to re-establish a permanent dialogue formally.

Soon after, on October 21, Cardinal Wyszyński discussed the tense situation in the country with First Secretary Kania. The social contract was not being realized. Local conflicts, degenerating into strikes, were paralyzing the normal functioning of the country. One of the problems that most worried Cardinal Wyszyński was the government's temporizing over the formal legal registration of the newly established independent, self-governing labor union, Solidarity. The Primate pointed out the need for quick action, and received assurances that it would be forthcoming. Two days later Cardinal Wyszyński left for Rome, where he wanted to discuss important church matters, including those of Poland, with Pope John Paul II. He entrusted the overseeing of the registration of Solidarity to Bishop Dąbrowski.

One of the key provisions of the Gdańsk agreement, which had not yet been realized, was the limitation of arbitrary censorship. On October 30, while Cardinal Wyszyński was in Rome, the Episcopate sent a lengthy letter on this matter to the new premier, Józef Pińkowski. The letter was signed by the vice-chairman of the Episcopate, Cardinal Macharski, and the assistant secretary, Father Alojzy Orszulik. This important document read, in part:

> The Church, respecting the freedom and dignity of the human being, opposes prior censorship by the state in principle. Such censorship should occur only in exceptional situations, resulting from special circumstances.
>
> Today everyone agrees that the present activities of the censor are doing and have done great harm to the nation and the state. It is worth recalling here the words of admonition spoken in the Warsaw Cathedral on January 6, 1978, when the Primate stated that social life demands openness and freedom of opinion. "That is why," he said, "greater alienation of public opinion, particularly through the excessive development of censorship under the pretext

of state secrets, must be avoided. In fact, this claps blinders on the people, disinforms them, and worst of all releases them from responsibility for the nation. Quite often people who do not know the truth do not know how matters really stand and, as a result, feel no responsibility for the state of social, moral, or economic life."

This quotation shows how the Church moved ahead of public opinion. It did so consistently, and when the state's obligations with regard to censorship were not met, the Episcopate stated in its October 30 communiqué that

the present policy on publishing and the powers and functioning of the Central Bureau for the Control of the Press, Publishing, and Performances [i.e., the censor] constitute glaring contradictions of one of the fundamental human rights—the right to truth. The negation of this right has led the Polish society and state to the edge of catastrophe.
    . . . The censor's present-day protection of the infallibility of the authorities and the inadmissability of making independent social initiatives public necessarily cause a negative reaction among the worthiest people and among those most sensitive to society's needs and most ready to act.

The Episcopate's document went further and pointed out the need to reform publishing policy generally.

Aside from the laws about censorship, there should be enacted in the immediate future corresponding laws about the press and publishing, which ought particularly to establish the following principles:
    a. All associations, trade unions, the Catholic Church, and other religious denominations have the right to set up freely their own periodicals and publishing houses;
    b. as long as it is not possible to buy paper without limitations, the allotment of paper should be carried out

in accordance with the real demands of readers as established by objective criteria, particularly on the basis of numbers of subscriptions and the opinion of responsible social bodies;

c. there should be no limitation of the length or press runs of publications printed on the paper that publishers have at their disposal;

d. paper bought for foreign currency or obtained from abroad may not be taxed;

e. limitations on the purchase, importation from abroad, and use of printing equipment by legally functioning institutions should be lifted;

f. the requirement that publishing schedules be approved by state organs may not be applied to publishers not financed by the state. In state-financed publishing houses, the approval of publishing schedules should have only a general nature, without interference in regard to particular titles, their volume, or the size of editions. There is no place for bans on particular areas of culture, themes, or authors.

Far from caring only about its own publishing, the Church thus expressed its concern for the needs of Polish culture in general. This also appeared in its demand that the organ of censorship be subordinated to the Sejm and be excluded from the government's administrative structure.

There were anxious moments while Cardinal Wyszyński was away in Rome. The judicial authorities refused the first attempt to register Solidarity, despite the earlier assurances to the Church. The Cardinal's closest colleagues intervened with the government, and he himself decided to return to the country on the day when the final decision was to be made, so that the possibility of his public protest would have to be taken into account. He returned on November 10 and received a Solidarity delegation led by Lech Wałęsa on the same day. That was also the day on which the Supreme Court finally registered Solidarity. The Primate spoke to the union delegation with great warmth, recalling his own prewar work in labor unions and wishing the new unionists many successes in their indispensable work. *Tygodnik Powszechny* published his remarks in full on November 23.

It was clear that his assistants, and in particular Bishop Bronisław Dąbrowski, had worked energetically in concert with the Cardinal on the registration of Solidarity. The registration created a climate in which the Joint Commission could meet, on November 20 and 21, then again on December 9. The Catholic Church received no special privileges at these meetings; in fact, it accomplished little more after August. The church-government meetings mainly concerned the general situation, particular steps that could be taken to ease the conflicts, the pressure of strikes, and the misunderstandings between Solidarity and the government. Even after they had formally and legally recognized it, the government representatives tended to ignore Solidarity. They could not bring themselves to accept that the union had close to ten million members and had become a major factor in social and political life. The Church did everything it could to drive this fact home while urging the government to ease numerous specific conflicts.

At the Episcopate's meeting on December 10 and 11, the bishops considered the general situation and called for an extensive renewal of national life. Everyone—in the party, the press, and the media—was talking about renewal. At the same time there was social stagnation, an indecisive government, and an active, strong conservative trend that wanted to stop reform in order to preserve its own privileges. In this situation, the Episcopate published a pastoral letter on December 14 under the title "The Polish Bishops Ask for Christian Responsibility for the Homeland." This letter was an important step toward overcoming stagnation and disposing the people and their rulers to a mutual dialogue that would lead to real reform.

A few days later, on December 16 and 17, representatives of the Church, the government, and Solidarity took part together in observances of the tenth anniversary of the tragic December events of 1970, in Gdańsk and Gdynia. This joint participation in unveiling monuments to the workers and dockers who had been shot was a great event and could have become the beginning of a national reconciliation. Some observers drew excessively far-reaching conclusions from it. They wanted to see signs of a historic compromise or of a coalition of the three great social forces in Poland. Such views embodied a certain misunderstanding. The idea of the "historical compromise," derived from Italy, postulated a compromise between communist and Christian Democratic political parties. But the Church did not strike compromises with political parties, because its own goals were religious and supernatural rather than political. The Church could come to understandings with temporal institutions in concrete matters and conclude accords with them. It acknowledged the state and "rendered unto Caesar," but it is difficult to speak of its entering into a historical compromise or coalition—especially with a Marxist state.

The Church had rigidly specified attitudes toward labor unions. Christian social teaching had always been based on the "auxiliary principle," according to which the highest social level—the state—ought not to replace or supersede the functioning of other communities, unions, or organizations at lower levels. If possible, these lower levels should execute their own social functions, within their abilities. On the basis of this principle, the Church did not just support the new labor unions but became in fact their chief ally. It did this on doctrinal grounds and in accordance with Christian social teaching, rather than as part of a political compromise or coalition. Thus there can really be no talk of a historical compromise in Poland.

On January 10, 1981, the Joint Commission met again and took up for the first time the fundamental question of how the secular nature of the Polish state could be reconciled with the ideological pluralism of society. The results of this important discussion have not been published.

On January 13, Lech Wałęsa and a Solidarity delegation arrived in Rome for a visit to the Pope. The situation in the country was still tense. A mass transit strike took place in Warsaw on January 16 and spread in the wake of sharp statements by First Secretary Kania, Central Committee Secretaries Grabski and Olszowski, and other party leaders. In the midst of the crisis, on January 19, Wałęsa returned from Rome and met with Cardinal Wyszyński and, later, with the premier. The main bones of contention were now free Saturdays and the registration of Rural Solidarity.* A day earlier, the National Committee of Solidarity had issued a suggestion from Gdańsk that all Saturdays be free of work except for workers who voluntarily agreed otherwise with the government. Then the union suggested that one Saturday a month be devoted to work. Instead of this idea's being accepted, there was another contest of strength. Representatives of the Solidarity National Committee met with Premier Pińkowski on the evening of January 21 without achieving an agreement. The government proposed a 42½-hour work week, while Solidarity wanted it an hour shorter. A warning strike was called in many places on the 22nd, and an all-day strike on Saturday the 24th. The government had to continue negotiating. The authorities also proposed the creation of a permanent joint commission to discuss and control systematically the realization of the Gdańsk accord and to examine the course of current events.

From today's perspective [June 1981], one can have doubts about the actions of Solidarity, which was principally concerned with free Saturdays and unleashed a wave of strikes all over the country while the economic situation was catastrophic and the nation badly needed stabilization. There is no way, on the other hand, to deny that society gave Solidarity its full support during these strikes. Because the people were irritated and fatigued by the government's tactics of delaying the introduction of reform and playing for time, the radical elements operating within Solidarity commanded obedience. This point bears emphasis, for it was the social allegiance to Solidarity that effected a transfor-

---

*As a result of the Solidarity movement of Lech Wałęsa, Polish farmers also founded their own Solidarity organization to promote their interests.

mation in government thinking. In the face of the growing protests, the authorities increasingly realized that it was necessary to reach a compromise and treat the new union as a partner.

On the afternoon of January 30, after a wave of strikes around the country, the government resumed negotiations with Solidarity. The main themes were the length of the work week, self-government for the peasants, and media access for Solidarity. The next day, at four in the morning, an understanding was reached on a forty-two-hour work week, along with an initial agreement about media access. The peasant question, left hanging, looked as if it would be answered in the negative. The next day, February 1, Wałęsa and Karol Modzelewski held a press conference at which they expressed their full support for Rural Solidarity.

* * *

On February 2, Cardinal Wyszyński preached an unusually important sermon in Gniezno. Having recognized an independent, self-governing trade union in the cities, the authorities did not want to hear anything about a similar organization in the villages. The authorities did not want to understand that family farms were the most productive form of agriculture any more than they wanted to understand that there was nothing about the family farm, on which all members shared in the work, that contradicted the existing system in Poland. Thus, while the authorities still opposed the farmers' union, Cardinal Wyszyński spoke in its favor on February 2. "If industrial workers have gained the right to associate," he said in his sermon, "truth demands that the same right be allowed to farm workers." Four days later, the Primate met with delegations of both industrial Solidarity, including Lech Wałęsa, and of a delegation from Rural Solidarity. He gave his full support to the farmers who had come to hear him in Warsaw and stressed the naturalness of the right to association. This meant that the right to associate was inalienable; no political authority could deprive people of it. Cardinal Wyszyński warned against attempts to undermine natural rights, but at the same time he cautioned the farmers and the unionists against the possibility that outsiders would try to influence their movement for political ends.

I want to return to the February 2 sermon at Gniezno, where Cardinal Wyszyński stated categorically:

This right [to associate] does not need to be "granted"— it simply exists, and no one can deny it. It is one natural right that applies in the same way to everyone, regardless of whether he works in a factory, in a mine, or on a farm. All have the same natural right to organize their strength and efforts to meet the common tasks that man must accomplish. Above and beyond this, it is also an individual right of the most personal kind. . . . Thus this delay in granting to farmers the right of association that they want is unwise. More—it is contrary to the natural and fitting rights of those great providers for our nation, the farming population.

It was characteristic of Cardinal Wyszyński to speak out repeatedly for the farmers. On February 6, he told them that months earlier he had sent a letter to the state authorities in defense of people who were being evicted from their land in Kampinos and Płudy.* He said that he knew the same thing was going on elsewhere.

Bishop Dąbrowski, as secretary of the Episcopate, is a witness to the numerous memoranda that the Episcopate has sent to the authorities over forced evictions. In the discussions that the Bishop has often conducted on behalf of the Episcopate with the state and political authorities, this theme continually arises. We have just created a spe-

*Villages in the area about twelve miles north of Warsaw.

cial pastoral commission for industrial workers, and we are considering doing the same for agricultural workers, especially those on the collective farms. Beyond that, we will talk about this issue from the pulpit, and we will talk about it with the party. I will talk to everyone, with the first secretary and the premier if need be. I say this so that you will know, brothers, that this problem in which you have such a lively and appropriate interest is also a problem very close to the Polish Episcopate. . . . You have all the right in the world to demand an organization that will meet your needs. That is my position, which I have expressed more than once. . . . It would be superfluous for me to say any more about it today, because the position of the Primate of Poland on this matter is known.

This same speech dealt with the existing political and social tensions and the Primate's fears that matters would slip through Polish fingers and be settled by outsiders.

I have just been saying to Mr. Wałęsa and the delegation from Bielsko-Biała that the movement for social and moral renewal that has arisen here is eminently Polish. This movement must above all serve Polish interests, which means the people of Poland. It must meet their needs, whether they are farmers or laborers. There must be caution, to avoid entangling yourselves with people who work from other assumptions and want to introduce non-Polish issues. It is impossible to mention names here. These people count on dragging Poland into some sort of political situation, while your movement is above all a social and a labor movement. Remember this for a long time, my dearest ones, because this social-labor work will finally strengthen your movement. For now you must take up the farm people and their needs, for better or for worse. You must try to organize as many farm workers as possible to work the land that has been given to you, to your families, to the people and to the homeland.

I have cited such a long passage because it expresses the wider problems that remained unsolved. The Church tried to represent the current of judiciousness and responsibility so that reform could be assured without running the risk of outside intervention. The Primate's misgivings on the latter count were so strong that he took a polemic stand that pained the radicals he criticized. But he felt deeply that excessive radicalism was both dangerous to the nation and harmful to labor-union affairs. To the many questions this emphasis aroused, there can be but one answer: Cardinal Wyszyński discriminated the overriding national interest from the particular interests of the political groups that were springing up on the fringes of Solidarity.

Rural Solidarity had become the major issue in January. On the 10th, Stanisław Kania decisively rejected the idea of a free farmers' union. It was this stance, maintained throughout January, that had led Cardinal Wyszyński to speak out early in February. On all matters of fundamental national importance he took an unyielding stand. On all secondary issues, however, he favored compromise. The Church and Solidarity worked together harmoniously; the government found itself in a corner when Solidarity called for a farmers' union on February 1 and the Church did the same the next day. Although the Church had clearly supported first industrial and then Rural Solidarity, it came under attack from radical critics. The foreign press echoed these criticisms. I believe that this criticism was unjustified, since the Church closely united the two threads of support for those who were struggling to win social self-determination and of caution against foreign intervention. It is impossible to disagree with the Primate's assertion that special political interests were at work in the union movement. Of course, one could ask whether any movement as massive as Solidarity could remain free of political influences. But although Cardinal Wyszyński never called these interests by name, he criticized them decisively.

The unity of Solidarity, the Church, and the people finally compelled the party to revise its policy. During the Eighth

Plenum of the Central Committee, on February 9, Premier Pińkowski became the sacrificial goat for having delayed necessary decisions for so long, and lost his job. General Wojciech Jaruzelski, the minister of defense, became the new premier. Members of the party leadership attacked KSS-KOR for radicalizing Solidarity, but the truth was more complex—a strong wave of radicalism was sweeping the workers, especially the younger ones.

On February 10 the Supreme Court ruled that farmers had the right to organize, but not to form a labor union. Despite the change of premiers, the government was sticking to a position it could not defend against the feelings of Solidarity, the Church, and society. That day, Cardinal Wyszyński had a discussion with First Secretary Kania but they disagreed on the subject of Rural Solidarity and the usual communiqué was not issued. On February 11 the Sejm formally named General Jaruzelski as premier and Mieczysław F. Rakowski as one of the vice-premiers. The next day, while the Solidarity National Committee was meeting in Gdańsk, Premier Jaruzelski asked the Sejm for ninety days of calm and warned against "a fratricidal conflict." Solidarity decided to suspend a printers' strike and left the door open for talks with the authorities. This was the first sign of a thaw and of the ascendancy of moderation and thoughtfulness in public opinion. A week after the nomination of the new premier, an agreement was concluded that created an Independent Students' Association. The authorities also signed an agreement with striking farmers in Rzeszów and Ustrzyki Dolne that guaranteed their property rights but put off the question of a farmers' union. Then the next conflict erupted. On March 19 an incident took place during a meeting of the local council at the United People's Party in Bydgoszcz, where a sit-in by private farmers had been under way. The militia ejected Solidarity representatives who had been invited to the meeting, and three unionists were badly injured and taken to the hospital. The next day a nationwide warning strike was proclaimed, and on Sunday the 25th, Wałęsa and Rakowski tried without result to settle the crisis. There was a real danger of a general strike, which the Church did all it could to avert. Such a strike would certainly be met with force and involve outside intervention in consequence.

Signs of progress appeared in successive negotiating sessions on March 27 and 28. The Ninth Plenum of the Central Committee, on March 29, announced itself in favor of an accord with Solidarity, under strong pressure from the party grass roots. Thus began the "horizontal structure" movement in which such party figures as Stefan Bratkowski called for authentic respect of social self-government. On March 30 the Rakowski-Wałęsa commission reached an agreement, and the next day Solidarity called off the strike.

At the beginning of April the Western media were insistently reporting on Soviet preparations for an invasion of Poland. This time the main reason was to be the erosion of the party as evinced in the Ninth Plenum.

Although Cardinal Wyszyński's health began to fail in mid-March, he followed developments with uneasy interest. The Episcopate, which met on March 11, sent the clergy a message (made public on the 23rd) that included both suggestions to the authorities and warnings to society. "The effort to broaden the limits of justice and social freedom," the bishops wrote, "is moral and justified."

> Work to spread the principle of healthy social order, the defense of individual rights, and especially those of working people, has been the concern of the Church not only today but from the first years of the new phase of Polish history. Some fail to remember that when all fell silent under the pressure of political terror, only the Church did not back down, and that for their bravery its bishops and priests paid the price of imprisonment, removal from spiritual posts, and heavy fines. The Church, the Episcopate, the bishops have stood in defense of people who were repressed and wronged by the authorities in different periods of social tension in our country. It suffices to recall 1968, 1970, and 1976. On these issues the Church has

spoken out publicly and directed letters and memoranda to the authorities. It has provided help, including material help, in various forms—such as the church collections taken up in 1971 for the families of workers who had perished on the Coast. . . .

All . . . the wrongs that have befallen the nation and its consciousness will not be righted today or tomorrow. Such is life: soil that has gone sour demands long cultivation. In Poland there are a great many forces, enterprises, and institutions that want the best, and as soon as possible.

But this also requires deliberation and the concerted action of all national, moral, social, and official forces acting honorably and to a single end—to do the best, without creating new wrongs and losses for the nation.

While supporting all forms of self-determination in the spirit of Catholic social teaching, the bishops wrote that "Priests and clergy, who have a fundamental and vast religious and pastoral task, should not associate their priestly work with political causes, because the Polish Church has never in its history made itself dependent on any of the political or pseudo-political groupings that have been established and never yielded itself to serving them." The ideas and the style here seem to belong to Cardinal Wyszyński, who favored social renewal with all his heart but did not wish to see the clergy tied to even the noblest of political groups.

The same March 11 Episcopal conference approved a pastoral letter, to be read on April 26, in which the bishops clearly limned the iniquities of Polish life:

Whatever served the system or certain persons was called moral, and whatever bothered them was called immoral or evil. In this way morality was made a slave to people and the system. . . . Words lost their value. Untruth reigned in the means of social communication, falsified information, the truth passed over in silence, perverse commentaries given. Everyone said that the press lies, the radio lies, the television lies, school lies. Until in the end the lies turned back on the liars.

The bishops also stirred the consciences of the faithful:

Many people gave in to intimidation. Fear commanded them to fall silent, not to stigmatize evil, not to stand in defense of the good. Fear did not allow many people to go to church, to receive the sacraments, to enter Catholic marriages, to baptize their children and send them to cate-chism. . . . Some affected unbelief, some disowned their faith publicly. They feared censure and the loss of good positions.

Although they called for moderation in a tense situation, the bishops were maintaining their unequivocal stance on matters of principle. Cardinal Wyszyński's illness was beginning as this letter was edited, and by the time it was read his condition was grave. All the time, however, he kept his finger on the worrisome pulse of events.

Controversy broke out in Solidarity over the Wałęsa-Rakowski agreement that prevented the general strike. It was not a controversy over substantive matters, but over the right of negotiators to enter into agreements. The party was also full of differing assessments of the political situation. At this point the main national issues were the setting of a date for a party congress, the registration of Rural Solidarity, and the clarifica-tion of the Bydgoszcz beating. The Solidarity National Com-mittee decided to hold negotiations with the government on April 9, demanding that the discussions be broadcast, an un-realistic suggestion that testified to the influence of the radical wing in the union. On April 10, Premier Jaruzelski dropped a bombshell by demanding two months without strikes from the Sejm. The legislature passed a nonbinding resolution to that effect. The Solidarity National Committee reacted negatively in principle but did nothing to escalate tensions. The party "grass roots," the horizontal-structure exponents, demanded reform at an April 18 assembly in Toruń. Now ferment within the party itself seemed to be the main political problem, though there were other trouble spots as well. Farmers began a sit-in at a building in Inowrocław. Professor Szczepański, the head of a special Sejm commission, announced that the legislature would append to the labor-union law a paragraph permitting the formation of a private farmers' union. Thus the government finally changed its course, a month and a half after Cardinal Wyszyński had taken a categorical stand on the issue. The government and Rural Solidarity signed an understanding in Bydgoszcz on April 17, and on May 12, after the Sejm had acted, the Independent Self-Governing Labor Union of Private Farmers was legally registered.

Unfortunately, social peace was still not assured. And shattering news would soon come: an attack on the life of Pope John Paul II occurred in Rome on May 13, the same day that a communiqué about Cardinal Wyszyński's deteriorating health was released. Before relating the events of May, however, I must return to the affairs of the Church, which as usual were being managed by Cardinal Wyszyński. On February 10 the Episcopal Steering Committee had stated, "The use of force, pressures, threats, and galling propaganda will not lead to domestic peace; on the contrary, they give rise to new tensions and forms of protest." The bishops also used that meeting to call again for the guarantee of private farmers' property rights and right to organize. On March 2 the Joint Commission met to discuss the Church's access to the media, the censorship of religious publications, and the social tensions in the country. The March 11–12 Episcopal conference considered the Church's tasks in the face of a delicate and besieged situation. Besides the documents that we have already cited, the Episcopate publicized its concern for the freedom and sovereignty of the country—a response to the growing conviction at home and abroad that events in Poland could lead to intervention from outside.

Once again the Church gave its full support to the union movement, and especially the private farmers. Its com-

muniqués appealed for careful action so that Poles could overcome the crisis with their own efforts. The shared desideratum
of the Primate and the bishops was the same: to help society
in its struggle for self-determination while preserving social
peace and stabilizing the situation on the safe side of the limits
that would lead to intervention if crossed. During the radio
Mass on March 22, "The Primate's Words" were read. The
message appealed to the nation for "calm, poise, and responsibility," and to the government for "respect for the physical and
moral integrity of each citizen."

Such appeals bore a close and clear relation to the beatings
of unionists in Bydgoszcz and the subsequent threat of a general strike. While urging calm, Cardinal Wyszyński asked the
government not to resort to the unlawful exercise of authority.
On March 26, during the period of high tension, the ailing
primate discussed ways out of the crisis with Premier Jaruzelski. Once the threat of a general strike passed, the authorities
thanked Pope John Paul II,* Cardinal Wyszyński, and the
Episcopate for helping to bring about a peaceful solution. The
government highly valued the Church's influence with Solidarity and particularly appreciated Cardinal Wyszyński's persuasion, since he was the only authority almost universally
respected by society. Only the radical elements who had favored the general strike had failed to consider the danger from
outside.

On April 2, Cardinal Wyszyński received the presidium of
the national committee that was setting up Rural Solidarity. In
his remarks he again expressed support of the unionists. At
Easter a year earlier, the Primate had spoken of Christian hope
for life: that it would not stop at death, but keep renewing
itself. Those words became particularly moving for those who
knew how ill Cardinal Wyszyński was. Soon the publication
of communiqués on his health would begin.

---

*Specifically, for sending Premier Jaruzelski a telegram at the height of the March
crisis exhorting the people and the authorities to negotiate and preserve social peace.

* * *

As I have mentioned, it was obvious from the middle of March that Cardinal Wyszyński was being consumed by a serious illness. The course of the disease led the Primate's secretariat to issue a communiqué on April 15 that spoke of an illness of the alimentary canal and asked for prayers in Cardinal Wyszyński's intention. The next communiqué came from the Episcopal secretariat, on April 26; it mentioned that the Primate was continuing to receive medical care at his home, and again asked the faithful to pray for the Cardinal's health. The Primate had wanted very much to attend religious observances in Gniezno in honor of Saint Wojciech on April 23, and to go on to Częstochowa on May 3, but his increasing physical weakness made these pastoral journeys impossible. During the celebrations of Mary, Queen of Poland, on May 3, 1981, the bishops gave the archepiscopal blessing to the faithful at Jasna Góra, and the ailing Cardinal Wyszyński pronounced the blessing at the same time from the archbishop's residence in Warsaw. On May 14 a communiqué on the Cardinal's health, signed by a team of eminent physicians, was published, stating:

> In the course of diagnosis it has been established that the illness involves the organs of the pit of the stomach and the lymphatic system. The diagnosis has been established on the basis of clinical and laboratory tests conducted with the participation of specialists. Pharmaceutical means are being used to treat the primary illness and to strengthen the organism. The consulting specialists have stated that, in spite of the treatment, the disease has a progressive character. The Primate's condition is grave.

It did not take a doctor to conclude from this communiqué exactly what the illness was, or that it was beyond treatment. Society reacted to the communiqué with despondency. The attack on the Pope had occurred in Rome the day before, and the people were literally in shock. Prayers for the Pope and the

Primate were being said everywhere in Poland. During a solemn Mass in Warsaw, "The Primate's Words" were played from a tape recording.

Today there is only one thing for us to do. We must try to add all our personal sufferings and afflictions to this great anguish of the world. Certainly the Holy Father thinks of and experiences it thus, so that his personal anguish can be enfolded in the hands of the Mother of the Church, to whom he entrusted himself at Jasna Góra. This is his greatest work. In contrast to this great work our personal sufferings become minuscule. That is why, my dearest ones, stricken at present with my various physical ailments, I must regard them as modest and small in comparison with those that have struck the head of the Church.

As he spoke, the Primate was facing death, and he knew well where he stood. He appealed again for his guiding idea of entrusting everything to Mary. Few people could show such fortitude and spiritual integrity at the approach of their own death. Along with the entire Polish nation, the Primate followed the successful postoperative treatment of the Holy Father. On May 18 he sent the following telegram to the Pope:

Beloved Holy Father, hearing your *Urbi et Orbi* blessing on your birthday is a great hope for the human family, for the country, the bishops, the clergy, and the nation that is praying in the churches for your health. And yet the words of truth, love, peace, and hope for a better future cannot be brought to a conclusion because the Lord's discourse lasts forever. It is in vain to protest against the little obstacles. From Poland we send you these wishes, submitting your life to the Jasna Góra Mother of the Church, as you yourself have entrusted it along with us. United with you in your trial, the Episcopate and the Primate of Poland, Stefan Cardinal Wyszyński.

Cardinal Wyszyński had again demonstrated his personal heroism by writing of hopes for a future that he knew would not be his. These words become the more striking when contrasted to two communiqués issued a day earlier:

On Sunday, May 17, the Polish Press Agency received a communiqué from the secretariat of the Primate of Poland.

There have been no important changes in the health of the Primate of Poland in the course of the last days. A disturbance in the action of the heart was noted on May 14 and quickly responded to treatment.

By his express wish, the Primate is still being cared for at his home by a team of specialists. The conditions for intensive care and monitoring of the Primate's illness and for constant observation by physicians have been established.

While the secretariat of the Primate of Poland expresses warm thanks for all forms of medical help, the Primate is making use exclusively of the therapy provided by the team of attending physicians.

Another communiqué was published the same day:

The Polish Press Agency received the following communiqué from the secretariat of the Primate of Poland:

On Saturday, May 16, 1981, His Eminence Cardinal Stefan Wyszyński, Primate of Poland, Archbishop of Gniezno and Warsaw, received the Sacrament of the Sick in solemn form in his Warsaw residence. His personal confessor, Father Edmund Boniewicz, Pallotine, administered the sacrament. . . . [Cardinal Wyszyński's long-time associates Bishops Dąbrowski and Modzelewski and Monsignor Goździewicz were among those present.] After receiving the sacrament, His Eminence spoke to those who were with him. He first made a public profession of his faith, then entrusted the Church to the particular protection of the Blessed Mother of Częstochowa, thanked those present for their many years of cooperation, and gave them his blessing.

Cardinal Wyszyński was preparing for the end with the great dignity and calm that result only from deep faith. On May 22 he presided at the opening of a meeting of the Episcopal Steering Committee. He thanked the members for their cooperation. Then he turned the meeting over to Cardinal Franciszek Macharski, who reported on his visit to the Holy Father in Rome. The steering committee discussed the participation of a twenty-man delegation from the Polish Episcopate to a world assembly of episcopal representatives called by Pope John Paul II. The assembly was to take place in Rome on the Feast of the Descent of the Holy Spirit, on the sixteen hundredth anniversary of the First Council of Constantinople and the 1550th anniversary of the Council of Ephesus. The bishops also discussed relations with the government, concentrating on the Caritas issue, the Church's access to the media, and the building of churches.

The next communiqué on the Cardinal's health was published on May 23:

> Since the doctors' communiqué of May 14, the state of His Eminence the Primate's health has worsened.
>
> Transitory disturbances of circulation and respiration, which responded to treatment, were noted on May 14 and 21. Besides pharmacological treatment, several transfusions of blood, plasma, and albumin have been performed.
>
> On his further express wish, His Eminence remains at his residence. The conditions for intensive medical care have been created there, and modern equipment is being used. Specialist physicians are present around the clock.
>
> Clinical observations and the results of laboratory tests indicate the further progress of the primary disease.
>
> The condition of His Eminence the Cardinal Primate is very grave.

The direct threat to the Primate's life was unfortunately obvious, and the Polish Church continued to pray.

Until he had realized the extent of his illness, Cardinal Wyszyński had longed to go to Rome on June 7 in connection with the anniversaries of the two great councils. To speak with the Holy Father was perhaps one of his last fervent wishes. These hopes had been dashed by the almost simultaneous attack on the Pope and the drastic worsening of his own health. As he recovered from his operation, Pope John Paul was informed about the hopelessness of Cardinal Wyszyński's condition. He knew how much the Primate wanted to see him. The Pope placed a call to the Primate from the Gemelli Clinic on May 24. The conversation never took place, however, because the telephone cord did not reach to the Primate's bed. This must have been a painful stroke for the Cardinal: a symbolic thread linking his life with the outside world, with the Apostolic See, had been snapped.

Naturally, technicians were called to lengthen the cord, and the Pope called again the next day, May 25. Cardinal Wyszyński wished the Holy Father a speedy recovery. Although both conversants knew the truth, the Pope could convey to the Primate only words of religious comfort, expressions of love, of fellowship in suffering and prayer, his best wishes, and the apostolic blessing. The drama of these conversations—the first, which did not take place, and the second, in which the two great hierarchs wanted to say so much and yet were unable to say it—is difficult to imagine. How many sentiments must have penetrated the hearts and minds of the Pope and the Primate during this brief conversation, when they both knew that they would not see each other again! There is reason to believe, however, that the Primate had already shared his thoughts with the Pope in a special document. We also know that the Primate was aware that a very difficult spell lay ahead for the country and, not wanting to constrain him in any way, he entrusted the affairs of the Polish Church into the Holy Father's hands.

The next day, May 26, the physicians stated in a communiqué that the Primate's health had worsened that morning and was critical.

What was approaching was inevitable, and yet it would be a shock to a society that had grown accustomed to thinking that the ailing Primate would go on working, that until the end he would be interested in the country's difficulties, signing documents and making church decisions.

Many of those who revered and respected Cardinal Wyszyński somehow trusted in his spiritual strength to triumph again, as it had already triumphed over a sickly and frail constitution. His departure, although expected, was thus a thunderbolt out of a clear sky, a great shock to all of Polish society.

At 4:40 in the morning of May 28, 1981, the Feast of the Ascension, Stefan Cardinal Wyszyński, Archbishop Metropolitan of Gniezno and Warsaw, Primate of Poland, head of the conference of bishops, returned to God. The physicians' communiqué stated that the cause of death was "the spreading of a tumor of exceptional malignancy and rapid progress in the pit of the stomach."

* * *

The Cardinal died two months and six days before his eightieth birthday. He had been a priest for fifty-seven years, a bishop for thirty-five, Archbishop of Gniezno and Warsaw and Primate of Poland for thirty-two, and a member of the College of Cardinals for twenty-eight. His life had been so rich in events, it fell in such tempestuous times, and the Primate had been such an atypical and great personality, that there is no way to attempt a full and synthetic appraisal of his character. He was a man of unusual spiritual integrity. Each of his ideas, acts, decisions, even his gestures and his style seemed to characterize his whole personality. In a most admirable way he managed to join the majesty of the Roman Church, the dignity and pride of a Polish statesman, harsh demands upon himself, frank protest or censure of everything he deemed improper, with an open heart, good humor, and love for the people with whom his life brought him into contact. His respect for man and readiness to listen attentively, his skill at forgiving and forgetting the evils of the past, his desire to understand the motives and mentality of his persecutors—these are only a few of his traits. He held each person in reverence. I have seen him kiss the hands of the chaplain who served him at Mass, in thanks for participation in the offering of the Eucharist. He never remained seated when a woman was standing. Raised to the summit of the social order, he retained complete simplicity. He never forgot his parents, but visited their graves and his native village. He was responsive to the little ones of the world. Thoroughly educated, he still remained close to the people and knew how to win them to the Church. In everything that he wrote he was first of all a pastor. Without creating any new directions in theology, he charted a pastoral program and course that led to victory for the Church. This victory came through his motto: *Soli Deo—Per Mariam.* He always thought in historical terms and drew on the most enduring traditions of his nation. John Paul II himself said that without the Primate, there would have been no Polish pope. The Holy Father called him "the Primate of the Millennium," which means not only that he created the program in celebration of the Millennium, but also that he was one of the greatest Polish church figures of ten centuries.

Throughout his life, the Primate remained faithful to the traditions of his youth, in which the defense of religion and of Polishness made up a single absolute imperative. Yet while remaining a traditionalist, he met all the demands of modernity. He took seriously the words of one of his teachers who, sensing the times to come, said that priests "would have spikes driven through their tonsures." Ready for such an eventuality, educated in the principle that martyrdom, especially for a bishop or a cardinal, is a clear obligation, he remained a flexible and acute observer of social transformation and the nuances of intellectual development. He was one of the first in Poland to discern the possibility of evolution in the communist system.

He could make himself understood by communist leaders of such various dimension and stamp as Bolesław Bierut, Władysław Gomułka, and Edward Gierek. After one conversation in Komańcza he sensed the gulf between the mentalities of Zenon Kliszko and Władysław Bieńkowski. As a Catholic sociologist he saw the ideological impracticality of Marxist materialism and the inevitability of social reform with equal clarity. He loved Rome and the Vatican, but the Western world was fundamentally foreign to him, distant because of its practical materialism. He believed in the third road and somewhat messianistically dreamed of its realization in Poland. That is why he became such a fervent ally of independent labor unions, and especially of the union of private farmers. But his program went beyond Poland. He forced the acknowledgment of the Blessed Mother as the Mother of the Church through the council, and arranged for John Paul II to place the world and the Church under her protection.

In relation to the Marxist ideological state, he adopted a twofold line. Aware that it would not vanish from one day to the next, he tried to regard it as a normal "Caesar," to whom one renders what is Caesar's. He negotiated with all the leaderships, but opposed them decisively when they began to break the law. For this he was imprisoned. Yet as soon as the signs of evolution that he had expected appeared, he facilitated it and reached out his hand in concord, though he never compromised his principles. He created a course of action in the face of the system. Cardinal Wyszyński never allowed himself to be provoked into a conflict that he did not want, and he never entered into an agreement that would have been a capitulation. He never let the initiative pass entirely to the other side, because he always had his church program and considerations for the national interest. He was a great statesman, and it is hard to imitate the great.

This does not mean that his policies cannot be continued. As long as conditions in Poland do not change and the ideological state endures, simultaneous opposition and efforts at understanding are the only rational road. But things changed irreversibly in 1980. There may be temporary retreats, but a full return to the earlier conditions is unimaginable. That is why the continuation of the Cardinal's line must be creative. The new elements that change realities must constantly be taken into consideration. Before his death he foresaw great shocks and difficulties, but until the end he believed in the victory of the Church and of Poland.

Society and the Church itself are certainly changing. Cardinal Wyszyński's pastoral art lay in the ability to ensure the triumph of mass Catholicism and popular piety in a society that was becoming urban and industrialized, and to correlate that religiosity with the spirit and decisions of Vatican II. A man formed in the provincial, patriarchal society of the early twentieth century, Cardinal Wyszyński knew how to preserve those older values in modern civilization. Yet his undoubted traditionalism cannot be identified with conservatism. In general, Cardinal Wyszyński does not fit into the categories of right and left, progressive and conservative. In the West he passed for a conservative—but what sort of conservative would begin his work among labor unions, astonish the world by participating in the first understanding between an episcopate and a communist government, and eventually rescue the communist state at moments of crisis, for the good of the nation?

The Primate did remain wary of Western theological currents. For years he guarded the Polish Church like a besieged fortress. Marxism was always foreign to him, but the idea of democratic socialism stirred his interest. Even in his last testament he felt obliged to write about the need for social reform. Personally, I regret only that he never managed to answer Leszek Kołakowski's question: was he against the system because it was atheist, or because it was not pluralistic? In any case, he rejected totalitarianism of all stripes and colorations throughout his life. It is therefore difficult to suspect him of Catholic monopolism or antipluralism. Instead, it was his role as Christian and bishop to witness and preach the Gospel, which he did throughout his life.

In his last testament, Cardinal Wyszyński expressed his allegiance and gratitude to the three very different popes—Pius XII, John XXIII, and Paul VI—during whose pontificates he led the Polish Church. He was able to make himself understood by, and even to win the respect and love of, all three. This does not mean that he never encountered painful difficulties in the Vatican. But after the sensation over the accord with a communist government, and then the accusations of opposing a wider dialogue and *modus vivendi* with the Eastern bloc, there finally came the recognition that he had been right and had judged the relations of Church and state accurately and soberly at each stage. He introduced each resolution of the council into Poland through his own pastoral program. Again, he eludes categories. His dimensions, I think, were greater than any categories. Greatness is difficult to define and classify.

What he left behind is a measure of his greatness. For three days and nights after his death, the streets of Warsaw were full, in pouring rain, of kilometers-long lines of the faithful from the capital and all over the country who wanted to file past the coffin and pay brief, final homage to their beloved shepherd. Innumerable crowds of the faithful took part in his funeral on May 31, 1981. The Pope himself was absent only because he had not yet recovered from the attempt on his life. Cardinal Agostino Casaroli, secretary of State of the Holy See, preached and celebrated the funeral Mass in Polish. Cardinal Franciszek Macharski read a moving message in which the Holy Father had written that he would yet find an occasion to pay his respects in person. Then Cardinal Macharski, the metropolitan of Cracow, spoke for himself, in what was to me one of the most moving moments of the funeral solemnities. The Cardinal spoke loudly, emphatically, and distinctly, but his voice kept breaking from emotion. With people around him crying and tears in his own eyes, the Cardinal proclaimed aloud that we need not hide our tears. The most important tribute was the one that Cardinal Macharski paid to the people of the capital and of Poland. He said that after the death of the Primate, Poles were showing the kind of values that could gather and unite them. This was a great truth. The deceased primate had united and gathered the nation around the Church. Abnormal living conditions, wretchedness, and the demoralization born of a flawed economic system were obscuring the everyday spiritual life of Poland. At the moment of the Primate's death, at moments of social and national crisis, a deeper layer of the national consciousness, its lasting adherence to Christian values, emerged. The Cardinal of Cracow thanked the whole nation for this, and his words left a deep impression. They will bear fruit in our social, national, and religious consciousness.

At the end of the obsequies in the Basilica of Saint John, Jerzy Modzelewski, the friend and auxiliary bishop of the late Primate, read fragments of the spiritual testament that Cardinal Wyszyński had composed in 1969. The Primate gave posterity an account of his struggle with atheism, with false brothers and mistaken state policies. He forgave all, including those who had attacked and imprisoned him. This testament had been written in one of the most difficult periods of the Primate's life, and twelve years later it had primarily a historical significance.

The Primate's experiences of the last twelve years had been completely new and startling. First, his greatness had been acknowledged universally, even by his adversaries and the rulers of Poland. Next, the Primate had had to play the role of arbiter in the dramatic conflicts that swept the country, supporting the renewal and the free union movement, while striving to prevent the changes from crossing the border of reason and moderation. He told the Solidarity activists that they should not try for everything at once, but should instead begin by consolidating their impressive achievements.

In some circles, this is regarded as too little. Some people criticize the Primate's sermon of August 26, 1980, without always remembering that on the same day the Episcopate approved, and on the next day publicized, a resolution in complete support of the establishment of free labor unions. The Cardinal and his associates certainly played a colossal role in the registration of Solidarity and Rural Solidarity. I will not elaborate here on the Primate's role in freeing members of the opposition from prison in 1977 and 1981, or his other acts of help to democratic circles.

The Primate based his sympathy for the liberation movements in Poland on the faith in the resistance of the people, first of all. He was not inaccurate in remarking that the intellectuals showed too great an inclination to compromise. The Letter of Thirty-four in 1964, the Jasienica affair, and the years 1968 and 1976 changed this. The Primate observed the "revolt of the intellectuals" and the entry of the young working class into the political arena with great interest, but he always insisted on the Church's independence of politics and politicians. This gave rise to some misunderstandings and controversies, particularly in view of the different strategies of a thousand-year-old Church and of democratic movements that had come into being only recently and had nothing but their own fortunes to put at risk. It must be understood that for historical reasons, and because of the position and strength of Polish Catholicism, every public act of a primate can have consequences for the whole Church and nation.

The Primate was an enthusiast of grass-roots, autonomous initiatives. He stressed that politics is the business of laity, and not of the Church. He had not the least inclination to monopolize public life for the Church and for Catholics. Although he became a statesman in fact, he always intended first of all to be a pastor. He supported the establishment of a Christian-social orientation in Poland, but he did not think that the time for a Catholic political party had come. In general, he did not want to tie himself to any political movement, not even to the most honorable. In view of the supernatural character and mission of the Church, such was the only logical position.

Instead, the Primate defended all who had been wronged and persecuted, as well as those suffering political repression. This was completely in accord with his general policy of defending human rights and the moral rights of the nation.

The Primate reached accords with the state, but he never thought of a historical compromise. This stance had to do not only with a Marxist ideological state. As a canonist and sociologist, Cardinal Wyszyński was too well aware of the different natures and goals of Church and state to desire their political symbiosis. The Italian historical compromise, after all, joined two political parties, and not Church and state. Besides, nothing ever came of it.

The Primate did not believe in political coalitions. He wanted the Church to remain a Church. He bestowed his sympathy upon politicians, activists, and journalists who expressed a system of social and moral values close to his own. He admonished and chastised those who erred in doctrinal and church matters. Witnessing, at the end of his life, a conceptual revolution that embraced all social circles, the Primate—not always understood by those who think schematically—was capable of contact with people and groups who did not enjoy social recognition. Cardinal Wyszyński believed in man and his inclination to good and truth. The fact that the spiritual transformation of Poland is almost universal confirms this view.

The Primate's major concern in his last years was that Polish affairs not slip out of Polish control to be settled by outsiders. In light of the trend of military-political alliances, that is a real possibility. Thus the Primate laid great stress on maintaining social calm, on limiting strikes, on conducting a dialogue and negotiations between the labor unions and the government. This has been interpreted as a sign that the Primate became yielding and allowed himself to be intimidated by the possibility of intervention. Cardinal Wyszyński showed too many signs of courage, even in the last years of his life, to be accused seriously of having been intimidated. Rather, he simply paid attention to the worst possibilities. From a historical point of view, that is an obligation for every Polish statesman. Yet no one can accuse the Cardinal of mistaken compromise. He was naturally one of the most informed men in Poland and knew about all moments of real danger. He did not allow himself to be intimidated, as his uncompromising position on the registration of Solidarity and Rural Solidarity shows. It is nevertheless a fact that he tried to ease tensions and that he opposed such radical solutions as a general strike after the beatings of the unionists in Bydgoszcz in March 1981. I would ask, however, whether any wise person, as we understand the word, would really have favored a general strike then, or would generally favor a method of permanent strikes as a road to renewal.

In each great process of change there is always a radical wing and a more moderate wing. Only later is it apparent who was right. In his later years, the Primate was a decided advocate of restraint and moderation. We do not yet have the historical perspective in which the different strategies of the Polish liberation movement can be evaluated. The greatest testimony to his policy is the fact that because of it he became an arbiter and gained a position of superiority in the nation and in the government of souls, and at the same time garnered the thanks of the rulers. Thus he could accomplish much and shape the most important social issues.

Later we will understand what Poland has lost in the person of Cardinal Wyszyński. He had great social intuition, a statesman's instincts, and an unerring moral compass, which allowed him to face the most difficult situations and steer the Church and the nation through tempests and the sharp turns of history. When new problems, pressures, and crises arise, we will understand how much we miss Cardinal Wyszyński. This sketch of his biography is intended only as initial research into his life, which many generations of Poles will study. This first attempt, full of gaps and inadequacies, is intended to satisfy the first demands of the reader.

In truth, there is no brief way to tell who Stefan Wyszyński was. Naturally he was a primate and statesman, a pastor and a good man, a prince of the Church and a leader of the nation, a defender of man, a guardian of law and morality. But that is not all. His greatness, in specifically Polish conditions, lies in the fact that without creating new doctrines or ideologies he wove together the national tradition and the system of Christian values. In this he erected a bastion that is not to be razed. For centuries, the fact that Poland has remained unconquered will be linked with his name. The Cardinal preserved its spiritual, national, and European identity.

Index